A Glimpse of China's Fine Traditional Culture

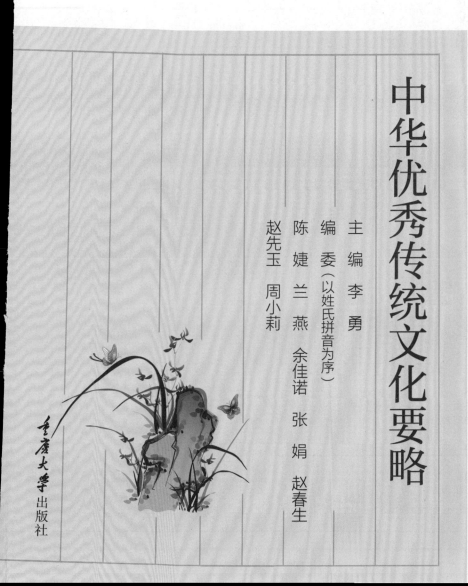

中华优秀传统文化要略

主编 李 勇

编 委（以姓氏拼音为序）

陈 婕 兰 燕 余佳诺 张 娟 赵春生

赵先玉 周小莉

重庆大学出版社

内容提要

《中华优秀传统文化要略》共13章,内容涉及哲学(孔子、老子、百家争鸣)、宗教(道教、佛教)、文学、艺术、科技、节日、菜肴、手工艺品、体育和园林,突出中华思想文化内容的讲述和术语翻译。

本书全英文编写,配有插图,语言力求新颖地道,格式力求醒目别致,部分章节里融入中华思想文化术语的引例,以增强读者对有关中华思想文化术语内涵的理解;每个单元后面都设计有配套的知识性练习和思辨性练习,既可帮助学生巩固所学单元内容,又能培养学生的思辨能力。

本书不但可以作为高等院校学生的教材,而且可以作为大学英语教师的教学参考资料,还可供来华留学生和对中国文化感兴趣的外国友人阅读使用。

图书在版编目(CIP)数据

中华优秀传统文化要略:英文 / 李勇主编.-- 重庆:重庆大学出版社,2023.6
大学英语选修课系列教材
ISBN 978-7-5689-3859- 4

Ⅰ.① 中… Ⅱ.① 李… Ⅲ.① 中华文化—高等学校—教材—英文 Ⅳ.① K203

中国国家版本馆 CIP 数据核字(2023)第 077851 号

中华优秀传统文化要略

主 编:李 勇
策划编辑:安 娜
责任编辑:罗 亚 版式设计:罗 亚 叶抒扬
责任校对:王 倩 责任印制:赵 晟
*
重庆大学出版社出版发行
出版人:陈晓阳
社址:重庆市沙坪坝区大学城西路21号
邮编:401331
电话:(023)88617190 88617185(中小学)
传真:(023)88617186 88617166
网址:http://www.cqup.com.cn
邮箱:fxk@cqup.com.cn(营销中心)
全国新华书店经销
印刷:重庆永驰印务有限公司
*
开本:787mm×1092mm 1/16 印张:20.75 字数:559千
2023年8月第1版 2023年8月第1次印刷
ISBN 978-7-5689-3859-4 定价:55.00元

Preface
前　言

　　随着世界经济的日益全球化,国际文化交流也日益频繁,展示"软实力"的文化传播活动成为许多国家对外交往的战略选择。璀璨的华夏文明越来越受到世界的关注。"加强国际传播能力建设"已经写入2015年中国政府工作报告。2022年10月16日,习近平总书记在中国共产党第二十次全国代表大会上的报告中指出:"增强中华文明传播力影响力。坚守中华文化立场,提炼展示中华文明的精神标识和文化精髓,加快构建中国话语和中国叙事体系,讲好中国故事、传播好中国声音,展现可信、可爱、可敬的中国形象。加强国际传播能力建设,全面提升国际传播效能,形成同我国综合国力和国际地位相匹配的国际话语权。深化文明交流互鉴,推动中华文化更好走向世界。"

　　展现文化大国形象,提高中华文化传播影响力,讲好中国故事,助力中国更好走向世界、让世界更好了解中国,是当代大学生义不容辞的责任与担当。然而,当前中国一些高校的英语教学中的母语文化要素有所欠缺,部分大学生用英语表达中华文化的能力偏低,从而造成对外交流的障碍,影响中华文化的国际传播,妨碍中国国际传播能力的建设。为了助力教师更好地引导学生传承和弘扬中华优秀传统文化,实现英语专业学科的内涵化高质量发展,打造优秀的校级规划教材,我们参阅了大量中英文文献,编写出了这本《中华优秀传统文化要略》。

　　《中华优秀传统文化要略》可供高等院校英语专业学生以及非英语专业学生学习使用,也可供相关旅游传媒专业学生、留学生和对中国文化感兴趣的外国友人使用。

　　《中华优秀传统文化要略》共13章,包括哲学(孔子、老子、百家争鸣)、宗教(道教、佛教)、文学、艺术、科技、节日、菜肴、手工艺品、体育、园林等内容,突出中华优秀传统文化内容的讲述和术语翻译,并配有插图。教材每章都设计有配套的知识性练习和思辨性练习,并在书后提供了练习答案和参考文献;部分章节提供了中华思想文化术语及引例。

　　《中华优秀传统文化要略》全书13章的内容由重庆交通大学的李勇编写,各章的校对与练习编写分工如下:陈婕负责第3章、第12章,兰燕负责第7章、第11章,张娟负责第1章、第2章,赵春生负责第6章、第8章,赵先玉负责第4章、第5章,周小莉负责第9章、第13章,余佳诺负责第10章。

　　由于编者的水平有限,书中不足之处在所难免,敬请广大读者批评指正。

编　者

2022年11月

Contents

目 录

Chapter 1
Confucius: Supreme Sage and Foremost Teacher

Confucius was the first and most famous scholar of the Spring and Autumn Period. As a great thinker, statesman, educator and the founder of Confucianism, Confucius is an ancient sage to the Chinese people, and his thought has for many years exerted a deep influence on China and other countries in East Asia.

Confucius

Confucius was born into an impoverished aristocratic family at Zouyi (陬邑) in the State of Lu (鲁), in Qufu (曲阜) of the present-day Shangdong Province, in 551 B.C.E. Kong (孔) was his family name; his given name was Qiu (丘) and his literary name Zhongni (仲尼). But he is often referred to by his title of honor, Kong Fuzi (孔夫子), meaning Master Kong. A legend goes that before his birth, his parents had prayed to the god of Mount Niqiu (尼丘山) for a son, so they called him Qiu and Zhongni. Confucius is his Latinized name, which has been widely used in the West ever since he was known abroad.

Confucius was only three years old when his father died. In Qufu, the capital of Lu, the mother and her son had a hard life. Young Confucius was smart and showed a great interest in study, and his mother did everything possible to encourage him. But his mother died when he was 16 or 17 and could not see her son established as a learned scholar.

Later, recalling his earlier days, Confucius said, "At 15 I was determined to study; at 30 I was established; at 40 I was not perplexed; at 50 I knew what destiny was; at 60 I was open to different opinions; at 70 I could do whatever I wanted and would not break any rules. (吾十有五而志于学,三十而立,四十而不惑,五十而知天命,六十而耳顺,七十而从心所欲,不逾矩。)" It appears that he had in his youth studied many classic works and formed his own views about the most important problems of history, society and mankind. *The Analects of Confucius* (《论语》), a collection of 500 sayings of Confucius and his major disciples, and their comments and answers to questions, is the earliest and most reliable source of the life and teachings of Confucius and is regarded as the basic "scripture" of Confucianism.

In his early twenties, Confucius served as a keeper of the granary and later as a supervisor of flocks in the State of Lu. It is said that he once became the Minister of Justice and the Prime Minister of Lu. For a few years, his work as an official brought about very good results. But those aristocrats who gained real control of the government disliked his measures and made it difficult for him to carry out his ideals. So he, full of disappointment, resigned his position at 55.

During the next 13 years, accompanied by several faithful disciples, Confucius wandered from state to state to preach his theories and seek a position suitable for his talent. When he was 68 years old, he returned home at the invitation of a new generation of nobles who came into power in the State of Lu. In his last years he did not work in the government, but devoted himself to teaching his disciples and editing the six classics. It is said that the six classics compiled by Confucius include *The Book of Songs* (《诗经》), *The Book of History* (《书经》), *The Book of Rites* (《礼经》), *The Book of Changes* (《易经》), *The Book of Music* (《乐经》), and *The Spring and Autumn Annals* (《春秋》). In 479 B.C.E., when he was 73, he fell ill and passed away.

Confucius received numerous posthumous title, "Supreme Sage and Foremost Teacher (至圣先师)", "Great Perfect, Most Holy Culture Spreading King (大成至圣文宣王)", "A Great Sage in the Fateful World, and an Ideal Teacher for Myriads of Years (命世大圣,亿载师表)", to mention just a few.

/ A Great Thinker /

As one of the greatest thinkers in the history of China, Confucius constructed a system of philosophical thought with humanity as its basic virtue, which is the central theme of *The Analects of Confucius*. He considered *ren* (仁) or humanity as the first and highest criterion of man's behavior and the core of morality. The Chinese word for humanity is composed of the character meaning "man" and the character for two, denoting vividly that which is common in two men, and suggesting the notion of a common denominator in mankind and a demarcation between man and animal. According to Confucius, humanity or benevolence means to love other men and love one's parents, brothers and sisters first. If a man of humanity wants to stand up, he should help others to stand up first; if he wants to understand things himself, he should help others to understand things first. Meanwhile, one should not impose on others what one does not desire oneself. Thus, humanity is a word embracing all those moral qualities which should govern one man in his relations with others.

Confucius stressed the importance of man's morality. He said, "To be humane is to be a man," which means that humanity or humaneness is the fundamental quality of man, and it is this quality that makes a man a true man. As man has a moral nature, to adhere to moral principles should be everyone's first consideration. Moral principles are more important than all other things including position, wealth and even life. He said, "Wealth and high position are desired by all men, but I would not have them if they were not won in the right way. Poverty and low position are hated by all men, but I would not leave them if they could not be rid of in the right way. (富与贵,是人之所欲也,不以其道得之,不处也。贫与贱,是人之所恶也,不以其道得之,不去也。)"

Humanity is the supreme moral principle or the supreme virtue. To realize it, one should, if necessary, abandon everything else including life itself. Confucius said, "A determined or humane man never give up humanity to save his life, but he may sacrifice his life to realize humanity.(志士仁人,无求生以害仁,有杀身以成仁。)"

In connection with humanity, Confucius advocated many other virtues, such as justice or righteousness (义), propriety or rites (礼), knowledge or wisdom (智), good faith or trustworthiness (信), allegiance or loyalty (忠), forbearance (恕), filial piety (孝), fraternal duty or brotherly love (悌) as well as incorruptness (廉). He called a man who had virtues a gentleman (君子) and a man who was not virtuous a petty man (小人). A man of virtue is always open and sincere, ready to help other men, free from worries and fears, and at peace with himself and the world.

The basic meaning of *yi* (义) is "reasonable" and "proper". It has two extended meanings. One is the proper basis and standard for people's actions. The other is to adjust one's words or deeds to meet certain standards, under the guidance of moral judgments.

Li refers to rituals, traditions and norms in social life. Of these, Confucius regarded burial rituals and ancestral worship rituals as the most important, because they arose from human feelings. The ritual of wearing mourning for a deceased parent for three days was an expression of the child's love and remembrance. He once said, "Do not look when your action would be contrary to rites; do not listen when your action would be contrary to rites; do not speak when your action would be contrary to rites; do not touch when your action would be contrary to rites. (非礼勿视,非礼勿听,非礼勿言,非礼勿动。)"

Confucius put emphasis on *li* with the aim of maintaining social order, stability and harmony.

Confucius's views on the golden mean and harmony also had a great influence on the thinking of the Chinese people.

Zhongyong (golden mean) was considered to be the highest level of virtue by Confucius and Confucian scholars. *Zhong* (中) doesn't mean "compromise" but a "moderate" and "just right" way in one's words and deeds. Everything has its limits, and neither exceeding nor falling short of the limits is desirable. *Yong* (庸) has two meanings. One is common or ordinary and the other is unchanging. Moderation can be maintained for a long time only when one practices it in everyday life. *Zhongyong* means the standard of moderation that one should follow in dealing with others and in one's everyday conduct.

The Chinese term *hexie* (harmony) originally referred to the simultaneous combination of different tones that gave rise to a musical work. Later, it came to mean a state of governance in which there are good social relations of coexistence based on respect for difference and diversity. In such a society, all people give free rein to their talent and find their proper place to live together in harmony, order and health. Harmony is a core Confucian ethical principle for dealing with interpersonal relationships and guiding social and political activities. It now generally refers to the harmonious, peaceful, and amicable relationship between people, between groups, and between countries. Harmony represents the Chinese cultural value of opposing violence and conflicts and cherishing peace and order.

/ An Outstanding Statesman /

To some extent, Confucius might be respected as an outstanding statesman in ancient China for his wise and farsighted political ideas. As to the way to govern a state, on the one hand, Confucius emphasized the rule by virtue and humane government. He said, "Governance based on virtue is like the North Star taking its place in the sky, while all the other stars revolve around it. (为政以德,譬如北辰,居其所而众星拱之。)" He disagreed with the use of harsh laws and severe punishments, which were common in those days. Tyrannical measures, according to him, would only make ordinary people try hard to avoid punishments, and would not help them to distinguish between right and wrong or give them a sense of shame. Governance based on virtue does not, however, exclude the use of punishment, but rather highlights the decisive role of virtue in governance, and regards moral edification both as the fundamental principle and the essential means for achieving good governance.

Confucius also claimed that the ruler himself should be an upright man, and should guide the common people with virtue, and regulate their conduct and behavior with the rites, which were standards of conduct laid down by the rulers of the Western Zhou. What's more, Confucius urged selecting only virtuous and talented people to serve as government officials.

With regard to the way to govern a state, on the other hand, Confucius asserted that people should be made rich first and then educated. This political view might be a good principle even today, for it covers both material and spiritual civilization, which have to be developed at the same time to ensure the stability of the state and the happiness of the people.

/ China's First Educator /

Confucius, who was China's first educator and no doubt one of the world's first educators, was a pioneer in running private schools and developed significant educational principles and methods of teaching which were considered his great contributions to education in ancient China.

Before Confucius, only the nobility had the right to receive education. He was the first figure in Chinese history to initiate private education. A teacher all his adult life, he set up a school and taught about 3,000 disciples, 72 of whom excelled in the "six arts", i.e., ritual, music, archery, (carriage) driving, calligraphy, and mathematics.

"I teach everyone without making distinction (有教无类)," Confucius said. This was an open rebellion against the tradition that education was accessible to the noblemen only. By bringing education to ordinary people, he made an immeasurable contribution to the advancement of Chinese culture.

Confucius believed that all men were educable because men had a similar nature. "By nature men are pretty alike (性相近也)," he said, "but learning and practice set them apart (习相远也)." This assertion, which opposed the popular view of his time that aristocrats were born superior to common people, expressed his belief in equality.

Confucius advocated equality between teachers and students and expected students to become men of virtue. He preserved a close relationship with his students, cared for and loved them, always ready to answer their questions and give them guidance they needed. His students, in return, were loyal and respectful to him; some of them accompanied him on his journey through the states, sharing with him weal and woe. It is natural that this teacher-student relationship should be regarded as a model in later ages.

Confucius believed that the basic goal of education was to cultivate "persons of virtue (君子)", who should possess sound character, uplifted minds and high caliber. Such persons should be able to shoulder social responsibilities and to make contributions to society. Zi Lu (子路) asked what a man of virtue is like. Confucius said, "He cultivates himself so as to be reverent. (修己以敬。)" Zi Lu asked, "Is that all? (如斯而已乎?)" Confucius said, "He cultivates himself so as to benefit others. (修己以安人。)" Zi Lu asked, "Is that all?" Confucius said, "He cultivates himself so as to benefit all people. Comforting all people, even Yao and Shun would have found it difficult! (修己以安百姓。修己以安百姓, 尧舜其犹病诸!)"

Confucius regarded lofty ideals, great virtue, love for people, and the "six arts" as the general principles of education. Of those, virtue was the most important. Confucius said, "People in ancient times learned to cultivate their own moral characters. People today learn to impress others. (古之学者为己, 今之学者为人。)"

Confucius paid much attention to aesthetic education. He said, "Studying *The Book of Songs* inspires the spirit and helps one appreciate beauty. Studying *The Book of Rites* enables one to behave properly as a person of enlightenment. Studying music lifts the spirit and helps one to enjoy life." He also said, "Simply knowing the highest standard of virtue (i.e., love for people) is not as good as setting it as one's goal. Setting it as one's goal is not as good as enjoying the practice of it. (知之者不如好之者, 好之者不如乐之者。)"

Confucius's main teaching method was the elicitation method, which means conversation, or question and answer. Sometimes he would give a student a clear answer who came to him with a question. Sometimes he would comment on a view expressed by his student. Sometimes the master would start a conversation with a student to explain a theory to him, or direct his attention to a question, or point out the way forward for him.

In his conversations with his students, Confucius often commented on real events and people, and took into consideration the needs of the listener. He also encouraged his students to combine learning and thinking and warned them not to learn without thinking or think without learning. He said, "He who learns without thinking will be bewildered; he who thinks without learning will be perilous. (学而不思则罔, 思而不学则殆。)"

The elicitation method invented by Confucius was nearly one hundred years earlier than the Socratic dialogue. His conception of teaching according to the student's aptitude is still considered an important educational principle in China today.

All in all, Confucius was a transmitter as well as a creator of Chinese culture. He emphasized the importance of humanity and regarded it as the highest ideal of morality. He also stressed that rites should be combined with humanity, and that humanity should be practiced within the strict boundary of rites. He initiated private teaching and advocated universal education without class distinction. It is no wonder that Confucius is revered as one of the top ten thinkers in the world. Many of his ideas, such as sacrificing life in order to fulfill humanity, thinking of righteousness before profit, learning insatiably and teaching without identification, and pursuing truth and sticking to it, have been embodied in Chinese culture and have enabled Chinese people to create such a splendid culture and survive many perils in history.

Key Terms

1. 当仁不让

When Facing an Opportunity to Exercise Benevolence, Do Not Yield.

◎子曰："当仁不让于师。"(《论语》)

Confucius said, "When faced with an opportunity to be benevolent, one should not yield even to one's own teacher." (The Analects of Confucius)

2. 见义勇为

Act Bravely for a Just Cause

◎见义不为,无勇也。(《论语》)

One who does nothing when encountering injustice is a coward. (The Analects of Confucius)

3. 见利思义

Think of Righteousness in the Face of Gain

◎见利思义,见危授命,久要不忘平生之言,亦可以为成人矣。(《论语》)

He, who when faced with gain thinks of righteousness, who when confronted with danger is ready to lay down his life, and who does not forget a past promise despite enduring poverty, may be considered a true man! (The Analects of Confucius)

4. 见贤思齐

When Seeing a Person of High Caliber, Strive to Be His Equal.

◎子曰："见贤思齐焉,见不贤而内自省也。"(《论语》)

Confucius said, "When you see a person of virtue and capability, you should think of emulating and equaling the person; when you see a person of low caliber, you should reflect on your own weak points." (The Analects of Confucius)

5. 克己复礼

Restrain Yourself and Follow Social Norms

◎颜渊问仁。子曰:"克己复礼为仁。一日克己复礼,天下归仁焉。为仁由己,而由人乎哉?"(《论语》)

Yan Yuan asked about benevolence. Confucius said, "To restrain yourself and practice propriety is benevolence. Once you can restrain yourself and practice propriety, everyone else will praise you for your benevolence. You must practice benevolence yourself; how can others practice it for you?" (The Analects of Confucius)

6. 以直报怨

Repay a Grudge with Rectitude

◎或曰:"以德报怨,何如?"子曰:"何以报德? 以直报怨,以德报德。"(《论语》)

Someone asked, "How about repaying a grudge with kindness?" Confucius said, "Then how would you repay kindness? Repay a grudge with rectitude, and repay kindness with kindness." (The Analects of Confucius)

7. 政者正也

Governance Means Rectitude.

◎季康子问政于孔子,孔子对曰:"政者,正也。子帅以正,孰敢不正?"(《论语》)

When asked by Ji Kangzi about governance, Confucius replied, "Governance is all about rectitude. If you lead along the right path, who would dare not to follow you?" (The Analects of Confucius)

8. 君子义以为质

Righteousness Is Essential for a Person of Virtue.

◎子曰:"君子义以为质,礼以行之,孙(xùn)以出之,信以成之。君子哉!"(《论语》)

Confucius said, "A person of virtue takes righteousness as a fundamental principle to guide his acts, practices ethics and justice according to etiquette, demonstrates ethics and justice by way of discreetness, and fulfills ethics and justice in honesty. This is what a person of virtue does." (The Analects of Confucius)

9. 君子固穷

A Man of Virtue Maintains His Ideals Even in Frustrations.

◎子曰:"君子固穷,小人穷斯滥矣。"(《论语》)

Confucius said, "A man of virtue will uphold his ideals even in frustrations, but a petty man will stop at nothing." (The Analects of Confucius)

10. 博施济众

Deliver Extensive Benefits to the People and Relieve the Suffering of the Poor

◎子贡曰:"如有博施于民而能济众,何如? 可谓仁乎?"子曰:"何事于仁,必也圣乎! 尧舜其犹病诸。"(《论语》)

Zi Gong asked, "If a ruler delivers extensive benefits to his people and relieves the suffering of the poor, how would you rate him? Do you consider him benevolent and virtuous?" Confucius said, "He is not only benevolent but virtuous. I would call him a sage. Even virtuous rulers such as Yao and Shun could not match him." (The Analects of Confucius)

11. 三思而行

Think Thrice Before Acting

◎季文子三思而后行。子闻之,曰:"再,斯可矣。"(《论语》)

Ji Wenzi acted after having reflected thrice. When Confucius heard it, he remarked, "Twice is sufficient." (The Analects of Confucius)

12. 民无信不立

Without People's Trust the State Will Not Survive.

◎子贡问政,子曰:"足食,足兵,民信之矣。"子贡曰:"必不得已而去,于斯三者何先?" 曰:"去兵。"子贡曰:"必不得已而去,于斯二者何先?"曰:"去食。自古皆有死,民无信 不立。"(《论语》)

Zi Gong asked about what was needed in governance. Confucius said, "Enough food, enough weapons and people's trust in the ruler." Zi Gong said, "If you had no choice but to forgo one thing, which of those three should be the first?" Confucius said, "Forgo weapons." Zi Gong said, "If you had no choice but to forgo one thing, which of those two should be the first?" Confucius said, "Forgo food. Since ancient times, there has always been death, but if the people have no trust, the state does not survive." (The Analects of Confucius)

13. 四海之内皆兄弟

All the People Within the Four Seas Are Brothers.

◎君子敬而无失,与人恭而有礼,四海之内皆兄弟也。(《论语》)

A man of virtue always does things conscientiously without making any mistakes and treats people respectfully and appropriately. Then all within the Four Seas will be his brothers. (The Analects of Confucius)

14. 和为贵

Harmony Is the Most Precious.

◎有子曰:"礼之用,和为贵。先王之道,斯为美,小大由之。有所不行,知和而和,不以礼节之,亦不可行也。"(《论语》)

You Zi said, "Make harmony a top priority in the application of rites. That is a key feature that characterized governance by sovereign rulers in the ancient past. Always act upon the rule of harmony, no matter whether the issue at hand is minor or major. Sometimes, however, this rule may fail to work. If one insists on seeking harmony just for the sake of harmony instead of qualifying it with rites, then there will be no hope of success." (The Analects of Confucius)

15. 习

Practice

◎学而时习之,不亦说乎?(《论语》)

Isn't it a pleasure to practice what one has learned from time to time? (The Analects of Confucius)

16. 兴

Evocation

◎兴于诗,立于礼,成于乐(yuè)。(《论语》)

One uses poetry to evoke volition, rituals and etiquette to regulate behavior and music to shape one's character. (The Analects of Confucius)

17. 俭

Thriftiness

◎林放问礼之本。子曰:"大哉问! 礼,与其奢也,宁俭;丧,与其易也,宁戚。"(《论语》)

Lin Fang asked Confucius about the essential meaning of ritual ceremonies. Confucius replied, "What you are asking is a big question. For rites, it is always desirable to be simple rather than excessive. In the case of mourning, such rites should be determined by degree of grief rather than by over-consideration of rituals." (*The Analects of Confucius*)

Exercises

Part One　Comprehension

Fill in the following blanks with the information you learn in Chapter 1.

1. As a great thinker, statesman, educator and the ____ ____ of Confucianism, Confucius is an ancient sage to the Chinese people, and his thought has for many years exerted a deep influence on China and other countries in East Asia.

2. Humanity is the _____ moral principle or the supreme virtue.

3. Harmony is a core Confucian _____ principle for dealing with interpersonal relationships and guiding social and political activities.

4. As to the way to govern a state, on the one hand, Confucius emphasized the rule by _____ and humane government.

5. The _____ method invented by Confucius was nearly one hundred years earlier than the Socratic dialogue.

Part Two　Translation

Term Translation

1. 当仁不让
2. 见利思义
3. 见贤思齐
4. 克己复礼
5. 和为贵

Passage Translation

　　孔子(Confucius)是一位思想家、政治家、教育家,也是中国儒家学说(Confucianism)的创始人。冯友兰,20世纪中国思想史上的伟大权威之一,把孔子在中国历史上的影响与西方的苏格拉底相提并论。因为人有德性,所以恪守道德原则应当成为每个人的首要考虑之事。道德原则比其他任何东西包括地位、财富甚至生命都更重要。子曰："富与贵,是人之所欲也,不以其道(in the right way)得之,不处也;贫与贱,是人之所恶也,不以其道得之,不去也。"

Part Three   Critical Thinking and Discussion

Is Confucianism out-of-date today? Is it necessary for us to promote Confucianism in modern society? Why or why not?

Chapter 2
Lao Zi: The Founder of Taoism

If Confucianism was the mainstream of Chinese thought for about 2,000 years, then the second deepest influence on Chinese thought was no doubt Taoism, which opposed but supplemented and enlivened Confucianism.

Lao Zi, the founder of Taoism, was born in the State of Chu (楚), in present-day Henan Province, a little earlier than Confucius. His family name was Li, his given name was Er and his nickname was Lao Dan (老聃). He lived during the Spring and Autumn Period. Due to his great learning, even Confucius was said to have traveled miles to consult him. According to *Records of the Grand Historian* (《史记》) by Sima Qian, Lao Zi was a librarian or archivist in the royal court, in charge of the archival records of Zhou Dynasty. Seeing the decline of the Zhou Dynasty, he quit his job to live in seclusion. On his way he

Lao Zi

reached a gate which he had to go through. Yin Xi (尹喜), the gate keeper, begged him to write a book. Lao Zi agreed and wrote about 5,000 words on *Dao* (道) and *De* (德), or the Way and its Virtue. The book is called *Dao De Jing* (《道德经》), or *Classic of the Way and Its Virtue*, but more commonly known as *Lao Zi* (《老子》). The philosophy interpreted in it is described as Taoism, for *Tao*, not *Dao*, which was how the Chinese word was represented in English in the past.

The book of *Lao Zi* consists of just about 5,000 Chinese characters, and contains 81 chapters which are divided into two parts, namely *Dao* and *De*. Short as it is, the book has played a significant role in the development of Chinese culture. It became the basis of Taoism, the school of philosophy parallel to Confucianism in ancient China. The thought of Lao Zi formed the foundation of the Taoist religion, the most influential indigenous school of religion in China. It has also had a direct impact on the characteristics, trends of thought and aesthetic sensibilities of the Chinese nation. The classic is written in verse, in very succinct language, with many lines capable of different interpretations. It has been translated into many foreign languages and modern Chinese. It was first introduced into Europe, possibly as early as the 15th century, and has been one of the most translated philosophical works of ancient China. Indeed, few books have attracted as much attention and aroused as much interest in China and abroad as the *Dao De Jing* (《道德经》), which has won Lao Zi the title of World Cultural Celebrity. Many of Lao Zi's enlightening views are based on his philosophy of *Dao*, naturalness (自然), non-action (无为), and non-contention (不争).

/ *Dao* /

The keynote of Lao Zi's philosophical system is *Dao*, or the Way, which is the origin, the principle, the substance, and the standard of all things, to which all of them must conform. *Dao* gives birth to the universe and makes all things in the universe what they are. In other words, it is the law that governs the development and change of all things in the universe. It is invisible, intangible, and indescribable. It is even nameless, and *Dao* is just an inadequate name forced upon it.

Dao is one and simple, like the uncarved block. In its essence, it is eternal, absolute, and beyond space and time; in its operation, it is spontaneous, everywhere, constant and unceasing, always in transformation, going through cycles and finally returning to its root. It is modeled after Nature and is called the "self-so (自然)." It is good like water, always benefiting things without claiming credit. It takes no unnatural action, and yet all things flourish. Furthermore, it is nonbeing itself, not in the sense of nothingness but as not being any particular thing. When it is possessed by an individual thing, it becomes its Virtue (德), which is the principle underlying the individual thing. *Dao* creates all things under heaven while *de* (德) nurtures them. Lao Zi was progressive for his time in that he replaced a god, a Heaven, or a supreme authority that was believed to govern the universe with the Way, an absolute, overriding spirit that transcends time and space, but his theory represents the standpoint of objective idealism.

Lao Zi put forward a series of profound views on the laws governing the workings and changes of all things in the universe. According to Lao Zi, things and concepts are relative. In Chapter of the *Dao De Jing* (《道德经》), Lao Zi claimed, "When the world recognizes the beautiful as beautiful, there is the ugly; when the world recognizes the good as good, there is the bad (or the evil). Being and nonbeing produce each other; the difficult and the easy complement each other; the long and the short shape each other; the high and the low contain each other; the sound and the voice accord with each other; and what is before and what is after follow each other." Generally speaking, of every pair of opposite concepts, one produces the other, or the existence of one depends on the existence of the other.

From the above mentioned relativity of things and concepts, Lao Zi continued to draw an important conclusion: "Reversion is the movement of *Dao*," or turning back is how the Way moves. This saying, which means that a state or quality has its process of development, and when it reaches the extreme, it will eventually turn back to its opposite state or quality, contains some naive ideas about dialectics. To him, anything that develops extreme qualities will invariably revert to the opposite qualities. Thus the named and nameless, being and nonbeing, strength and weakness, honor and shame, wisdom and stupidity, etc., are all interdependent and grow out of one another. He said, "It's upon calamity that happiness leans; it is upon happiness that calamity rests." Because of this truth, Lao Zi taught that, to weaken something, one should first strengthen it; to diminish something, one should first increase it. In this way, even the weakest in the world can overcome the strongest. That is to say, weakness is the function of *Dao*. Lao Zi unveiled the unity of opposites in the world and realized the contradictions in things and the transformation of the opposites. In his opinion, however, change did not develop in a forward fashion; instead, it went on in an endless cycle. In addition, the transformation of the opposites was absolute and unconditional.

/ Naturalness /

"Naturalness", as an important concept of Lao Zi's philosophy, refers to a natural state of being, an attitude of following the way of nature. In Lao Zi's eyes, *Dao* takes naturalness as its law. He emphasized that everything in the world has its own way of being and development: birds fly in the sky; fish swim in the water; flowers bloom and fall. All these phenomena occur independently and naturally without following any human will, and humans should not struggle to change anything natural. Lao Zi admonished people to give up any desire to control the world. Following the way of nature is the way to resolving conflicts between humans and the world. While in political philosophy, "naturalness" specifically denotes the natural state enjoyed by ordinary people free from the intervention of government supervision and moral edification. Taoism holds that in governance, a monarch should conform to the natural state of the people.

/ Non-action /

"Non-action", as another vital concept of Lao Zi's philosophy, is the guarantee of "naturalness". Lao Zi said, "*Dao* acts through non-action and it always makes all things possible through non-interference with them," by which he did not mean that one should do nothing and passively wait for something to be achieved. Neither did he deny human creativity. What he meant is that human enterprising actions must be built on the basis of naturalness, not on any attempt to interrupt the rhythm of nature. Human creativity should be in compliance with the ways of nature.

As far as government and social order, Lao Zi advocated rule through non-action. Here non-action does not mean doing nothing, but instead taking no action that is not natural, and that is against the original nature and wishes of people. It means letting people and the society take their own course without being taught and directed. In Lao Zi's view, a state is badly governed when the ruler does too much. He said, "The more prohibitions there are in the world, the poorer the people will be; the more sharp weapons people have, the more turbulent the state will be; the more skills man possesses, the more strange things will appear; the more laws and orders are made, the more thieves and robbers there will be." On the other hand, "If the ruler takes no action, the people will be transformed by themselves; if he loves tranquility, the people will become correct by themselves; if he engages in no activity, the people will become prosperous by themselves; if he has no desire, the people will become simple by themselves." Many centuries later, there was in the West a similar political view: The best government is the one that governs least.

Taoist school of thought contrasts "action" to "non-action". "Action" generally means that the rulers impose their will on others or the world without showing any respect for or following the intrinsic nature of things. "Non-action" is the opposite of "action", and has three main points: through self-control containing the desire to interfere; following the nature of all things and the people; and bringing into play the initiative of all things and people. "Non-action" does not mean not doing anything, but is a wiser way of doing things. Non-action leads to the result of getting everything done.

/ Non-contention /

On the basis of "naturalness" and "non-action", Lao Zi proposed the view of "overcoming the strong by being weak", which means what appears soft and weak can defeat or overcome what is hard and strong. A tree that is strong is fragile and can easily be broken in the wind; while a weak tree is supple, it bends with the wind but will not be broken.

The era in which Lao Zi lived was replete with endless wars. Therefore, war was a significant theme for philosophers, and anti-war thinking was the norm. According to Lao Zi, war springs from humans' bloated desires. Conflicts arise out of people's struggles to satisfy their desires, and conflict escalates into war. Therefore, Lao Zi put forward the philosophy of "non-contention". To him, human competitive strife is the source of decline; desiring nothing is the natural way of life.

Lao Zi said, "The greatest virtue is just like water." He compared his philosophy of "non-contention" to water, to distinguish it from the law of the jungle. He went on to say, "Water nurtures everything but contends for nothing." To Lao Zi, humans tend to seek higher positions while water always flows to lower places. Driven by desire, humans like whatever they think is superior while depreciate whatever they think is inferior. As the source of life, water nourishes all living things on Earth and no life can exist without it. A virtuous ruler should govern with gentle and accommodating qualities as demonstrated by water. He should assist and provide for people just like what the water does, instead of competing with them for resources. People should nourish all things as water does and try their best to help others without seeking fame or profit.

As to the way to live, behave and handle things, Lao Zi advised people to be peaceful, quiet, submissive, tolerant, modest, contented and humble, to live a simple life and not to strive for wealth, fame or power, which will only give them worries and troubles. Even when one has won a great success, one had better withdraw from the scene without claiming credit for it. He said, "He does not show himself, and so is conspicuous; he does not consider himself right, and so is famous; he does not brag, and so is given credit; he is not conceited, and so can endure for long. It is just because he does not contend that no one in the world can contend with him." He also said, "To yield is to be preserved; to bend is to become straight; to be low is to be full; to be worn out is to be renewed; to have little is to gain; to have plenty is to be perplexed. (曲则全,枉

则直,清则盈,敝则新,少则多,多则惑。)"

Similarly, the ideal life of the individual is a life following the principles of *Dao*. In addition to simplicity, spontaneity and vacuity, a good life is one of tranquility, which characterizes the natural state; of weakness, which eventually overcomes strength; and above all, of non-action, that is, to lead a natural life. Lao Zi proposed "Three Treasures (三宝)" for life: kindness (慈), which enables one to be brave; frugality (俭), which makes one profuse; and humility, never being the first in the world or not venturing anything no others have done (不敢为天下先), which enables one to become chief of the state. However, Lao Zi exhorted people to banish wisdom and discard knowledge in order to reduce their desires. When people have few desires and are content with what they have, they will suffer no humiliation, and will be forever safe and sound.

By and large, Lao Zi was a venerable philosopher to Confucian scholars, a saint or a god to the people, and a fountainhead of *Dao* and one of the greatest divinities to the Taoists. His philosophy has influenced Chinese culture in many ways. His emphasis on harmony with all things in nature gave rise to subsequent schools of philosophy, poetry, painting and garden designing. Lao Zi's theory, that the movement of *Dao* consists in reversion, helped cultivate the forbearance and resilience of people in adversity. Moreover, his theory, that *Dao* always makes all things possible through non-interference with them and yet nothing can be achieved without acting this way (道常无为而无不为), was taken as a guiding principle by the enlightened monarch.

Key Terms

1. 道法自然

Dao Operates Naturally.

◎人法地,地法天,天法道,道法自然。(《老子》)

Man patterns himself on the operation of the earth; the earth patterns itself on the operation of heaven; heaven patterns itself on the operation of Dao; Dao patterns itself on what is natural. (Lao Zi)

2. 反者道之动

The Only Motion of *Dao* Is Returning.

◎反者道之动,弱者道之用。(《老子》)

The motion of Dao is transforming into the opposite or returning to the original state; and Dao is soft and humble while it is functioning. (Lao Zi)

3. 治大国若烹小鲜

Governing a Big Country Is Like Cooking Small Fish.

◎治大国,若烹小鲜。以道莅天下,其鬼不神;非其鬼不神,其神不伤人;非其神不伤人,圣人亦不伤人。夫两不相伤,故德交归焉。(《老子》)

Governing a big country is like cooking small fish. When the country is ruled by Dao, demons can neither disrupt it nor harm the people. Even sages acting on Dao principles will not bring harm to people either. Free from harms by demons and sages, people stand to gain all the benefits. (Lao Zi)

4. 不言之教

Influence Others without Preaching

◎是以圣人处无为之事,行不言之教。(《老子》)

Therefore, the sage deals with worldly affairs through non-action, and influences others without preaching. (Lao Zi)

5. 福祸相倚

Fortune and Misfortune Are Intertwined.

◎祸兮,福之所倚;福兮,祸之所伏。(《老子》)

Fortune lies beside misfortune; misfortune lurks within fortune. (Lao Zi)

6. 光而不耀

Be Bright but Not Dazzling

◎是以圣人方而不割,廉而不刿,直而不肆,光而不耀。(《老子》)

The sage is ethical but not hurtful, incorruptible but not disdainful, candid but not offensive, bright but not dazzling. (Lao Zi)

7. 见素抱朴

Maintain Originality and Embrace Simplicity

◎绝圣弃智,民利百倍;绝仁弃义,民复孝慈;绝巧弃利,盗贼无有。此三者,以为文不足,故令有所属,见素抱朴,少私寡欲。(《老子》)

Cast aside all the wisdom, and the people will benefit greatly; cast aside the demands of righteousness and the people will revert to their natural dutiful feelings; cast aside deceit and gain and thieves will disappear. Teachings, righteousness and deceit are all the embellishments of man and are inadequate. People must maintain and depend on their natural condition, and desire less. (*Lao Zi*)

8. 玄德

Inconspicuous Virtue

◎道生之,德畜之,物形之,势成之。是以万物莫不尊道而贵德。道之尊,德之贵,夫莫之命而常自然。故道生之,德畜之,长之育之,成之熟之,养之覆之。生而不有,为而不恃,长而不宰。是谓玄德。(《老子》)

Dao is the origin of all things; virtue nurtures all things, which thus assume their different forms, and grow in different environments. That is why all things and beings revere Dao and cherish virtue. This reverence and cherishing arise because there are no demands imposed on the natural state of things and beings. Instead this state is respected. Thus Dao creates all things, virtue nurtures them, and the environment makes them grow and mature. Create without possessing, influence without showing off one's ability, and cultivate without controlling. Such is the quality of inconspicuous virtue. (*Lao Zi*)

9. 兵强则灭

Relying on Force and Flaunting One's Superiority Lead to Destruction.

◎人之生也柔弱,其死也坚强。草木之生也柔脆,其死也枯槁。故坚强者死之徒,柔弱者生之徒。是以兵强则灭,木强则折。(《老子》)

When a man is alive, his body is soft and weak. Upon his death, it becomes hard and stiff. When grass and trees live, they are soft and fragile. Upon their death, they turn withered and dry. Therefore, the hard and stiff are followers of death; the soft and weak are followers of life. That is why when an army flaunts its strength, it will soon perish, while when a tree becomes strong it snaps. (*Lao Zi*)

10. 知常达变

Master both Permanence and Change

◎归根曰静,静曰复命。复命曰常,知常曰明。(《老子》)

Returning to the basics leads to tranquility. Tranquility leads to the return of life. The return of life means permanence, and understanding permanence is to be enlightened. (*Lao Zi*)

11. 上善若水

Great Virtue Is like Water.

◎上善若水。水善利万物而不争,处众人之所恶,故几于道。(《老子》)

Great virtue is like water. Water nourishes all things gently and does not compete with anything, content to be in a low place not sought by people. Water is therefore closest to Dao. (Lao Zi)

Exercises

Part One   Comprehension

Fill in the following blanks with the information you learn in Chapter 2.

1. The book of *Lao Zi* consists of just about _____ Chinese characters, and contains 81 chapters which are divided into two parts, namely *Dao* and *De*.

2. The keynote of Lao Zi's philosophical system is *Dao*, or the Way, which is the _____, the principle, the substance, and the standard of all things, to which all of them must conform.

3. Lao Zi unveiled the unity of opposites in the world and realized the _____ in things and the transformation of the opposites.

4. In Lao Zi's eyes, *Dao* takes _____ as its law.

5. As far as government and social order, Lao Zi advocated rule through _____.

Part Two   Translation

Term Translation

1. 道法自然

2. 不言之教

3. 福祸相依

4. 见素抱朴

5. 上善若水

Passage Translation

《老子》又称《道德经》,是春秋时期的老聃所作,主要研究政治哲学和人生哲学。受其思想影响,中国古代产生了道教,这是华夏民族本土产生的最具影响力的宗教。《老子》的思想直接影响了中国人的民族特性、思想倾向和审美趣味。直到今天,《老子》仍是我们民族思想的一部分。此外,《老子》也是译本最多的中国古代哲学著作之一。

Part Three　Critical Thinking and Discussion

1. What are the main characteristics of Taoism?

2. What is your attitude towards Taoism?

Chapter 3

The Contention of a Hundred Schools of Thought

From the Eastern Zhou Dynasty, the slave-owning system began to decay and crumble with a notable rise in the value of the common people with a corresponding increase in disenfranchised nobility. The result was the appearance of a new class, consisting of scribes, counselors, and teachers, many of whom had an aristocratic background. Deeply concerned with the social chaos and moral decline brought about by the collapse of slavery and by constant wars among the states, these people contended vigorously in proposing solutions, thus forming various philosophical schools. These schools began to take shape during the Spring and Autumn Period, and flourished in the Warring States Period. Historically known as the classical age, this period is also referred to as the age of the "Hundred Philosophers (诸子百家)."

The "Hundred Philosophers" were classified by Sima Tan (司马谈), father of Sima Qian (司马迁), as belonging to six schools: Confucianism (儒家), Taoism (道家), Mohism (墨家), the Logicians (名家), the *Yin-Yang* School (阴阳家) and the Legalist School (法家). To these six schools, Liu Xin (刘歆), a late Western Han philosopher, added four others: the Agriculturists (农家), the Strategists (兵家), the Eclectic School (杂家), and the Story-tellers (小说家), thus bringing the total up to ten. Each school of thought had its main theorist and followers. They wrote books and gave lectures to propagate their views and criticize their opponents' fallacies. Later, people described this lively academic environment as "The Contention of a Hundred Schools of Thought". In the following pages we shall have a concise discussion of the leading figures and principal tenets of some main philosophical schools.

/ Confucianism /

Confucianism is a school of thought represented by Confucius and Mencius. Primarily a code of ethics and a system of philosophy, Confucianism has left its mark on Chinese politics and government, family and society, and art and literature. In a certain sense, Confucianism even functioned as a religion in the ancient community. Its influence is so predominant that if anyone should be asked to characterize traditional Chinese life and culture in one word, that word would be "Confucian". Confucianism is not confined to China. Neighboring countries such as Japan and Vietnam embraced Confucianism in their national life and culture. In Europe, Confucianism also has a lot of famous admirers, such as Gottfried Leibniz (戈特弗里德·莱布尼茨) and Voltaire (伏尔泰). Other men of letters in Europe who came under the influence of Confucian included Geothe (歌德), Alexander Pope (亚历山大·蒲柏) and Charles Lamb (查尔斯·兰姆).

To understand Confucianism thoroughly, we need a survey of its origin. Confucianism sought its origin in the institutions of the "Former Kings (先王)", that is, the pre-dynastic sage-emperors Yao (尧) and Shun (舜) and the founders of the first three dynasties, Xia, Shang, and Zhou. Many basic Confucian principles, such as the worship of ancestors, the Mandate of Heaven and the government by virtue, were popular at least during the Zhou Dynasty. However, the Confucian School began to take shape only during the Spring and Autumn Period when Confucius and his disciples were traveling from one state to another to spread their ideas. Therefore, Confucius is regarded as the founder of Confucianism. There is no special word in Chinese meaning "Confucian" or "Confucianist". Members of the Confucian School have always been called *ru* (儒), a word that may be translated as "literati". With regard to this term, *The Explanation of Script and Elucidation of Characters* (《说文解字》) by Xu Shen (许慎), one of the earliest dictionaries, says: "The word *ru* means 'yielding'. It's a term used to refer to scholars proficient in the arts." This would indicate that *ru* was originally a term denoting all persons who possessed education and were versed in the arts. But later on, the use of the term was restricted exclusively to the Confucian School.

The Confucianists were specialists in the rituals that played an important role in the lives of the aristocracy. The result is that Confucianism became the rationalized expression of upper-class morality. This explains its emphasis on correct ritualistic behavior, on such cultural activities as music, on a graded love, and on the ruler as a moral example to his people.

Mencius, also known as Meng Zi (孟子), the second sage of Confucianism, was born in the kingdom of Zou (邹) in the State of Lu (鲁), more than 100 years after Confucius's death. His family name was Meng (孟) and his personal name Ke (轲). His family was poor when he was young. It was said that his mother moved house three times so that her son could live in a good neighborhood. In several respects his life was similar to that of Confucius. After finishing his study under a disciple of Zi Si (子思), grandson of Confucius, he became a well-known scholar and for a brief period served as an official in the State of Qi (齐). He went to many states to talk with their rulers about government by humanity. When he found that no ruler would adopt his views, he devoted himself to teaching and writing. He wrote the *Mencius* (《孟子》) with the help of some of his disciples.

Mencius

Mencius considered himself the man able to perpetuate (使不朽，延续) Confucius's teachings in a time of disorder and intellectual confusion. He tried his utmost "to rectify men's hearts, and to put an end to perverse doctrines; to oppose one-sided actions and put away licentious expressions, thus to carry on the work of the sages. (正人心，息邪说，距诐行，放淫辞，以承三圣者。)" Therefore, the philosophic ideas of Mencius might be regarded as an amplification of the teachings of Confucius.

Mencius reaffirmed the basic Confucian tenet that government is primarily for the good of the people and not the ruler. He said, "The people rank the highest in a state; the spirits of the land and grain come next; and the ruler counts for the least. (民为贵，社稷次之，君为轻。)" To him, the relationship of the ruler and the people was reciprocal. "When a ruler regards his subjects as his hands and feet, they regard him as their belly and heart; when he regards them as dogs and horses, they regard him as a common fellow; when he regards them as dirt and grass, they regard him as robber and enemy. (君之视臣如手足，则臣视君如腹心；君之视臣如犬马，

则臣视君如国人；君之视臣如土芥，则臣视君如寇仇。）"

Mencius made the original goodness of human nature the keynote to his system. To him, everyone has feelings of sympathy or commiseration, the feeling of shame and resentment, the feeling of respect and modesty, and the feeling of the distinction between right and wrong. Such feelings are universal among mankind and they come as naturally as the taste of food, and the sight of beauty. Therefore, human nature is originally good, and will be good if it is guided by its innate feelings, just as water is inclined to flow downward. According to Mencius, from these feelings grow the following four moral qualities or the "Four Initiators (四端)": humanity, righteousness, propriety, and wisdom. These qualities are inherent in man, for they are endowed by Heaven, or they arise from the inner springs of the human heart.

Since human nature is originally good, then where does evil arise? Why are some people degenerate, even evil? Mencius argued that when a man is not good, it is not because he lacks the "Four Initiators" described above. His evil results from the fact that he has either not developed, or has suppressed and destroyed these initiators. It is the material longings that have obscure these moral qualities. Therefore, all-important is the function of education, self-cultivation and self-discipline, so that one does not lose his original "child's heart" and so that the "Four Initiators" may become the four full-flowing virtues.

For self-cultivation, Mencius advocated the method of nourishing the great morale or the vast moving force (浩然之气), which is produced by the accumulation of righteous deeds. When this force is developed to the fullest extent, one will attain the highest spiritual state. Then, "Riches and honor cannot make him dissipate, poverty and mean condition cannot make him swerve, and power and force cannot make him bend himself. (富贵不能淫，贫贱不能移，威武不能屈。)"

/ Taoism /

Taoism, together with Confucianism, is one of the two major indigenous religio-philosophical traditions that have shaped Chinese life for more than 2,000 years. Taoist thought permeates Chinese culture and has also found its way into all Asian cultures influenced by China, especially those of Vietnam, Japan, and the Republic of Korea. More strictly defined, Taoism includes philosophical Taoism, that is, the ideas and attitudes peculiar to *Lao Zi* (《老子》), *Zhuang Zi* (《庄子》), *Lie Zi* (《列子》), and related writings, and religious Taoism, which is concerned with the ritual worship of *Dao* (道) or the Way. In this chapter only philosophical Taoism, which was founded by Lao Zi and Zhuang Zi, will be discussed.

As we know, Taoism, as a school of thought, advocates the doctrine that *Dao* is the origin of the universe, the course, the principle, the substance, and the standard of all things, to which all people must conform. Based on *Dao De Jing*, Taoism promotes the belief that a person should live a simple life, not to strive for wealth, fame or power, which will only bring one worries and troubles. With proper behavior and self-restraint, a person can achieve great inner strength and a prolonged life. This school favors the political principle of "achieving good governance through non-action".

Zhuang Zi, also known as Zhuang Zhou (庄周), was born in the State of Song (宋) (in the present-day Henan Province), and lived a hermit's life. He was famous for his ideas and writings and once declined a prime minister in the State of Chu (楚) to retain his freedom because he preferred to live like a fish in muddy water and enjoy himself. *Zhuang Zi* (《庄子》), which is believed to have been written by him, consists of 33 chapters, presenting his ideas through imagery, anecdote and parable, as well as allegory and parody. Written in beautiful poetic prose, many of the chapters are considered to be literary masterpieces.

Zhuang Zi

Zhuang Zi inherited and developed Lao Zi's philosophy. Following Lao Zi, Zhuang Zi took *Dao* or the Way to be the all-embracing first principle through which the universe has come into being. *Dao* is a formless material and might be called *wu* (无) or nonbeing, but it produces all things with forms. *Dao* is also *qi* (气) or air, which integrated and became concrete things. When concrete things disintegrated, they returned to *qi*. This also applies to human beings. In other words, *Dao* is nonbeing, and exists by and through itself without a beginning or an end. But Zhuang Zi advanced the concept of *Dao* and gave Taoism a dynamic character. To him, *Dao* as Nature is not only spontaneity but also a constant flux, for all things are in a state of perpetual self-transformation, each according to its own nature and in its own way. In this unceasing transfiguration, things appear and disappear. Although they are different, *Dao* equalizes them as one. Therefore, all things and opinions should be dealt with equally, and there should be no distinction between right and wrong, good and evil, life and death, beauty and ugliness, etc. All distinctions and oppositions are merely relative. This is Zhuang Zi's famous doctrine of the equality of all things (齐物论). The master overemphasized the relativity of things, and went so far that he denied any distinction among them. This, of course, is contrary to both truth and reality, and can only lead to relativism.

Zhuang Zi held that man should live a life that suited his original nature. If he could get rid of desires for fame, wealth, and position, he would be able to obtain peace, freedom, and leisure. Things that are natural are good, and things that are artificial are bad. An ideal person is one who is entirely at one with nature, accepts whatever happens to him, has no goal, and makes no conscious effort to achieve anything. Zhuang Zi blamed not only the heroes and the inventors of culture praised by the Confucianists, but also the sages who shaped the rites and rules of the society. Even "coveting knowledge" is condemned because it engenders competition and fights over profit. His ideal society is one in which "there were no roads over the mountains or boats and bridges to cross the waters, and men dwelt together with birds and beasts. (山无蹊隧,泽无舟梁,万物群生。)" The master denied all human efforts and made what is of nature and what is of man absolutely diametric. His total denial and condemnation of human civilization reflected the deeper pessimism of the Taoists facing greater chaos during the Warring States Period.

In contrast to Confucian sages and cultural heroes, Zhuang Zi's ideal personality is the perfect man (至人), or the true man (真人). According to him, the perfect man "fasts in his mind (心斋)," that is, to keep his mind void and tranquil, and "sits down in forgetfulness (坐忘)", which means to discard knowledge, forget first the outer world, then the body, then the mind, and become one with the infinite. Since the perfect man has transcended all distinctions, he is happy in any form of existence. The transformation of life and death is to him as the succession of day and night, and cannot affect him, to say nothing of the worldly gain and loss, good luck and ill luck. In this way, the perfect man is in perfect identity with the universe and goes up and down with evolution. Therefore, he is absolutely free and happy. Of course, such a perfect man can only appear in Zhuang Zi's imagination and can never be found in the mundane world.

/ Mohism /

Founded by Mo Zi (墨子), Mohism was an eminent school of philosophy that rivaled Confucianism in prominence during the Warring States Period. The followers of this school were mostly commoners, and the Mohist philosophy was a rationalized expression of the ethics of the lower classes in general. Being well organized, Mohism later became somewhat a religious congregation with the Elder Master (钜子) as its leader. Both the Elder Master and his followers admonished zealously to promote benefits and remove evil while leading an extremely simple life themselves. In order to help the weak and poor, the Mohists devoted themselves to the techniques of defensive war, including the building of instruments for resisting the siege of cities, which in turn explains the interest of the Later Mohists in mathematics and physics. Mohism was pushed into the background if not into complete oblivion by the ascendancy of Confucianism for the next 2,000 years and was rediscovered only in the 20th century.

Mo Zi, whose name was Mo Di (墨翟), was the founder of Mohism. Born into the State of Song, he was widely read and well versed in the classics. A craftsman in his youth, he later became a scholar. After serving for a brief period as a civil servant, Mo Zi spent a number of years as a traveling counselor to feudal lords and princes, and having never been given the opportunity to put his teachings into practice or the world in order, he had eventually to be content with conducting a school and preparing his disciples for public office. It is said that Mo Zi was at first a follower of

Mo Zi

Confucianism but later opposed it to found a system of thought of his own. He was critical of Confucianism for its emphasis on the codes of rituals and social elegance, which were, to him, burdensome and wasteful. He left a work known as *Mo Zi* (《墨子》) consisting of 71 chapters.

Mo Zi's important views included exalting the worthy (尚贤), conforming upwardly (尚同), practicing economy (贵俭), simplifying funerals (节葬), discarding music and other enjoyments

(非乐), rejecting fatalism (非命), denouncing unjust wars (非攻), and practicing universal love (兼爱). The best-known one of these views was the theory of universal love. Mo Zi advocated it to replace selfishness and partiality, or graded love. Universal love, according to him, means to love all people equally regardless of their nationality, social status, or relationships. Mo Zi said, "One should consider other people's bodies as one's own, other people's families as one's own. (必为其友之身若为其身，为其友之亲若为其亲。)" He taught people to love other people's parents, families, and countries as their own. What is more, universal love should be combined with mutual benefit. To love people means to bring benefits to them, and to bring benefits to people is the result and proof of the love. As previously stated, Mo Zi was the philosopher of the people, especially the lower class people. All of his doctrines are the manifestations of his great sympathy and attentive care for the poor and weak. Mo Zi's greatness lies in his proposal of the doctrine of universal love and its combination with mutual benefit more than 2,000 years ago.

Another distinctive feature of Mo Zi's thought was his stress on methodology. He attached great importance to the threefold test and the fourfold standard. The threefold test refers to the basis, the provability, and the applicability of a proposition. This test was employed to examine a proposition for its compatibility with the best of the established conceptions, its consistency with experience, and its contribution to desirable ends when put into operation. The benefits resulting form the application of a proposition, the last part of the threefold test, are conceived in terms of the fourfold standard, namely enrichment of the poor, increase of the population, removal of danger, and regulation of disorder. Because of this theory, Mo Zi was sometimes called a pragmatist, or a utilitarian by contemporary scholars.

/ Legalism /

Legalism or the Legalist School did not concern itself with ethical, metaphysical, or logical concepts, as other schools did. Guan Zi (管子) was the pioneer of Legalism. Its chief objective was the concentration of power in the ruler. In its early period, this school was divided into three groups, one of which laid emphasis on power or authority (势); the second highlighted statecraft (术), or the art of conducting affairs and handling men; and the third laid stress on the concept of law (法). The first group was headed by Shen Dao (慎到), who was a Taoist as well as a Legalist. The leader of the second group was Shen Buhai (申不害), who was a minister in the State of Han (韩). The leader of the third group was Shang Yang (商鞅), a descendant of the royal family of the State of Wei (卫), who for many years served as a minister in the State of Qin (秦). *The Book of Lord Shang* (《商君书》), one of the main works of the Legalist School, was attributed to him. Combining the three tendencies and forming his doctrines of Legalism, Han Fei (韩非) became the most outstanding exponent of this school. Generally speaking, Legalism values the necessity to lay down laws to unify the thoughts of people, to promote agriculture to achieve affluence, to wage wars to gain strength and power, and to establish a system of bureaucracy. The Legalists also hold a belief that contradiction is present everywhere, and the two sides of a contradiction are changeable. The Legalist School triumphed over the other schools in the 3rd century B.C.E., and its philosophy was put into strict practice during the brief period of the Qin Dynasty.

Han Fei

Han Fei, the representative philosopher of the Legalist School and the synthesizer of the Legalist theories, was born into a noble family in the State of Han (韩). He delighted in the study of punishment, names, law and statecraft, while basing his doctrines upon the Yellow Emperor (黄帝) and Lao Zi. Owing to his speech impediment, he was not good at talking, but was skilled at writing. Together with Li Si (李斯), he studied under the guidance of Xun Zi (荀子). Seeing the weakness of his state, Han Fei wrote many letters to the king, suggesting ways to make it strong, but his advice went unheeded. Then he devoted his time to writing a book explaining his ideas. It was called *Han Fei Zi* (《韩非子》). The King Ying Zheng of Qin (秦王嬴政), who later unified China, happened to read the book, and admired the writer's ideas. The King forced Han to send Han Fei to Qin. Unfortunately, soon after he arrived in Qin, he was first thrown into prison and then poisoned to death by Li Si, Qin's chief minister.

Most of the Legalists believed that man's nature was evil, and Han Fei, as the disciple of Xun Zi, was particularly clear on this point. All men, he insisted, acted from motives of selfishness and self-profit, and so showed calculating minds toward one another. Relations between men were determined by nothing but personal gains and losses. Because of this state of human nature, men must be administrated by governmental organizations and kept in their place by punishments if the world is to be put into proper order. Accordingly, law, statecraft, and power must be employed by the government.

Han Fei made a comprehensive synthesis of the enforcement of law, the manipulation of statecraft and the exercise of power. In his opinion, the "intelligent ruler (明主)" should rule the state by laws, and laws should be made public to all people and should be strictly enforced. After the laws have been made, everyone in the state, both the ruler and the ruled, must obey them and cannot change them at will. In fact, the highest ideal of the Legalist School is that the ruler and the ministers, the superior and the inferior, the noble and the humble, all of them obey the laws. Laws, then, are the highest standards by which to judge the words and actions of the people of a state. All words and actions that are not in accord with the laws must be prohibited. Therefore, "In the state of the intelligent ruler, there is no literature of books and records, but the laws serve as teachings. There are no sayings of the early Kings, but the officials act as teachers. (明主之国，无书简之文，以法为教。无先王之语，以吏为师。)" "Statecraft" means the skill or technique and wisdom of the ruler in managing public affairs. To select and evaluate officials, the ruler should adopt his statecraft. After assigning posts according to individual capacities, the ruler should demand satisfactory performance of the responsibilities devolving on their posts and punish anyone who is derelict of duty or abuses his power. Statecraft is also Han Fei's answer to the problem of usurpation, through which the rulers lose their power. It behooves the ruler to trust no one; to be suspicious of sycophants; to permit no one to gain undue power or influence; and, above all, to use wile to unearth plots against the throne. "Power" or "authority" refers to the highest position and supreme power of the ruler to issue orders and to make others obey. A ruler's authority is outwardly manifested in his rewards and punishments, which act as the "two handles (二柄)" of his administration.

Han Fei held that society was always going forward, and would never go backward. He told interesting fables like "Waiting for a Rabbit by the Tree (守株待兔)" to ridicule those people who thought that the past was better than the present. He saw the relevance between material wealth and the population. If the population grew faster than material wealth, there might be social turmoil. This is a correct view even today.

The term *maodun* (矛盾) or contradiction came from one of his fables. A man from the Kingdom of Chu was selling spears and shields. He boasted about his shield, saying, "It is so tough that nothing can pierce it." He then boasted about his spear, saying, "It is so sharp that it can pierce anything." Someone asked him, "What will happen if you pierce your shield using your spear?" The man was speechless. A spear that can pierce anything and a shield that can be pierced by nothing cannot exist at the same time. Han Fei indicated that contradiction was present everywhere, and the two sides of a contradiction were changeable, that is to say, good fortune might change into misfortune, prosperity into decline, strength into weakness, and so on.

To sum up, Han Fei's opposition to conservatism was clear-cut and his advocacy of reform positive. His doctrine of the equality of all people before established laws was refreshing in a society of rigid hierarchy and various privileges. However, his emphasis on absolute concentration of power of the ruler led the first emperor to practice totalitarian regimentation, "burning the books and burying the literati (焚书坑儒)". Representing the interests of the rising landlord class, Han Fei laid the ideological foundation for the advent of the feudal aristocracy.

Besides the philosophy during Pre-Qin times, the Han Dynasty featured orthodox thought. Emperor Wu launched the campaign of "discrediting the hundred schools of thought and respecting only Confucianism (罢黜百家, 独尊儒术)". Consequently, the political, social and educational institutions were developed according to the Confucian principles and the Confucian classics became the corpus of learning studied by all scholar-administrators through the ages. Confucianism became an orthodox philosophy that served as the ideological foundation of the feudal rule as well as the state cult.

Orthodox philosophy inspired by Dong Zhongshu (董仲舒) claims that Heaven affects human affairs and human behavior finds response in Heaven (天人感应) and that the power of emperors is endowed by Heaven (君权神授). The disasters and anomalies are interpreted as Heaven's ways of warning the ruler and the people to examine their personal conduct and correct their mistakes. This theory, to modern people, is preposterous and wry. In the Eastern Han Dynasty, a brave scholar, Wang Chong (王充), criticized and refuted Dong's theory of the interaction between Heaven and man. Wang Chong spent over 30 years writing his work entitled *Balanced Discussions* (《论衡》), in which he also stressed the importance of effect in testing the correctness of a theory.

Dong Zhongshu

Dong Zhongshu also propounded his doctrine of "Three Cardinal Guides (三纲)", that is, a sovereign is the guide of his subjects, a father is the guide of his son, and a husband is the guide of his wife. To be the guide means to have absolute authority. Moreover, he popularized the set of "Five Constant Virtues (五 常)", which includes humanity, righteousness, propriety, wisdom, faithfulness or trustworthiness. All the above mentioned ethics were a severe burden on the majority of the Chinese people in the long years of feudal society.

Philosophers during the Wei and Jin Dynasties went beyond phenomena to find reality behind space and time. They were interested in what is profound and abstruse, and consequently their school is called the Metaphysical School or Metaphysics (玄学) containing three famous classic works of *The Book of Changes* (《易经》), *Dao De Jing* and *Zhuang Zi*, known as the "three profound studies (三玄)." These philosophers, mostly young literary men, often engaged in "pure conversations (清谈)," an unconventional way of life expressed in elegant, refined, carefree, and witty conversations. The most outstanding figures of this school are Wang Bi (王弼) and Guo Xiang (郭象).

Buddhism reached its apex during the Sui and Tang Dynasties. The Buddhist philosophy formed an alliance with the wisdom of Chinese philosophers. By analyzing spiritual phenomena and human rationality, it attempts to understand thoroughly the universe and human life.

During the Song and Ming Dynasties, the rationalistic Confucian philosophy or Neo-Confucianism, which combined Taoism with Buddhism, became influential. It mainly discussed the nature of human beings, the relationship between human beings, between man and nature, and between man and society. Neo-Confucianism was divided into two schools, the School of Principle (理学), and the School of Mind (心学). The typical representatives of the former were Zhou Dunyi (周敦颐), Cheng Hao (程颢), Cheng Yi (程颐) and Zhu Xi (朱熹), who held that

"rationalism (理)" was eternal and was a spiritual existence before the world existed, and that all things in the world were derived from "rationalism". The representative figures of the latter included Lu Jiuyuan (陆九渊) and Wang Shouren (王守仁). Lu Jiuyuan, a contemporary and rival of Zhu Xi, regarded the mind as the origin of the universe and identified the mind with principle. "The universe is my mind; my mind is the universe. (宇宙便是吾心，吾心便是宇宙。)" he said. This thoroughgoing subjective idealism shows not only the influence of Meng Zi but also the impact of Buddhism. Wang

Wang Shouren

Shouren, the Ming Dynasty Neo-Confucianist, revised and refined Lu's theory, and advocated that "There is nothing outside the mind and no rationalism or reason outside the mind. (心外无物,心外无理。)"

The philosophy during the Ming and Qing Dynasties was called application philosophy. It focused on "self-examination" and sticking to the application of philosophy on state affairs. The answers to specific issues instead of abstract study were explored.

Key Terms

1. 仁民爱物

Have Love for the People, and Cherish All Things

◎孟子曰:"君子之于物也,爱之而弗仁;于民也,仁之而弗亲。亲亲而仁民,仁民而爱物。"(《孟子》)

Mencius said, "Men of virtue cherish all things, but this is not benevolent love, have compassion for others, but this is not love of family. Men of virtue love and care for their loved ones, they are therefore kind to other people. When they are kind to people, they treasure everything on earth." (Mencius)

2. 仁者无敌

The Benevolent Person Is Invincible.

◎孟子对曰:"地方百里而可以王(wàng)。王如施仁政于民,省刑罚,薄税敛,深耕易耨;壮者以暇日修其孝悌忠信,入以事其父兄,出以事其长上,可使制梃以挞秦楚之坚甲利兵矣……故曰:'仁者无敌'。"(《孟子》)

Mencius replied, "With a territory of a hundred square li, it is possible for one to rule as a true king. If Your Majesty governs with benevolence, refrains from imposing harsh punishment, and lightens taxes and imposts on the people, they will plow deeply and weed thoroughly. The able-bodied will, on their days off, care for their parents, and they will show fraternal love, loyalty and good faith. At home, they will serve their fathers and brothers, and away from home, their elders and superiors. So they are able to defeat the Qin and Chu troops even with wooden sticks... That is why I believe that the benevolent person is invincible." (Mencius)

3. 保民而王

Protect the People and Then Rule as a King

◎曰:"德何如则可以王(wàng)矣?"曰:"保民而王(wàng),莫之能御也。"(《孟子》)

King Xuan of Qi said, "What kind of virtue should one pose to be able to rule as a true king?" Mencius replied, "Protect the people and ensure their well-being, and you can rule as a king of all the land. No one can challenge you." (*Mencius*)

4. 心悦诚服

Be Completely Convinced and Follow Willingly

◎以力服人者,非心服也,力不赡也;以德服人者,中心悦而诚服也,如七十子之服孔子也。(《孟子》)

Coercion will only win those who follow because they are too weak to resist; it is moral qualities that will persuade others to gladly and willingly follow, just as in the case of Confucius's seventy disciples who followed him out of true conviction. (*Mencius*)

5. 浩然之气

Noble Spirit

◎"敢问何谓浩然之气?"曰:"难言也。其为气也,至大至刚,以直养而无害,则塞于天地之间。其为气也,配义与道。无是,馁也。"(《孟子》)

"May I ask what noble spirit is?" "It is something hard to describe," Mencius answered. "As a vital force, it is immensely powerful and just. Cultivate it with rectitude and keep it unharmed, and it will fill all the space between heaven and earth. Being a vital force, noble spirit becomes powerful with the accompaniment of righteousness and Dao. Without righteousness and Dao, noble spirit will be weak and frail." (*Mencius*)

6. 舍生取义

Give One's Life to Uphold Righteousness

◎生亦我所欲也,义亦我所欲也,二者不可得兼,舍生而取义者也。(《孟子》)

Both life and righteousness are important to me. However, if I cannot have both, I will give my life so as to uphold righteousness. (*Mencius*)

7. 得道多助,失道寡助

A Just Cause Enjoys Abundant Support While an Unjust Cause Finds Little Support.

◎域民不以封疆之界,固国不以山溪之险,威天下不以兵革之利。得道者多助,失道者寡助。寡助之至,亲戚畔之。多助之至,天下顺之。以天下之所顺,攻亲戚之所畔,故君子有不战,战必胜矣。(《孟子》)

People are not confined by boundaries, the state is not secured by dangerous cliffs and streams, and the world is not overawed by sharp weapons. One who has Dao enjoys abundant support while one who has lost Dao finds little support. When lack of support reaches its extreme point, even a ruler's own relatives will rebel against him. When abundant support reaches its extreme point, the whole world will follow him. If one whom the whole world follows attacks one whose own relatives rebel against him, the result is clear. Therefore, a man of virtue either does not go to war, or if he does, he is certain to win victory. (Mencius)

8. 荣辱

Honor and Disgrace

◎先义而后利者荣,先利而后义者辱。(《荀子》)

Those who put righteousness before personal interests will be honored. Those who put personal interests before righteousness will be disgraced. (Xun Zi)

9. 明分使群

Proper Ranking Leads to Collaboration.

◎离居不相待则穷,群而无分则争。穷者患也,争者祸也,救患除祸,则莫若明分使群矣。(《荀子》)

Living alone without group support leads to poverty; living together without appropriate ranking causes disputes. Poverty and disputes are all disastrous. The best way to solve these problems is to establish different ranks, which makes collaboration possible. (Xun Zi)

10. 君者善群

A Ruler Should Keep People Together.

◎君者,善群也。群道当,则万物皆得其宜。(《荀子》)

A ruler is someone whose duty is to bring people together. If he follows this principle in organizing the people into a community, all things will fall into the right place. (Xun Zi)

11. 载舟覆舟

Carry or Overturn the Boat / Make or Break

◎君者,舟也;庶人者,水也。水则载舟,水则覆舟,此之谓也。(《荀子》)

The ruler is the boat and the people are the water. Water can carry the boat but can also overturn it. This is the very truth. (*Xun Zi*)

12. 王者富民

A Ruler Should Enrich People.

◎故王者富民，霸者富士，仅存之国富大夫，亡国富筐箧、实府库。筐箧已富，府库已实，而百姓贫……则倾覆灭亡可立而待也。(《荀子》)

So a ruler who conducts benevolent governance will enrich his people. But a ruler who wants to control all dukes and princes can only enrich his army. A state that only enriches its ministers can barely survive; a state that only keeps the ruler's coffer and his storehouses full is doomed. Inevitably, the people in such a state will be plunged into poverty··· It will not be long before such a state collapses. (*Xun Zi*)

13. 爱民者强

Power Comes from Caring for the People.

◎爱民者强，不爱民者弱。(《荀子》)

A state that takes good care of its people is strong and prosperous; a state that does not care about its people is waning and weak. (*Xun Zi*)

14. 积善成德

Moral Character Can Be Built by Accumulating Goodness.

◎积土成山，风雨兴焉；积水成渊，蛟龙生焉；积善成德，而神明自得，圣心备焉。(《荀子》)

Heaped earth makes mountains where wind and rain are born; water pools into deep lakes where dragons dwell; many good deeds build moral character that creates discernment, and prepare for the heart and mind of a sage. (*Xun Zi*)

15. 兼爱

Universal Love

◎天下兼相爱则治，交相恶则乱。(《墨子》)

Universal love will bring peace and order to the world, while mutual animosity can only throw the world into disorder. (*Mo Zi*)

16. 非攻

Denouncing Unjust Wars

◎今欲为仁义，求为上士，尚欲中圣王之道，下欲中国家百姓之利，故当若非攻之为说，

而将不可不察者此也。(《墨子》)

If one wishes to be humane and just and become a gentleman with high moral standards, he must both observe the way of the sage kings, and advance the interests of the state and the people. In order to achieve these goals, the principle of prohibiting unjust wars cannot be disregarded. (Mo Zi)

17. 非命

Rejecting Fatalism

◎执有命者,此天下之厚害也,是故子墨子非也。(《墨子》)

Those who hold that there is fate are harmful to the world. For that reason, Mo Zi is opposed to their stand. (Mo Zi)

18. 尚贤

Exalting the Worthy

◎故古者圣王甚尊尚贤,而任使能,不党父兄,不偏贵富,不嬖(bì)颜色。(《墨子》

Therefore, in antiquity the sage kings greatly honored the principle of exalting the worthy. They employed the virtuous and capable, forming no cliques with their fathers and brothers, showing no partiality to the rich and noble, nor favoring those with handsome features. (Mo Zi)

19. 尚同

Conforming Upwardly

◎上之所是,必亦是之。上之所非,必亦非之。己有善,傍荐之。上有过,规谏之。尚同义其上,而毋有下比之心。(《墨子》)

What your superior affirms, you must also affirm. What your superior rejects, you must also reject. If you have a good idea, manage to go to your superior and recommend it. If your superior commits an error, admonish him and remonstrate. Upwardly you should conform to your superior, not to your subordinates. (Mo Zi)

20. 达名

Unrestricted Name

◎名,达、类、私。(《墨子》)

A "name" consists of the unrestricted, classified, or private. (Mo Zi)

21. 达闻知

Knowledge from Hearsay

◎知,闻、说、亲。(《墨子》)

Knowing comes from hearsay, explanation, or personal experience. (Mo Zi)

22. 言必信,行必果

Promises Must Be Kept; Actions Must Be Resolute.

◎言必信,行必果,使言行之合,犹合符节也,无言而不行也。(《墨子》)

Promises must be kept; actions must be resolute. They should fit together like the two parts of a tally stick: everything said must be put into practice. (Mo Zi)

23. 庄周梦蝶

Zhuang Zi Dreaming of Becoming a Butterfly

◎昔者庄周梦为胡蝶,栩栩然胡蝶也,自喻适志与!不知周也。俄然觉,则蘧(qú)蘧然周也。不知周之梦为胡蝶与?胡蝶之梦为周与?周与胡蝶,则必有分矣。此之谓物化。(《庄子》)

Once I, Zhuang Zi, dreamed that I became a flying butterfly, happy with myself and doing as I pleased. I forgot that I was Zhuang Zi. Suddenly I woke up and I was Zhuang Zi again. I did not know whether Zhuang Zi had been dreaming that he was a butterfly, or whether a butterfly had been dreaming that it was Zhuang Zi. There must be a difference between the two, which is what I call "the transformation of things". (Zhuang Zi)

24. 逍遥

Carefree

◎芒然彷徨乎尘垢之外,逍遥乎无为之业。(《庄子》)

People should seek carefree enjoyment beyond the constraints of the human world. (Zhuang Zi)

25. 坐忘

Forget the Difference and Opposition between Self and the Universe

◎曰:"回坐忘矣。"仲尼蹴然曰:"何谓坐忘?"颜回曰:"堕肢体,黜聪明,离形去知,同于大通,此谓坐忘。"(《庄子》)

Yan Hui said, "I forget." Startled Confucius asked, "What do you mean by forgetting?" Yan Hui answered, "Pay no attention to my body and give up what I hear and see, leave the physical form, get rid of what occupies

my mind, and become one with the universe. This is what I call forgetting the difference and opposition between myself and the universe." (*Zhuang Zi*)

26. 忘适之适

Effortless Ease

◎始乎适而未尝不适者,忘适之适也。(《庄子》)

If a person feels at ease in mind, he will feel so anytime and anywhere. This is effortless ease. (*Zhuang Zi*)

27. 无用之用

The Advantage of Appearing Useless

◎山木自寇也,膏火自煎也。桂可食,故伐之;漆可用,故割之。人皆知有用之用,而莫知无用之用也。(《庄子》)

The trees in the mountain invite the axe; lamp oil illuminates by burning itself. The bark of the cinnamon tree is edible, and therefore it is cut down; the lacquer tree produces useful varnish, and therefore it suffers incisions. People all know the advantages of being useful, but no one knows the advantages of being useless. (*Zhuang Zi*)

28. 目击道存

See the Way with One's Own Eyes

◎子路曰:"吾子欲见温伯雪子久矣。见之而不言,何邪?"仲尼曰:"若夫人者,目击而道存矣,亦不可以容声矣!"(《庄子》)

Zi Lu said, "You, Master, have been wanting to see Wenbo Xuezi for a long time. But you did not say a word when you saw him. Why?" Confucius replied, "As soon as I saw him, I realized that he possesses Dao. So there was no need for me to say anything." (*Zhuang Zi*)

29. 安时处顺

Face Reality Calmly

◎且夫得者,时也;失者,顺也。安时而处顺,哀乐不能入也。(《庄子》)

And what is gained in life is due to changes in nature; loss of life is the natural course of things. I face the functioning of nature calmly and follow its path; thus neither sorrow nor joy will affect me. (*Zhuang Zi*)

30. 君子之交

Relations between Men of Virtue

◎君子之交淡若水,小人之交甘若醴。君子淡以亲,小人甘以绝。(《庄子》)

The relations between men of virtue are plain like water, while those between petty men are delicious like sweet wine. For the men of virtue the bland flavor leads to closeness; for the petty men the sweet flavor easily leads to rupture. (Zhuang Zi)

31. 静因之道

Governance by Being Aloof

◎是故有道之君,其处也若无知,其应物也若偶之。静因之道也。(《管子》)

Therefore, a ruler who practices the Way (Dao), when being by himself, seems without knowledge. And he adapts to things which follow their natural course of development. This is called being aloof in governance. (Guan Zi)

32. 法与时变,礼与俗化

Laws Change Along with Evolving Times; Rites Shift Along with Changing Customs.

◎故古之所谓明君者,非一君也,其设赏有薄有厚,其立禁有轻有重,迹行不必同,非故相反也,皆随时而变,因俗而动。(《管子》)

Hence there was more than one so-called wise ruler in ancient times. They gave out rewards which varied from big to small, their proscriptions might be harsh or light, and their methods were not always the same. This is not because they were deliberately trying to be different, but because they changed with the evolving times and shifted as customs changed. (Guan Zi)

33. 以国为国,以天下为天下

Rule a State or a Country with Different Methods

◎以家为乡,乡不可为也;以乡为国,国不可为也;以国为天下,天下不可为也。以家为家,以乡为乡,以国为国,以天下为天下。(《管子》)

To rule a town with the methods for governing a clan, the town will not be run well. To rule a state with the methods for governing a town, the state will not be run well. To rule a country with the methods for governing a state, the country will not be run well. To rule a clan, one must meet the requirements for governing a clan. To rule a town, one must meet the requirements for governing a town. To rule a state, one must meet the requirements for governing a state. To rule a country, one must meet the requirements for governing a country. (*Guan Zi*)

34. 兴利除害

Promote the Beneficial; Eliminate the Harmful

◎先王者善为民除害兴利,故天下之民归之。所谓兴利者,利农事也;所谓除害者,禁害农事也。(《管子》)

Wise ancient rulers promoted what was beneficial for the people and eliminated what was harmful, thus winning their allegiance. The beneficial means what is good for farming, the harmful what is not. (*Guan Zi*)

35. 法不阿贵

The Law Does Not Favor the Rich and Powerful.

◎法不阿贵,绳不挠曲。法之所加,智者弗能辞,勇者弗敢争。刑过不避大臣,赏善不遗匹夫。 (《韩非子》)

The law does not favor the rich and powerful, as the marking-line does not bend. What the law imposes, the wise cannot evade, nor can the brave defy. Punishment for wrongdoing does not spare senior officials, as rewards for good conduct do not bypass the common man. (*Han Fei Zi*)

36. 抱法处势

Upholding Law by Means of Power

◎中者,上不及尧、舜,而下亦不为桀、纣,抱法处势则治,背法去势则乱。(《韩非子》)

An ordinary ruler, not as good as Yao or Shun, yet not descending to the ways of Jie or Zhou, upholds the law by means of power to realize social stability. If he turns his back on the law and abnegates his power, society will fall into disorder. (*Han Fei Zi*)

37. 治内裁外

Handling Internal Affairs Takes Precedence over External Affairs.

◎三王不务离合而正,五霸不待从横而察,治内以裁外而已矣。(《韩非子》)

The founding rulers of the Xia, Shang, and Zhou Dynasties did not try to impose order on the land by keeping their distance from some or becoming close to others, nor did the Five Most Powerful Kings of the Spring and Autumn Period discern the broad trends in the world by forming vertical or horizontal alliances. They managed external affairs only after they had handled their internal affairs well. (*Han Fei Zi*)

38. 不战而胜

Win without Resorting to War

◎百战百胜,非善之善者也;不战而屈人之兵,善之善者也。故上兵伐谋,其次伐交,其次伐兵,其下攻城。攻城之法,为不得已。(《孙子兵法》)

Winning every battle is not the wisest use of force. Making the enemy surrender without fighting is the best military strategy. The preferred way is to foil the enemy's plans, the next best to use diplomacy, failing that to attack the enemy's forces, and the least desirable is to assault the enemy's cities. Assaulting cities is a last resort when all else has failed. (Sun Zi's Art of War)

39. 兵形象水

Troops Should Charge Forward like the Flow of Water.

◎夫兵形象水。水之形,避高而趋下;兵之形,避实而击虚。水因地而制流,兵因敌而制胜。故兵无常势,水无常形,能因敌变化而取胜者谓之神。(《孙子兵法》)

Troops should charge forward like water. Water takes its shape by flowing from high to low; troops attack weak points and avoid the strong. Water flows according to the shape of the land; troops achieve victory according to the situation of the enemy. Hence there is no set formation for troops and no set shape for water. One who can win by understanding the enemy's situation can be called a godlike commander. (Sun Zi's Art of War)

40. 天时地利人和

Favorable Weather Conditions, Geographic Advantages, and the Unity of the People

◎天时、地利、人和,三者不得,虽胜有殃。(《孙膑兵法》)

Favorable weather conditions, geographic advantages, and the unity of the people must be all in place. If not, victory will be costly. (Sun Bin's Art of War)

Exercises

Part One   Comprehension

Fill in the following blanks with the information you learn in Chapter 3.

1. For self-cultivation, Mencius advocated the method of nourishing the great _____ or the

vast moving force, which is produced by the accumulation of righteous deeds.

2. Zhuang Zi held that man should live a life that suited his _____ nature.

3. Universal love, according to him, means to love all the people _____ regardless of their nationality, social status, or relationships.

4. Another distinctive feature of Mo Zi's thought was his stress on _____.

5. In fact, the highest ideal of the Legalist School is that the ruler and the ministers, the superior and the inferior, the noble and the humble, all of them obey the _____.

6. _____ philosophy inspired by Dong Zhongshu claims that Heaven affect human affairs and human behavior finds response in Heaven and that the power of emperors are endowed by Heaven.

7. Philosophers during the Wei and Jin Dynasties went beyond phenomena to find _____ behind space and time.

8. During the Song and Ming Dynasties, the rationalistic Confucian philosophy or Neo-Confucianism, which combined Taoism with _____, became influential.

Part Two   Translation

Term Translation

1. 仁民爱物

2. 保民而王

3. 舍生取义

4. 得道多助,失道寡助

5. 明分使群

6. 载舟覆舟

7. 言必信,行必果

8. 忘适之适

9. 兴利除害

10. 法不阿贵

Passage Translation

　　诸子百家始于公元前770年,终于公元前222年。这一时期被誉为中国思想的黄金时期和百家争鸣时期,见证了不同思想学派的兴起。儒家思想是对于国人生活最具有长远影响

中华优秀传统文化要略 *A Glimpse of China's Fine Traditional Culture*

的本体思想。法家思想是深刻影响国家管理形式的哲学基础。道家思想则关注人与自然的关系,指出每个人的生活目标应该是调整自我来适应自然世界的节奏,顺应宇宙的模式,并和谐生活。而墨家学派是基于墨子思想创立的,被认为是百家争鸣时期儒家思想的主要竞争对手。诸子百家,特别是老子和孔子的思想,在世界哲学史的发展过程中占据了重要地位。

Part Three   Critical Thinking and Discussion

1. How did Han Fei make a synthesis of the Legalist Ideas? What do you think of rule by law and rule by morality?

2. Make a comment on "The people rank the highest in a state; the spirits of the land and grain come next; and the ruler counts for the least."

Chapter 4
Taoist Religion

Taoist religion is essential to Chinese culture. Taoist attitudes, ideas, and values have helped shape the minds and characters of millions of people in China, in East and Southeast Asia, and wherever Chinese communities have become established throughout the world. Not exclusive to Chinese cultures, Taoist religion has entered the mainstream of many Western societies. A brief introduction of Taoist religion in English demonstrates the popularity of Taoist ideas and practices throughout the world.

/ Origins of Taoist Religion /

One of the three major religious traditions in China, Taoist religion consisted of a series of organized religious movements that worshiped *Dao* or the Way and its emanations and observed magical, physical, alchemical and meditative practices (炼金术和冥想练习) aiming at immortality. Taoist religion sought its origins in three aspects: the worship of gods and ghosts in ancient times, the theories and practices of the immortals advocated by necromancers of alchemists and philosophical Taoism, and the learned tradition of Huang-Lao masters.

People of the Shang Dynasty worshiped an anthropomorphic supreme God (赋予人性的至高神仙) who was thought to dominate the whole world. Under this supreme God, there was a large group of various minor gods and ghosts that helped the supreme God to mete out reward and punishment in various aspects of life according to men's good or evil behaviors. People also believed that man's soul would not perish after death, and therefore they constantly made sacrifices to the departed ancestors in order to obtain their blessings. Moreover, divination and other magic techniques were developed to consult the will of gods and the ancestors for decisions on important affairs. The wizard acted as an intermediate between man and the other world of gods, ghosts, and ancestors. Some of the gods and ghosts later "served" in the Taoist pantheon, and most of the Taoist masters (道士), like wizards, were magicians who were believed to possess occult techniques.

Beliefs in immortal beings and practices aiming at immortality were quite popular during the Warring States Period, especially in the north-eastern coastal regions. The people who engaged in such practices and claimed to possess magical powers were called necromancers or wonder-workers (方士). A number of such wonder-workers visited the courts of Qin and the early Han. They talked about islands in the ocean and people by immortal beings that were described in the ancient books, and so convincing were their accounts that sizable expeditions were fitted out and sent in search of them. The necromancers (巫师, 方士) persuaded emperors to climb holy mountains and perform sacrifices in order to receive from immortals the elixir of longevity. One of these necromancers, Li Shao-jun (李少君), taught Emperor Wu of the Han Dynasty to perform sacrifices into the furnace, which would enable him to summon spiritual beings. They, in turn, would allow him to change cinnabar powder (mercuric sulfide) into gold, from which vessels were to be made, out of which the Emperor would eat and drink. This would increase his span of life and permit him to behold the immortals who dwell on the Isles of Penglai (蓬莱岛), in the midst of the sea. Many people believed that immortals frequently appeared disguised among men to transmit their immortality formulas and magical powers to worthy humans. This idea that humans could become immortals was later incorporated into the Taoist religion, and became one of its most important tenets.

Also originating in the eastern coastal region, alongside these same thaumaturgic tendencies, was the learned tradition of Huang-Lao masters, devotees of the legendary Yellow Emperor and Lao Zi. Lao Zi was the initiator of philosophical Taoism, and later was venerated also as the founder of Taoist religion. Lao Zi's work, *Dao De Jing*, or *Classic of the Way and Its Virtue*, in which he discoursed upon *Dao*, the arts of government and the method of longevity, became the most holy scripture of the Taoist followers. The Yellow Emperor was believed to be a ruler of the Golden Age who achieved success through following the principle of non-action. He was also celebrated as the patron of technology; and the classic works of many arcane arts, including alchemy, medicine, sexual techniques, cooking and dietetics, were all placed under his aegis.

/ Primitive Taoist Religion /

In the early Han Period, the teachings of Huang-Lao masters spread throughout learned and official circles in the capital. Many early Han statesmen became their disciples and attempted to practice government by non-action; among them were also scholars who cultivated esoteric arts. Although their doctrine lost its direct political relevance during the reign of Emperor Wu Di, their ensemble of teachings concerning both ideal government and practices for prolonging life continued to evoke considerable interest and is perhaps the earliest real Taoist movement of which there is clear historical evidence.

At the end of the 1st century B. C. E., a certain necromancer, Gan Zhongke (甘忠可), presented to the emperor a *Classic of the Great Peace* (《太平经》) which, he claimed, had been revealed to him by a spirit, who had come to him with the order to renew the Han Dynasty. His temerity cost him his life, but other works bearing the same title continued to come out. These works, miscellaneous in contents, contained some of the tenets of early Taoist religion, and were taken as holy scriptures by the Taoist masters.

The tradition of fully developed Taoist religious movements began in the second century with the Way of the Great Peace (太平道) and the Way of the Celestial Masters (天师道).

The Way of the Great Peace was organized by Zhang Jiao (张角) who led the great Yellow Turban Rebellion (黄巾起义) in 184. Zhang Jiao declared that the "blue heaven" was to be replaced by a "yellow heaven"; and his followers wore yellow turbans in token of this expectation. Worshiping a "Huang-Lao Lord (黄老君)", the movement gained a vast number of adherents throughout eastern China. Though they were eventually defeated by the imperial forces, the tendency towards messianic revolt continued to manifest itself at frequent intervals.

Zhang Jiao

The Way of the Celestial Masters, also known as the Way of the Five *Dou* of Rice (五斗米道) after a famous tax levied by the organization on its members, was founded in the mountains of modern Sichuan Province by Zhang Daoling (张道陵) who is said to have receive a revelation from Lao Zi or Lord Lao the Most High (太上老君). Lao Zi was honored as the originator of this religion, and *Dao De Jing* as the bible.

Zhang Daoling

For ceremonial and administrative purposes, the Way of the Celestial Masters organized 24 (later 28 and 36) parishes (教区, 堂区), where the Masters offered political as well as spiritual government. The focal point of each parish was the oratory, or "chamber of purity" which served as the center for communication with the powers on high. Here the *jijiu* (祭酒), the priestly functionary of the nuclear community, officiated. Zhang Daoling was later honored by his disciples as the Celestial Master (天师), whence came the name of the Way of the Celestial Masters.

Both the Way of the Great Peace and the Way of the Celestial Masters are in a sense associated with peasants, whose wishes they reflecte to some extent. The two movements lacked systematic theories as well as practices, therefore they were called by later people Primitive Taoist religion in contrast to the Taoist religion by later aristocrats.

/ Development of Taoist Religion /

As stated above, the Way of the Great Peace was suppressed by the Eastern Han Dynasty and only circulated secretly among people of lower class. The Way of the Celestial Masters, however, survived. In 215, the celestial master Zhang Lu (张鲁), grandson of Zhang Daoling, submitted to the authority of the Han general Cao Cao (曹操), which resulted in official recognition of this sect, though it was closely controlled. In the Wei-Jin chaotic years, Neo-Taoism flourished and the prominent scholars of the age were almost all engaged in discussions about *Dao* or the Way, non-action and techniques for longevity and immortality. This served as a catalytic agent for the development of the Way of the Celestial Masters. Consequently, this sect made marked progress at the courts of the Wei and Western Jin Dynasties until, by the end of the 3rd century, it counted among its adherents many of the most powerful families in North China.

This period also witnessed the mutual interaction of Religious Taoism and Buddhism. Taoism participated in the widening of thought because of the influence of a foreign religion and Buddhism underwent a partial "Taoicization" as part of its adaptation to Chinese conditions. The Buddhist contribution is particularly noticeable in the developing conceptions of the afterlife; Buddhist ideas of purgatory had a most striking effect on Taoism. Also during this period appeared *The Classics of Lao Zi's Conversion of the Barbarians* (《老子化胡经》) which claimed that Lao Zi, after vanishing into the west, became the Buddha and that Buddhism was a debased form of Religious Taoism.

To serve the needs of the aristocracy, some aristocratic adepts of Religious Taoism altered the Way of the Celestial Masters: eliminating the vulgar elements and systematizing its theories and practices. The new Religious Taoism was called Aristocratic Religious Taoism, the representatives of which included Ge Hong (葛洪), Kou Qianzhi (寇谦之), Lu Xiujing (陆修静) and Tao Hongjing (陶弘景).

Ge Hong, a Taoist master, alchemist and medical scientist of the Eastern Jin Dynasty, was a native of contemporary Jiangsu Province. After a strenuous life in civil and military service, in the course of which he managed to write voluminously on many subjects, this great eclectic scholar is said to have undertaken a long journey to Southern China in quest of the pure cinnabar found there. He stopped at Luofu Mountain, near contemporary Guangdong Province, however, where he died.

In his major work, *The Man Who Holds to Simplicity* (《抱朴子》), Ge Hong systematized and elaborated the theories and practices of immortals beginning with the Warring States Period. He discussed in detail the various formulas and practical operations for making the "gold elixir" and hence he was regarded by some scholars as the founder of the Way of Gold Elixir (金丹道). Ge Hong also incorporated into Religious Taoism Confucian ethical teachings, such as the Three Cardinal Guides and the Five Constant Virtues (三纲五常), and thus laid the theoretical basis of Aristocratic Religious Taoism.

Kou Qianzhi, a Taoist master of the Northern Wei Dynasty, was in his early years a follower of the Way of the Celestial Masters. Later, he alleged that he received the revelation from Lord Lao the Most High, who designated him celestial master and ordered him to undertake a total reformation of Religious Taoism. Not only were all popular messianic movements claiming to represent Lao Zi unsparingly condemned, but Kou's mission was particularly aimed at the elimination of abuses from the Way of the Celestial Masters itself. Sexual rites and the taxes contributed to the support of the priesthood were the principal targets of his denunciations. The proposed reform was radical and the Religious Taoism thus established was called by later people the Northern Way of the Celestial Masters (北天师道). Political and economic factors favored the acceptance of Kou's message at court; Emperor Tai Wu of the Northern Wei Dynasty put Kou in charge of religious affairs within his dominions and proclaimed this sect the official religion of the empire.

Lu Xiujing, a Taoist master of Song during the Southern Dynasties, codified the Taoist liturgies according to the requirements of the rulers, and by fusing several Southern Taoist sects he established the Southern Way of the Celestial Masters (南天师道). Lu also examined and distinguished 1, 228 volumes of Taoist scriptures, including precepts (戒律), ceremonies, alchemical drugs, and charms and talismans, which he divided into three Caves (三洞). Thus he laid the basis for the divisions of Taoist canons (教规).

Tao Hongjing, a great Taoist master between Qi and Liang during the Southern Dynasties, was also a poet, calligrapher, natural philosopher and the founder of critical pharmacology. He spent years searching out the manuscript legacy of Yang Xi (杨羲) and Xu Mi (许谧), two Taoist masters of the age, and in 492 retired to Maoshan (茅山), where he edited and annotated the revealed texts and attempted to re-create their practices in their original setting. The result was the writing of *Declaration of the Perfected* (《真诰》) and *Secret Instrument for Ascent to Perfection* (《登真隐诀》). His another important work is *Chart of the Ranks and Functions of the Gods* (《真灵位业图》) in which he integrated the Confucian hierarchy into Religious Taoism, and divided gods into several grades. Tao Hongjing founded the Maoshan Sect (茅山宗) which survived the prescription of all other Taoist sects in 504. It is reported that both Buddhist monks and Taoist priests officiated at his burial rites, because he was an intimate friend of Emperor Wu of Liang. Tao was also a Buddhist follower, and his writings evidence a complete familiarity with Buddhist literature.

After all these reforms, Religious Taoism became an effective tool to rule the people, and hence won the support of the rulers. In the following hundreds of years, it gained great popularity and ranked as one of the three main Chinese religions.

The Tang Dynasty marked the beginning of Religious Taoism's most spectacular success. The dynasty's founder, Li Yuan (李渊), claimed to be descended from Lao Zi and the Tang emperors were commonly referred to as "sages". Many officially sponsored shrines (神龛) were erected to worship Lord Lao the Most High, and even the Taoist priests and nuns were regarded as belonging to the imperial family. There appeared during this period many Taoist writings and prospective candidates who were examined in Taoist classics for the civil service. Also during this period, some important Taoist classics were translated into foreign languages and Religious Taoism thus spread to other Asian countries.

During the Northern Song Dynasty, Religious Taoism continued to hold a strong position, and was further strengthened by the comedies of the Song emperors' mystification. A whole series of "revelations" was arranged—the finding of letters from Heaven congratulating the dynasty, the announcing of auspicious omens, the conferring of titles on spirits and genii by the emperors, the sending of magic mushrooms to the court and so on.

After the retreat of the Song government to the south of the Changjiang River, a number of new Taoist sects were founded in the occupied North and soon attained impressive dimensions. Among them were: the Supreme Unity sect (太一道) founded in 1140 by Xiao Baozhen (萧抱珍); the Perfect and Great Way sect (真大道) founded in 1142 by Liu Deren (刘德仁); and the Perfect Realization sect (全真道) founded in 1167 by Wang Chongyang (王重阳). This last sect advocated the syncretism of the three religions and placed emphasis on meditation as a means to return to one's original nature and thus to prolong life. This sect enjoyed great popularity, and its establishments of celibate monks continued to be active into the 20th century, with the famous White Cloud Monastery (白云观) at Beijing as headquarters.

In the South, the Maoshan sect (茅山道) continued to prosper. In 1131, a Taoist master He Zhengong (何真公) claimed to have received a revelation from Xu Xun (许逊), a Taoist master of the 4th century, and founded the Pure and Luminous Way of Loyalty and Filial Piety (净明忠孝道). This sect preached the Confucian cardinal virtues as being essential for salvation, and consequently won many followers in conservative intellectual and official circles.

After the Song Dynasty, however, there was a decline. The Mongols were suspicious of Taoism on account of its continuing subversive political nature, which so easily took the form of anti-foreign agitation. In spite of the persecutions in the Yuan Dynasty, Religious Taoism continued to develop. In 1304, Zhang Yucai (张与材), the 38th descendant of Zhang Daoling, was honored as the head of the Way of Orthodox Unity (正一道), and all the sects characterized by the practices of charms and talismans were put under his control. Since then, there have been only two Religious Taoist schools: the Way of Orthodox Unity which gathered all the sects of charms and talismans and the Way of Perfect Realization which practiced the inner elixir techniques.

/ Principal Tenets and Practices of Taoist Religion /

The primary concern of the Taoist religion has been the Way, the origin of all things. The supreme way in its concealed state, itself permanent and unchanging, is seen as the first in a series of generating causes. In a typical formulation, the invisible Way gives birth to material forces in a state of a primordial chaos. This in turn gives rise by movement to the active principle of *Yang*, and by stillness to the principle of rest of *Yin*. The interaction of these two principles engenders the phenomenal world. But material forces are of different levels, and that of the highest level produces the world of immortals. In the cosmos, there are heavens beyond heavens, and altogether there are 36, all populated by immortals. Apart from these heavens, there are still cavern-heavens (洞天) and sanctuaries (福地) peopled by immortals in the human world. It is believed that there are 10 great cavern-heavens, 36 lesser cavern-heavens and 72 sanctuaries in this world.

The premise of Religious Taoism is that life is good and to be enjoyed. Like all things, the individual self is not set apart from the rest of nature but is a product of *yin* and *yang* as the creative processes of the Way. Neither the ego nor the rest of the phenomenal world is illusory—both are completely real. The religious quest is for the liberation of the spiritual element of the ego from physical limitations, so that it may enjoy immortality or at least longevity. In other words, the goal is the triumph: one will become an immortal.

Material forces not only engender the phenomenal world but also give birth to great gods, for example, the Three Celestial Worthies (三天尊) or the Three Pure Gods (三清), namely Celestial Worthy of the Original Beginning (元始天尊), Celestial Worthy of the Sacred Treasure (灵宝天尊) and Celestial Worthy of the Way and Its Virtue (道德天尊) who is identified with Lao Zi. The Three Celestial Worthies govern the Three Pure Heavens (三清天), and they are the highest Taoist gods under whom there is still a vast group of minor gods and immortals, such as Town God (城隍), Door God (门神), God of the Hearth (灶君), God of Blessings (福星) and God of Longevity (寿星). In fact, there are as many gods as there are aspects of the Way that can become visible to the believers. The Taoist master Tao Hongjing attempted to codify the sprawling multiplicity in his *Chart of the Ranks and Functions of the Gods* (《真灵位业图》).

The Taoist pantheon, like the Han Dynasty imperial government, is constructed as a vast other-worldly bureaucratic administration. These gods rule in the manner of earthly emperors with ministers, armies, and local bureaucratic functionaries.

The Chinese ideogram for "immortal (仙)" depicts a man and a mountain, suggesting a hermit; the older form of "immortal", however, shows a man dancing around, flapping his sleeves like wings. To become immortal is to be "transformed into a feathered being". This image comes from the mythology of eastern Chinese tribes who claimed bird ancestors, worshiped bird deities, and held religious rites with bird dances performed on stilts.

There are many categories of immortal. The highest are those who "ascend to heaven in broad daylight". There are also those who live in terrestrial paradises (on holy mountains or islands) for centuries without growing old and later appear disguised in this world to transmit their immortality formulas and magical powers to worthy adepts. Lower immortals do not reach paradise before dying an apparent death (尸解), leaving their sandals or their canes in the coffins to take on the appearance of their corpses.

Religious Taoism assimilated the Buddhist doctrine of karma (因果报应) and reincarnation (轮回) and the Confucian moral teachings. In Religious Taoism, moral conduct was rewarded with health and long life; immorality caused sickness, premature death, and, according to later texts, suffering in hell. Numerous deities came to be the "directors of destiny (司命)" who record man's virtues and vices. A complex heavenly bureaucracy received annual reports on the deeds of the family or the individual from the God of the Hearth at New Year or from the malevolent "three worms (三虫)" residing in the human body. A proliferating literature of merits and demerits, including schedules of points for good and bad deeds (the most famous being *The Tract on the Most Exalted One on Actions and Retributions*《太上感应篇》), probably shaped the minds of the masses more than any other religious texts in China.

/ Techniques of Longevity and Immortality /

Daoists hope to have a long earthly life and they try to do everything possible to see that they will have such a life. Living according to Daoist principles requires self-discipline, self-awareness, and self-control. They hope, through the practice of various life-enhancing activities such as exercise, meditation, and healthful diet, to live a very long time. They believe that by so doing, they will become Xian, able to achieve immortality in present life.

Hygienic and Dietary Techniques

Religious Taoists believe that the five major organs of the body correspond to and partake of the Five Elements or Five Agents: lungs corresponding to metal, heart to fire, spleen to earth, liver to wood, and kidneys to water. These sense organs are orifices which are passageways for entry and exit of vital forces. Desires are seen as leading to the loss of vital forces, and therefore the senses have to be carefully kept in balance lest disease be caused through overindulgence in any one of the corresponding desires.

All dietary regimens are intended to nourish the respective organs in right proportions with foods and medicinal herbs containing the energy corresponding in quality to their respective elements. A preliminary step in diet is "complete abstinence from all cereals (辟谷)" in order to starve and kill the "three corpses (三尸)" or the "three worms (三虫)", which caused disease, old age, and death.

Gymnastic Techniques

In order to make all energies in the body reach their proper place and to maintain a continuous circulatory process, the adepts practice gymnastics called *Dao Yin* (导引), to attract them to the proper places. Massage and Chinese boxing were also performed. Such practices can render the body flexible and make the energy circulate everywhere. They eliminate any internal obstructions, which can cause disease, and untie internal knots so that everything inside the organism can communicate freely.

Respiratory Techniques

Ordinary people breathe through the throat but the Taoist saint breathes through the whole body, starting from the heels. The Taoists breathe not only atmospheric air but solar, lunar, and stellar emanations. They absorb the characteristic energies of the five directions, guiding the green emanation of the east to the liver, the red emanation of the south to the heart, and so on. They absorb the emanations of the sun at noon (the peak moment of *Yang*) and of the moon at midnight (the peak moment of *Yin*). Another method teaches how to "feed on air (服气)" by retaining breath and conducting it throughout the body. One who could hold his breath for the time of 1,000 respirations would become immortal.

About the time of the Tang Dynasty, ordinary respiration was replaced by the respiration of inner breath, or "embryonic breathing (胎息)". This inner breath was viewed as man's share of the primordial life breath contained in the lower of three "elixir fields (丹田)" of the body. This life breath is conducted, in a closed circuit like that of the embryo, through the body and directed by means of the "inner sight (内观)", an inward-turned vision of the eyes. In case of sickness, the inner breath is conducted to the diseased organ and heals it.

Heliotherapuetic Techniques

The Taoists seem to have discovered some of the virtues of heliotherapy, not recognized by European medicine until the modern age. The "method of wearing the sun rays (服日芒之法)" consisted in the exposure of the body to the sunlight, while holding in the hand a special character (the sun within an enclosure) written in red on green paper. Women adepts were to expose their bodies likewise to the moon, holding a special character (the moon within an enclosure) written in black on yellow paper.

Alchemical Techniques

Dietary and breathing techniques only prolong life so as to give time for the preparation of the elixir of immortality, of which there are two kinds: an "outer elixir (外丹)" and an "inner elixir (内丹)". The outer elixir is made by compounding cinnabar, orpiment, red-orpiment and magnetite according to certain formulas and tempering them in a crucible several times. It was believed that the taking of the elixir would confer immortality. Sarcastically, many people seeking immortality died shortly after taking such "elixir of immortality".

The failure of the outer elixir resulted in quest of an inner elixir. Instead of compounding and tempering minerals, the inner elixir alchemists endeavored to make the "elixir of life" within the human body. The human body was taken as the alchemical crucible, semen and vital energy became the "minerals", and spirit was used as "fire" to temper them. The process consisted of conserving semen to produce vital energy, nourishing vital energy to produce spirit, and nourishing spirit to return to vacuity, that is, to identify with the Way. The inner elixir practice was based on the Taoist doctrine that all things, including human kind, are the emanations of the Way, and thus, to gain immortality meant to reverse the normal vital process leading to old age and death and become one with the Way.

Magical Techniques

Some religious Taoists tried to prolong life through magical charms and talismans used to control the deities and ghosts and drive away disease. The basis for the Taoists' control over ghosts and deities was a form of name magic. They could summon and dismiss the deities of macrocosm and microcosm by virtue of the knowledge of their names, true descriptions, and functions. They further controlled them by means of cabalistic writing, talismans or charms, which were, in effect, orders or commands issued by the Taoist masters, and thereby they kept away ghosts and invoked the beneficence of the deities. Charms and talismans were also used to cure disease. To the religious Taoists, illness was caused by demons and ghosts. Accordingly, talismans drawn by the Taoist masters would be burned and the ashes, mixed with water, swallowed by the demon's victims. Furthermore, charms and talismans served as badges of office and as the signs by which divine ruler or his emissaries would distinguish the virtuous "chosen people" from the villains and reward them with official appointments in the heavenly bureaucracy. Other magic tools employed included mirrors, swords, compass, fans, lamps and flags.

/ Eight Immortals in the Taoist Religion /

The Eight Taoist Immortals were adored by Taoist believers as well as ordinary people. They were Han Zhongli (汉钟离), Zhang Guolao (张果老), Lü Dongbin (吕洞宾), Li Tieguai (铁拐李), He Xiangu (何仙姑), Lan Caihe (蓝采和), Han Xiangzi (韩湘子) and Cao Guojiu (曹国舅). There exists a famous saying about them: "When the Eight Immortals cross the sea, each demonstrates their divine power. (八仙过海,各显神通。)"

The Eight Immortals Crossing the Sea

For Chinese people, the Eight Immortals stand for eight categories of people in their daily life: men and women, the old and the young, the rich and the poor, the noble and the lowly. What's more, the Eight Immortals held common, everyday items in their hands—fan, fisherman's drum, sword, gourd (葫芦), lotus, flower basket, flute and castanets (响板)—endearing these items to Taoist followers and to ordinary Chinese people. This explains why stories about the Eight Immortals have been so popular and influential in China. Special halls have been dedicated to the Eight Immortals in most Taoist temples.

/ The Most Sacred Taoist Mountain—Dragon-Tiger Mountain /

The Dragon-Tiger Mountain is located in the southwestern suburb of Yingtan, Jiangxi Province. It is the birthplace of the Taoist religion and a key scenic tourist resort. It is said that the founder of the Taoist religion, Zhang Daoling, started to distill elixirs (长生不老药) here. The legend has it that when the elixirs were made, a dragon and a tiger were observed above the mountain. So the mountain was renamed after those two celestial animals.

The Dragon-Tiger Mountain

Taoists believed that immortals usually lived in high mountains where they assumed that they would find elixirs to obtain immortality. And the Dragon-Tiger Mountain is regarded as the most sacred mountain of the Taoist religion.

/ Religious Taoism and Chinese Culture /

Religious Taoism is the original native religion of China. It originated and developed in Chinese culture, and at the same time, exerted a great influence on the formation of Chinese culture. Its influence is apparent in almost all aspects of Chinese life, particularly in the fields of science, literature and art.

Some scholars have stated that the Taoists initiated the sciences of chemistry, mineralogy (矿物学), botany (植物学), zoology and pharmaceutics (药剂学) in East Asia. Though the aims of Taoist alchemy are ridiculous, the processes are similar to those of scientific experiments. In their efforts to transmute baser metals into silver and gold and to make the elixir of life, the Taoists made a lot of discoveries and inventions in chemistry, mineralogy, and pharmaceutics, such as the invention of the dynamite. To preserve health and to prolong physical life, many Taoist masters gained a lot of knowledge of medicine and became famous doctors and pharmacists, of whom Ge Hong, Tao Hongjing and Sun Simiao (孙思邈) were all first-rate doctors in Chinese history and contributed a great deal to the development of Chinese medicine. Many medical works were written by Taoist masters. The earliest surviving medical book, *The Yellow Emperor's Canon of Internal Medicine* (《黄帝内经》), for example, presents itself as the teachings of a legendary Celestial Master addressed to the Yellow Emperor.

The Taoist idea of immortals has been the constant theme of Chinese authors who produced romantic and fascinating masterpieces about well-known immortals. Esoteric Taoist writings also held great fascination for men of letters. Their responses might vary from a mere mention of the most celebrated immortals to whole works inspired directly by specific Taoist texts and practices. Many a poet recorded his search, real or metaphorical, for immortals or transcendent herbs, or described his attempts at compounding an elixir. A certain number of technical terms became touchstones of poetic diction. The revealed literature of the Maoshan sect made a decisive contribution to the development of Tang romance stories. Literary accounts of fantastic marvels also drew heavily on the wonders of Maoshan hagiography and topography. The Maoshan influence on the Tang poetry was no less important. Precise references to the literature of this sect abound in the poems of the time, while many of the greatest poets, such as Li Bai (李

白), were formally initiated into the Maoshan organization. As awareness of these influences increases, scholars are faced with the intriguing question of the possible religious origins of whole genres of Chinese literature.

Chinese arts are also closely associated with Religious Taoism. Ancient Chinese mirrors, bowls, dishes and other porcelain and pottery wares were often ornamented with delicate pictures of Taoist immortals. Graphic guides existed from early times to aid in the identification of sacred minerals and plants, particularly mushrooms. A later specimen of such a work is to be found in the Taoist Canon. This practical aspect of Taoist influence resulted in the exceptionally high technical level of botanical and mineralogical drawing that China soon attained.

In calligraphy, too, Taoists soon set the highest standard. One of the greatest of all calligraphers, Wang Xizhi (王羲之), was an adherent of the Way of the Celestial Masters, and one of his most renowned works was a transcription of *Huang Ting Scripture* (《黄庭经》).

Figure painting was another field in which Taoists excelled. China's celebrated painter Gu Kaizhi (顾恺之), a practicing Taoist, left an essay containing directions for painting a scene in the life of the first Celestial Master, Zhang Daoling. Many works on Taoist themes, famous in their time but now lost, have been attributed to other great early masters. Of these, many have been painted for use in ritual, and religious paintings of the Taoist pantheon are still produced today.

Exercises

Part One   Comprehension

Fill in the following blanks with the information you learn in Chapter 4.

1. The necromancers persuaded emperors to climb holy mountains and perform sacrifices in order to receive from immortals the _____ of longevity.

2. Both the Way of the Great Peace and the Way of the _____ Masters are in a sense associated with peasants, whose wishes they reflected to some extent.

3. Ge Hong also incorporated into Religious Taoism _____ ethical teachings, such as the Three Cardinal Guides and the Five Constant Virtues, and thus laid the theoretical basis of Aristocratic Religious Taoism.

4. And the Dragon-Tiger Mountain is regarded as the most _____ mountain of the Taoist religion.

5. Some scholars have stated that the Taoists initiated the sciences of chemistry, mineralogy, botany, _____ and pharmaceutics in East Asia.

Part Two   Translation

Passage Translation

道,原指"道路",意指"治""理"。老子用"道"来提出(propound)自己的思想体系;因此,他的思想流派被称为道家。在东汉时期,它成为一种宗教。这种宗教追求不朽和健康;且最终是要长生不老。

道是无为(non-action)。无为就是要遵循自然规律而不是超越自然规律。道遵从自然规律,什么都不做,却又无所不能。道使一切顺利进行,不夸耀自己的成就。

道教也有缺点。例如,中国知识分子遭遇挫折时,就会遁世(hermitic way of life);当他们成功时,他们会说"大隐隐于市,小隐隐于山"。这种内、外分明的世俗态度使中国的知识分子在积极的儒家和消极的道教之间左右摇摆(hover)。

Part Three   Critical Thinking and Discussion

1. What are the techniques for achieving longevity and immortality of Religious Taoism? How can we best understand them?

2. Are there similar tales about people like those Eight Immortals in the Taoist religion? What can immortals be compared to?

Chapter 5
Buddhism in China

Buddhism, a philosophy as well as religion, was founded by an Indian prince, Siddhartha Gautama, also known as Sakyamuni (the sage of Sakyas), the son of the ruler of a small state in what is now Nepal. He is said to have lived during the years of 565—485 B.C.E. Tradition has it that at the age of 29, he left the luxurious life of the palace to become a wandering mendicant, determined to seek a solution to the problem of

Sakyamuni

suffering and understand the true meaning of life. At the age of 35, through mediation, he found the solution, became enlightened, and henceforth became known as the Buddha (佛), or the enlightened one.

After this momentous event, the Buddha spent his remaining years wandering up and down the Ganges Valley (恒河谷), preaching his message to ascetic and lay persons alike. More and more people accepted the truth he had found and became his disciples and followers. The general tenets of Buddha may be summarized as following.

/ Teachings of Buddha /

Karma and Reincarnation

From traditional Hindu thought, Buddhism accepts the theory of reincarnation (轮 回), according to which a living being will be reborn endlessly in the ceaseless cycle of existence in accordance with his karma (业或因果, fruits of actions). Karma results from acts or deeds as well as the intentions behind those deeds, and represents the "fruits" arising from those thoughts and actions. Every deed or thought produces karma which may be good or evil. According to the karma of the past, a living being will undergo repeated rebirths and assume a different form in each rebirth. These rebirths take place on several different levels: that of beings in the various hells, of animals, of human beings, of divine beings in the various heavens and so on. In their totality, they constitute the wheel of life and death.

The Four Noble Truths

In connection with human life, Sakyamuni preached the Four Noble Truths (四圣谛):

The noble truth of suffering (苦谛). Life is suffering. Birth, decay, sickness, and death are all sufferings. To meet a person whom one hates, to be separated from a person whom one loves, to seek something that cannot be obtained, and physical and mental pains are all sufferings.

The noble truth of the origination of suffering (集谛). The cause of suffering is desire, or thirst, or greed. It is the craving thirst that causes rebirth, accompanied by sensual delights; this thirst seeks satisfaction as a craving for lust, for existence, or for nonexistence.

The noble truth of the cessation of suffering (灭谛). If desire can be removed, all human suffering will come to an end. The ideal state where there is no desire, no passion and no suffering is called nirvana (涅槃), which means freedom from the endless cycle of personal reincarnation. Suffering ceases with the complete cessation of that craving—the giving up, the getting rid of, the release from, and the detachment from this craving thirst.

The noble truth of the right path to the cessation of suffering (道谛). To attain nirvana, one has to follow the right path or the right way that leads to the cessation of suffering—the Noble Eight-Fold Path (八正道).

The Twelve Nidanas

According to the Buddha, everything in the universe is transient and in a state of constant flux. This means that phenomenal "existence", as commonly perceived by the senses, is illusory; it is not real inasmuch as, though it exists, its existence is not permanent or absolute. Nothing belonging to it has an enduring entity or "nature" of its own; everything is dependent upon a combination of fluctuating conditions and factors for its seeming "existence" at any given moment. This is the Buddhist theory of the Twelve Nidanas (十二因缘) or dependent origination, expressed in the following formula: (1) the original condition of ignorance leads to (2) will-to-action, which in turn leads to (3) consciousness, which leads to (4) psycho-physical existence, which leads to (5) the six organs of sense (eye, ear, nose, tongue, body or sense of touch and mind), which leads to (6) contact, which leads to (7) sensation or feeling, which leads to (8) craving, which leads to (9) attachment or grasping which leads to (10) becoming or worldly existence, which leads to (11) birth, which leads to (12) decay, death, grief, lamentation, physical suffering, dejection and despair.

The Noble Eight-Fold Path

Given the awareness of the law of dependent origination, the question arises as to how one may escape the continually renewed cycle. It is not enough to know that misery pervades all existence and the way in which life evolves; there must also be a purification that leads to the overcoming of this process. This can be achieved through the avoiding of extremes, and following a middle path. This, the Noble Eight-Fold Path, consists of eight steps: right view (正见), right thought (正思), right speech (正语), right conduct (正业), right livelihood (正命), right effort (正进), right mindfulness (正念) and right concentration (正定).

Nirvana

The ultimate goal to be achieved through following the Noble Eight-Fold Path is nirvana, but the Buddha does not explain what it is or what it is not because it cannot be expressed in general terms and escapes all definitions. Nirvana is a condition that is realized when karma and the consequential succession of lives and births have been definitely overcome. The resulting state is of oneness with reality and the Buddhas are those beings who belong to this state.

/ Hinayana Buddhism and Mahayana Buddhism /

The above tenets underlie Buddhism, in the elaboration of which, however, infinite variations exist within the individual schools. Among the schools, the two main groups are those of the Hinayana or the Small Vehicle (小乘), and the Mahayana or the Great Vehicle (大乘). Hinayana Buddhism, which is closer to the tenets of original Buddhism, has to this day remained dominant in the Buddhist countries of Southeast Asia. Mahayana Buddhism, which is an enormously elaborated and sophisticated development of primitive Buddhism, received its chief growth in the countries north and northeast of India: Central Asia, China and Japan, especially China.

Among the many differences between the two groups, we need to cite three: The difference in theory centered on the ontological problem. To the Hinayana schools, our karma-producing actions are caused by the delusion that we are real selves, that the ego is a permanent identity, and therefore this self or ego is dominated by egoistical desires or attachments which shackle us to the ever-revolving wheel of birth-life-death-rebirth. Therefore, the key to release from this wheel is the understanding that there is no self or ego and consequently that desires and the satisfaction of desires are the illusory products of ignorance. Though the Hinayana schools deny the existence of the self, they accept the existence (at least the temporary existence) of a number of elements and aggregates. The elements, called dharmas (法), include such things as sensation, form, memory, space, and energy. The aggregates, called skandhas (蕴), include material form and the spiritual items of sensation, ideas, concepts, and understanding. To the Mahayana schools, neither does self or ego exist, nor do the hypothesized dharmas and skandhas exist. There is literally nothing that has true existence, and nothing that can be called a thing-in-itself.

In Hinayana Buddhism, salvation is a personal matter; the individual concerned must work out his own salvation and can do little to help others to achieve theirs. In Mahayana Buddhism, on the contrary, the concept of the Bodhisattva (菩萨) is prominent. It is the being who seeks Buddhahood but seeks it altruistically; he wants enlightenment, but wants it to enlighten others; he willingly sacrifices himself for others, and therefore, even after enlightenment, voluntarily remains within the wheel of life and death.

In Hinayana Buddhism, the Buddha is only an enlightened human being, whereas in Mahayana Buddhism the Buddha is the Godhead, the savior who possesses limitless power. Apart from the Buddha, there are various Bodhisattvas such as Avalokitesvara (观音), Amitabha (阿弥陀佛) and Maitreya (弥勒佛), who represent personifications for the popular mind of various aspects of reality.

/ The Spread and Development of Buddhism in China /

It is generally recognized that Buddhism was brought to China by missionaries at the very beginning of the Christian Era. Tradition has it that Buddhism was introduced after Emperor Ming (汉明帝) of the Han Dynasty had a dream of a flying golden deity, which was interpreted as a vision of the Buddha. Accordingly, the Emperor dispatched emissaries to India who subsequently returned to China with *The Sutra in Forty-two Sections* (《四十二章经》), which was deposited in a temple known as the White Horse Temple outside the capital of Luoyang. Today there is still a White Horse Temple on that site.

The Buddhism that first became popular in China during the Han Dynasty was deeply colored with magical practices. In the succeeding centuries, Chinese pilgrims constantly went to India to study the religion at first hand and to bring back the sacred texts, and Indian and Central Asiatic monks came to China to assist in the translation of the texts into Chinese. The work of translation contributed greatly to the rapid growth of Buddhism from magical practices into both a religion and a philosophy.

When Buddhists came into contact with the Chinese literati, especially the Neo-Taoists, in the Wei-Jin Period, they matched Buddhist concepts with those of Taoism, identifying Tathagata (如来佛) with the Taoist "original nonbeing", for example. Under Neo-Taoist influence, early Buddhist schools in China all engaged in discussions about being and nonbeing. There are seven , among which the most famous are the School of Original Nonbeing (本无宗) represented by Dao An (道安), the school of Matter as Such (即色宗) by Zhi Daolin (支道林) and the School of Nonbeing of Mind (心无宗) by Zhi Mindu (支愍度).

Buddhism had marked progression during the Northern and Southern Dynasties. From the time of Emperor Wen of Song (宋文帝), many venerable Buddhist monks came to China from the West, and Buddhism of various sects flourished. Large numbers of Sanskrit Buddhist scriptures were translated into Chinese. Among the emperors and princes, the most devout Buddhists were Xiao Ziliang, Prince of Jinling of Qi, and Emperor Wu of Liang. Emperor Wu of Liang many times retired to a Buddhist temple to become a novice and each time had to be brought out of the temple by his ministers. At one time, Jiankang (modern Nanjing) alone boasted more than 500 Buddhist monasteries housing upwards of 100,000 monks and nuns. Famous Buddhist monks were held in awe by people of rank and title.

The Northern and Southern Dynasties also witnessed bitter controversies over Buddhist issues. Many Buddhist thinkers sought to combine Buddhism with Confucianism and Taoism, and there were also some orthodox Chinese scholars, usually Confucianists and Taoists, who attacked Buddhism as the religion of the barbarians and accused the Buddhists of neglecting social and personal responsibilities by abandoning family life. The most spectacular controversy centered around the destructibility or the indestructibility of the soul. The Buddhist adherents maintained that the soul would not perish after the decay of the body, and would undergo successive transmigration with the load of karma, whereas their opponents, such as Fan Zhen (范缜), contended that the body and the soul cannot be separated, and that the soul exists when the body exists and the soul will perish as the body decays. A number of the resulting polemics have been preserved in two compilations: *Collected Essays on Buddhism* (《弘明集》) and *Further Collection of Essays on Buddhism* (《广弘明集》).

By the seventh century, Buddhism reached its apogee, claiming as converts all elements of Chinese society—the imperial household, the nobility, the great and wealthy families, and the common people. Scattered all over China were monasteries large and small, and associated with the monasteries were vigorous and influential schools of Buddhism founded by creative Chinese monks. Eminent Buddhist schools founded during the Sui and Tang Dynasties include the Three-Treatise School (三论宗), the Consciousness Only School (唯识宗), the Tiantai (Flower Splendor) School (天台宗), the Hua Yan School, the Pure Land School (净土宗), and the Chan or the Meditation School (禅宗).

The Song Dynasty was the age of the Neo-Confucianists, most of whom, though incorporating into their systems Buddhist theories, fought it strenuously and continuously. Consequently, Buddhism embarked on the way of decline. However, Buddhism was still a major force at that time, and it was recorded that there were 40,000 monasteries housing more than 450,000 monks and nuns. Several versions of Buddhist canons were published. In the Yuan, Ming and Qing Dynasties, Buddhism, in the main, continued to decline. Though there were short-time revivals for some of the Buddhist schools, they never regained the popularity they enjoyed before. In modern China, Buddhism suffered greater eclipse, but its influence still cannot be too lowly estimated.

The following is a brief introduction to the major Chinese Buddhist schools.

The Three-Treatise School

This school was based on three Indian scriptures—*The Treatise on the Middle Doctrine* (《中论》) by Nagarjuna (龙树), *The Twelve Gates Treatise* (《十二门论》), also by Nagarjuna, and *The One Hundred Verses Treatise* (《百论》) by Aryadeva (提婆), a pupil of Nagarjuna. Founded by Ji Zang (吉藏), the school holds that all things come into being through dependent origination, and they themselves have nothing of their own. That is, they do not have their own true natures. According to the famous doctrine of this school—the Eight-No-Middle Way (八不中道)—there is no production and no extinction; no enduring and no cutting off; no unity and no diversity; no arriving and no departing. Both being and nonbeing are viewed as extremes whose opposition must be resolved in a synthesis. The synthesis, itself a new extreme with its own antithesis, also needs to be synthesized. In the end, all oppositions are dissolved in the True Middle or emptiness. This school was especially nihilistic and is often called the School of Nonbeing (空宗).

The Consciousness Only School

This school was founded by Xuan Zang (玄奘), one of the greatest figures in the history of Chinese Buddhism. Entering the monastery at 13, Xuan Zang traveled from monastery to monastery for more than ten years and came across many conflicting doctrines. Impelled by a burning desire to seek the true doctrines and visit the sacred places of Buddhism in India, he started alone in 629 on the pilgrimage and arrived in India in 633. There he spent the next ten years traveling and studying before starting his journey home, this time carrying with him 657 Buddhist texts. Under imperial patronage, he set up a school of translation and devoted the next 20 years to the translation of 75 of these works, most of these being Yogachara (瑜伽行唯识宗) works. He left a famous work, *Treatise on the Establishment of the Doctrine of Consciousness-Only* (《成唯识论》).

The Consciousness Only School maintains that what people call the "ego" and "dharmas", or things, have only a false basis and lack any real nature of their own; their manifestations are all mental representations dependent upon the evolution of consciousness. That is, they are products of consciousness, which acts as their evolving agent. This school divides consciousness into eight kinds: those of the five senses (sight, hearing, smell, taste and touch), plus a sixth consciousness which coordinates these senses, that of intellection, or the manas consciousness (末那识), and the maturing consciousness, variously called the alaya consciousness (阿赖耶识), the seed consciousness or storehouse consciousness. Whereas the ego and things, considered as external to the mind, are not in their essential nature existent, the consciousness upon which this ego and these things depend is itself real. Therefore the ego and things cannot be said to be absolutely empty or unreal. Accordingly, the Consciousness Only School follows a middle way, denying the existence of external things as such, but affirming that of consciousness.

The Consciousness Only School, like the Three-Treatise School, was essentially no more than an Indian school transplanted to Chinese soil. It lacked the spirit of synthesis and was too extreme for the Chinese. Consequently, it declined after a few centuries, a relatively short time compare to other schools.

The Tiantai School

This school was founded by Zhi Kai (智凯), and named after the Tiantai Mountain in Zhejiang where Zhi Kai lived and taught. This school took *The Lotus Sutra* (《法华经》) as its basic text, and it is sometimes referred to as the Lotus School (法华宗). As in all schools of Buddhism, the Tiantai School teaches a middle way, but it achieves a typically Chinese synthesis. According to this school, all dharmas (elements of existence) are empty because they have no self-nature and depend on causes for production. This is the Truth of Emptiness. But since they are produced, they do possess a temporary and dependent existence. This is the Truth of Temporary Truth. Thus dharmas are both empty and temporary. This is the Truth of the Mean. Each truth involves the other two, so that three are one and one is three. This mutual identification is the true state of all dharmas. In the realm of temporary truth—that is the phenomenal world—all realms of existence, whether of Buddhas, men, or beasts, and all characters of being, such as cause, effect, and substance, involve one another, so that each element, even an instant of thought, involves the entire universe. As put by the Buddhists, "The Three Thousand Worlds are immanent in an instant of thought (一念三千)." Accordingly, all beings are of the same Buddha-nature, and hence all are to attain Buddhahood eventually. The methods of attaining Buddhahood include both the method of concentration and that of insight.

One of the most famous early Chinese Buddhist Schools, the Tiantai School, lasted for several centuries. In the early ninth century, it spread to Japan and, in the late 11th century, to Korea.

The Hua Yan School

The Hua Yan School was established by Fa Zang (法藏) and based on *The Avatamsaka Sutra*, or *The Flowery Splendor Sutra* (《华严经》). This school propagates the doctrine of the universal causation of the realm of dharmas. This realm is fourfold. It contains the realm of facts, the realm of principle, the realm of principle and facts harmonized, and the realm of all facts interwoven and mutually identified. Principle is emptiness, satic, the noumenon, whereas facts are specific characters, dynamic, constituting the phenomenal world. They interact and interpenetrate and in this way form a perfect harmony. This doctrine rests on the theory of the six characteristics of universality, speciality, similarity, difference, integration and disintegration. Thus, each dharma is both one and all. The world is, in reality, a perfect harmony in all its flowery splendor.

The Pure Land School

The Pure Land School was founded by a Tang Buddhist Shan Dao (善导). The basic doctrines of this school differ widely from the doctrines of the early Buddhists. The Pure Land School's Buddhists have generally taught that a man reaches salvation from this earth not by individual effort or the accumulation of merits but through faith in the grace of the Buddha Amitabha (阿弥陀佛). The main practice of those who follow the Pure Land teachings is not the learning of the texts, nor meditation on the Buddha, but rather the constant invocation of the name Amitabha. Furthermore, in Pure Land Buddhism, the attainment of nirvana is not the goal; it is rather to become reborn in the Pure Land of Amitabha.

These doctrines and practice of invoking the name Amitabha later gained great popularity in China, where it was believed that the world had reached a degenerate period, in which the

Buddhist doctrines were no longer clear and men no longer possessed the purity of heart or determination to attain salvation by self-endeavor. Therefore, all men of every section of society could only hope to be saved by the grace of Amitabha.

The Chan School

Of all the schools of Chinese Buddhism, the most uniquely Chinese and the best known is that of Chan. This name is an abbreviation of Channa (禅那), which is the Chinese phonetic rendering of the Sanskrit dhyana, meaning meditation. The Japanese term for Chan Buddhism is called Zen Buddhism, which has been more commonly used abroad.

According to Chan tradition, the school originated with certain esoteric teachings allegedly expounded by the historical Buddha to a disciple, and thereafter transmitted through a series of Indian patriarchs of the school. There was a transmission from mind to mind without the use of written texts. Finally the twenty-eighth of these patriarchs, the famous Bodhidharma (菩提达摩), came to China during the reign of Emperor Wu of the Liang Dynasty, thus becoming the first Chan patriarch in China. After his death, the school was successively headed by his disciple Hui Ke (慧可) as the second Chinese patriarch, by Seng Can (僧璨) as the third, by Dao Xin (道信) as the fourth, and by Hong Ren (弘忍) as the fifth.

Following Hong Ren, Chan Buddhism was divided into two schools: a northern school led by Shen Xiu (神秀), stressing "gradual enlightenment (渐悟)"; and a southern school led by Hui Neng (慧能), stressing "sudden enlightenment (顿悟)". The southern school gradually overcame the powerful northern school, and the doctrines now associated with Chan are those of the southern school. The position may be suggested by the story of Hui Neng's accession to power. An itinerant seller of firewood, Hui Neng, was attracted to the monastery where the fifth patriarch was instructing his disciples. For eight months, he worked in the stables. When the reigning patriarch, near death, decided to pick as his successor the one who wrote the best gatha (偈, short poem, Buddhist hymn) summarizing the teaching of Chan, the favorite candidate, Shen Xiu, inscribed his poem on the wall outside the master's hall:

The body is a bodhi tree,	身是菩提树，
The mind is the bright mirror.	心如明镜台。
They need dusting from time to time,	时时勤拂拭，
So that no dirt may gather.	莫使染尘埃。

When the master saw the poem, he commented, "Shen Xiu has not seen the truth yet. More meditation is necessary."

Hui Neng, who was illiterate, heard his fellow monks talking about Shen Xiu's poem, and composed another one to comment on it. He asked someone to write his verse on the wall:

Originally the bodhi is not a tree,	菩提本非树，
Neither is there a bright mirror.	明镜亦非台。
Since originally there is nothing,	本来无一物，
Where can dirt gather?	何处染尘埃？

When the master saw Hui Neng's poem, he sensed that Hui Neng had a deeper comprehension of the truth of Chan Buddhism and appointed him the sixth patriarch. As there were so many jealous monks in the temple, the master told Hui Neng to go back to Guangdong and live in hiding, to wait for a proper opportunity to reveal his status and perform his duties.

Back in Guangdong, Hui Neng lived a secluded life in the mountains for many years. Then one day, when he was 39 years old, he went to a temple to listen to the learned abbot's interpretation of Buddhism. Two monks were arguing the fluttering of a pennant. One said, "The pennant is fluttering (时有幡动)," and the other said, "The wind is fluttering the pennant (时有风吹幡动)." Hui Neng interpreted them by saying, "Neither the pennant not the wing is moving (不是风动，不是幡动). It is your own mind that is moving (仁者心动)." The abbot was surprised by what Hui Neng said, so he invited the stranger in and began to talk with him.

In this way, Hui Neng's status as the sixth patriarch of the Chan sect became known. Shortly afterwards, he started preaching in a temple in Shaoguan in northern Guangdong. His talks on Buddhism were recorded by some of his disciples, which made up a book entitled *Scripture from the Platform* (《坛经》) containing the basic theories of the Chan sect.

Principles of Chan Buddhism were summarized in these four lines: "The belief is passed on outside the religion (教外别传). There is no reliance on written scripts (不立文字). It goes straight into the human heart-mind (直指人心). One becomes a Buddha the moment he sees his own Buddha nature (见性成佛).

Sixth Patriarch Hui Neng

Energizing powerfully in China until the 13th century, Chan Buddhism found a home in Japan in 1191, where it was known under the Japanese name Zen Buddhism. It is today an important factor in Japanese life.

Hui Neng, the sixth Patriarch of Chan Buddhism, should not be ignored. The principles of Chan Buddhism are summarized in these four lines: "The belief is passed on outside the religion (教外别传). There is no reliance on written scripts(不立文字). It goes straight into the human heart-mind(直指人心). One becomes a Buddha the moment he sees his own Buddha nature(见性成佛)." These lines have become the first thing to pop into the mind when people think of Chan Buddhism. In 730, Hui Neng's disciples won debates with other sects and Chan Buddhism was strengthened in China. Chan Buddhism was introduced to Korea in the 8th Century and to Japan at the end of the 12th Century.

/ Monastic Community and Buddhist Holidays /

The Buddhist community is composed of monks and nuns, male and female novices, who usually live in Buddhist monasteries, and laymen and laywomen, who observe the precepts though living in their own home. Government of the monastery was in the hands of the abbot, who was elected by the monks. The power of the abbot within the monastery was, like that of the senior person in any Chinese institution, paternalistic, and it extended to the expulsion of any monk who committed a grave sin or who was incorrigibly nonconformist.

The life of the monks and s in the monastery was strictly regulated by the Vinaya. There were 250 precepts for the monk and 348 for the nun. The five precepts for the layman prohibit killing, stealing, engaging in sexual misconduct, lying, and drinking intoxicating liquor. There were five additional precepts for monastic novices and laity committed to this stricter regime: not to eat during prohibited hours; not to take part in festivals and amusements; not to use garlands, perfumes, or ointments; not to use a bed or a chair that is too large or luxurious; not to accept money for one self. Taken together, these comprise the ten precepts (十戒). The monks and nuns were also required to practice the Six Acts (六度), which include charity or giving, keeping the commandments, patience under insult, zeal and progress, meditation and wisdom.

A person often joins the Sangha (僧伽) by applying, or being given as a child, to the master of some small temple. Here he would receive training as a novice. A peculiarly Chinese aspect of this practice is that the relationship of the master and the novice was often considered the equivalent of the natural father-son relationship. After preliminary studies, the novice would travel to some monastery noted for its great tradition of famous masters, and there he would apply for ordination (传戒). Ordination involved a longer or shorter period of study and training and was conferred in three stages. In later times, these three stages, each originally requiring extensive preparation, were for practical reasons combined into a three-part ceremony that concluded within a period of a few weeks or days. The Bodhisattva vows were the important ones. There were (1) to lead all beings to salvation, (2) to seek to put an end to all pains and sufferings, (3) to study all teachings of the Buddha, (4) to seek to perfect oneself. After pronouncing these vows in impressive rituals supervised by duly authorized senior monks, the candidates were branded by burning incense on their shaven pates and became full-fledged monks.

There are various Buddhist holidays. The three major events of the Buddha's life—his birth (佛诞), enlightenment (成道), and entrance into final nirvana (涅槃) are commemorated in all Buddhist countries but not everywhere on the same day. In Southeast Asia, the three events are celebrated together on the full moon day in May of the Gregorian calendar. In China, the three anniversaries are observed on separate lunar calendar days (the birth April 8, the enlightenment December 8, and the nirvana February 15).

For the Buddhists in China, the Republic of Korea, and Japan, there is the Ullambana (盂兰盆会) or All-Souls' Feast, celebrated on the fifteenth day of the seventh lunar month. This festival is based on the legend concerning one of the chief disciples of the Buddha, Moggallana (目犍连), who descended to the deepest of Buddhist hell to search for his mother, reborn there because of her greed and deceit. To rescue her from her sufferings, the Buddha suggested that Moggallana and the community of monks make a united donation of food, clothing, and wealth, not only on behalf of Moggallana's mother, but also for the sake of all departed ancestors. This was accordingly done and the mother was rescued. Because of its identification with the Chinese virtue of filial piety, the All-Soul's Feast became the most popular annual Buddhist festival in China.

/ Buddhism and Chinese Culture /

Buddhist influence on Chinese culture is far and wide. In actuality, Buddhism has become one of the important components of Chinese culture. It affected almost all aspects of Chinese life, be it philosophy, religion, arts, literature or science.

As has been stated before, it was under Buddhist pressure and influence that the Tang and Song Neo-Confucianists established Neo-Confucianism in which both Buddhist theories and terms were incorporated. The classification of principles and things made by the Hua Yan School was taken into the Cheng-Zhu School as the distinction between principle and material force. The Chan method of meditation became a chief means of spiritual cultivation in the Lu-Wang School. It was after taking in Buddhist theories and practices that Religious Taoism grew, from magical practices into a real religion. The Taoist five precepts and eight precepts are totally those of the Buddhists.

With the introduction of Buddhism into China, there appeared a new art of architecture—the art of building Buddha's temples and pagodas. These temples and pagodas, unique in building, magnificent in form and ancient in time, now serve as main scenic spots and historical sites. For example, the oldest extant wooden structure in China is the main hall of the Buddha's Halo Monastery (佛光寺) of Wutai in Shanxi. The main hall of the Hua Yan Temple (华严寺) in Datong, is a huge single-storey structure with single-decked eaves. Built in about 1038, it is one of the largest Buddhist structures in China. There are various types of masonry pagodas: one-storey pagodas, multistory pagodas, multi-eave pagodas, stupas and diamond-based pagodas, all of which are monuments marking the sites where Buddhist relics are buried. The wooden pagoda of Yingxian County, Shan'xi Province, for instance, is the finest example of multistory timber construction in China. Erected in 1056, it is a five-storey structure with four additional mezzanine storeys, built on an octagonal plan.

Associated with these temples and pagodas are paintings and sculptures of Buddhist scenes of paradise and hell, of images of the Buddha, Bodhisattva, demons and other legendary beings. The most eminent paintings and sculptures of this kind are found in the three great grottoes: the Yun-gang Grotto (云冈石窟), Longmen Grotto (龙门石窟) and Mogao Grotto (莫高石窟). All these grottoes were designed and made to invoke the Buddha's blessing, and now they are world-famous art treasures.

Buddhism also contributed a great deal to Chinese literature. Genuine Chinese fiction was developed in the Tang Dynasty, during which Buddhism flourished. Earlier works had been mere fables and naive tales. *The Tang Tales of Marvels* (《唐传奇》) derived from Buddhist visions, however, developed intriguing plots and vivid characterizations. The great masterpiece *Journey to the West* (《西游记》) by Wu Cheng'en (吴承恩) is a fictionalized account of the pilgrimage of the Chinese monk Xuan Zang to India in the 7th century. In addition, the Buddhist idea of karma and retribution becomes the never-tired-of theme of Chinese authors. It is no exaggeration to say that without knowledge of Buddhism, it is difficult to read Chinese literary works.

Exercises

Part One Comprehension

Fill in the following blanks with the information you learn in Chapter 5.

1. At the age of 35, through mediation, he found the solution, became enlightened, and henceforth became known as the Buddha, or the _____ one.

2. The ideal state where there is no desire, no passion and no suffering is called nirvana, which means freedom from the endless cycle of personal _____.

3. The Buddhism that first became popular in China during the _____ Dynasty was deeply colored with magical practices.

4. Of all the schools of Chinese Buddhism, the most uniquely Chinese and the best known is that of _____.

5. With the introduction of Buddhism into China, there appeared a new art of architecture—the art of building Buddha's temples and _____.

Part Two   Translation

Passage Translation

公元一世纪左右,佛教通过丝绸之路从古印度传到中国中部。此后,众多佛经(sutras)传入中国,印度高僧(dignitaries)也被邀请来宣讲佛法。在同一世纪,中国的第一个佛教圣地——白马寺——在河南洛阳建成。

佛教在发展初期受到贵族的肯定和接纳,但也遭到百姓的反对和抗拒。他们更喜欢儒家和道教。

禅宗六世祖师慧能(638～713)将儒家思想引入佛教,推动了中国佛教的发展。慧能认为每个人都有佛性,都可以成佛。他坚信,佛教信徒只要心中有佛,就可以不诵佛经、不遵从其他仪规而成佛。他的主张受到了学者、官员和普通百姓的欢迎。在他的努力下,佛教终于在中国流行,并迅速传播开来。

Part Three   Critical Thinking and Discussion

1. What are the main teachings of Buddhism?

2. What are the important differences between Hinayana Buddhism and the Mahayana Buddhism?

3. What are the characteristics of the Chan School?

Chapter 6
Chinese Classical Literature

China has a long and rich literary history, but to many westerners, Chinese literature remains an enigma. Many Chinese classics are unavailable in translation, as most Chinese classical literary works are too difficult to be translated despite scholarly efforts.

For over 5,000 years, Chinese literature has included diversified genres and forms such as mythology, poetry, prose, fiction and drama. It rivals the literature of other countries in the world.

Chinese classical literature refers to literary works from the days before the Qin Dynasty to the year of 1919, and is virtually an unbroken strand undergoing dynastic changes.

Beginning with primitive mythology, Chinese classical literature developed with *The Book of Songs* (《诗经》), *The Songs of Chu* (《楚辞》), the prose of the Pre-Qin times, *hanfu* and *yuefu* folk songs of the Han Dynasty, the literary criticism of the Wei and Jin Dynasties, the Tang poetry, the Song *ci* poetry, the Yuan dramas in the Yuan Dynasty and the Ming and Qing novels. The literary achievements at the end of the Qing Dynasty are mainly poems and novels.

/ Mythology /

In China, as elsewhere, mythology served to explain the otherwise esoteric, by attributing the origin and current structure of the universe to the operations of supernatural beings. Meanwhile it, as a whole, reflects people's strong desire to survive in the universe and to overcome difficulties and disasters in nature.

Chinese mythology is particularly about the actions of gods and other supernatural creatures as they affect man and the world in which he lives. It interprets not only the origins of things but also the continuing role of supernatural beings in the day-to-day life of the Chinese people. Most of it removed the frightful aspects of terrifying natural phenomena, such as lightning and thunder, by placing individual gods in charge of each natural force and thus making them accessible to men.

Chinese mythology presents a double image: the relatively few myths of antiquity, about which little is known, and the numerous myths of later ages, about which a great deal is known. There certainly were myths in ancient China, but, unlike Greece and Rome, which had great epics embodying mythological lore, such tales can only be found in sketches and fragments in ancient books, for example, *The Book of Mountains and Seas* (《山海经》), *Zhuang Zi* (《庄子》), *The Book of Master Huainan* (《淮南子》), and *The Songs of Chu* (《楚辞》). And many were probably reworked and reinterpreted by later scholars of the Zhou and Han dynasties. That is why there are several different descriptions of a certain god or supernatural hero.

Chinese mythology contributed much to the forming of Chinese religion, especially Religious Taoism and Buddhism. And conversely, the religious situation that prevailed in China added to it more new gods that generally had clearly defined functions and definite personal characteristics and became prominent in art and literature, and meanwhile, modified many early myths to the extent that some deities and figures were rationalized into abstract concepts and others were euhemerized into historical figures.

In the process of evolution, some new deities were successively created or sanctioned by imperial authorities in various dynasties, such as the two door-gods, Qin Shubao (秦叔宝) and Yuchijingde (尉迟敬德). According to the record, when Emperor Tai Zong was ill, ghosts started disturbing him at night. When the two door-gods were informed of that, they volunteered to stand guard outside the door of the emperor's bedroom. So there was no further alarm and later the emperor had their portraits painted and hung on both sides of his palace gate and the ghosts ceased to disturb him since then.

Although Chinese mythology has no epics or collections, it is still rich and prolific in content and theme, dealing with almost every field of the universe, the major categories being myths of the cosmos, myths about man, myths about heroes, myths about gods, and myths about animals.

Myths of the Cosmos

The most conspicuous and popularly recognized figure in the creation of the world is Pan Gu (盘古). Usually pictured as a giant (in some books he is depicted as a creature with a dragon's head and a snake's body) clothed in bearskin, or merely in an apron of leaves, he has two horns on his head and holds a hammer in one hand and a chisel in the other. When he came into being, the universe was in primordial chaos like an egg. His task is to chisel the universe out of chaos.

With its splitting asunder, the pure and bright element became heaven, the impure and dark element became earth, while Pan Gu underwent nine transformations in one day, turning into a god in heaven and a sage on earth. Heaven grew one *zhang* (丈, about 3.33 meters) higher, earth grew one *zhang* thicker everyday, and Pan Gu also grew one *zhang* taller each day. The stupendous labor, and his life as well, lasted as long as 18,000 years, until heaven was exceedingly high, earth exceedingly thick, and he exceedingly tall. Having finished the task, he himself dissolved into the various concrete parts of the visible universe: His head became the mountains, his breath the wind and clouds, his voice the thunder, his eyes the sun and the moon, his limbs the four extremities of the earth, his blood the rivers, his flesh the soil, his beard the constellations, his skin and hair the herbs and trees, his teeth, bones, and marrow the metals, rocks and precious stones, his sweat the rain, and the insects creeping over his body human beings.

Though heaven and earth separated, there were deficiencies with them since they were made of matter. So Nü Wa (女娲), a female deity pictured with a woman's head and a snake's body or described in some other forms, filled out the deficiencies by using multi-colored melted rock and cut off the feet of the celestial tortoise to set upright the four extremities of the earth. Later Gong Gong (共工) contended against Zhuan Xu (颛顼) for the throne but failed. In his rage, he struck his head against the Buzhou Mountain (不周山), one of the heavenly pillars, and broke it. Then heaven tilted down to the northwest, and the sun, the moon and stars all go that way. The earth has a gap in the southeast, and there all the streams and rivers flow.

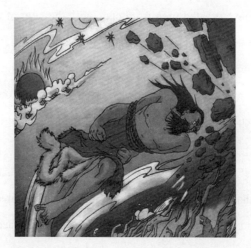

Gong Gong Striking His Head against the Buzhou Mountain

As for the sun, one text speaks of the goddess Xi He (羲和), one of the wives of Di Jun (帝俊), to whom she bore ten suns. In what seems to be the original version of the myth, Xi He bathed the suns every morning in a lovely pond to restore their brightness before they set out, one each day, on their journey. The nine suns which were not on duty would perch on a giant *fusang* (扶桑) tree on the eastern edge of the world. The sun is limned as traveling in a chariot, occasionally drawn by a dragon, with Xi He sometimes as the charioteer.

Much less evidence remains of early moon myths, though the loveliness of Chang Xi (常羲), also named Chang Yi (常仪), or Chang E (嫦娥), also named Heng E (姮娥), the moon goddess, has often been celebrated in poems and novels. As a wife of Di Jun, Chang Xi gave birth to 12 moons, 11 of which somehow eventually disappeared. In another legend, Chang E is considered the wife of Hou Yi (后羿). She flew to the moon after she swallowed the pill of immortality given to her husband by the Empress of Heaven (王母娘娘). Hou Yi's chasing was impeded by the hare, who would not permit the irate husband to pass until he promised reconciliation. Each year on the 15th day of the 8th lunar month, the Chinese celebrate the memory of Chang E's flight to the moon with the Mid-Autumn Festival; many go outdoors to look for the contour of a toad on the moon for, according to an account, Chang E was changed into a toad.

Myths about Man

Very obvious in Chinese mythology is a lack of detailed myths concerning the origin of man. As already noted, one that is well-known is that mankind came from the lice on the decaying body of Pan Gu. Nü Wa, the deity who reconstructed the four pillars supporting heaven, was also said to have created men from clay, with the help of other gods and goddesses, some with care, others by dragging a string through mud because they wanted to produce more and faster. Another tale goes that Nü Wa and her elder brother Fu Xi got married, which marked the beginnings of the human race. Later when they found that young people lived together irregularly, to the great detriment of morality, they prohibited marriage between members of the same family.

Myths about Heroes

Of Chinese hero myths, that of Hou Yi is among the most elaborated. One day the ten suns all appeared simultaneously in the sky, searing the earth with scorching heat. Hou Yi shot down nine of the ten suns with arrows and thus saved the world from destruction. This remarkable exploit was matched by such other Herculean tasks as saving the world from six destructive monsters.

Hou Yi Shooting Down Nine Suns

Other prominent heroes are the Yellow Emperor (黄帝), Yao (尧), Shun (舜), and Yu (禹), who were probably legendary historical figures and chieftains of ancient tribes.

The Yellow Emperor, who is also called Xuan Yuan (轩辕), is the legendary founder of the Chinese Empire after his victory over Chi You (蚩尤) and all other tribes. He is said to have introduced mathematical calculations, made musical instruments, constructed boats, carriages and carts for oxen, studied medicine to prolong the life of his people and made many other inventions and discoveries such as clothes and the script.

Both Yao and Shun were the best-loved legendary heads whose reigns were China's "golden age". But Yu the Great was perhaps a more outstanding saviour-hero. During Yao and Shun's reign, a great mass of water covered the land and prevented people from engaging in agriculture for a time. A man called Gun (鲧), being ordered to control the flood, planned to accomplish his task by damming up the water. He stole from heaven a piece of magic soil or swelling clod of earth for this purpose. The theft angered Heaven so much that the harder Gun worked, the higher the water rose and at last God ordered him to be executed on Mt. Yushan (羽山). Then Gun's son Yu continued this task. In time, Yu sought to reduce the water by dredging, and, after years of strenuous labor, provided outlets to the sea.

In Chinese mythology we have many other heroes. All of them bear the characteristics that in front of the primordial or terrible nature they, by every means, win great successes over disasters or enemies.

中华优秀传统文化要略 *A Glimpse of China's Fine Traditional Culture*

Myths about Gods

Mentioning myths about gods, we should keep in mind that popularly known gods are closely intermingled with religions, mainly Religious Taoism and Buddhism. The famous novel *Journey to the West*, on the basis of legends and folk tales, provides such an unusual world of gods for us, in which the supreme lord is the Jade Emperor (玉皇大帝) who had his Court, palace, ministers, and so on. The major gods, among others, were the Queen Mother of the West, the Eight Immortals (八仙), the Bodhisattva (菩萨), the four Heavenly Kings (四大天王), the Constellations (二十八宿), Buddhas (佛), Arhats (罗汉), and so on, each being in charge of one kind of duty.

In addition, Chinese mythology has many local deities and gods of professions. For instance, each city or town has its own supernatural official called Town God (城隍), each district a local deity, each river a river deity, each mountain a mountain deity, and each household a god of the kitchen. As for gods of professions, there are almost countless, such as the god of grain, the god of literature, the god of wealth, the deity of trees, and the gods of guilds.

Myths about Animals

Among Chinese animal myths, dragon lore is the earliest and most famous of the symbolic animals. It is legendary that before becoming the symbol of sovereign power, it had been the emblem of the Xia Dynasty. According to the refashioned tales in the Han Dynasty, the Yellow Emperor had a dragon-like countenance, and the mother of Yao conceived him as a dragon.

The dragon is a mystique and auspicious animal in Chinese mythology, with its image having the features of a number of animals: horse's head, deer's antlers, shrimp's eyes, donkey's mouth, bull's ears, human beard, snake's body, and eagle's claws. It can walk, fly, swim, and even raise clouds and make rain. It holds boundless supernatural powers and can transform itself into different creatures at will.

As one of the oldest totems of the Chinese nation, the dragon became a symbol of the emperor or the imperial house after the Qin and Han Dynasties. Later, it further evolved into a common spiritual and cultural symbol of the Han ethnic group and all Chinese people.

Dragons live in the heavens or in the deep waters. The Dragon King, controling streams, floods, seas, and rains, is usually a beneficent force that dispenses blessings both in the supernatural and natural worlds. He moves through the heavens and gathers clouds to disperse life-giving rains where they are needed. In this regard, the European dragon is quite different for it is usually portrayed as a cruel monster and the enemy of man.

The phoenix, counterpart of the dragon in Chinese symbolism, was the totem of some tribes at first. In time, it became the venerated mythological king of all birds and a symbol of peace and prosperity. It is also used to bless marriages, as it represents nobleness, harmony, auspiciousness, and happiness.

Whereas the dragon and the phoenix are highly fanciful (奇特的) creatures, other animals also frequently appear in Chinese myths, such as the unicorn (独角兽), the tortoise, the bear, and the hare.

Why, for thousands of years, has Chinese mythology remained in separate fragments since it is so rich in content? Mr. Lu Xun (鲁迅) listed several reasons in his *A Brief History of Chinese Fiction* (《中国小说史略》). Here let's quote them as the summary of this part: "First, the early dwellers in the Yellow River valley were not imaginative people; and since their life was hard and they devoted most of their energy to practical matters without indulging in flights of fancy, they did not combine all the old legends into one great epic. Secondly, Kong Zi appeared with his teaching about the way to cultivate morality, regulate the family, rule the state and bring peace to the world. Since he disapproved of talk of the supernatural, the old myths were not quoted by Confucian scholars, and instead of undergoing further development many of them were lost.

"But a more fundamental reason was probably the absence of a strict division between gods and ghosts. In the earliest times, there was apparently some line of demarcation between the deities of heaven and earth and the ghosts of dead men, yet ghosts could become deities, too. Since men and gods intermingled in this manner, the early religion was never fully developed, and as more new legends appeared, the old ones died out, and the new legends lacked lustre."

/ Poetry /

Poetry, one of the earliest artistic forms, originated from folk songs before the existence of written Chinese. Its content evolved out of people's everyday life, and revealed their labor and entertainment. *The Book of Songs* (《诗经》) and *The Songs of Chu* (《楚辞》) are regarded as the two peaks of China's earlier literary history.

Poetry in the Pre-Qin Period

The Book of Songs, the earliest anthology of 305 poems, is the first monument in the Chinese poetic tradition. It may be dated from the 11th to the 6th century B. C. E. or from the early

Western Zhou Dynasty to the middle of the Spring and Autumn Period, and is viewed as the earliest realistic literature in China. As the starting point of Chinese literature, the classic has provided a deep insight into all aspects of social life of the Zhou Dynasty and truly reflected the rise and fall of the Chinese slavery society. In the light of their rhythms, the poems can be divided into three sections, namely *feng* (风, folk ballads), *ya* (雅, odes) and *song* (颂, hymns), each being subdivided. The 160 poems in the first section are mainly folk songs from the various vassal states, so they are the finest and perennially lovely. They are rich in content, dealing with labor, love affairs, marriage, despair and hardships of the underprivileged, and protests against tyranny and war. The second section contains 105 poems, one part of which is called *Greater Odes* (《大雅》) and the other *Lesser Odes* (《小雅》). The last section is divided into *Zhou Hymns* (《周颂》), *Lu Hymns* (《鲁颂》) and *Shang Hymns* (《商颂》), most of which are formal ritual hymns performed in sacrifices to praise the ancestors. The realistic songs in the collection offer a comprehensive, vivid and truthful picture of social life and customs of that period.

The style of the poems, chiefly written in four-character lines with some irregular stanzas here and there, in general, is straightforward and natural, typical of ancient literature in terms of the immediacy of imagery and pervasive musical quality. The modes of expression, however, are by no means simple: they are not only rich in end rhymes and internal rhymes, but ample and imaginative use is made of metaphors and similes to convey ideas and feelings forcefully. In terms of its writing technique, it can be classified into *fu* (赋, narration), *bi* (比, metaphor) and *xing* (兴, evocation). Roughly, *fu* poems are those with straightforward narrations; *bi* are those with implicit comparisons; *xing* are like the prelude of a song, setting the scene for the poem. All these poems can be sung.

The Book of Songs, as the fountainhead of realism, occupies an important place in the history of Chinese literature. Many great poets throughout history drew inspiration from the anthology. So it is no exaggeration to say that *The Book of Songs* has exerted a profound influence upon the entire course of the development of Chinese poetry.

Second only to *The Book of Songs*, whether in chronological order or in importance in the history of Chinese poetry, is *The Songs of Chu*, also originating from music and dance. *Chu Ci* (楚辞), as the classic's Chinese name indicates, is derived from the songs of the southern state of Chu during the Warring States Period. It pioneered romanticism in the history of Chinese poetry. Liu Xiang (刘向) and Wang Yi (王逸) collected and compiled the works of the noted poet Qu Yuan (屈原) and some others as *The Songs of Chu*.

The verses of *The Songs of Chu* are freer than those of *The Book of Songs*. They are not fixed to four characteristics per line, and the character "*xi* (兮)" is often put in the middle or at the end of some lines such as Qu Yuan's sentence "The road ahead will be long; I'll search up and down. (路漫漫其修远兮，吾将上下而求索。)"

Basing on folk songs in the state of Chu, the towering genius Qu Yuan, China's first known poet, developed these folk songs into a genre of poetry with a number of his immortal poems. The main ones are: *Nine Songs* (《九歌》), which is in fact made up of eleven instead of nine, for the word "nine" here is not in the sense of an exact number; *Questions to Heaven* (《天问》), in which he poses 172 questions about natural phenomena, ancient myths and legends and historical figures, demonstrating the author's valuable spirit of

Qu Yuan

truth seeking; *Nine Elegies* (《九章》), which are short lyrics about the poet's own experiences and difficulties, anguish and anger; and *Sorrow After Departure* (《离骚》).

Sorrow After Departure is Qu Yuan's masterpiece and the most important lyric and romantic poem of The Songs of Chu. Slandered by his wick political enemies and banished from the court, Qu put all his aspirations and emotions into this poem of 373 lines.

Qu Yuan, filled with patriotic sentiments and with a lofty and unsullied personality, "used the Chu written language, followed the Chu pronunciation, described Chu places and named Chu things (书楚语，作楚声，纪楚地，名楚物)". One of the main themes of his works is his great anxiety about dangers and troubles Chu met and his strong aspirations for building a powerful Chu state, though they are indirectly expressed.

Qu Yuan created a new literary genre. His new form and his adoption of positive romanticism have exerted a lasting influence on Chinese literature and been imitated or admired by many writers from the Han Dynasty onward.

Song Yu (宋玉), among many poets after Qu Yuan, was another important author of this genre. His *Nine Arguments* (《九辩》) shows that he closely followed the tradition of Qu Yuan.

Poetry from the Han to the Northern and Southern Dynasties

After the establishment of the Han empire, literature, as well as the economy, flourished. When Emperor Wu came to power, he founded an institution called the Music Bureau (乐府) to compose music, train musicians, perform rites, and collect folk ballads which would enable the government to learn about the local customs and the people's reactions to the central government and political situation. In time, the term Music Bureau was extended to include songs by common people as well as works by men of letters which drew on titles, tunes, and narrative motifs of the original folk ballads. These songs finally came to be known as music-bureau poems (乐府诗), a famous genre in the history of Chinese poetry.

The most important anthology of this form is *The Collection of Music-Bureau Poems* (《乐府诗集》) compiled by Guo Maoqian (郭茂倩) in the 11th century. The poems were composed or sung by common people when "moved to sorrow or joy and eager to voice their minds (感于哀乐，缘事而发)". The language is generally simple and unadorned; the plots are often straightforward and uncomplicated. In this respect, they follow the tradition of *The Book of Songs*, and give us a very comprehensive picture of the lives of working people and social contradiction at that time. For example, *The Song of an Orphan* (《孤儿行》) tells the hardships and wretched lot about an orphan whose elder brother and sister-in-law compel him to work like a slave.

Other poems, such as *The Ailing Wife* (《病妇行》), *Fighting South of the City* (《战城南》), *The Eastern Gate* (《东门行》), and *Roadside Mulberry Tree* (《陌上桑》), vividly depict the sufferings of the common people, the macabre desolation on a battlefield or the spirit of rebellion of a poor man driven to desperation.

The most outstanding folk ballad of this period is *Southwest the Peacock Flies* (《孔雀东南飞》). The longest poem (353 lines) for several hundred years, it relates the tragedy of a young married couple, Jiao Zhongqing (焦仲卿) and Liu Lanzhi (刘兰芝), sharply denounces the feudal ethics, exposes its evil and shows great sympathy for women who were chief victims of the ethics.

Since songs of the genre were employed to express the author's feelings spontaneously, they were usually written in lines of irregular lengths, varying from three to six characters, but more and more they began to assume five-character lines. The assumption of the form and realism in content influenced and inspired later poets. Hence came the gradual genesis of the poetry of five-character line, or five-character ancient-style poetry (五言古诗), one of the most enduring and versatile Chinese poetic forms. These poems were mostly literati compositions, and became mature during the reign of Emperor Huan (桓帝) adn Emperor Ling (灵帝) of the Eastern Han Dynasty. The representative poems are those in *Nineteen Ancient-Style Poems* (《古诗十九首》) compiled by Xiao Tong (萧统) of the Liang Dynasty. In the poems the pensive melancholy and pessimism is heightened, but the artistic value is highly treasured in the history of Chinese literature. Metaphor, allegory and symbolism are widely utilized and diverse ways of executing them are adopted, which enables sentiments to subtly blend with the objects of comparison and the moral lesson to move the emotions.

The period of the Three Kingdoms is known as the Jian'an period (建安时期) in literature, Jian'an being the reign title of the last Han emperor. Its literary leading figures are the father and sons of the Cao family (曹氏父子) and the Seven Masters (建安七子): Wang Can (王粲), Kong Rong (孔融), Liu Zhen (刘桢), Chen Lin (陈琳), Ruan Yu (阮瑀), Xu Gan (徐干), and Ying Yang (应玚) headed by Wang Can.

Of Cao Cao (曹操)'s poems written in the style of the music-bureau poetry, only over twenty are extant, such as *Overgrown with Brambles* (《蒿里行》), *A Short Song* (《短歌行》) and *The Sea* (《观沧海》).

Cao Pi (曹丕) and Cao Zhi (曹植), two sons of Cao Cao, were also famous as writers, but Cao Zhi achieved much more in poetry. Noted for his lyricism, he had greatly developed and given definite artistic form to the poetry of five-character line, making it more expressive and varied in its themes.

Wang Can is commonly regarded as the most brilliant of the Seven Masters of the Jian'an period. His extant work is fairly extensive, and more conspicuous for originality. His most deservedly famous compositions are written in five-character lines, as was then the fashion, especially his *Poems of Seven Lamentations* (《七哀诗》). The group of poems effectively and truly portrays in an impassioned and energetic way the evils of his day: ravages of war, unbearable exile, endless vagrancy and extreme destitution.

In sum, during this brief but memorable period, poetry reached new heights. The writings were individual and beautiful, rich in true feelings and vigorous in expression. Many of them, voicing the spirit of the age, showed emotional depth and spiritual exaltation. The poets, with lofty ideals and tough, upright and ambitious personalities, revealed through their writings the pursuit of accomplishment that would profit generations to come and of a fame that would remain for an eternity, and as Liu Xie (刘勰) says: give free rein to their aspiration and let their pen obey only the dictates of their talent (慷慨以任气，磊落以使才). This style, honored by later critics as the thematic and stylistic feature of the Jian'an literature (建安风骨), was vibrant and widely imitated, especially in the Tang Dynasty.

By the end of Wei, power fell into the hands of the Sima family (司马氏). Literature of this period mainly reflects the feeling of the people under terror and oppression. The representative poets of this era are the Seven Worthies of the Bamboo Groves (竹林七贤) who used to meet to discuss literature in bamboo groves. Ruan Ji (阮籍) and Ji Kang (嵇康) stand out among them.

In the year of 265, the Sima family finally established the Western Jin Dynasty. During its early years, literature flourished to a certain extent with a new school of poets known as the Taikang poets (太康诗人), Taikang being the reign title of the first emperor of the Jin Dynasty. Lu Ji (陆机) and Pan Yue (潘岳) are relatively important poets, who are often yoked together and have come down to us as a pair. They paid much attention to the manner of expression, namely their poetic artifice. But they were, along with other poets of the generation, superficial and empty in content and euphuistic and florid in style.

Zuo Si (左思), however, stood apart in style from his contemporaries. He wrote both good *fu* (赋, combination of poem and prose) such as *Rhapsody on the Three Capitals* (《三都赋》) and charming five-character poems. His most celebrated works are the eight *Poems on History* (《咏史诗》). He inherited and promoted the spirit of Jian'an literature and influenced a lot of later authors.

In the Eastern Jin Dynasty, many poets were heavily influenced by the philosophy of Lao Zi and Zhuang Zi, which resulted in many mysterious and abstruse poems. But Tao Yuanming (陶渊明) is an exception.

Tao Yuanming or Tao Qian (陶潜), disillusioned with the corruption of the government, disgusted with the bureaucracy, and eager to return to nature, put an end to his short official career, resigned to his home village and wrote many outstanding poems.

Tao's poems featured his vivid and sensitive descriptions of natural scenery, which established him as the creator of the pastoral or idyllic poetry (田园诗) in Chinese literature. His poems of this sort are as pure and simple as nature itself, without an iota of embellishment or artificiality. The best examples are his *Miscellaneous Poems* (《杂诗》), *Drinking Wine* (《饮酒》) and *On Returning to My Garden and Fields* (《归园田居》).

During the Northern and Southern Dynasties, the music-bureau poems revived to some extent. In the South, unlike their counterparts in the Han Dynasty, the poems were mainly lyrical or love songs. The speakers in *The Songs at Midnight* (《子夜歌》), for example, are occupied with love and often do not hesitate to express it in suggestive terms. Only Bao Zhao (鲍照) is different, whose music-bureau poems are of five- or seven-character line. The most famous is *In Imitation of The Weary Road* (《拟行路难》), which has often been imitated.

Such poems from the Northern Dynasties, on the whole, are more militant and heroic. The one reflecting the spirit most fully is *The Ballad of Mu Lan* (《木兰诗》), which sings praise of a girl who disguised herself as a warrior and won glory on the battle-field. These lyric songs are much more unified than those of the Han Dynasty and are known for their skillful manipulation of language, especially their numerous use of puns and evocative images arousing associations, metaphors and similes.

Xie Lingyun (谢灵运), Shen Yue (沈约) and Xie Tiao (谢朓) are also famous poets of that period.

Poetry during the Tang Dynasty

The Tang Dynasty is generally acknowledged as the golden age of Chinese poetry. In the number of poems and variety of forms, in the beauty of imagery and broadness of themes, Tang poetry surpassed that of all ages before it. *The Complete Anthology of Tang Poetry* (《全唐诗》), edited in the early Qin Dynasty, is the biggest-ever collection of Chinese poetry, which collects nearly 50,000 poems by more than 2,000 poets. This means that in 300 years, the Tang poets wrote more poems than all the poets before them.

The development of poetry in the Tang Dynasty can be classified into four stages: Early Tang (初唐), High Tang (盛唐), Middle Tang (中唐) and Late Tang (晚唐).

The Early Tang poetry was marked by a demand for a return to classical simplicity and clarity, for since the two Jin Dynasties, especially in the Chen, Liang and Sui Periods, poetry with eulogistic themes which was extremely ornate and grand in form, possessing a subtly woven texture, prevailed and flourished. The pioneers of poetic innovation at that time were the Four Literary Eminences (初唐四杰): Wang Bo (王勃), Yang Jiong (杨炯), Luo Binwang (骆宾王) and Lu Zhaolin (卢照邻), who were minor officials who were politically frustrated. They denounced the prevailing style of the period as "the complete absence of motif for representing and glorifying the upright and ambitious personality, and the total rejection of stylistic vigor and toughness (气骨都尽，刚健不闻)". So in their poems they strove to demonstrate this essence and intension of the tough and upright personality. Lu Zhaolin's *Panorama of Chang'an* (《长安古意》), Luo Binwang's *The Capital of the Empire* (《帝京篇》) and *Cicada's Song Heard in a Cell* (《在狱咏蝉》), and Wang Bo's landscape poetry all represented a marked break from the narrow confines of that of the court. Other famous poets in the Early Tang Period were Chen Zi'ang (陈子昂) and Zhang Ruoxu (张若虚).

During the High Tang Period, when the society enjoyed prosperity and stability, there appeared a whole generation of literary giants whose names are known all over the world, and whose immortal poems are basic to the history of Chinese literature.

First of all, a group of excellent pastoral poets emerged such as Wang Wei (王维), Meng Haoran (孟浩然), Chu Guangxi (储光羲), Liu Changqing (刘长卿) and Wei Yingwu (韦应物), among whom Meng Haoran and Wang Wei were two representatives. They followed and developed the tradition of Tao Yuanming and Xie Lingyun to depict country life and reflect the beauty of nature. *Returning to South Mountain on the Eve of the Year* (《岁暮归南山》), *A Song on Returning at Night to Deer Gate* (《夜归鹿门歌》) and some others are Meng's most famous and widely cited poems.

Wang Wei was skillfully in communicating thought in unpolished, exquisite and symbolic language through his poems which evince a great harmony of the self and the world, or even the submergence of man in nature. *The Gully of Twittering Birds* (《鸟鸣涧》), *Seeing Yuan the Second off on a Mission to Anxi* (《送元二使安西》) and *Wei River Farm* (《渭川田家》) are the best examples.

Secondly, another group of frontier poets (边塞诗人) also appeared such as Gao Shi (高适), Cen Shen (岑参), Wang Changling (王昌龄) and Li Qi (李颀). The frontier poems describe the frontier scenery, military life and soldiers' homesickness, passionate patriotism, and devotion to the state. The best-known were Gao Shi's *A Song to the Frontiers* (《塞下曲》) and *A Song of Yan* (《燕歌行》), Cen Shen's *In Farewell to General Feng at the Running-Horse River on His Western Expedition* (《走马川行奉送出师西征》), Wang Changling's *On the Frontier* (《出塞》) and *A War Song* (《从军行》), and Li Qi's *An Old War Song* (《古从军行》). These poems were in fact vehicles for expressing will power, ambition or chagrin regarding a defeated career of the poets.

Finally, Li Bai (李白) and Du Fu (杜甫) who shone in a galaxy of poetic luminaries, have been regarded as the most famous poets in the High Tang Period.

Li Bai, the "Immortal of Poems (诗仙)", has long been considered the greatest romantic poet in the history of Chinese literature. He wrote as many as 900 poems. Some of them describe the lives of the people; some describe the magnificent scenery he saw; others express his own wishes and sorrows. His poems are characterized by unusual imagination, exaggeration, wit, elasticity, flexibility, unpredictability, and vitality. His love of life, generous spirit and closeness to the people make his romanticism healthy and positive. Some of Li Bai's most famous poems include *Thinking in the Silent Night* (《静夜思》), *Hard is the Road to Shu* (《蜀道难》), and *Dreaming of Sightseeing in the Tianmu Mountains* (《梦游天姥吟留别》).

Li Bai

Du Fu, the "Sage of Poems (诗圣)", has been regarded as the greatest realistic poet in the history of Chinese literature. He was a master of many styles both in regulated and non-regulated forms and so broad had been his range of styles that his corpus contained the prototype of most later stylistic developments in poetry.

Du Fu

Most of Du Fu's best poems were written after the An Lushan-Shi Siming Rebellion (安史之乱). So, as a realist poet, he wrote many poems that chronicled the political upheavals and sufferings of the people of his years with a gift for direct observation and an ability to relate without maudlin feeling his own suffering to that of the country and to denounce the social evils. Because he reached perfection in developing a depressing and meticulous literary style, his works have been considered the classics of realism. The best of these poems are the "Three Officers (三吏)" and the "Three Partings (三别)". The former includes *The Xin'an Officer* (《新安

吏》), *The Shihao Officer* (《石壕吏》), and *The Officer at Tongguan Pass* (《潼关吏》); whereas the latter contains *Parting of the Newly-Wed* (《新婚别》), *Parting of the Old* (《垂老别》), and *Parting of the Homeless* (《无家别》). Many of his other poems express faith in mankind's future while some are about his friends and natural beauty. The examples are *A Spring View* (《春望》), *On a Tower* (《登楼》), and *Watching a Sword Dance Performed by the Pupil of the Elder Sister of Gongsun* (《观公孙大娘弟子舞剑器行》).

In the Middle Tang Period, though their works are devoid of the high ambition and heroism demonstrated in the poetry of the High Tang Period, many writers produced numerous excellent poems which forcefully exposed the social vices of their time. Eminent ones were Bai Juyi (白居易), Yuan Zhen (元稹), Han Yu (韩愈), Liu Zongyuan (柳宗元), Liu Yuxi (刘禹锡), Meng Jiao (孟郊), Li He (李贺), and Jia Dao (贾岛).

Bai Juyi and Yuan Zhen were good friends and exchanged poems constantly. With other poets, such as Zhang Ji (张继), Wang Jian (王建), Li Shen (李绅), they initiated the New Music-Bureau Movement (新乐府运动) to liberate poetry from the rigid rules of prosody. It is true that the music-bureau poetic form had been revived by earlier poets, such as Li Bai and Du Fu, but Bai Juyi, Yuan Zhen and their friends went beyond the structural freedom of metre and rhyme advocated by others and stressed the simplicity of language and seriousness of purpose. They firmly believed that poetry could effect social and political changes.

A prolific writer, Bai Juyi, wrote nearly 3,000 poems, about 2,000 of which were regulated poems and around 170 were satirical and allegorical. The latter category includes his poetic treasures. For instance, *The Old Man with a Broken Arm* (《新丰断臂翁》) attacks militarism and the horrors of war; *The Old Charcoal Seller* (《卖炭翁》) is a plaint against official harassment and class oppression; *The White-Haired Lady of Shangyang Palace* (《上阳白发人》) is a lament on the fate of palace ladies. However, the most popular of his poems are his romantic narrative ballads: *Song of Everlasting Sorrow* (《长恨歌》) and *Song of the Pi Pa Lute* (《琵琶行》).

Yuan Zhen also wrote satirical poems, such as *Lianchang Palace* (《连昌宫词》), but they are less forceful than Bai's. Yuan is famous for his love and mourning poems.

Han Yu and Liu Zongyuan were two champions of the Tang classical movement (古文运动). They were both great essayists and important poets. Han created a style that was at once bursting with force, strange beauty, grotesque images, and freakish imagination. According to himself, he always strove for an accuracy and clarity appropriate to the content of the poem and its social context, though some critics think these poems are a little too intricate and even baroque in style. Anyhow, he pioneered an entirely new school of poetry that influenced many later poets, such as Li He and Li Shangyin (李商隐).

Liu Zongyuan's poems are different. On them one can see little influence of Han Yu's prosification of poetry; instead, they are considered to have been influenced by earlier "nature poets": Wang Wei, Meng Haoran, Wei Yingwu, and others. Nature and social themes were his primary concerns. His *River in the Snow* (《江雪》) is a poem known to all Chinese literati.

After the An Lushan Rebellion, the Tang empire declined with increasing rapidity. Up to the Late Tang, national revival proved to be hopeless. Although their patriotic fervor was occasionally rekindled by what remained of their dedication to the imperial court, the literati were increasingly aware that the situation was irremediable. Faced with such conflicting emotions, poets of the Late Tang Period fell either to reminiscence and meditation on the past, or to family love or boudoir. Poets turned to the theme of nostalgia for the former splendor of old times. Some of them expressed their delicate sentiments through delicate techniques and wrote some good poems. The most outstanding were those written by Li Shangyin and Du Mu (杜牧).

Another great contribution of the Tang Dynasty to Chinese poetry was the emergence of the *ci* poetry (词).

Originating in Tang and coming into maturity in the Song Dynasty, the *ci* poetry was one of the major poetic genres and a new form of lyric verse in China. It was originally a song text set to existing musical tunes which have been called tune patterns. These tunes for which the poems are composed came to be viewed as definite verse patterns (词牌). This unique practice of *ci* composition is called "filling in words (填词)." The *ci* poetry is characterized often by lines of unequal length, in sharp contrast to the regulated verse in strictly five- or seven-character lines.

Something like the *ci* poetry had appeared long before the Late Tang Period. Li Bai was usually considered the first poet to experiment with it. Later Bai Juyi, Liu Yuxi and others also composed this genre of poetry occasionally. The first prolific *ci* poet in China is Wen Tingjun (温庭筠). About 70 of his *ci* poems have survived. Wen's representative *ci* poems were *Buddhist Dancers* (《菩萨蛮》), *The South Recalled* (《忆江南》) and some others. Most of them describe women and lovesickness. His solitary female figure is characteristically enclosed behind layers of veils, curtains, and mirrors in a self-reflective state of imagination and memory. The luxurious surroundings make up an ironical contrast with the lonely woman's emotional deprivation. Wen's writing style is somewhat extravagantly ornate and the diction a little overly embellished. However, he paved the way for the *ci* creation, influenced many contemporary *ci* poets and became the originator of the Among-the-Flowers School of *ci* poetry (花间词派). It is he that established the *ci* poetry as an independent poetic genre in China.

A few decades later, Li Yu (李煜), the last emperor of the Southern Tang, wrote some noteworthy *ci* poems, especially after he was taken prisoner in 975, for, after that, he gradually opened the vista of the *ci* from women's apartments to larger concerns such as philosophical and political reflections on and lamentation for the downfall of his kingdom and the brevity of life. The exemplifications are his *Ripples Sifting Sand* (《浪淘沙》) and *The Beautiful Lady Yu* (《虞美人》). In these poems, Li Yu breaks through the conventional style of floweriness and euphuism and puts his own self into the foreground. This kind of subjectivity was innovative in the *ci* creation at that time. His emotions, sentiments, and sufferings are so vividly and truly expressed that they arouse a universal set of emotions which could be shared by the readers. In this sense, Li Yu is regarded as the first true master of *ci* poetry.

Poetry during the Song Dynasty

In the Song Dynasty, the *ci* poetry came into full flower and grew into the most distinguished poetic genre, which is known as *Song ci* poetry. Instead of regulated poetry, *Song ci* poetry could convey more refined and delicate feelings with an irregular meter. Besides poets, emperors and ministers, actresses and prostitutes, also tried to write *ci* poetry. There were over 200 Song poets whose *ci* works were later collected and preserved, and they used as many as 870 different tunes.

Depending upon its length, *Song ci* poetry can be divided into *xiaoling* (小令, short tunes, less than 59 characters), *zhongdiao* (中调, medium tunes, 59—90 characters), and *changdiao* (长调, long tunes, more than 90 characters). Some have only one verse, some two, and others have three or four, each having its own style.

As stated above, *ci* originated from music or the words of songs. So each *ci* has a title as well as a *cipai* (词牌). *The Beautiful Lady Yu* (虞美人), *Moon on the Western River* (西江月), *Butterfly Loves Flowers* (蝶恋花), and *Immortals Meeting on the Magpie Bridge* (鹊桥仙) are all names of *cipai*.

There appeared two major *ci* styles in the Northern Song Dynasty. One style is called the "Graceful and Restrained School (婉约派)" represented by Liu Yong (柳永), Li Qingzhao (李清照), Yan Shu (晏殊) and Ouyang Xiu (欧阳修). Most of their works are about personal joys and sorrows, love and parting, and reflect the elite literati taste and the sophisticated aristocratic lifestyle of leisure and luxury.

Liu Yong made a great contribution to the *ci* poetry and has been universally acknowledged to be the first master of the "Graceful and Restrained School". He was good at tonal patterns and rhyme scheme, and well-versed in literature. Liu's style absorbed much from contemporary popular folk music. His *Collection of Yuezhang* (《乐章集》) reflects strongly the popular tradition of banquet music and the aesthetic tastes of common urban people. Through him, the *ci* lyrics were taken from the upper class boudoir back to the people in the

Liu Yong

street, and addressed a much broader range of society. His *Collection of Yuezhang*, with its lively diction and subtle description of folk customs, breathed fresh vitality into the *ci* poetry of the Northern Song, especially the two pieces of *Bells Ring in the Rain* (《雨霖铃》) and *Eight Beats of a Ganzhou Song* (《八声甘州》). What's more, Liu Yong was the first *ci* poet conversant with long tunes. Of all his *ci* pieces, approximately 130 tune-titles are employed; some 30 pieces are written to the short tunes and 80 percent to the long tunes.

Li Qingzhao, as China's greatest poetess with erudition and versatile talents, also rose to prominence in this period. Her *ci* poems could be classified into two groups. Her early poetry, full of vitality and elegant diction, paints vignettes of her carefree days as a woman of high society, such as *Tipsy in the Flower's Shade* (《醉花阴》) and *A Twig of Mume Blossoms* (《一剪梅》). But the poems written after the loss of the country and her husband's death portray her as grief-stricken, mourning the loss of her homeland and her beloved. The representative ones are *Joy of Eternal Union* (《永遇乐》) and *Slow, Slow Tune* (《声声慢》). Basing on real events and personal experience, she describes her worries and woes, frustration and bitterness with such vivid depth of emotional intensity that few poets could rival her. Despite her meticulous observance of the metrical rules of the *ci* poetry, the poetess was able to depict, in everyday language and without affection, her true state of mind. Her sensitivity to music and cadence, her gift for fresh imagery, and her impeccable craftsmanship place her among the best of *ci* masters.

Yan Shu's best works are gracefully fluent, musical, and slightly colloquial, not burdened by allusions or intensity like Wen Tingjun's, and his exquisite imagery and delicate suggestivity create a fine effect, such as the *Sand of Silk-Washing Stream* (《浣溪沙》) and *Treading on Grass* (《踏莎行》).

During the second half of the Northern Song Dynasty, important *ci* poets were Qin Guan (秦观), He Zhu (贺铸), and Zhou Bangyan (周邦彦). All of them belonged to the members of the

"Graceful and Restrained School".

The other style is called the "Powerful and Free School (豪放派)" represented by Su Shi (苏轼) and Xin Qiji (辛弃疾).

Another great *ci* poet of the first half of the Northern Song Dynasty was Su Shi, whose *ci* pieces are different in style and content from those of Liu Yong. With his extraordinary vigorous style of poetry, Su Shi brought innovations to *ci* and helped broaden its scope, elevate its status and set up the "Powerful and Free School". He produced about 350 *ci* poems, the most famous of which are his *To the Tune of Charm of a Maiden Singer: Recalling Antiquity at the Red Cliff* (《念奴娇·赤壁怀古》), *Prelude to the Melody of Water: The Mid-Autumn Festival* (《水调歌头·明月几时有》), and *To the Tune of a Riverside Town: Dreaming of His Deceased Wife* (《江城子·十年生死两茫茫》). Su's another important contribution was his reform in the *ci* form by "making the *ci* more poetic (以诗为词)". The result was that the uneven lines of *ci*, originally developed simply to match the music, now became an independent lyrical verse form in which emotions and aspirations found direct expression. This marked a great step forward though his verses were sometimes out of tune and too much like didactic prose.

Su Shi

Since the 1120s, facing the troubled motherland, many *ci* poets wrote with patriotic sentiments and produced a lot of excellent poems. The most remarkable one was Xin Qiji among other poets such as Yue Fei (岳飞), Zhang Yuangan (张元干), Zhang Xiaoxiang (张孝祥), and Chen Liang (陈亮).

Xin Qiji, born in the last years of the weak Song Dynasty, could not put his great abilities to use, and his indignation found no vent. Therefore, his plaintive songs, his passions, his pent-up feelings all found expression in his *ci* poetry. He elevated *ci* writings of the "Powerful and Free

School" to a new height by enriching their content and improving their form. He wrote about the great, impassioned themes of opposing Jin (金) invasions and recovering lost territories, which represents a major change in the history of the *ci* poetry. *Water Dragon Chant* (《水龙吟》), *Song of a Southern Country* (《南乡子》) and *Dance of the Cavalry* (《破阵子》) are examples of this theme written in a heroic and unrestrained style.

In the late Southern Song, *ci* writers who had a fairly great influence were Jiang Kui (姜夔) and Wu Wenying (吴文英). They were traditionally regarded as poets of the "Graceful and Restrained School". In fact, they are different.

Jiang Kui modeled himself at first upon Huang Tingjian (黄庭坚), the founder of the Jiangxi School (江西诗派). Several years later he found that emulation was stifling and he began to turn his attention to originality and spontaneity in his literary creation. So he said, "In poetry writing, it is better to attempt to be different from our predecessors rather than conform to them. But better yet is to be different without attempting to either conform or be different."

Compared with the *ci*, the Song regulated poetry was not so outstanding, but among nearly 4,000 poets, quite a few produced noteworthy poems of a lasting influence. They are Wang Yucheng (王禹偁), Ouyang Xiu, Mei Yaochen (梅尧臣), Su Shunqin (苏舜钦), Su Shi, Huang Tingjian, Lu You (陆游), Fan Chengda (范成大), Yang Wanli (杨万里) and Wen Tianxiang (文天祥).

Poetry from the Yuan to the Qing Period

During the Yuan Dynasty, a new lyrical poetic genre, *sanqü* (散曲) came to maturity. *Sanqü* was in fact a kind of folk music and song at first. It considered either an independent song called *xiaoling* (小令, short tonal poem) or the suite style named *santao* (散套, a sequence of *sanqü* songs of a certain musical mode). The text of *sanqü* is written, like the *ci* poetry, according to different metrical patterns and tunes. *Xiaoling* could be a single stanza to one tune, or two, three or four stanzas to different tunes in the same mode. A suite is a string of single-stanza arias and cluster arias from the same mode, whose rhyme and metre are arranged according to a favored sequence pattern characteristic of the mode. It has also a head aria and a coda, which are the most predicable and constant elements. *Sanqü* could not only exist independently as a kind of lyrical poetry but also form a part of Yuan drama.

The *sanqü* poetry, originating from the common people, is freer and more lively than its *ci* counterpart. The composer can add any number of what are called padding words to a line, which permits considerable variation in the number of characters per line.

Important *sanqü* writers in the first half of the Yuan Dynasty were Guan Hanqing (关汉卿), Bai Pu (白朴), and Ma Zhiyuan (马致远), all of whom came from the lower society. They wrote mainly about partings and love, landscape and nature or personal sorrows and woes. Their poetry is usually natural in style, earthy and lively in language. Ma Zhiyuan's *Autumn Thought* (《秋思》), a *xiaoling*, enjoys great popularity. He sketched a picture with only 28 words showing the wilderness of a strange land and expressing his loneliness and sadness. In the second half, Zhang Yanghao (张养浩), Zhang Kejiu (张可久), Qiao Ji (乔吉), and Sui Jingchen (睢景臣) paid much more attention to literary language and versification, thus losing some of their freshness. But their poems were beautifully constructed and some verses, with a deep and angry mood, poignantly criticize the social evils of that time and the wicked nature of the ruling class, such as Zhang Yanghao's *Meditation on the Past at the Tongguan Pass* (《潼关怀古》) and Sui Jingchen's *Emperor Gao Zu Returning to His Native Village* (《高祖还乡》).

The Yuan Dynasty did not achieve much in creating regulated poetry though there were some poets such Liu Yin (刘因), Sadula (萨都剌) and Wang Mian (王勉).

The Ming Dynasty lacks outstanding poetic masters like Su Shi of the Song Dynasty, though some are noteworthy.

First of all, Liu Ji (刘基) and Gao Qi (高启) were two early important poets. Experiencing the turmoil at the end of the Yuan Dynasty, they wrote some poems substantial in content, especially those of Gao Qi's. His *A Bird-Eye View of the Changjiang River on the Rain-and-Flower Stone Terrace of Jinling* (《登金陵雨花台望大江》), written in the heroic and gallant style with proper allusions, fully describes China's grandeur and beauty and exactly expresses his excitement at its unification.

Then for about 60 to 80 years after Liu Ji and Gao Qi, the poetic field was dominated by poems of the Secretariat Style (台阁体) represented by Yang Shiqi (杨士奇), Yang Rong (杨荣) and Yang Pu (杨溥), who were all high officials in the court, hence the name. They advocated writing poems of eulogistic themes in ornate and grandiose form. It was not until 1470s that this style came to be gradually broken by the Former Seven Masters (前七子) and then the Latter Seven Masters (后七子).

These two groups of poets, the former headed by Li Mengyang (李梦阳) and He Jingming (何景明) while the latter by Li Panlong (李攀龙) and Wang Shizhen (王世贞), in order to correct the so-called Secretariat Style, launched the movement of archaism.

Realizing that the archaism of the revivalists was a kind of retrogression, Yuan Hongdao (袁

宏道) and his brothers Yuan Zongdao (袁宗道) and Yuan Zhongdao (袁中道) campaigned against it form the late years of the 16th century. They are known in history as the three Yuans from Gong'an (公安三袁) or the Gong'an School (公安派), a name derived from their native place, Gong'an County of Hubei.

At the end of the Ming Dynasty, facing its fall, some writers created many poems showing their anxiety and strong desire to save the country. The outstanding ones were Chen Zilong (陈子龙) and the young hero Xia Wanchun (夏完淳), both of whom died for the Ming Dynasty.

In the first 80 years of the Qing Dynasty, poetic creativity was quite flourishing and surpassed the Ming Dynasty. The poets could be divided into two groups, one belonging to the Ming-Qing transitional period with the other coming to maturity after Qing was established.

The foremost poets of the first group were Gu Yanwu (顾炎武), Qian Qianyi (钱谦益), Wu Weiye (吴伟业), Gui Zhuang (归庄), Qu Dajun (屈大均), and others. Most of them are remember for their works based on their experiences and reflections about the collapse of the Ming and the conquest of the Qing.

Poems of the second group are different in themes and sentiments for the authors grew up and began their career in the Qing Dynasty. They are chiefly Wang Shizhen (王士禛), Zhu Yizun (朱彝尊), Nara Xingde (纳兰性德), and Chen Weisong (陈维崧).

Wang Shizhen, the leading poet after Qian Qianyi and Wu Weiye, was remarkable in writing nature poetry with a fresh and beautiful style and fluent and natural rhythm. He, opposing archaism, advocated a serene and lucid style and stressed implicit diction.

Zhu Yizun, like Wang Shizhen, was also one of the most learned scholars and prolific authors of his time. He was good not only at regulated poetry but also at the *ci* poetry and is traditionally regarded as the father of the Western Zhejiang School of the *ci* poetry (浙西词派), who promoted the revival of the *ci* writing. His works, simple, fresh and vigorous, covered mainly social reality, landscapes and his own feelings and wished.

During the Yongzheng and Qianglong Period (雍正与乾隆时期), there appeared two major schools of theory: the theory of classical style and the theory of natural sensibility.

The former was put forward by Shen Deqian (沈德潜). The core of his theory was that poetry should be formally didactic in the theme, honestly mild in diction and classically refined in form. In fact, he advocated that poetry should serve the feudal rule. His theory was appreciated by Emperor Qianlong and permeated the poetic field for some years. Yuan Mei (袁枚), disagreeing with Shen's theory and rejecting any blind imitation of past masters, put forward his own, holding that poetry should serve as an expression of personal nature and sentiments and be written with individual technique. His theory has gaind a widespread influence and many followers.

From the reign of Daoguang (道光) to that of Xianfeng (咸丰) the ruling class became terribly corrupted, and foreign imperialists tried every means to invade China. The Qing Dynasty began to decline rapidly and, faced with this situation, some poets became indignant and wrote poems incisively reflecting the reality, especially Gong Zizhen (龚自珍) and Wei Yuan (魏源).

Gong Zizhen, one of the most influential figures, with broad and varied literary and scholastic achievements at that time, is particularly famous as a poet for his seven-character *jueju* poems (七言绝句). The representative ones are his several pieces of *Miscellaneous Poems of the Year of Jihai* (《己亥杂诗》).

Wei Yuan, personally witnessing the Opium War, wrote poems full of patriotism and hatred for the aggressors. As famous as Gong, Wei's poetic style was also similar to Gong's: heroic, lofty, lucid and lively.

Lin Zexu (林则徐), Zhang Weiping (张维屏), and Zhang Jiliang (张际亮) are also patriotic poets of that period.

In the years of Tongzhi (同治) and Guangxu (光绪), voices of reformism grew gradually louder and many poets, through their verses, propagandized reformist ideas, paving the way for the reform movement. In style, they advocated "poetic revolution (诗界革命)", calling for expressing new ideas with new diction in the traditional form. The foremost figures were Huang Zunxian (黄遵宪), Kang Youwei (康有为) and Liang Qichao (梁启超) though Tan Sitong (谭嗣同), Yan Fu (严复) and others also did a lot.

After the failure of the reform of Kang Youwei and Liang Qichao, many revolutionaries launched other movements to overthrow the Qing Dynasty to establish a democratic republic. Some of them, with lofty and revolutionary aspirations, wrote many heroic and impassioned poems in an unrestrained and forceful style, such as Qiu Jin's (秋瑾) *A Song of Autumn Wind* (《秋风曲》) and *A Song of the Sword* (《宝刀歌》), Zhang Taiyan's (章太炎) *To Zou Rong from Prison* (《狱中赠邹容》), and Chen Qubing's (陈去病) *A Visit to Anru* (《访安如》). Their poems, in the traditional form, were mostly written with plain and lucid language. These poems and the authors themselves contributed greatly to the overthrow of the Qing Dynasty.

/ Prose /

The English word "prose", coming closest to the notion of Chinese *sanwen* (散文), is derived from the Latin term *prorsa oratio* that means "straight-forward talk" as opposed to verse. So the greatest virtue of prose, in this sense, is clarity. Unfortunately, the term has taken on negative connotations in English, so such phrases as "a prosy old fellow" and "a prosaic problem" are often seen. But in Chinese, *sanwen* is a literary category with a history as long as, or even longer than that of poetry. It is often exalted as one of its pillars and has a position of prominence in Chinese literature.

Chinese classical prose covers a wide range of different genres. Though in history, scholars have different ideas about the classifications, the chief genres are agreed upon. They are mainly discourses and arguments (论说), miscellaneous records (杂文), prefaces and colophons (序跋), essays presented at parting (赠序文), letters (书牍文), elegies and funeral orations (哀祭文), admonitions and inscriptions (箴铭), biographies and obituaries (传状文), and epitaphs (碑志文).

Prose in the Pre-Qin Period

Prose of this period can be dated back to as early as the Shang and Zhou Dynasties, but the prosperous era was the Spring and Autumn and the Warring States Periods. The prose in the Pre-Qin times includes historical prose (历史散文) and philosophical prose (诸子散文).

As far as the historical prose is concerned, the main representative works are *The Book of History* (《书经》or《尚书》), *The Spring and Autumn Annals* (《春秋》), *Zuo's Commentary* (《左传》), *Intrigues of the Warring States* or *Strategies of the Warring States* (《战国策》) and *Discourses on Governance of the States* (《国语》).

The Book of History is the most ancient collection of Chinese prose writings with fragments of disconnected and diverse individual official papers.

The Spring and Autumn Annals is the earliest chronicle (编年史) in China with concise and meticulous language.

Zuo's Commentary, said to have been written by Zuo Qiuming (左丘明), a contemporary of Kong Zi or a little earlier, and also called *The Spring and Autumn Annals of Mr. Zuo* (《左氏春秋》), is not only the first comprehensive historical account of the major political, social and military events of the Spring and Autumn Period, but also the first widely imitated prose model.

Intrigues of the Warring States is a collection of historical narratives, fictionalized stories, and persuasive speeches that reflect the important events of politics, military and diplomacy between states in the Warring States Period.

Discourses of the States is a chronological recording of the statements of the aristocrats of various states.

During the Spring and Autumn and Warring States Periods, Chinese society was undergoing radical changes, and various schools of thought, such as the Confucian School, the Mohist School, the Taoist School, and the Legalist School, all strived to put their ideas into practice by writing books and expounding their theories. Some outstanding pieces of philosophical prose include *The Analects of Confucius* (《论语》), *Mencius* or *The Book of Master Meng* (《孟子》), *Dao De Jing* (《道德经》) or *Lao Zi* (《老子》), *Zhuang Zi* (《庄子》), *Mo Zi* (《墨子》), and *Xun Zi* (《荀子》).

The Analects of Confucius, compiled by the disciples of Confucius, is the Bible of Confucianism, consisting of Confucius's sayings and speeches which express his viewpoints of politics, his ideas of education, his understanding of ethics and his principle of morality in the simple, lively, and straightforward spoken language of that time. Many of his famous sayings have become proverbs that have been appreciated by one generation after another.

Mencius, written by Mencius, is a collection of speeches and conversations of Meng Ke (孟轲), the second prominent Confucian master and expositor. It makes full use of the expressive power of spoken language in forging an eloquent verbal style.

Dao De Jing, written by Lao Zi, is regarded as the scripture of Taoism. Through using a rhyme (韵) like prose poems imbued with philosophical ideas, the classic features the superlative compactness in language and the mixture of prosaic and poetic form in style.

Zhuang Zi, written by Zhuang Zi, has established the model of an exuberantly imaginative form that defies classification. In lively, sometimes paradoxical language, Zhuang Zi gave free play to his imagination and thought, without following any particular school or committing himself to any line. With sharp insight and acute observation, he widely used anecdotes, allegories, analogies, fables, and satires to reveal profound truths in some respects of life, though some of his philosophical ideas were quite passive, for example, the fables *In the North Ocean There Is a Fish* (《北冥有鱼》), *Autumn Floods* (《秋水》) and the anecdote *Cook Ding Carves Oxen* (《庖丁解牛》).

Mo Zi, written by Mo Zi, is known for its extensive and effective methodological reasoning.

Xun Zi is written by Xun Kuang (荀况), and most of the pieces are mature prose with a complete structure, which marks the replacement of the dialogue and conversation form. His compositions, with clear central ideas, great unity and coherence, and tight arguments, are penetrating and convincing. His *On Heaven* (《天论》) and *Exhortation to Learning* (《劝学》) are good examples.

It is worthy to mention that *The Book of Rites* (《礼经》) and *The Book of Changes* (《易经》) were also two famous works of this kind.

Han Fei (韩非) is also a rare master of the ancient Chinese prose style. His masterpieces, such as *Difficulties in Persuasion* (《说难》), *Five Vermins* (《五蠹》), and *Solitary Vexation* (《孤愤》), are plain, compact, forceful and incisive, though fables and anecdotes are used.

Prose during the Han, Wei and Six Dynasties

In a sense, the Han prose is the continuation of that of the Pre-Qin era, for the political, philosophical and historical works were still the best prose written in this period.

In the early years of the Western Han the most outstanding prose writers were Jia Yi (贾谊) and Chao Cuo (晁错). *On the Faults of Qin* (《过秦论》), a masterpiece by Jia Yi, recounts the waxing and waning of the Qin Dynasty from Duke Xiao (秦孝公) to Prince Ying (子婴), depicts and analyzes Qin's political failures and short-lived rule, and points out that the root cause of Qin's collapse is that "it failed to rule with humanity and righteousness". Chao Cuo's *Memorial to Discourse upon Valuing Grain* (《论贵粟疏》), which is lucid and simple in language, was written in the same style as that of *On the Faults of Qin*. *Discourses on Salt and Iron* (《盐铁论》) by Huan Kuan (桓宽) is the most influential prose work in the Mid Western Han Period, though it is more limited in scope, dealing specifically with a debate between the supporters of government monopoly of those commodities and their opponents. Apparently it is merely a stenographic account of the debate; actually it is, in the form of dialogue, a well-knit, unique prose work with substantial content.

The most influential writer of the Han Dynasty and one of the major stylists in the entire prose tradition was Sima Qian (司马迁). He was the first historian to record and narrate historical events in the form of individual biographies. *Records of the Grand Historian* (《史记》) is a first monumental work of general history that records Chinese history from the time of the legendary figure Emperor Huang up to Emperor Wu of the Han Dynasty, over a period of about 3,000 years. The book consists of five parts, 130 chapters, in half a million words. The five parts are: Basic Annals (本纪, 12 biographies of prominent rulers and emperors), Chronological Tables (表, 10 tables of dates of important events), Treaties (书, 8 essays devoted to the history and description of various subjects such as rites, music and economy), Hereditary Houses (世家, 30 biographies of notable rulers, nobility and bureaucrats) and Collected Biographies (列传, 70 biographies of important grass-root figures). Sima Qian's clear, vivid description of persons, from emperor to fortune-teller, such as Liu Bang (刘邦), Xiang Yu (项羽), and Lin Xiangru (蔺相如), has been looked upon as the model of biographical prose.

The first distinguished follower of Sima Qian was Ban Gu (班固), author of the first dynastic history in China, *The History of the Han Dynasty* (《汉书》). Another famous follower of Sima Qian was Fan Ye (范晔), author of the other dynastic as well as biographic history in China, *The History of the Later Han Dynasty* (《后汉书》).

In the late period of the Han Dynasty, prose began to break though the limits of the two genres: philosophical and historical, and became varied in form, for example, the appearance of epitaphs, inscriptions, admonitions, various types of letters, and parallel prose (骈文). By the Wei and Jin Period, Chinese prose began to deviate from the old frame of philosophical and historical form and pay much more attention to the artistic value, diction, and lyric color and taste. As a result, three types of prose became dominant after the Han Dynasty: landscape depiction, lyrical portrayals of the author's emotions, and description of objects.

The Literary Mind and the Carving of Dragons (《文心雕龙》) written by Liu Xie (刘勰) in parallel prose is the first work of literary criticism in the history of Chinese literature. He put forward the following six criteria (六观) on literary appreciation and criticism which are also six key elements in writing: structural layout of writing (位体, 谋篇布局), choice of words to construct sentences (置辞, 遣词造句), acceptance and innovation in the style of earlier writers (通变, 对前人作品风格的继承与创新), inheriting and transforming traditional ways of expression (奇正, 表现手法上的守正与新变), citing examples to support an argument (事义, 援引事例以证立论), and musical rhythm (宫商, 音律节奏). The reason why he produced this book lied in the attempt to criticize the efforts of his contemporaries to seek the beauty of form at the cost of meaning, and to advocate the presence of social and political content in literature.

Cao Cao's best-known work is *Mandate Clarifying My Intention in Giving up My Prefectural Post* (《让县自明本志令》). Written in a lively, limpid, and unrestrained style, the prose, full of emotion and energy, is of individual character and creates a completely fresh trend in prose writing. Cao Cao's two sons, Cao Pi and Cao Zhi, are famous for their letters. Cao Pi's *A Letter to Wu Zhi* (《与吴质书》) has a lyric quality in the depiction of nostalgic memories of friendships and happy gatherings in a limpid and delicate style. Both poetry and prose of Cao Zhi, a literary genius, are of greater note than his elder brother Cao Pi's. His *A Letter to Rang Dezu* (《与杨德祖书》) is an excellent essay on literature as well as lyrical prose expressing his emotions.

Among the Shu writers Zhu Geliang (诸葛亮) was certainly the best. His *First Memorial on Sending Out the Troops* (《前出师表》) has been praised as a model for memorials for nearly 2,000 years.

During the Eastern Jin Dynasty, Wang Xizhi (王羲之) and Tao Yuanming were the two best prose writers. Wang Xizhi, a noted calligrapher as well, wrote many short essays, of which *Preface to the Orchid Pavilion Collection* (《兰亭集序》) is the best. The preface fully shows his style—clear, pure, relaxed, but charming. Tao Yuanming, as a prose writer, has been highly admired and esteemed for his *On Returning Home* (《归去来兮辞》), *Record of the Peach-Blossom Fount* (《桃花源记》) and *Biography of Mr. Five Willows* (《五柳先生传》).

While the parallel prose was dominant in the literary field of the Southern Dynasties, and few pieces of worthy prose were produced, three influential prose works appeared in the Northern Dynasties, namely, *A Commentary on the Classic of Waterways* (《水经注》) by Li Daoyuan (郦道元), *Record of Buddhist Temples in Luoyang* (《洛阳伽蓝记》) by Yang Xuanzhi (杨衒之) and *Family Admonitions* (《颜氏家训》) by Yan Zhitui (颜之推).

Prose during the Tang and Song Dynasties

From the Southern Dynasties to the High Tang Period, the parallel prose in a vain (空虚), bombastic (夸张) and euphuistic (辞藻华丽) style had been dominant in the literary field. The four eminences of the Early Tang Period tried hard to alter the situation but achieved little. Only by the late 8th century, when Han Yu and Liu Zongyuan had started the great full-fledged Classical Prose Movement (古文运动), did Chinese prose creation turn into a healthful track.

Han Yu, the core of the literary reform as well as the leading figure of the eight great prose masters of the Tang and Song Dynasties (唐宋八大家), was the revival of the classical prose style, especially that of the Confucian classics, in opposition to and deviation from the decadent and over-elaborate style of the parallel prose. He wanted a style better suited to the needs of a more flexible, utilitarian prose. According to him, "Just imitate their intent instead of language (师其言不师其辞)," while "all stereotyped phrases and words must be got rid of (唯陈言之务去)." His representative works include *On Horses* (《马说》), *On the Teacher* (《师说》) and *An Epitaph for Liu Zihou* (《柳子厚墓志铭》).

Liu Zongyuan is another writer of Tang Dynasty who belongs to the eight prose masters, the other six of whom were Ouyang Xiu, Sun Xun (苏洵), Su Shi, Su Zhe (苏辙), Wang Anshi (王安

石) and Zeng Gong (曾巩). Liu's masterpiece include *Eight Notes of Yongzhou* (《永州八记》), *Discourse of a Snaker-Catcher* (《捕蛇者说》), *Humpback Guo the Gardener* (《种树郭橐驼传》) and *On Feudalism* (《封建论》).

Zeng Gong, the last figure of the eight masters, distinguished himself by his ability to model his writings on classics and to give his subject matter a slow, limpid and simple treatment. The best example is *The Inky Pond* (《墨池记》), an essay on the pond in which the famous calligrapher Wang Xizhi is said to have washed his writing brushes, causing the water to turn inky black.

Aside from these major writers, there were others who were remembered as outstanding essayists. Worthy of mentioning was Fan Zhongyan (范仲淹). Fan's prose is lucid, straightforward, functional and realistic in style. His *Yueyang Pavilion* (《岳阳楼记》) has been one of the most widely read pieces, from which comes the famous quotation "the first to worry over the country's problems and the last to enjoy the country's pleasures (先天下之忧而忧, 后天下之乐而乐)."

The Southern Song Dynasty failed to produce great prose masters, but there were some impressive and moving works which were pieces full of patriotic enthusiasm, such as Hu Qian (胡诠)'s *Memorial to Emperor Gao Zong* (《戊午上高宗封书》), Li Qingzhao's *Postface to the Record of Bronze and Stone Inscriptions* (《金石录后序》) and others by Ye Shi (叶适), Chen Liang (陈亮), Wen Tianxiang and Xie Ao (谢翱).

Prose during the Ming and Qing Dynasties

The Yuan Dynasty witnessed a great depression in prose creation. Some writers are sometimes mentioned by scholars, such as Liu Yin, Wu Cheng (吴澄), Ouyan Xuan (欧阳玄) and Yu Ji (虞集), but most of their works were narrow in scope and shallow in subject and perception.

The development of prose in the Ming Dynasty can be broken into a number of schools related to historical periods. In the early stage, dominant positions were held by Song Lian (宋濂) and Liu Ji, whose works were of great social significance in subject and fresher in skill and style. Song Lian was well-known for his biographical writings, the best of which were *Notes on Gentleman from Qin* (《秦士录》), *A Biographical Sketch of Du Huan* (《杜环小传》) and *Biography of Wang Mian* (《王冕传》).

Contemporary with the Latter Seven Masters, the Tang-Song School (唐宋派) headed by Tang Shunzhi (唐顺之), Mao Kun (茅坤) and Gui Youguang (归有光), reacted to the archaism and held up as models the prose of Eight Masters of Tang and Song, but they did not think it a right way to slavishly imitate the ancients; on the contrary, they held that the important thing was to capture their spirit.

Influenced by the Tang-Song School, Xu Wei (徐渭) and Li Zhi (李贽) put forward the theory that literature must reflect the true feelings and must arise from the real nature of people.

The spirit of revolt against convention and imitation was shared by another school known as the Jingling School (竟陵派) represented by Zhong Xing (钟惺) and Tan Yuanchun (谭元春). They advocated profundity, detachment, espoused and refined diction, and original inspiration.

At the end of the Ming Dynasty, the most famous and successful prose writer was Zhang Dai (张岱). Bringing into full play the literary merits of Gong'an and Jingling Schools and then developing his own unique skills, Zhang Dai produced many beautiful and delicate writings compiled in two collections—*Recollections of Past Dreams of Tao'an* (《陶庵梦忆》) and *In Search of Past Dreams at the West Lake* (《西湖梦寻》).

In the early Qing Dynasty, prose writings continued the tradition of the classical prose, both in style and in subject, but because of contradictions between nationalities and social turmoil, another subject was covered in prose by many writers, that is, the resistance against the Manchus. Characteristic were *A Letter to Mother from Prison* (《狱中上母书》) by Xia Wanchun and *The story of Courtesan Li* (《李姬传》) by Hou Fangyu (侯方域). The former reveals the young man's heroic spirit of fearing no death and his sorrow and indignation at the country's disaster, while the latter describes the faithful love of Li Xiang (李香) for her fiance and her patriotic zeal. The latter was also the subject of a famous drama of *The Peach Blossom Fan* (《桃花扇》) by Kong Shangren (孔尚任).

The Mid-Qing Period was dominated by Tongcheng School (桐城派), a school named after the hometown of its three leaders, Fang Bao (方苞), Liu Dakui (刘大櫆), and Yao Nai (姚鼐). As their guiding principle they put forward the theory of "substance (义)" and "form" or "techniques (法)." Similar to the views of Tongcheng School at that time was Yanghu School (阳湖派) named after the birthplace of its chief advocator, Yun Jing (恽敬). Writings of Yun Jing and his followers were more lively but far less influential than those of Tongcheng School.

In the first dozens of years of the 19th century, some prose writers, such as Mei Zengliang (梅曾亮) and Guan Tong (管同), still followed what the Tongcheng School advocated. The most prominent figure of that period was Gong Zizhen. As one of the most powerful and far-sighted thinkers of the late Qing Dynasty, most of his prose was political and forceful, reflecting his desire to reform the society and to protest against Western powers. The best examples are *My Plum Tree s Infirmary* (《病梅馆记》) and *An Account of Juyong Pass* (《说居庸关》).

Among the reformists, many publicized their ideas by means of prose. Liang Qichao was one of the most prolific prose writers of his age and exerted a great influence on the development of the Chinese prose style. Many new terms were coined, syntax simplified, and old rhetorical devices avoided. Liang's prose, such as *A Discourse on the Youthful China* (《少年中国说》), written in a grand and vibrant way like a rolling river, is forceful, persuasive and encouraging.

At the turn of the century, a number of revolutionary prose was created, Zhang Taiyan's *A Biographical Sketch of Zou Rong* (章太炎,《邹容传》) and Lin Juemin's *A letter to My Wife* (林觉民,《与妻书》) being the most typical of them.

/ Fiction /

Chinese classic fiction was based on and developed from two sources. One is mythology, many fragments of which came down from generations and were employed repeatedly as elementary material for some short stories in the early stage; the other is historical writings with fictional elements.

Fiction during the Han, Wei and the Six Dynasties

The noteworthy works of elaborations of history and folk legends into a fictional form were soon produced during the Han Dynasty and the best examples are *Garden of Anecdotes* (《说宛》) by Liu Xiang (刘向), *Annals of Wu and Yue* (《吴越春秋》) by Zhao Ye (赵晔), and *Lost Records of Yue* (《越绝书》) by Yuan Kang (袁康) and Wu Ping (吴平). Some other works also belong to this category, such as *Miscellanies of the Western Capital* (《西京杂记》) describing events and personages in Chang'an during the Western Han Dynasty, *Tales of Emperor Wu of the Han Dynasty* (《汉武帝故事》) and *Private Life of Emperor Wu of the Han Dynasty* (《汉武帝内传》).

The Six Dynasties Period was noted in Chinese history for its political turbulence and economic decline; however, new strengths and vitality in literature were developed, steps toward genuine fiction were taken, and Chinese fiction began to take form. Fiction of that time included two categories: tales of the supernatural spirits (志怪小说) and tales of men (志人小说).

The important tales of the supernatural spirits are *Records of Strange Things* (《博物志》) by Zhang Hua (张华) of the Jin Dynasty, *Garden of Marvels* (《异苑》) by Liu Jingshu (刘敬叔) of the Song of the Southern Dynasty, *Forgotten Tales* (《拾遗记》) by Wang Jia (王嘉) of the Eastern Jin Dynasty, *Records of Light and Dark* (《幽明录》) by Liu Yiqing (刘义庆) of the Song Dynasty, and *Records of Spirits* (《搜神记》) by Gan Bao (干宝) of the Eastern Jin Dynasty.

The tales of men dominantly dealt with short anecdotes about famous personages from all walks of life. Many of the happenings had an earlier origin and can be found in some books in the Warring States Period. An early book of this genre is *Forest of Sayings* (《语林》) by Pei Qi (裴启) of the Eastern Jin Dynasty. Then *The Forest of Jokes* (《笑林》) by Handan Chun (邯郸淳) of the Three Kingdoms Period and *A New Account of Social Talk* (《世说新语》) by Liu Yiqing appeared.

These Six Dynasties tales of the supernatural spirits and of men paved the way for the development of the more complex and lengthier Tang romances (唐传奇小说).

Romances during the Tang Dynasty

The Tang Dynasty marked the beginning of the conscientious practice of fiction as an art in China with the appearance of romance tales. No longer imitating history or recording strange events or the supernatural only, Tang romance writers began to create genuine imaginative literature.

The romances, products of men of letters in literary language, are quite different in many ways from the Six Dynasties tales. Short (350—3,500 Chinese characters) and dramatic, the Tang romances are often noted for their narrative skill, vivid characterization and complete structure. Thematically powerful and moving, many present a complex plot, memorable characters and extravagant settings. So they are indeed what we call short stories.

In the Early Tang, romance stories, heavily influenced by the tales of the Six Dynasties, were still dominated by ghosts, spirits, and feats of magic. Typical examples are *The Ancient Mirror* (《古镜记》) and *The Story of the White Monkey* (《补江总白猿记》).

The Mid-Tang Period witnessed the transformation of the themes of romances from the supernatural spirits to the daily life of the human world, widening the range of themes to a great extent. Those describing love affairs formed the most remarkable group of the period and of all the Tang romances. These stories generally stress romantic attachment in realistic settings. The most moving and enjoyed ones are Bai Xingjian's *The Story of Li Wa* (白行简,《李娃传》), Yuan Zhen's *The Story of Ying Ying* (《莺莺传》), Jiang Fang's *The Story of Huo Xiaoyu* (蒋防,《霍小玉传》), Li Chaowei's *The Story of Liu Yi* (李朝威,《柳毅传》), Chen Xuanyou's *The Disembodied Soul* (陈玄祐,《离魂记》), and Shen Jiji's *The Story of a Girl Named Ren* (沈既济,《任氏传》).

In the Late Tang Period, social disorder and rivalry among warlords lasted for many years. This is truthfully depicted in tales about swordsmen. The representative ones are *The Story of the Red Thread Maid* (《红线女传记》), *The Story of Nie Yinniang* (《聂隐娘传》), *The Kunlun Slave* (《昆仑奴》) and *The Curly-Bearded Stranger* (《虬髯客传》).

In addition to the above stories, another category worth mentioning is tales about dreams, such as *The Story of the Pillow* (《枕中记》) and *The Governor of the Southern Tributary State* (《南柯太守传》).

Storytellers' Scripts (话本) in the Song and Yuan Period

The emergence of urban centers created a need for entertainment and spurred the growth of professional storytellers who developed a fairly sophisticated and increasingly specialized art. Furthermore, in the Southern Song, guilds were organized by storytellers to promote their trade by writing new scripts and carrying on other activities. It was also during the Southern Song that stories of this genre, which had long been an art of oral narration and recitation, were eventually written down, edited and printed.

Being the texts of storytellers, the scripts were produced in a peculiar form. They usually begin with a poem that has little to do with the story itself. Then follows an introductory anecdote that has a similar theme or some relationship to the story. The story itself is interspersed with narrative, verses, dialogues, comments, and questions. Another feature of the stories, especially those long historical ones, is that the storytellers often left some dramatic episodes half told with the words "If you want to know what will happen afterwards, you have to find the answer next time," thus to attract the audience to come again.

The short stories of the Song Dynasty indicate a further development in Chinese fiction by portraying a fuller picture of real society and life with peddlers, craftsmen, maids, servants, monks, nuns and other commoners as the main characters. Surviving contemporary Song accounts show that different types of stories such as religious tales, historical stories, love stories, and stories based on judicial cases were popular at that time. The last three types are of greater importance and value.

Stories of detective and judicial cases (诉讼公案小说) obviously reflect the corruption of the ruling class and the darkness of the society, such as *The Erroneous Execution of Cui Ning* (《错斩崔宁》) in which the fatuous official dealt with the case perfunctorily and erroneously sentenced Cui Ning and Chen Erjie (陈二姐) to death.

Love stories of this period are different from those of the Tang Dynasty in describing love affairs between commoners rather than those between singsong girls and young men from the upper class. The best example is *The Jade Avalokitesvara* (《碾玉观音》).

The scripts of historical stories (讲史话本) were just roughly written during the Song and Yuan Dynasties, but they paved the way for the Ming novels. The better and influential one are *The Great Tang Tripitaka's Quest for Buddhist Sutras* (《大唐三藏取经诗话》) and *Tales of the Xuanhe Period of the Great Song* (《大宋宣和遗事》) which recounts the decline and fall of the Northern Song and contains an early, brief version of the story of Song Jiang (宋江) and his group. *Popular Tales of the Three Kingdoms* (《三国志平话》), *Popular Tales of the Former Han Dynasty* (《前汉书平话》), *Popular Tales of the Annexation of the Six States by Qin* (《秦并六国平话》), *Popular Tales of the Seven States* (《七国春秋平话》) and *Popular Tales of King Wu's Conquest of King Zhou* (《武王伐纣平话》) were called "five popular works of fiction with illustrations (全相平话五种)" when they were published by the Yu Family of Xin'an (新安虞氏) of the Yuan Dynasty.

The influence of these Song storytellers' scripts is very great, for most later fiction is based on their works, such as *Wonderful Tales New and Old* (《古今奇观》) and *Romance of the Three Kingdom* (《三国演义》).

Fiction during the Ming Dynasty

After nearly a thousand years of development up to the Ming Dynasty, Chinese fiction reached a period of maturity and prosperity. During the Ming Dynasty, China produced its first novels in the fullest sense of the word, which are important landmarks in the history of Chinese fiction and represent significant achievements of Chinese literature. At the same time, short stories were still advancing, even at a better pace. Some authors wrote many outstanding ones which exerted a great influence on their later counterparts. The most important literary form of the Ming Dynasty was the fiction written in the language spoken by the common people. Ming fiction, being much wider and more extensive in thematic subjects, mainly includes romances of history (历史演义小说), stories of heroes (英雄传奇小说), tales about deities and demons (神魔小说), and novels of manners or worldly novels (人情小说). Its three masterpieces include *Romance of the Three Kingdoms* (《三国演义》), *Water Margin* (《水浒传》) and *Journey to the West* (《西游记》).

Romance of the Three Kingdoms

Romance of the Three Kingdoms, the earliest chapter-by-chapter historical novel (章回体历史小说), has been attributed to Luo Guanzhong (罗贯中), who was also the author of *Romance*

of the Sui and Tang History (《隋唐志传》) and *The Sorcerer's Revolt and Its Suppression by the Three Suis* (《北宋三遂平妖传》). Of all the sources adopted by Luo Guanzhong, the most important is Chen Shou's *History of the Three Kingdoms* (陈寿，《三国志》), a reliable official history of the Three Kingdoms Period. Luo also utilized much of the information found in Pei Songzhi (裴松之)'s detailed commentary on Chen's book. Based on history books and folk legends, the book describes the rise and fall of the three kingdoms of Wei, Shu and Wu,

Luo Guanzhong

and the complex political, military and diplomatic struggles during that period. One main theme advocated by the author is brotherhood (义气).

The basic expressive technique of *Romance of the Three Kingdoms* is realism, but the plot arrangement and the portrayal of historical figures are full of romantic color. The novel is written in plain, concise and vivid language. The dialogues in the novel play an important role in revealing the characters' personalities. Luo's views on the Three Kingdoms are amply demonstrated in his character portrayals by making Liu Bei and Zhu Geliang of Shu come out as much more positive characters than those of Wei and Wu. To him, the rivalry between the Kingdoms of Shu, Wei and Wu is a contest between legitimacy and illegitimacy; therefore, he portrays most leaders of Shu as heroes and those of Wei and Wu often as villains, which makes the characters too black and white.

Water Margin

Water Margin, or *Outlaws of the Marsh*, by Shi Nai'an (施耐庵) tells the story of the rebellion of the 108 heroes at the end of the Northern Song Dynasty. It is the first novel to deal with the subject matter of peasant uprisings in China. Under the banner of "practicing the Way (or justice) on behalf of Heaven (替天行道)," the 108 heroes bravely rose up in arms against the social corruption, injustice and darkness and defeated the government's repeated attacks and suppressions. In this sense, the novel glorifies the heroes and uses them as symbols of social protest against the despotic government and

Shi Nai'an

corrupted officials. But the work has a fatal fault with the subject, that is, the acceptance of amnesty (招安) and the surrender of the heroes to the government.

Shi Nai'an was skilled at revealing the inner world of characters through their behavior and language. His expressive technique originated from storytelling scripts. He was also adept at portraying each character's appearance and personality, demonstrating the characters' dispositions and resistance to oppression through depicting their life experiences.

The novel has a relatively weak and loose internal structure, which was also one of the features of the storyteller's scripts. However, the novel presents a charming and well developed portrayal of some peasant rebels, such as Song Jiang (宋江), Li Kui (李逵), Lin Chong (林冲), Wu Song (武松), and Lu Zhishen (鲁智深). In addition, it is noted for its unity of theme, smooth and expressive colloquial style, exciting episodes, effective dialogue, vivid imagination, limited dependence on historical sources, and realistic descriptions of the common people. Together with *Romance of the Three Kingdoms*, it marked the coming of the golden age of the Chinese novel.

Journey to the West

Owing to the great influence of Buddhism, Taoism and alchemy, stories about clashes between deities and demons became quite popular during the Yuan and Ming Dynasties. In the first half of the 16th century, stories about deities and demons finally constituted one of the main fictional trends. The most conspicuous were *Journey to the West*, *Canonization of the Deities* (《封神榜》), and *Expedition to the Western Ocean* (《三宝太监西洋记》), among which *Journey to the West* is the representative work.

Journey to the West, or *Pilgrimage to the West*, by Wu Cheng'en (吴承恩), is an outstanding romantic work replete with fantastic tales. It is generally recognized as a masterpiece about deities and demons. The novel tells mainly the story of how the Tang-dynasty monk, Xuanzang or Tripitaka (唐僧), and his three disciples, Monkey King (孙悟空), the Eight-Commandment Pig (猪八戒), and Monk Sha (沙和尚), overcoming 81 hardships and perils, and defeating various monsters and demons before finally reaching India in quest of Buddhist scriptures and finally returning to China.

Wu Cheng'en

Wu Cheng'en illuminated the intelligence, bravery, and loyalty of the Monkey King, the piety of Monk Xuanzang, the straightforwardness and good nature of the Eight-Commandment Pig, and the kindness of Monk Sha. In fact, the hero of the novel is Monkey King. Loyal, intelligent, resourceful and courageous, he is not only the protector but often the instructor of Tripitaka as well. His actions throughout the novel suggest a defiance of established authority and rule. Though he has the body of a monkey, he stands for the best of human qualities. In the book, Tripitaka is merely a comic figure and an object of satire. The Eight-Commandment Pig and Monk Sha also serve as the foils. What's more, through telling tales of deities and demons, Wu Cheng'en exposed the darkness and corruption of feudal society, criticized the social realities, and implicitly expressed people's different forms of resistance.

Jin Ping Mei (《金瓶梅》)

Jin Ping Mei, a famous worldly novel, written by an author under the pseudonym of the Scoffing Scholar of Lanling or Lanling Xiao Xiao Sheng (兰陵笑笑生) in the late 16th century, is a long, complex and sophisticated novel which provides realistic descriptions of social life of that time. The novel gives a detailed depiction of the economic life of a newly-emerging class of businessmen and other social classes and reveals a moral world that existed in both matrimonial practices and sexual relations at that time. So its appearance ushers in a new genre—the novel of manners—in the history of Chinese fiction. Its title comes from the names of three important women in the novel: Pan Jinlian (潘金莲, the Golden Lotus), Li Ping'er (李瓶儿, the Vase), and Pang Chunmei (庞春梅, the Spring Plum).

Taking the daily life of ordinary men and women, their expectations, desperation and struggles for money and status as the background, the author, with penetrating insight into the life of his time, actually condemns the whole ruling class and reveals the internal collapse of the dynasty by describing an impressive array of representative characters at all levels, the heartless and vicious Ximen Qing (西门庆) being the central figure among the 200 and more. So it is a great and realistic work about social, political, economic and psychological situations in the 16th-century China in an extremely charming and persuasive style. Many Western scholars think it is a landmark in the development of narrative art, not only from a special Chinese perspective, but in a worldwide historical context, for there is no earlier work of prose fiction of equal sophistication in the world literature. The large fault of this novel is the too many and too explicit descriptions of sexual activities, many of which do not seem necessary for the manifestation of the theme.

Short Stories

After a long and slow process of development from the late Tang and Song times, short stories of the Late Ming, influenced by many factors, became flourishing and mature with thousands of pieces written. "Three Volumes of Words (三言)" and "Two Volumes of Slapping (二拍)" belong to townsfolk literature during this period.

Illustrated Stories Ancient and Modern (《古今小说》), which was collected, edited and created by Feng Menglong (冯梦龙), includes "Three Volumes of Words", namely *Instruction Stories to Enlighten the World* (《喻世明言》), *Comprehensive Stories to Admonish the World* (《警世通言》), and *Lasting Stories to Awaken the World* (《醒世恒言》). Each volume contains 40 stories. They constitute the bulk of the surviving vernacular stories produced from the Song Dynasty to the Ming Dynasty.

Feng's stories have well-developed themes and plots, moving scenes and genuine character development, and mark a high point in the history of the Chinese vernacular story.

Shortly after Feng's collections, Ling Mengchu (凌濛初), under the influence of his contemporary Feng Menglong, published his own creative stories in two volumes, namely *Slapping the Table in Amazement at the Wondrous Stories* (《初刻拍案惊奇》) and *The Second Series of Slapping the Table in Amazement at the Wondrous Stories* (《二刻拍案惊奇》), on which Ling's position in literary history rests. The creation by Ling alone explains the unity of style, theme, viewpoint, and technique in the collections of 78 stories in all.

Here what should be pointed out is that both Feng and Ling's stories contain somewhat backward, such as signs of preordained fate and retribution, which was a common failing in the Ming fiction.

Fiction during the Qing Dynasty

The Qing Dynasty, especially the 17th and 18th centuries, was the golden age of Chinese fiction writing and it was the first time in history that fiction prevailed over the old-style poetry. Fiction of this period became much more varied in style and theme with the appearance of excellent stories of the supernatural, masterly novels of satire, manners, romance, history, and novels about heroes and gallants. Of far more importance, they are incomparably high and mature in literary technique and value. Continuing the fine tradition of the preceding works, they, in content, reflect the contemporary society with fuller and deeper insight. The most outstanding works are *Strange Tales of the Tale-Telling Studio* (《聊斋志异》), *The Scholars* (《儒林外史》), *A Dream of the Red Mansions* (《红楼梦》), *Exposure of the Official World* (《官场现形记》), *Flowers in the Mirrors* (《镜花缘》) and *The Travel Records of Lao Can* (《老残游记》).

Strange Tales of the Tale-Telling Studio

A collection of about 490 short stories in a simple but elegant style, the book was composed and created in classical Chinese by Pu Songling (蒲松龄), a native of Zichuan (淄川), Shandong Province. Many stories contained in the collection are about love affairs between men and foxes, ghosts or demons, which manifest youth's yearning to break away from the feudal ethical code and for free marriage. Pu's characters are well rounded and adeptly portrayed. The language is fluent and vivid, the plot is intricate, and the structure is tight.

At first glance, the stories, derived from a variety of sources, seem an amalgamation of the earlier traditions represented by the Six Dynasties tales of the supernatural spirits—fairies, foxes, ghosts, goblins, and Tang romance stories; in fact, they differ markedly from earlier stories in that they reflect more clearly the author's mind and view. By making the improbable seem probable and many of his supernatural characters quite human and even morally better than some persons, Pu Songling vents his disappointments, frustrations, and disillusionment with the Qing government and society. Clearly speaking, he expresses his social and political criticism through the supernatural and strange stories in an allusive style. So his stories are often referred to as a combination of realism and romanticism.

The Scholars

Generally regarded as China's best satirical novel, *The Scholars*, a book of 55 chapters, was written by Wu Jingzi (吴敬梓) from Anhui Province. The novel portrays a group of feudal scholars and directs criticism at the eight-part essay (八股文) and the imperial civil examination system (科举制度). What *The Scholars* reveals and poignantly satirizes is just the demoralization, sordidness, vulgarity, pedantry, and folly of the scholars who were dominated by the examination system. Du Shaoqing (杜少卿) in the novel is generally believed to partly represent a self-portrait of the author, who is uninterested in worldly pursuits of wealth and fame but leads a simple, generous life of integrity and self-cultivation. With a variety of techniques and a high degree of sophistication, the author presents many characters of complexity in considerable depth—not simply in good or evil terms, but from different angles.

There seems to be no hero running through the novel but a sequence of separate episodes; the organization is actually based on internal harmony, balance, and correspondence.

The Scholars is distinguished for its characterization, satirical art, and narrative technique. It is not only the first book to create a variety of images of numerous scholars and intellectuals, but also the first to openly challenge the idea of making academic studies only for the sake of taking official positions. It occupies an important place in the history of Chinese fiction and has exerted a considerable impact on later Chinese satirical novels.

A Dream of the Red Mansions

Written by Cao Xueqing (曹雪芹) and Gao E (高鹗), *A Dream of the Red Mansions* reached the pinnacle of Chinese classical novels. It has been acknowledged as the greatest novel in Chinese classical literature and also a world literary masterpiece. Cao is generally believed to be the author of the first 80 chapters called *The Story of the Stone* (《石头记》). It was until 1791 that a complete 120-chapter edition prepared by Gao E and printed by Cheng Weiyuan (程伟元) became available under the title *A Dream of the Red Mansions*.

Cao Xueqin

The novel presents a vast panorama of the wealthy and aristocratic Jia family. Having enjoyed imperial favor for a long time, one generation after another of the family lived a life of luxury and dissoluteness. But with the coming collapse of feudalism, the family, once prosperous and prominent, could not escape decline and destruction either.

Cao's experience in his childhood made him conversant with the lifestyle and customs of the feudal noblemen. The decline of his family and adverse conditions of his later years helped him to see through the corruption and decadence of the people in his early memories. With this experience and understanding, he was able to paint a most broad, varied, truthful and colorful picture of the society of his day.

The hero and heroine of the book are Jia Baoyu (贾宝玉) and his cousin Lin Daiyu (林黛玉), two young rebels against feudalism. Jia Baoyu, born with a piece of jade in his mouth and considered a promising successor to carry on the family line in the future, shows little interest in fame and an official career, and, what is more, detests the social conventions of orthodox Confucian morality. Having developed many identical views and attitudes, such as both hating feudal bondage and longing for freedom to develop their individuality, they two fall passionately in love with each other. But such a rebel as Lin Daiyu could not be tolerated by a family of that kind. She dies in bitter despair of an illness and with a broken heart at the very moment of the wedding of Jia Baoyu and Xue Baochai (薛宝钗), Jia Baoyu's another cousin, who is a conforming, pleasant and dutiful girl. Soon afterwards, Jia Baoyu leaves the family and becomes a monk to escape from the filthy world, which suggests that Jia Baoyu finally awakes from the illusions of life as if from a dream. Instead of just telling the love story between Xue Baoyu and Lin Daiyu, the novel taps the social origins of the tragedy through probing deeply into the characters' minds and complicated relationships. Clearly, the author purposely stresses the tragic aspects of the love affair to express his ideas about arranged marriage (包办婚姻), the Confucian family system, the conventional morality, the low status of women, and other aspects of the feudal society.

As a novel of realism, the classic offers a profundity of complex and diverse themes in reflecting that society and few other novels can be compared to it in terms of depth and scope.

Technically, the novel exhibits important advances. First of all, it is wonderfully framed, well organized, and tightly and methodically knitted though hundreds of characters and many episodes are involved. Secondly, the book, written in a highly expressive colloquial style, skillfully reveals the images and personalities of major characters through various means, including dialogue, contrasts, and the uses of dreams and poetry. Jia Baoyu's personality, for instance, is revealed through his words, behavior, reactions to different situations, and through his dreams and poems. So most of the figures are well-developed and each has his own individual personality identical with his social status and moral characters. Finally, its narration uses mature colloquial language, plain but elegant, explicit but expressive. The novel contains poems, *ci*, lyric verses and prose essays, which fit the plot and the fate of the characters. It is really a panorama of feudal society and has been considered an encyclopedia of Chinese literature.

One more point worthy of mentioning is that the so-called Four Great Classical Novels (四大名著) include *Romance of the Three Kingdoms*, *Water Margin*, *Journey to the Wes*, and *A Dream of the Red Mansions*. They have been eulogized for centuries for their historical and cultural significance.

/ Drama /

Compared with Chinese poetry and prose, the drama is a genre of later development in Chinese literature, for it was not until the Song and Yuan Dynasties that the Chinese drama gradually grew mature.

Miscellaneous Play during the Song Dynasty

In the first half of the Northern Song, the Miscellaneous Play (杂剧, *zaju*, poetic drama), in fact, was still one of the numerous forms of entertainment. Only by about the end of the Northern Song did it take on the tender form of drama in the present-day sense of the word, for the plot began to center on a single theme in a relatively longer and more complete structure. During the Southern Song and Jin Period, the Miscellaneous Play began to become numerous and popular and to hold a dominant position in the state, though with only one piece it was still too short to constitute an independent program of entertainment.

Southern Drama during the Song and Yuan Dynasties

The earliest two notable plays of the Southern Drama (南戏, also *nanxi*) were *Miss Zhao, a Chaste Woman* (《赵贞女》) and *Wang Kui* (《王魁》). Considering other early comments, we are sure that the Southern Drama had its birth in the late Northern Song, but attained full popularity only with the advent of the Southern Song Dynasty. There they entered a new phase of sophistication, initiated by the two innovative plays. After the founding of the Yuan Dynasty, the Southern plays were still performed while the Northern Yuan Miscellaneous Drama (元杂剧) arose and prevailed.

The Southern plays were distinguished by their greater length and ability to treat full stories. The authors of the Southern Drama were usually members of writing clubs (书会) organized by authors of various forms of vernacular literature. They not only wrote dramas but also performed personally. The most famous groups were the Nine Mountains Writing Club (九山书会) and the Yongjia Writing Club (永嘉书会) in Wenzhou, the Scarlet and Green Association (绯绿书会) in Hangzhou.

The main content of the plays covered a wide range. First were those that showed the heroes' infidelity to their wives. Both of the first two notable Southern plays allegedly depicted such stories.

Secondly, many of the Southern plays described how young men and young women enthusiastically and staunchly sought true love in their struggle against the conventions and bondage of feudalism and other dark forces. The best example was *Wang Huan* (《王焕》).

Plays of the third group are odes to patriotic heroes and merciless castigation of treacherous officials and traitors. *Su Wu Tending Sheep* (《苏武牧羊记》) and *Tale of the Eastern Window* (《东窗记》) are the representative ones.

The fourth group profoundly exposed the evils and cruelty of the feudal society and wicked forces. The most well-known plays are *Little Butcher Sun* (《小孙屠》) and *Zujie* (《祖杰》).

In addition, other themes, such as those about deities, Taoists and filial piety, are also reflected in plays of the Southern Drama, but they are far fewer than the above groups.

As the Southern plays were written by authors from the lower society, they were usually created in the vernacular and were easily accepted by the contemporary common people.

Miscellaneous Drama during the Yuan Dynasty

While the Southern Drama was flourishing in the South, the Yuan Miscellaneous Drama emerged in the North. Some scholars regard them as the earliest two mature genre, sharing common roots in the literary and theoretical sources of the Song Dynasty. Exactly speaking, the Miscellaneous Drama was the first completely mature genre of Chinese drama, for, after a long period of incubation in history, it showed a great advance and became more comprehensive in any dramatic sense than any of its predecessors. Taking in the advantages of various performances before it, the new form of drama immediately became the most vital literary expression of the time and has been elevated to the same position as that of the Tang Poetry and the Song *ci* poetry.

The Yuan Miscellaneous Drama usually consists of four acts (折子) and occasionally a prelude before the first act or an interlude between acts, with each containing Northern opera melodies of the same tune and rhyme as the spoken parts.

The Yuan Period was unrivaled in its abundance of excellent plays. Dramatists of great renown were so many as about 230, who wrote thousands of dramas, though only over 200 scripts have survived. Among them the most outstanding are Guan Hanqing, Wang Shifu (王实甫), Bai Pu, Ma Zhiyuan, Yang Xianzhi (杨显之), Ji Junxiang (纪君祥), Kang Jinzhi (康进之), Gao Wenxiu (高文秀), and Shi Junbao (石君宝), who belonged to the first half of the Yuan Dynasty; Zheng Guanzu (郑光祖), Gong Tianting (宫天挺), and Qin Jianfu (秦简夫), who belonged to the second half.

Guan Hanqing was the first leader and the most productive playwright of that period in regard to both chronology and technique, with some 60 plays attributed to him. Despite his immense creative power and his fame as the father of traditional drama, only scanty biographical data about him exist. He lived in the 13th century; the dates of his birth and death are uncertain. A native of Dadu (大都, the present-day Beijing), he worked there as a

Guan Hanqing

doctor, but was known for the many plays he wrote. His works include tragedies, comedies and historical plays. Some of them describe the lives of the people of his day; others are based on historical events. All of them sing praises of the oppressed or expose the evils of the ruling class. The characters in his plays are all very vivid, convincing and impressive, and they reveal their personalities in dramatic conflicts.

About 13 of his 60 plays are completely extant, the most famous being *The Injustice Suffered by Dou E* (《窦娥冤》), *The Butterfly Dream* (《蝴蝶梦》), *The Rescue of a Courtesan* (《救风尘》), and *The Pavilion above the River* (《望江亭》). The first play describes Dou E, a good young widow, who is accused of murder when she obstinately refuses to marry a depraved young man named Zhang Lü'er (张驴儿) who has poisoned his own father by mistake. To spare from the pain of torture suffered by her mother-in-law who is accused of the murder, Dou E has to admit the false crime and is executed by the corrupt governor who takes the bribe from Zhang Lü'er before trying the case. But her ghost continues to fight against injustice. When her father comes to the region as a high-ranking official, her ghost appears in his dream and tells him the truth of the case. Her father then examines the case, corrects the wrong verdict, and punishes the evil Zhang Lü'er and the corrupt governor.

The Injustice Suffered by Dou E praises Dou E's fighting spirit and exposes and condemns the dark society and unjust legal system. In many of his plays, Guan Hanqing gives truthful pictures of the people's sufferings under Yuan rule. Realism in his drama is intense and powerful.

Another dramatist of distinction in the 13th century was Wang Shifu, who also lived in Dadu. Less productive than Guan Hanqing, Wang Shifu was the author of 14 plays, of which only three are preserved. His reputation rests chiefly on *The Romance of the Western Chamber* (《西厢记》), which has been praised by both traditional and modern critics as one of the masterpieces of Chinese drama. The source of the story is the Tang Romance tale *The Story of Yingying* by Yuan Zhen. The immediate predecessor and main source, however, is *Melody in Multi-modes, Romance of the Western Chamber* (《西厢记诸宫调》) by Dong Jieyuan (董解元).

Besides Guan and Wang, there appeared many other playwrights and excellent plays in that period, for instance, Ji Junxiang's *The Orphan of the Zhao Family* (《赵氏孤儿》) which is probably best known to the Western world through translation and adaptation (Voltaire, the well-known French writer, historian and philosopher, adapted it and changed its name to *The Orphan of China*.), Yang Xianzhi's *Rain of Xiaoxiang* (《潇湘雨》), Shi Junbao's *Qiu Hu Taking Liberties with His Wife* (《秋胡戏妻》), Ma Zhiyuan's *Autumn of the Han Palace* (《汉宫秋》), Bai Pu's *Rain on the Phoenix Tree* (《梧桐雨》), Shang Zhongxian's *The Story of Liu Yi* (尚仲贤,《柳毅传书》), and Li Haogu's *Boiling the Sea* (李好古,《张生煮海》).

In the second half of the Yuan Dynasty, South China became the center of drama creation, but it was much less flourishing than that in the first period. The most important authors and works were Zheng Guanzu's *Wandering Soul of a Beauty* (《倩女离魂》) and Qiao Ji's *Dream at Yangzhou* (乔吉,《扬州梦》).

Romance Drama during the Ming Dynasty

In the Ming Dynasty, Miscellaneous Play was still on show and some playwrights produced quite a number of plays though they were not very influential. The better ones among them were *Du Fu's Roams in the Spring* (《杜甫游春》) by Wang Jiusi (王九思), *The Wolf of Zhongshan* (《中山狼》) by Kang Hai (康海), and Xu Wei's *Four Shrieks of the Monkey* (《四声猿》), a collectively entitled drama that consisted of four short separate plays: *The Mad Drummer* (《狂鼓吏》), *The Heroine Mulan* (《雌木兰》), *Monk Yu Tong* (《玉禅师》) and *The Female Top Graduate* (《女状元》). But what became dominant was the Romance Drama (传奇) which also belonged to a Southern genre. Its predecessor was the Southern Drama of the Song and Yuan Period. It was thus called because the plots of the plays were mostly based on Romance Stories of the Tang and Song Dynasties. It came into being at the end of Yuan and the beginning of Ming, but competed with the Miscellaneous Drama for popularity in the early decades of the new dynasty and dominated the Chinese stage for several hundred years from the 15th to the 18th century. Records show that scripts of the Romance Drama are as many as about 2,600 pieces produced by 750 known authors and many anonyms.

During the transitional period, the most influential Romance plays were Gao Ming's *The Story of a Pi Pa Lute* (高明,《琵琶记》) and the four great Romance plays (四大传奇).

The Story of a Pi Pa Lute was rewritten by Gao Ming, one of the greatest playwrights in the history of Chinese drama, on the basis of earlier dramatic versions of *Miss Zhao, a Chaste Woman*. It tells the story of Cai Bojie (蔡伯喈) who, at the urging of his father, reluctantly leaves his old parents and newly wedded wife Zhao Wuniang (赵五娘) to go to the capital for the civil service examinations. There he wins the first place, upon which Grand Council Niu (牛宰相) pressures him into marrying his daughter. During that time, his parents die of starvation in the famine-stricken hometown. Having barely survived the famine herself, Wuniang, who filially waits on her parents-in-law for years, makes a meager living on her way to the capital in search of her husband by singing out her sad fate to the accompaniment of her lute. In the capital, instead of a refusal by Cai, who even tries to kill her in the former versions, Cai's second wife takes pity on her and arranges a reunion of the separated couple.

Many critics ranked the play among the best dramatic works for its moving plot, linguistic excellence and structural unity. Of course, the rewritten ending weakens the social significance of its earlier versions.

The so-called four great romances refer to *The Story of a Hairpin* (《荆钗记》), *Moon Prayer Pavilion* (《拜月亭》), *The Story of a White Rabbit* (《白兔记》), and *The Story of Killing a Dog* (《杀狗记》), whose authors have not been exactly made out so far. *The Story of a Hairpin* and *Moon Prayer Pavilion* are usually viewed as two of the most outstanding plays that treat the faithful and everlasting love between young people.

By the second half of the 16th century, especially during the Wanli (万历, 明神宗朱翊钧的年号) Reign, the Romance Drama attained full prosperity. Some greates authors of the age showed no hesitation in investing their talents, hence the appearance of Wujiang School (吴江派) headed by Shen Jing (沈璟) and Linchuan School (临川派) represented by Tang Xianzu (汤显祖).

Shen Jing, a native of Wujiang, Jiangsu Province, retired from official post at the age of 35 and spent the rest of his life writing plays and studying dramatic theories. His only successful and best-known play, entitled *The Story of An Upright Hero* (《义侠记》), based on Wu Song's exploits from killing a tiger to giving in to the court, was adapted from *Water Margin*.

Fortunately, many playwrights had a different view and stressed artistic ingenuity and spontaneity. The most talented, successful and influential of them was Tang Xianzu, a native of Linchuan, Jiangxi Province. Unlike Shen Jing, Tang Xianzu and his followers valued literary quality over strict musical form. Tang left behind him four Romance plays: *The Purple Flute* (《紫箫记》) or *The Purple Hairpin* (《紫钗记》), *The Peony Pavilion* (《牡丹亭》), *The Dream of Nanke* (《南柯梦》), and *The Dream of Handan* (《邯郸梦》). They are usually

Tang Xianzu

referred to collectively as *The Four Dreams of Linchuan* (《临川四梦》), for dreams play a critical role in all the four plays. Of the four, *The Peony Pavilion* is by general consensus the greatest of all Romance plays.

Besides Shen Jing and Tang Xianzu, there appeared many other important playwrights and dramas since the Mid-Ming Period. Gao Lian (高濂) was one of them. As a dramatist, Gao Lian wrote only two plays: *The Jade Hairpin* (《玉簪记》) and *Fidelity and Filiality* (《节孝记》).

Other noted plays of that period include Zhou Chaojun's *Red Plum* (周朝俊,《红梅记》)

which is about Li Huiniang (李慧娘) and her struggle against the wicked and treacherous officials in the Southern Song Court; Wang Yufeng's Incense Burning (王玉峰,《焚香记》) that retells the sad story of the ungrateful Wang Kui (王魁) and Guiying (桂英); Meng Chengshun's *Lady Jiao-niang* (孟称舜,《娇红记》), and many others.

The last decades of the Ming Dynasty saw two outstanding dramatists who should be mentioned for their artistic achievements. They are Ruan Dacheng (阮大铖) and Wu Bing (吴炳). Ruan Dacheng wrote 10 Romance plays in all. The best-known are *The Swallow-Carried Message* (《燕子笺》) and *The Spring Lantern's Riddles* (《春灯谜》).

Wu Bing was very loyal to the Ming Dynasty. He, unlike Ruan Dacheng who surrendered when the Qing army advanced to the south, committed suicide after his capture by the Qing army. He left behind him five plays. The better-known are *The Story of the West Garden* (《西园记》), *The Green Peony* (《绿牡丹》), and *Remedy for Jealousy* (《疗妒羹》).

Drama during the Qing Dynasty

Great changes took place since the year 1644, which marked the accession of the Qing Dynasty. First of all, the Romance Drama declined from the most flourishing moment in the Ming and Early Qing Period to almost neglect and oblivion. Then, regional operas began to rise to the dominant position on the Chinese stage, especially the appearance and maturation of Beijing Opera. Lastly, as novels increased, more and more dramas were adapted on their basis.

At the Ming-Qing transitional time, the most influential playwrights were those from the Suzhou area, for they stressed in their plays dramatic plots which brought about enjoyable stage effect, because they acquired a thorough knowledge of stagecraft and dramatic techniques through experience. The representative was Li Yu (李玉) who achieved more than any of the others among the group. A prolific author, Li Yu is said to have written about 60 plays, the most popular of which were *A Handful of Snow* (《一捧雪》), *Between Man and Animal* (《人兽关》), *Everlasting Reunion* (《永团圆》), *The Oil Peddler and the Queen of Flowers* (《占花魁》), and *The Upright and Loyal* (《清忠谱》). Zhu He (朱㿥) and Zhu Zuochao (朱佐朝) were two other important writers. Co-author of *The Upright and Loyal*, Zhu He wrote other 19 plays. As one of the most outstanding dramas in history, his masterpiece *Fifteen Strings of Cash* (《十五贯》) is still performed today. Zhu Zuochao's successful work was *Joys of a Fisherman's Family* (《渔家乐》).

You Tong (尤侗) was a well-known playwright with great creative talents after the Suzhou group. His popularly appreciated and important works were *Reading Sorrow after Departure* (《读离骚》) and *The Pleasures of Heaven* (《钧天乐》).

In the early period of the Qing Dynasty, the most notable playwrights were Hong Sheng (洪昇) and Kong Shangren (孔尚任) who respectively wrote excellent plays *The Palace of Eternal Life* (《长生殿》) and *The Peach Blossom Fan* (《桃花扇》). For the outstanding merits of the plays, people had in the drama-producing circle the saying at that time: "Hong in the south and Kong in the north (南洪北孔)," because Hong came from Qiantang, Zhejiang Province while Kong was a native of Qufu in Shandong Province.

Since the Mid-Qing the creation of the Romance Drama began to wane. So comparatively few dramatists of stature appeared. The foremost were Tang Ying (唐英), Jiang Shiquan (蒋士铨), and Fang Chengpei (方成培). Tang Ying produced 17 plays collected in *The Dramas from the Hall of the Old Cypress* (《古柏堂传奇》), among which *The Witty Exchange of Wife* (《巧换缘》) was his masterpiece; Jiang Shiquan was more prolific, producing about 30 dramas in all, though only about 16 are extant. His representative script was *The Evergreen Tree* (《冬青树》), a drama depicting the career of the national patriot Wen Tianxiang and greatly praising Wen for his loyalty to the Song Dynasty. More influential thant Tang and Jiang's plays was Fang Chengpei's *Leifeng Pagoda* (《雷峰塔》) which was adapted on the basis of the scripts by Huang Tubi (黄图珌) and Chen Jiayan (陈嘉言).

In the late decades of the Qing Dynasty both the Romance Drama and the Miscellaneous Drama declined. In their place arose different regional operas. Most of the dramatic scripts for them were traditional ones or newly adapted titles, such as *The General and the Minister Are Reconciled* (《将相和》), *The Drunken Beauty* (《醉美人》), *The Empty City Ruse* (《空城计》), *The Crossroads* (《三岔口》), *Havoc in Heaven* (《大闹天宫》), *Wild Boar Forest* (《野猪林》), and *The Fisherman's Revenge* (《打渔杀家》).

The second half of the 19th century witnessed bourgeois reforms and revolutions one after another. Reflecting and spreading their ideas, some reformers wrote a number of plays to serve for politics and their struggle. The outstanding example was Liang Qichao, who wrote *New Rome* (《新罗马》) and other plays. But their creation of plays was followed by a serious problem that, owing to their lack of performing practice, their plays were not suitable for performance on stage; thus, their dramas could not be very popular.

Those that were really appreciated by large audiences and brought into full play the function of propaganda of revolutionary principles were produced by famous actors or associations. Wang Xiaonong (汪笑侬) created many plays with a fresh note of patriotism and reform, which gained immediate popularity. The best-known were *The Factionist Stele* (《党人

碑》), *Scolding King of the Hells* (《骂阎罗》), and *Weeping at the Ancestor Temple* (《哭祖庙》). In Sichuan Opera, Huang Ji'an (黄吉安) wrote *Zhuxian Town* (《朱仙镇》) and *Lin Zexu* (《林则徐》) among others. All of these dramas incited the patriotic enthusiasm to a greater extent than Liang Qichao's.

Key Terms

1. 小康

Modest Prosperity

◎民亦劳止，汔可小康。(《诗经》)

People are living a hard life and they hope they can have peace and moderate prosperity. (The Book of Songs)

2. 它山之石，可以攻玉

Use Stones from Another Mountain to Polish One's Jade

◎乐彼之园，爰有树檀，其下维穀(gǔ)。它山之石，可以攻玉。(《诗经》)

The garden is so lovely, where tall sandalwood grows; below are short and slender mulberry trees. There are stones on its rockeries, which can be used to polish jade. (The Book of Songs)

3. 靡不有初，鲜克有终

All Things Have a Beginning, but Few Can Reach the End.

◎天生烝民，其命匪谌。靡不有初，鲜克有终。(《诗经》)

Heaven created all people. Decrees of government must be consistent. All things have a beginning, but few people can see them through to the end. (The Book of Songs)

4. 协和万邦

Coexistence of All in Harmony

◎克明俊德，以亲九族。九族既睦，平章百姓。百姓昭明，协和万邦，黎民于变时雍。(《尚书》)

(Emperor Yao) was able to promote moral values, so that amity prevailed in his clan. He then clarified the hierarchical order of tribal officials. Only when this was done could all vassal states, big and small, prosper in harmony, and people would become friendly with each other. (The Book of

History)

5. 满招损，谦受益

Complacency Leads to Failure; Modesty to Success.

◎满招损，谦受益，时乃天道。(《尚书》)

Complacency leads to failure, while modesty to success. This is a universal law governing all things under heaven. (*The Book of History*)

6. 辞尚体要

Succinctness Is Valued in Writing.

◎政贵有恒，辞尚体要，不惟好异。(《尚书》)

What is most valuable for governance lies in its sustained stability, advocating substantial and straightforward wording, not seeking novelty. (*The Book of History*)

7. 以义制事

Handle Matters According to Morality and Justice

◎王懋(mào)昭大德，建中于民，以义制事，以礼制心，垂裕后昆。(《尚书》)

The ruler must work hard to promote high moral standards and advocate the correct path among the people; he should handle affairs of state according to moral precepts and guide people's thinking to accord with the rules of etiquette, so as to leave a rich legacy to those who come after him. (*The Book of History*)

8. 德惟善政

The Virtue of Those Exercising Power Is Reflected in Good Governance.

◎德惟善政，政在养民。(《尚书》)

A ruler should manifest his virtue in good governance, and the goal of governance is to bring a good life to the people. (*The Book of History*)

9. 大同

Universal Harmony

◎大道之行也，天下为公，选贤与能，讲信修睦。故人不独亲其亲，不独子其子，使老有所终，壮有所用，幼有所长，矜寡孤独废疾者，皆有所养……是谓大同。(《礼记》)

When the Great Way prevails, the world belongs to all the people. People of virtue and competence are chosen to govern the country, and honesty and harmony is the way for people to treat each other. People not only love their parents, bring up their children, but also take care of the aged. The middle-aged are able to put their talents and abilities to best use, children are well nurtured, and old widows and widowers, unmarried old people, orphans, childless old people, and the disabled are all provided for... This is universal harmony. (*The Book of Rites*)

10. 教化

Shaping the Mind through Education

◎故礼之教化也微，其止邪也于未形。(《礼记》)

Educating and influencing people through li (礼) has the invisible impact of getting rid of immoral thoughts in the bud. (*The Book of Rites*)

11. 乡饮酒礼

Banquet for Community Leaders and Rural Elders

◎乡饮酒之礼，六十者坐，五十者立侍，以听政役，所以明尊长也。六十者三豆，七十者四豆，八十者五豆，九十者六豆，所以明养老也。(《礼记》)

At banquets hosted for village elders, those who were over sixties sat, and those who were only in their fifties stood to serve them, and this shows that the elders were honored. Those in their sixties had three dishes, those in their seventies four, those in their eighties five and those in their nineties six, thus demonstrating care for the aged. (*The Book of Rites*)

12. 礼尚往来

Reciprocity as a Social Norm

◎礼尚往来。往而不来，非礼也；来而不往，亦非礼也。人有礼则安，无礼则危。(《礼记》)

Etiquette values reciprocity and mutual benefit. It would go against it if someone who has received a gift does not reciprocate such goodwill. When one acts according to such etiquette, one will enjoy peace. Without it, one will cause trouble. (*The Book of Rites*)

13. 时中

Follow the Golden Mean

◎仲尼曰："君子中庸，小人反中庸。君子之中庸也，君子而时中；小人之中庸也，小人而无忌惮也。"(《礼记》)

Confucius said, "A man of virtue follows the mean and a petty man goes against it. A man of virtue seeks to be in keeping with the mean at all times, whereas a petty man goes against it and acts unscrupulously." (*The Book of Rites*)

14. 大信不约

The Greatest Trust Is Not Found in Pledges.

◎大德不官,大道不器,大信不约,大时不齐。(《礼记》)

Great virtue in a person does not come just from their official status. The application of a universal principle is not restricted to a single circumstance. The greatest trust does not necessarily need pledges. Changes in seasons need not follow a uniform pattern. (*The Book of Rites*)

15. 不诚无物

Without Sincerity, Nothing Is Possible.

◎诚者自成也,而道自道也。诚者,物之终始。不诚无物。是故君子诚之为贵。诚者,非自成己而已也,所以成物也。成己,仁也;成物,知也。性之德也,合外内之道也。(《礼记》)

Sincerity is what makes oneself whole, and its way shows how one conducts oneself. Sincerity makes things happen and delivers outcomes. Without sincerity, there is nothing. For this reason, a man of virtue reveres sincerity. Sincerity not only makes oneself whole but also makes other people and creatures whole. Making oneself whole is a virtue; making others whole is a vision. Virtue and vision are naturally born, and they are fundamental to achieving unity between oneself and the outer world. (*The Book of Rites*)

16. 和而不流

Living in Harmony with Others Without Losing Moral Ground

◎君子和而不流,强哉矫。(《礼记》)

A man of virtue lives in harmony with others without losing moral ground— such is his strength. (*The Book of Rites*)

17. 修齐治平

Self-Cultivation, Family Regulation, State Governance, Bringing Peace to All under Heaven

◎古之欲明明德于天下者,先治其国。欲治其国者,先齐其家。欲齐其家者,先修其身。(《礼记》)

The ancients, who wished to promote illustrious virtue under heaven, first had to rule their own states well. Wishing to govern their states well, they first had to manage their fiefdoms well. Wishing to manage their fiefdoms well, they first had to cultivate themselves. (*The Book of Rites*)

18. 教学相长

Teaching and Learning Promote Each Other.

◎学然后知不足,教然后知困。知不足,然后能自反也;知困,然后能自强也。故曰:教学相长也。(《礼记》)

Learning makes you find out your shortcomings, and teaching makes you find out that you still have room for improvement. When knowing your shortcomings, you can think about them and make improvements; knowing you still have room for improvement, you can work hard to close the gap. That is why we believe that teaching and learning promote each other. (*The Book of Rites*)

19. 举贤容众

Recommend People of Virtue and Be Magnanimous toward the Masses

◎博学而不穷,笃行而不倦;幽居而不淫,上通而不困;礼之以和为贵,忠信之美,优游之法,举贤而容众,毁方而瓦合。(《礼记》)

One must learn extensively and endlessly, never be weary of the pursuit. One must never give way to licentiousness even when living in isolation and acting alone, and always follow the right paths even though smoothly promoted in officialdom. One must act in accordance with etiquette, value generosity and harmony, regard loyalty and honesty as virtue, tolerance and benevolence as benchmarks. One should recommend people with virtue and talent, and yet tolerate and be magnanimous toward those of ordinary virtue and aptitude. If necessary, one may even bend principles in order to accommodate the wishes of the general public. (*The Book of Rites*)

20. 敬业乐群

Work Diligently and Keep Good Company with Others

◎一年视离经辨志,三年视敬业乐群,五年视博习亲师,七年视论学取友,谓之小成。(《礼记》)

In the first year, it was seen whether they knew how to analyze the phrases in the texts and develop motivation; in the third year, whether they worked diligently and achieved fraternity with their fellow students; in the fifth year, whether they extended their knowledge and were close to their teachers; in the seventh year, whether they could form judgments on what they had learned and select good friends. This was said to be an initial attainment. (The Book of Rites)

21. 国以义为利

A State Should Regard Righteousness as Its Benefit.

◎国不以利为利,以义为利也。(《礼记》)

A state should not take pecuniary gain as a benefit, but righteousness as its benefit. (The Book of Rites)

22. 苟利国家,不求富贵

Seek to Benefit the Country Rather than Personal Wealth and Position

◎君得其志,苟利国家,不求富贵。(《礼记》)

One should work to help the sovereign ruler to realize his ideals, doing everything for the benefit of the country, without seeking personal wealth and honor. (The Book of Rites)

23. 苛政猛于虎

Tyranny Is Fiercer Than a Tiger.

◎夫子曰:"小子识之:苛政猛于虎也。"(《礼记》)

Confucius says, "Remember this, young man. Harsh and tyrannical laws are worse even than a fierce tiger." (The Book of Rites)

24. 唇亡齿寒

Once the Lips Are Gone, the Teeth Will Feel Cold.

◎且赵之于齐楚,扞蔽也,犹齿之有唇也,唇亡则齿寒。今日亡赵,明日患及齐楚。(《史记》)

To the states of Qi and Chu, the State of Zhao serves as a protective shield, just like the lips protecting the teeth. Once the lips are gone, the teeth will feel cold. If Zhao is defeated by the State of Qin today, the same fate will befall Qi and Chu tomorrow. (Records of the Grand Historian)

25. 徙木立信

Establishing One's Credibility by Rewarding People for Moving a Log

◎令既具，未布，恐民之不信，已乃立三丈之木于国都市南门，募民有能徙置北门者予十金。民怪之，莫敢徙。复曰"能徙者予五十金"。有一人徙之，辄予五十金，以明不欺。卒下令。(《史记》)

After the decrees for reform being drawn but before being issued, Shang Yang, fearing that people wouldn't take the decrees seriously, had a 3-zhang-long (approx. 7 meters) log erected in front of the southern gateway of the market place in the capital city. He declared that whoever could move the log from the southern gateway to the northern gateway would be given a reward of 10 yi (equivalent of 200 taels of copper). People found it very strange and nobody came forward to move the log. Shang then said, "Whoever can move the log will be awarded 50 yi (equivalent of 1,000 taels of copper)." One man came up and moved the log to the market's northern gateway. Shang kept his words and immediately gave him the promised amount of reward. Thus, Shang was able to issue the decrees of reform thereafter. (Records of the Grand Historian)

26. 韦编三绝

Leather Thongs Binding Wooden Strips Break Three Times.

◎孔子晚而喜易……韦编三绝。(《史记》)

In his old age, Confucius loved to study The Book of Changes… He used this book so much that the leather thongs binding the wooden strips wore out three times. (Records of the Grand Historian)

27. 仓廪实而知礼节

When the Granaries Are Full, People Follow Appropriate Rules of Conduct.

◎故曰："仓廪实而知礼节，衣食足而知荣辱。"礼生于有而废于无。故君子富，好行其德；小人富，以适其力。渊深而鱼生之，山深而兽往之，人富而仁义附焉。(《史记》)

So Guanzi said, "When the granaries are full, people follow appropriate rules of conduct, and when there is enough to eat and wear, people know honor and shame." Proper social norms emerge from sufficient conditions for life, and disappear when those conditions are absent. That is why when people of high status become wealthy, they will widely advocate moral standards, and when ordinary people become wealthy, they will behave in a moral way according to their means. Where the water is deep, fish will congregate; where the mountains are vast, wild animals will gather; when people are well off, a society of compassion and righteousness will appear. (*Records of the Grand Historian*)

28. 修德振兵

Cultivate Virtue and Strengthen the Army

◎轩辕乃修德振兵，治五气，艺五种，抚万民，度四方。(《史记》)

The Yellow Emperor cultivated virtue and strengthened the army; he studied the changes of the five elements (metal, wood, water, fire, and earth), grew the five kinds of grain, reassured the people, surveyed the land and planned its use. (*Records of the Grand Historian*)

29. 道不同，不相为谋

Part Ways and Part Company

◎子曰："道不同，不相为谋。"亦各从其志也。(《史记》)

Confucius said, "People who differ in their principles do not work together." That is to say, they follow their own wills in their actions. (*Records of the Grand Historian*)

30. 止戈为武

Stopping War Is a True Craft of War.

◎仓颉作书，"止""戈"为"武"。圣人以武禁暴整乱，止息干戈，非以为残而兴纵之也。(《汉书》)

When Cang Jie created the Chinese script, he put zhi (止, stop) and ge (戈, dagger-axe) together to make wu (武, war). To stop wars, sages used military force to quell violence and turmoil. They did not abuse their military power to commit atrocities by killing and destroying their opponents. (*The History of the Han Dynasty*)

31. 量出制入

Spend-and-Tax / Expenditure Should Be Carefully Calculated before Making a Plan to Gather Revenue.

◎量吏禄，度官用，以赋于民。(《汉书》)

A ruler must calculate the total amount of salaries for officials and administration expenditure of all levels of government, and on this basis, determine the amount of tax to be levied on the people. (The History of the Han Dynasty)

32. 休养生息

Recover from a Social Upheaval and Restore Production / Develop the Economy and Increase the Population

◎(霍)光知时务之要,轻徭薄役,与民休息。(《汉书》)

Huo Guang understood that what the state needed most was to give time for the population to recover and multiply by lightening taxes, and cutting back on conscript labor. (The History of the Han Dynasty)

33. 水至清则无鱼

No Fish Can Survive If Water Is Too Clear.

◎水至清则无鱼,人至察则无徒。(《汉书》)

Fish cannot survive in water that is too clear. One will have no friends if he is too shrewd. (The History of the Han Dynasty)

34. 安居乐业

Living in Peace and Working in Contentment

◎普天之下,赖我而得生育,由我而得富贵,安居乐业,长养子孙,天下晏然,皆归心于我矣。(《后汉书》)

If I can ensure that all the people under heaven survive and develop, are well-off, live in peace and work in contentment, and raise their children in a secure world, then they will willingly pledge allegiance to me. (The History of the Later Han Dynasty)

35. 尊师重道

Honor Teachers and Respect Rules

◎明王圣主,莫不尊师贵道。(《后汉书》)

All enlightened rulers honor teachers and respect rules. (The History of the Later Han Dynasty)

36. 悬壶济世

Hanging a Gourd (Practicing Medicine) to Help the World

◎市中有老翁卖药,悬一壶于肆头。(《后汉书》)

There was an old man who sold medicine in the market. He hung a

medicine gourd at his market stand. (*The History of the Later Han Dynasty*)

37. 言有物,行有恒

Talk Substance; Act with Perseverance

◎君子以言有物而行有恒。(《易经》)

　　A man of virtue should talk substance and act with perseverance. (*The Book of Changes*)

38. 穷理尽性

Exploring the Nature of All Things

◎穷理尽性,以至于命。(《易经》)

　　Thoroughly explore the nature of humanity and all things and maximize their natural roles, and then the ideal realm of people acting in line with laws and living in peace with nature can be reached. (*The Book of Changes*)

39. 穷则变,变则通,通则久

Extreme—Change—Continuity

◎《易》穷则变,变则通,通则久,是以"自天佑之,吉无不利"。(《易经》)

　　The Book of Changes reveals that when things reach their extreme, change occurs. After the change they evolve smoothly, and thus they continue for a long time. That's how "Heaven bestows help to the human world and benefits all." (*The Book of Changes*)

40. 义以生利,利以丰民

Justice Brings Wealth, and Wealth Enriches People.

◎民之有君,以治义也。义以生利,利以丰民。(《国语》)

　　The reason people need a sovereign ruler is because they want him to uphold justice and establish rules. A ruler must generate wealth in accordance with justice and rules, and then use such wealth to help people prosper. (*Discourses on Governance of the States*)

41. 上医医国

Great Healers Heal the Country.

◎上医医国,其次疾人,固医官也。(《国语》)

　　The greatest healers treat the illnesses of a country; lesser ones only treat those of people. This is always the duty of physicians. (*Discourses on Governance of the States*)

42. 众志成城

Unity Is Strength.

◎ 众心成城,众口铄金。(《国语》)

If we are united as one, we will be as solid as a fortress. If we speak in one voice, we will be able to fuse metal. (*Discourses on Governance of the States*)

43. 和实生物

Harmony Begets New Things.

◎ 夫和实生物,同则不继。以他平他谓之和,故能丰长而物归之。若以同裨同,尽乃弃矣。(《国语》)

Uniformity does not lead to continuation; it is harmony that begets new things. Using one thing to complement another is harmonization, which leads to lasting abundance and attracts all things. If a thing is added to another of the same kind, it will be discarded when used up. (*Discourses on Governance of the States*)

44. 怀远以德

Embrace Distant Peoples by Means of Virtue

◎ 管仲言于齐侯曰:臣闻之,招携以礼,怀远以德,德礼不易,无人不怀。(《左传》)

Guan Zhong said to the Marquis of Qi, "I have heard it said: Win over the disaffected with respect and embrace distant peoples with virtue. With virtue and respect unchanging, there is no one that will not be embraced." (*Zuo's Commentary*)

45. 民生

Livelihood of People

◎ 民生在勤,勤则不匮。(《左传》)

People's livelihood comes from hard work, which in turn ensures no scarcity. (*Zuo's Commentary*)

46. 欲强兵者,务富其民

A Strong Army Depends on a Prosperous Populace.

◎ 欲富国者,务广其地;欲强兵者,务富其民;欲王者,务博其德。三资者备,而王随之矣。(《战国策》)

To make your nation strong, extend your boundaries; to make your army strong, enrich the people; to persuade all to accept your rule, govern with benevolence. If these three are accomplished, all under heaven is naturally yours. (Strategies of the Warring States)

47. 前事不忘,后事之师

Past Experience, If Not Forgotten, Is a Guide for the Future.

◎臣观成事,闻往古,天下之美同,臣主之权均之能美,未之有也。前事之不忘,后事之师。(《战国策》)

In observing past events and learnings of ancient times, I have found that the good things in the world are always the same, but it has never occurred that when a sovereign and his officials had equal power, they could still live harmoniously. We should not forget past experience, but instead use it as a guide for the future. (Strategies of the Warring States)

48. 知音

Resonance and Empathy

◎知音其难哉! 音实难知,知实难逢,逢其知音,千载其一乎!(《文心雕龙》)

It is such a challenge to understand music! Since music is so hard to understand, it is difficult to find people who can appreciate it. It may take a thousand years to find someone who understands music! (The Literary Mind and the Carving of Dragons)

49. 比显兴隐

Make Analogy Explicit and Association Implicit

◎《诗》文弘奥,包韫六义,毛公述传,独标"兴"体,岂不以"风"通而"赋"同,"比"显而"兴"隐哉!(《文心雕龙》)

Poetic works in The Book of Songs have both width and depth. They are represented by six basic elements: ballad, court hymn, eulogy, narrative, analogy and association. Mao Heng and Mao Chang, in interpreting The Book of Songs, singled out association for extra explanation. Isn't that because ballads are simple and crude, narratives are direct, analogies are obvious but associations are obscure? (The Literary Mind and the Carving of Dragons)

50. 情以物迁,意以情发

Feeling Varies with Scenery and Verbal Expression Arises from Feeling.

◎岁有其物,物有其容;情以物迁,辞以情发。(《文心雕龙》)

Scenery varies with seasons; each scene features different contours and shapes. Human feeling changes with scenery, with words arising from the bottom of the heart. (The Literary Mind and the Carving of Dragons)

51. 繁采寡情,味之必厌

Excessive Adornment and Lack of True Feelings Make One's Writing Dull.

◎言以文远,诚哉斯验。心术既形,英华乃赡。吴锦好渝,舜英徒艳。繁采寡情,味之必厌。(《文心雕龙》)

Beautiful wording with literary grace spreads far and wide. This has been proved sufficiently true. Once we know how to express our feelings and aspirations, we will be able to display our literary talent with ease. The brocades from the Wu area easily lose their splendor. Hibiscus flowers endure only for a short time. If intricate rhetoric lacks true feelings, it will soon lose its appeal. (The Literary Mind and the Carving of Dragons)

52. 舒文载实

Use Fine Wording to Voice Feelings and Aspirations

◎是以"在心为志,发言为诗",舒文载实,其在兹乎?(《文心雕龙》)

Therefore, "if hidden in his heart, it is his feelings or aspirations. Once expressed in words, it becomes poetry." Use fine wording to voice feelings and aspirations. That is what the writing of poetry is all about, isn't it? (The Literary Mind and the Carving of Dragons)

53. 腾声飞实

Spread Good Reputation Afar and Promote Virtue and Merit

◎岁月飘忽,性灵不居,腾声飞实,制作而已。(《文心雕龙·序志》)

As time passes by, no life or wisdom can be preserved forever. To spread good reputation afar and promote virtue and merit, writing is indispensable. (The Literary Mind and the Carving of Dragons)

54. 衔华佩实

Harmony Between Substance and Style

◎然则圣文之雅丽,固衔华而佩实者也。(《文心雕龙》)

Thus, the writings of the sages have class and beauty; they are graceful in wording and solid in content. (The Literary Mind and the Carving of Dragons)

55. 言与志反，文岂足征

Writing That Runs Counter to Its Author's Aspirations Is Worthless.

◎夫桃李不言而成蹊，有实存也；男子树兰而不芳，无其情也。夫以草木之微，依情待实；况乎文章，述志为本。言与志反，文岂足征？(《文心雕龙》)

Trees bearing peaches and plums do not have to talk, yet the world, attracted by the sweet fruits they yield, beats a path to them. A man once planted an orchid but its flowers did not exude any fragrance. Why? Because he did not put his heart into his cultivation. Even trees and flowers rely on sincere care to bear fruit or to give off a sweet scent. So it is with the business of writing, which is essentially about voicing one's feelings and wishes. If what is written contradicts the author's aspirations, what's the point of writing at all? (The Literary Mind and the Carving of Dragons)

Exercises

Part One   Comprehension

Fill in the following blanks with the information you learn in Chapter 6.

1. Chinese _____ literature refers to literary works from the days before the Qin Dynasty to the year of 1919, and is virtually an unbroken strand undergoing dynastic changes.

2. Chinese _____ contributed much to the forming of Chinese religion, especially Religious Taoism and Buddhism.

3. Of Chinese hero myths, that of _____ is among the most elaborated.

4. Among Chinese animal myths, _____ lore is the earliest and most famous of the symbolic animals.

5. Poetry, one of the earliest artistic forms, originated from _____ before the existence of written Chinese.

6. *The Book of Songs*, as the fountainhead of _____, occupies an important place in the history of Chinese literature.

7. Qu Yuan created a new literary genre. His new form and his adoption of positive _____ have exerted a lasting influence on Chinese literature and been imitated or admired by many writers from the Han Dynasty onward.

8. Tao's poems featured his vivid and sensitive descriptions of natural scenery, which established

him as the creator of the _____ or idyllic poetry in Chinese literature.

9. *The Complete Anthology of Tang Poetry*, edited in the early Qin Dynasty, is the _____ collection of Chinese poetry, which collects nearly 50,000 poems by 2,200 poets.

10. Li Bai, the "Immortal of Poems", has long been considered the greatest _____ poet in the history of Chinese literature.

11. Du Fu, the "Sage of Poems", has been regarded as the greatest _____ poet in the history of Chinese literature.

12. A _____ writer, Bai Juyi wrote nearly 3,000 poems, about 2,000 of which were regulated poems and around 170 were satirical and allegorical.

13. Instead of regulated poetry, Song *ci* poetry could convey more refined and delicate feelings with _____ meter.

14. Liu Yong (1004—1054) made a great contribution to the *ci* poetry and has been universally acknowledged to be the _____ master of the "Graceful and Restrained School".

15. Li Qingzhao, as the China's greatest _____ with erudition and versatile talents, also rose to prominence in this period.

16. With his extraordinary _____ style of poetry, Su Shi brought innovations to *ci* and helped broaden its scope, elevate its status and set up the "Powerful and Free School".

17. *The Book of History* is the most ancient collection of Chinese prose writings with fragments of disconnected and diverse individual _____ papers.

18. *Records of the Grand Historian* is a first monumental work of _____ history that records Chinese history form the time of the legendary figure Emperor Huang up to Emperor Wu of the Han Dynasty, over a period of about 3,000 years.

19. *The Literary Mind and the Carving of Dragons* written by Liu Xie in parallel prose is the first work of literary _____ in the history of Chinese literature.

20. The basic expressive technique of *Romance of the Three Kingdoms* is realism, but the _____ arrangement and the portrayal of historical figures are full of romantic color.

21. *Water Margin*, or *Outlaws of the Marsh*, by Shi Nai'an, tells the story of the rebellion of the 108 heroes at the end of the Northern Song Dynasty. It is the first novel to deal with the subject matter of _____ uprisings in China.

22. *Journey to the West*, or *Pilgrimage to the West*, by Wu Cheng'en, is an outstanding romantic work replete with _____ tales.

23. Written by Cao Xueqing and Gao E, *A Dream of the Red Mansions* reached the pinnacle of

Chinese classical novels. It has been acknowledged as the _____ novel in Chinese classical literature and also a world literary masterpiece.

24. *The Injustice Suffered by Dou E* praises Dou E's fighting spirit and exposes and condemns the dark society and _____ legal system.

25. In the early period of the Qing Dynasty, the most notable _____ were Hong Sheng and Kong Shangren who respectively wrote excellent plays *The Palace of Eternal Life* and *The Peach Blossom Fan*.

Part Two   Translation

Term Translation

1. 它山之石,可以攻玉

2. 协和万邦

3. 满招损,谦受益

4. 大同

5. 礼尚往来

6. 不诚无物

7. 修齐治平

8. 教学相长

9. 敬业乐群

10. 苟利国家,不求富贵

11. 唇亡齿寒

12. 韦编三绝

13. 仓廪实而知礼节

14. 道不同,不相为谋

15. 量出制入

16. 水至清则无鱼

17. 安居乐业

18. 悬壶济世

19. 前事不忘,后事之师

20. 言与志反,文岂足征

Passage Translation

曹雪芹的《红楼梦》是中国古典小说的顶峰之作。《红楼梦》长久以来被视作中国文学中最伟大的小说,也是世界文学的瑰宝。曹雪芹出身于一个从繁荣富贵走向贫穷没落的权贵家族。他能创作出《红楼梦》的原因在于他理解生活,思想进步,写作态度严谨,写作技能高超。

《红楼梦》描述了一个封建大家族的生活卷轴及其没落过程。贾宝玉和林黛玉的爱情悲剧构成了小说的主线。小说不只是讲述这场爱情悲剧本身,而是通过深入探究人物思想及其复杂的关系触及了悲剧的社会根源。小说情节安排独具匠心,采用成熟的口语进行叙事,朴素而优雅,明白易懂而富感染力。小说的确是一幅中国封建社会的全景画(panorama),被认为是中国文学的百科全书(encyclopedia)。

Part Three   Critical Thinking and Discussion

1. Why was the Tang poetry so flourishing?

2. Whose *ci* poems do you like best? Why?

3. What are the artistic features and the social significance of *A Dream of the Red Mansions*?

4. Whose fiction do you like best? Why?

5. Which traditional drama do you like best? Why?

Chapter 7
Traditional Chinese Arts

Traditional Chinese arts are diverse, rich, and splendid, which constitute one important part of the valuable cultural heritage of the Chinese nation. This chapter briefly deals with characters, calligraphy, traditional Chinese painting, traditional Chinese operas, folk performing arts, and traditional musical instruments.

/ Characters /

The Chinese written language is one of the various world languages with the longest history. Tradition has it that legendary kings or heroes, such as Shen Nong (神农), the Yellow Emperor, Shao Hao (少昊), Yao (尧) and Cang Jie (仓颉) all created different kinds of writing. Yet it can hardly be supposed that one man, be he a sage or however otherwise endowed, could have invented or shaped by himself an entire written language and then had it printed and issued for public use. What is more, we have not reliable material or records enough to verify its truthfulness. The only possibility is that writing was created by common people in the long period of laboring practice. According to archaeological excavations, Chinese characters can be traced back to a time when Yangshao Culture (仰韶文化) came into being 6,000 years ago, for pottery wares found in Banpo Village (半坡村) near Xi'an and in Dawenkou (大汶口) in Shandong Province bear signs and symbols of early writing, which is closely linked with later writing on oracle bones and bronze wares. They can surely be regarded as the forerunners of Chinese pictograms, especially those on the wares from Dawenkou relics. But instead of complete sentences, they are all individual characters or words.

In 1889, a large quantity, and later more, of tortoise shells and animal bones bearing inscriptions were discovered in Anyang (安阳), capital of the Shang Dynasty. So they are commonly known as the oracle bone (or shell-and-bone) inscriptions (甲骨文), which are considered by many scholars to be the earliest Chinese written language. The characters were incised with a sharp pointed knife or some other kinds of instrument on the hard surface of shells and bones. Only few traces of the brush could be seen, which shows that the brush was then definitely not a common writing instrument.

So far, roughly 150,000 oracle bones have been unearthed and analyzed, about 4,500 characters have been found, of which the meanings of some 1,700 have been ascertained. From studies, we are sure that the inscriptions are such diverse records as royal divination, ancestor worship, religious offerings, military campaigns, hunting expeditions, pregnancies, births, prayers for rain, and other allied subjects.

The development of bronze casting made it possible for bronze inscriptions (金文) to emerge in the late Shang Dynasty. Bronze inscriptions, carved first into the mould used in the casting, are mainly brief accounts of the private provenance or origin of the vessel, such as the name of the maker, the name of the ancestor to whom it is dedicated, and the name of the vessel. Only by the end of the Shang

Tripod of Duke Mao

Dynasty did bronze inscriptions become lengthier, recording political and other events. For instance, the inscription on the Tripod of Duke Mao (毛公鼎) of the Western Zhou was as long as 497 characters, and recorded an audience granted to the duke by the King of Zhou.

Besides on bronze vessels, we also have inscriptions on other materials. The most remarkable is the inscriptions on the ten Stone Drums (石鼓文) which were discovered in the 7th century during the Tang Dynasty. It is widely believed that the inscriptions were done in the late years of the Western Zhou, most probably in the 9th or 8th century B.C.E., though no specific date has been ascertained. As much of the stones' surfaces have been eroded, a modern rubbing shows only some 300 characters from the original total of over 600.

For pedagogical purpose during the reign of King Xuan (宣王) of the Zhou Dynasty, a court official, Shi Zhou (史籀) made a valiant attempt to codify the then-existing writing systems into a standard vocabulary. Despite the fact that the Chinese written language was far from uniform, the writing system he fashioned was called Zhou's Writing System (籀文), also known as the great seal script (大篆).

Up to then, Chinese as a written language had reached quite a high level, though its styles were still developing as time went on. Basing on the construction of the characters, Xu Shen (许

慎) of the Han Dynasty scientifically summarized and classified them into six categories (六书), namely pictographic characters (象形), self-explanatory characters (指事), associative compound characters (会意), pictophonetic characters (形声), phonetic loan characters (假借) and derivative characters (转注).

/ Calligraphy /

Chinese calligraphy, generally speaking, is the art of writing Chinese characters. It is a unique artistic form with a long history, for the Chinese people, not content with writing the characters correctly and legibly for the sole purpose of communication as most of the other languages in the world and urged by their love of beauty and creative impulse, make each character into an artistic unit through centuries of sustained and uninterrupted practice, and by putting many such units together, produce an artistic composition. By using the brush to write Chinese characters, calligraphers can convey their aesthetic ideas, thoughts and feelings, personalities and temperaments in a point or a line, so Chinese calligraphy is also called the art of lines. Although it adopts Chinese as its vehicle of expression, one does not have to know Chinese to appreciate its beauty.

Calligraphy retains the beauty of nature and shows the spiritual beauty of human beings. Chinese calligraphy stresses the overall layout and harmony between words and lines. The graceful shapes are profoundly artistic and arouse deep emotion. Thus, the popular Chinese saying like "The handwriting reveals the writer. (字如其人。)" is directly connected with calligraphy.

Five Styles of Chinese Scripts

Generally speaking, Chinese calligraphy came into being since the day when the shell-and-bone inscriptions appeared in the Shang Dynasty, for from the very beginning, Chinese characters, in a sense, were charming units with artistic taste. However, what should be kept in mind is that from the beginning up to the Han Dynasty, the Chinese writing system was in the process of development from the primitive to the mature. What scholars and experts paid much attention to was how characters should become more simplified, more convenient and more practical, though they tried hard to make them as beautiful as possible. So it is reasonable that some scholars and critics regard the Han Dynasty, or exactly speaking, the late Han as the beginning era when character-writing was purposely engaged in as an art.

Chinese scripts are generally divided into five styles: the seal script (篆书), the official script or the clerical script (隶书), the cursive script (草书), the regular script (楷书), and the running script (行书). These five writing styles are closely related, but each has its own shapes and features, so different methods are employed when writing them.

Discussed in chronological order, first comes the seal script, which can be subdivided into the great seal script (大篆) and the small seal script (小篆). In 221 B.C.E., China finally came under the unified rule of the Qin Dynasty; uniformity became the order of the day. The Emperor Qinshihuang (秦始皇) commanded the prime minister Li Si (李斯) to reform the written language and devise a writing system to be used throughout the empire. Li Si collected and categorized all the different systems of writing used

The Seal Script

throughout the country in an effort to unify the writing system. He simplified the ancient seal script and submitted the small seal script to Emperor Qinshihuang as a standard form of writing. Soft lines of strokes and upright rectangular shapes keep the seal characters more close to pictographs. Each of the characters has a balanced and symmetrical pattern. All the different scripts before Li Si's time: from the shell-and-bone inscriptions to the Zhou Dynasty script, have been exclusively regarded as belonging to the great seal script.

With the establishment of a central government and with the extension of the empire's frontiers, the small seal script, though a tremendous step forward, was obviously cumbersome for administrative efficiency and daily communication. A script with more easily and quickly executed characters was urgently

The Official Script

needed. So appeared the official script or the clerical script, for it was mainly used by officials and clerks (隶). Though the official script appeared in the Qin Dynasty, it did not prevail until the Han Dynasty for it was much easier to write. The introduction of the official script into extensive use was an immense breakthrough in the evolution of the Chinese script. It represented the most complete change from the past, opening an entirely new prospect for the future. It turned the remaining curved and round strokes of the seal script into linear and flat square shapes (扁方形).

The formal writing system of Han was the clerical script or the official script, which was more convenient and faster than its predecessors. But it could not meet the development and demand of the society. So the cursive script was born. In history there were many diversified types of cursive script, the most common and most representative ones were known as the Zhang cursive script (章 草) or the clerically cursive script (隶草) and modern cursive script (今草). The former, said to have been codified by Shi You (史游), evolving from the clerical script, still executed the individual strokes one by one though many strokes and elements

The Cursive Script

were eliminated. The latter, believed to have been developed by Zhang Zhi (张芝), was quite different, for its execution grew more and more "care-free and cursive". In a sense, it was used for artistic purposes or as a vehicle for expressing feelings rather than for practical use.

Generally speaking, this style of calligraphy is smooth and lively with strokes flowing and characters linking together. The characters are often joined, with the last stroke of one merging into the initial stroke of the next. They may vary in size in the same piece of writing, all seemingly dictated by the whims of the writer. The flow of the lines and the rhythm of the brush create an abstract beauty of the whole.

Probably because the cursive style was too abbreviated and erratic to be easily legible, the regular or standard, or orthodox script (楷书, 亦称真书或正书), as a way to bridge the gap between the official and the cursive, came into being in the late years of the Han Dynasty. The regular script was developed during the Wei and Jin Dynasties, and came to prominence in the Tang Dynasty. In its evolution, the famous calligrapher Wang Cizhong (王次仲) played a great role. Because it is easy to execute and suits everyday purposes, it is still today's standard form of writing. The characters of this style are square in form, and non-cursive in strokes.

Paralleled to the regular and the cursive styles at the end of the Han Dynasty was the running script. This style, as its name suggests, allows simpler and faster writing. In fact, it is a script between the cursive and the regular, some sort of compromise between the formality of the former and the cursoriness of the latter. When carefully written with distinguishable strokes, the running characters will be very close to the regular style, and can be called the "running regular script (行楷)". When swiftly executed, they will look like the cursive style, and can be called the "running cursive script (行草)".

The Regluar Script

The Running Script

Distinguished Calligraphers

Because of the lack of convincing material about calligraphers in the Qin and Han Dynasties, we usually talk about inscriptions or tablets when we mention calligraphy of that period. On the one hand, they represented the highest level of that period in certain styles; on the other hand, they were models on which later calligraphic works developed. The most famous and influential ones that belong to the Qin Dynasty were *Stone Inscription on Mount Tai* (《泰山石刻》) and *Stone Inscription On Langya Terrace* (《琅牙台石刻》) which, believed to be in the handwritten style of Li Si, are regarded as models of the small seal script with its vigorous manner and well-organized structure. The Han Dynasty was much more prolific in the inscriptions of the official style. The most outstanding are *Eulogy to Shimen* (《石门颂》) produced in the year of 148, *Yi Ying Inscription* (《乙瑛碑》) turned out in 153 or 154, *Inscription on Ritual Articles* (《礼器碑》) engraved in 156, *Shi Chen Inscription* (《史晨碑》) worked out in 169, *Cao Quan Inscription* (《曹全碑》) done in 185, *Zhang Qian Inscription* (《张骞碑》) made in 186, and so on. These masterpieces in varied styles differ greatly, ranging from unadorned boldness to sublime vigour or exquisite charm.

As we know, at the end of the Han Dynasty, the regular script was beginning to gain popularity. Tradition has it that Zhong Yao (钟繇) was the first known master of the regular script on which his enormous reputation was built, though he was also proficient in the seal and clerical hands. Critics consider that his style is a subtle balance of strength and pliability, every dot and stroke manifesting a peculiar appeal and charm. The specimens he left behind are *Memorial Recommending Ji Zhi* (《荐季直表》) and *Memorial Congratulating the Victory* (《贺捷表》).

During the two Jin Dynasties' Period, Chinese calligraphy had a great leap forward, the sign of which was the appearance of Wang Xizhi (王羲之) and Wang Xianzhi (王献之). Wang Xizhi from the Eastern Jin Dynasty has been honored and worshiped as the "Sage of Chinese Calligraphy (书圣)" in history. Among his works, those in the running style are recognized as his best. Unfortunately, none of his original works are extant today. Some of his best writings have been preserved on carved stone tablets. Stone rubbings taken from them have been reproduced and reprinted widely and studied by generations of students, used as models to practice. His most outstanding works are the transcriptions of *On Yue Yi* (《乐毅论》) and *Huang Ting Scripture* (《黄庭经》) in the regular style; *Preface to the Orchid Pavilion Collection* (《兰亭集序》) and *Model Copy of the Times of Troubles* (《丧乱帖》) in the running style; *Seventeen Model Copies* (《十七帖》) and *Letter Offering Oranges* (《奉橘帖》) in the cursive style.

Wang Xianzhi was Wang Xizhi's seventh and youngest son. Under the strict tutorship of his father, Xianzhi gained a reputation when he was young. He was especially excellent in the cursive style though he was also a master of other scripts. From his works left over to us, such as *The Mid-Autumn Letter* (《中秋帖》), one can see that he wrote a whole piece of characters with the twist and turn of a single continuous movement of the brush like that of dragons and snakes, so many people call his cursive script the one-stroke-writing (一笔书) or cursive script in the wild form (狂草). His famous work of the regular script is his transcription of *The Fu on Goddess of the Luo River* (《洛神赋》), by Cao Zhi.

During the period of the Northern and Southern Dynasties, stone inscription was forbidden in the Southern Dynasties where only epitaphs prevaild, while in the Northern Dynasties there was no prohibition on tablet-erecting. Among the kingdoms, Northern Wei was particularly outstanding by developing its own regular style with a flavor of the official script. So inscriptions of that period in such a style have been called Wei Inscriptions (魏碑). The most famous of thousands of such tablets, mostly made by anonymous calligraphers, are *Inscription in Memory of Zhang Menglong* (《张猛龙碑》), *Epitaph for Zhang Henü* (《张黑女墓志》), *Epitaph for a Crane* (《瘗鹤铭》), *Inscription in Memory of Bi Gan* (《吊比干碑》), and *Shimen Inscription* (《石门铭》).

The master of the short-lived Sui Dynasty was the monk Zhi Yong (智永), Wang Xizhi's seventh generation descendant and the most worthy upholder of the family tradition. He made 800 transcriptions of *One-Thousand-Character Text* (《千字文》) in two hands in alternating columns and distributed them among the Buddhist temples.

In the Chinese calligraphy history, there exist four great regular script masters whose styles are copied and admired by later generations. They are Ouyang Xun (欧阳询), Yan Zhenqing (颜真卿), and Liu Gongquan (柳公权) from the Tang Dynasty, and Zhao Mengfu (赵孟頫) from the Yuan Dynasty.

The forms of Ouyang Xun's characters in the regular style are square and erect, strong and angular. Every character stands rigidly and solidly by itself. The later generations find his calligraphy canonical and easy to learn by beginners, and call his calligraphy "*Ou Ti* (欧体)", referring specifically to his style of calligraphy. The excellent example is his transcription of *Eulogy to the Sweet Fountain at Jiucheng Palace* (《九成宫醴泉铭》).

Ou Ti

Yan Zhenqing, an upright, honest and qualified official, assimilated the best points of earlier and contemporary artists to create his own style of powerful appeal. His calligraphy is called "*Yan Ti* (颜体)" and his vigorous regular script set a good example in the Tang Dynasty. Power, exuberance, dignity and mastery of technique are his calligraphic features which can be verified in his stone inscriptions such as *The Pagoda of Many Treasures* (《多宝塔》), *Rites Observation of the Yan Family* (《颜勤礼碑》), *Family Temple of Yan* (《颜家庙》) and *Fairyland of the Lady Magu* (《麻姑仙坛记》).

Yan Ti

Liu Gongquan was a successful exponent of Yan's school, but he had his own bony and sinewy characteristics. The vigor of Liu's calligraphy is strong and the regulations strict and serious. His characters are famous for their powerful strokes and his calligraphy is called "*Liu Ti* (柳体)". His best works were *Mysterious Pagoda* (《玄秘塔》) and *The Imperial Guards* (《神策军》). Yan Zhenqing and Liu Gongquan together are called "Yan Liu (颜柳)", and their calligraphy is referred to as "Yan's tendon and Liu's bone (颜筋柳骨)".

Liu Ti

Zhao Mengfu was a descendant of the Song Dynasty's Emperor Zhao Kuangyin (赵匡胤). He was good at all the five styles of script, and was famous for the running and regular scripts especially. Synthesizing the merits of the past masters, Zhao produced characters that were full and fluent in strokes, and balanced and harmonious in structure, looking sweet and pretty though they, according to some critics, were not so manly and

Zhao Ti

heroic. His elegant and vigorous calligraphy with strict structure is often called "*Zhao Ti* (赵体)". The best manuscripts he left behind were *Epitaph for Chou E* (《仇锷墓志铭》) and *Notes on Miaoyan Temple* (《妙严寺记》).

Beside Zhao Mengfu, the other most prominent calligraphers of the Song Dynasty were Cai Xiang (蔡襄), Su Shi (苏轼), Huang Tingjian (黄庭坚) and Mi Fu (米芾), who have been collectively regarded as the Four Great Masters of the Song Calligraphy.

The great calligraphers of the Ming Dynasty excelled chiefly in the regular, the running and the cursive styles. Those in the early Ming carried on Zhao Mengfu's tradition and did not develop their own style. Up to the Mid-Ming appeared some important calligraphers such as Wen Zhengming (文征明) and Zhu Yunming (祝允明). In the Ming Dynasty, Dong Qichang (董其昌) was the most accomplished and influential calligrapher. The best-known of his works were *Epitaph for Xiang Yuanbian* (《项元汴墓志铭》), and some scrolls and colophons on or attached to pictures in the running or the cursive or the mixture of both.

At the dynastic turning point, well-known calligraphers were Zhang Ruitu (张瑞图), Wang Duo (王铎), Fu Shan (傅山), Zhu Da (朱耷) and Zheng Fu (郑簠). In the 18th century the most famous calligraphers were Jin Nong (金农) and Zheng Xie (郑燮), two of the "Eight Eccentrics of Yangzhou (扬州八怪)", and Deng Shiru (邓石如). In the last 100 years of the Qing Dynasty top calligraphers were Yi Bingshou (伊秉绶), Zhao Zhiqian (赵之谦), Wu Changshuo (吴昌硕) and Kang Youwei (康有为).

/ Traditional Chinese Painting /

Traditional Chinese painting, with its majestic and continuous tradition of thousands of years, is one of the greatest schools of painting that the world has seen. It dates back to the Neolithic Period, about six thousand years ago. The colored pottery with painted animals, fish, deer, and frogs excavated in the 1920's indicates that during the Neolithic Period the Chinese had already started to use brushes to paint.

General Characteristics

Traditional Chinese painting is highly regarded throughout the world for its theory, expression, and techniques. According to the means of expression, traditional Chinese painting can be divided into two categories: the *xieyi* school (写意派) and the *gongbi* school (工笔派). The *xieyi* school is marked by exaggerated forms and freehand brush work. The *gongbi* school is characterized by close attention to detail and fine brush work.

Xieyi, however, is the fundamental approach to traditional Chinese painting. It is a term coined by painters of scholarly painting and means freehand brushwork characterized by vivid expression and bold outline. It constitutes an aesthetic theory which, above all, emphasizes the sentiments. Even in ancient times, Chinese artists were unwilling to be restrained by reality. A famous painter of the Jin Dynasty, Gu Kaizhi (顾恺之), was the first to put forward the theory of "making the form show the spirit." In his opinion, a painting should serve as a means not only to convey the appearance of an object, but to express how the artist looks at it. Gu's views were followed by theories such as "Likeness in spirit resides in unlikeness." and "A painting should be something between likeness and unlikeness." Guided by these theories, Chinese painters disregard the limitations of proportion, perspective, and light. Take Qi Baishi (齐白石), the modern painter, for example. He does not paint shrimps, insects, birds, and flowers just as they are in nature; but only their essence has been shown as a result of the artist's long-term observation and profound understanding of the subjects.

Traditional Chinese painting has a social and moral function. No theme would be accepted in it that was not inspiring, noble, refreshing to the spirit, or at least charming. Nor is there any place in the Chinese artistic tradition for an art of pure form divorced from content, and the Chinese cannot conceive of a work of art in which the form is beautiful while the subject matter is unedifying. Hence we can just conclude that traditional Chinese painting is symbolic, for everything that is painted reflects some aspect of a totality of which the painter is intuitively aware.

Different from Western paintings, a Chinese painting is not restricted by the focal point in its perspective. Chinese painters may produce on a long and narrow piece of paper or silk all the scenes along the Yangtze River. The picture of *Mulan Returning Home* (《木兰还乡》) provides an example of this kind. It is based on an old story in which Mulan disguised herself as a boy, joined the army in her father's stead and returned home after the war was won. In the picture, one can see what people are doing both outside and inside the courtyard and the house.

It can be said that the adoption of shifting perspective is one of the characteristics of traditional Chinese painting. The reason why Chinese painters emphasize the shifting perspective lies in that they want to break away from the restriction of time and space and to include in their pictures both things which are far and things which are near. What's more, the artists find that in real life, people view their surroundings from a mobile focal point. As one walks along a river or in a garden, one sees everything along the way. The shifting perspective enables the artist to express freely what he wants.

Chinese painters dip their brushes in ink or paint to create classic pictures with lines and dots. Variations in shade enables the artists to execute human figures, landscapes, flowers, birds, and pavilions, which are the most common themes of traditional Chinese painting. A painting normally consists of calligraphic writing, a seal stamp, and the painting itself. Traditional Chinese painting is a combination in the same picture of fine art, poetry, calligraphy, and seal engraving to achieve an artistic unison. In ancient time, many artists such as Su Dongpo, Ni Yunlin (倪云林), and Dong Qichang were poets and calligraphers. To the Chinese, "painting in poetry and poetry in painting" has been one of the criteria for excellent works of art. Inscriptions and seal impressions help to explain the painter's ideas and sentiments and also add decorative beauty to the painting itself. Ancient artists liked to paint pines, bamboos, plum blossoms, and orchids. When inscriptions like "Exemplary conduct and nobility of character" were made, those plants were meant to embody the qualities of people who were virtuous and upright to be ready to help each other under hard conditions. For Chinese graphic art, poetry, calligraphy, painting, and seal engraving are necessary parts, which supplement and enrich one another. In addition, the paintings are usually mounted on a scroll by pasting them on a long piece of paper which can be rolled up or hung vertically on the wall.

Ink-Wash Painting, Figure Painting and Landscape Painting

Traditional Chinese painting usually refers to ink-wash painting (水墨画). It can be traced back to the Tang Dynasty and flourished from the Yuan Dynasty. Ink-wash painting also holds an important place in the history of traditional landscape painting.

From the Han Dynasty until the end of the Tang Dynasty, human figures occupied the dominant position in traditional Chinese painting. Figure painting flourished under a Confucian background, illustrating moral themes.

Landscaping painting for its own sake started in the fourth and fifth centuries. The practice of seeking out natural beauty and communing with nature first became popular among Taoist poets and painters. By the ninth century, artists began shifting their interest away from figures and, from the 11th century onwards, landscapes dominated traditional Chinese painting.

Remarkable Painters

Among the numerous ancient Chinese painters, Wu Daozi (吴道子) in the Tang Dynasty was regarded as the "Sage of Traditional Chinese Painting (画圣)" and the greatest master of

Tang figure painting. He was the first to make full use of the flexibility of the brush, and employed undulating lines varying in thickness, with third-dimensional effect. He had sufficient creative energy to execute 300 wall paintings in the temples of Luoyang and Chang'an. Wu's paintings have had a tremendous influence on later generations, and that is why he has been considered the forefather of painting by folk painters.

Riverside Scenes at Qingming Festival

There were many other prominent painters in ancient China after Wu Daozi. Zhang Zeduan (张择端) of the Song Dynasty, a master painter who specialized in such subjects as boats, carts, markets, bridges, city walls, streets, trees, water, and human figures. His representative work *Riverside Scenes at Qingming Festival* (《清明上河图》) is viewed as the most famous genre painting (风俗画) in the Song Dynasty. In late Yuan there appeared in Southern China four famous scholar painters called "Four Great Masters of the Yuan Dynasty (元朝四大画家)." The first is Huang Gongwang (黄公望), a Taoist recluse, scholar, and teacher whose greatest surviving work is the hand scroll *Living in the Fuchun Mountains* (《富春山居图》). The scholarly serenity was also expressed in the landscape of Wu Zhen (吴镇), a poor Taoist diviner, poet, and painter who, like Huang Gongwang, was inspired by Dong Yuan (董源) and Ju Ran (巨然), two landscape painters of the Song Dynasty. Wu's famous works include *Twin Junipers* (《双桧图》), *Pine and Spring* (《松泉图》), and *The Fisher* (《渔父图》). The third master was Ni Zan (倪瓒), a prosperous gentleman who gave up his estates and became a wanderer. As a landscapist he reduced the composition of Ju Ran to its simplest terms, achieving a sense of austere and monumental calm with the slenderest of means. He used ink, it was said, as sparingly as if it was gold. Quite different was the technique of the fourth Yuan master, Wang Meng (王蒙), a grandson of Zhao Mengfu. His brushwork was close-textured and luxuriant, and, unlike the other great scholar-painters, he made subtle use of color, which gives his pictures a visual charm and interest. During the Ming Dynasty, Dai Jin (戴进), a head of the Zhejiang School (浙派) as well as a famous court painter, was also adept at paintings of divine beings, human figures, animals, birds, and flowers. Such great landscape masters as Shen Zhou (沈周), Wen Zhengming (文征明), Tang Yin (唐寅), and Chou Ying (仇英) were known as the Four Great Maters of Ming (明朝四大画家).

The Qing conquest of Ming was resolutely resisted by the Ming loyalists, who, after their complete failure, retired to quiet hermitage. Among them are four remarkable painters, known as the Four Monks. They are Hong Reng (弘仁), Kun Can (髡残), Zhu Da (朱耷) and Shi Tao (石涛). The most original of the four was Zhu Da who was also known as Bada Shanren (八大山人) because he signed most of his pictures with this name. A descendant of Zhu Yuanzhang (朱元璋), founder of the Ming Dynasty, Zhu Da grew up in Nanchang (南昌), Jiangxi Province. He learned poetry and art while he was only a

Zhu Da

little boy. His peaceful life ended when the Ming Dynasty was overthrown by the Manchu northerners in 1644. The Qing army took over Nanchang the next year and the nineteen-year-old Zhu Da and his family were forced to flee and hide in the mountains.

A series of misfortunes followed. Zhu Da's father, wife, and son died. Under such heavy blows, Zhu Da, then twenty-three, changed his name and became a monk. He studied Dhyana or Zen (禅宗), the tenets of a Buddhist sect in ancient China which asserted that enlightenment could be attained through meditation and self-contemplation rather than through reading scriptures. In his thirties, Zhu Da became interested in Taoist teachings. He often went to Qingyunpu (青云谱), a Taoist temple near Nanchang, to study Taoist scriptures. One day, in his mid-fifties, when he heard that some of his poems had been used by an official to flatter the rulers of the Qing Dynasty, he went mad. He wandered through the streets of Nanchang, wailing and laughing alternately. When he was 62, he decided to return to a secular life and earned his living by painting and teaching. At this time, he started to use the name of Bada Shanren for many of his works. Although he was poor, he refused to paint for officials and rich people. He died in 1705 at the age of eighty.

Bada Shanren painted, often under the influence of drink, wild landscapes in monochrome ink in which the style of Dong Yuan and Ju Ran is transformed almost beyond recognition. In his brilliant paintings of birds and fish, he captured the essence of life in a few strokes. Bada

Shanren's paintings look strange to the public and even to many artists. The birds and fish in his pictures always hold their heads high. Their eyes were drawn big and even square to demonstrate the painter's feelings. His bitter experience in those years of social turmoil and his hatred for the Qing rulers helped to shape his distinctive style. In his *Picture of Peacocks* (《孔雀牡丹图》), two peacocks squat on a strangely-shaped and unsteady stone. They are very ugly and have strange big eyes. Each has three tail plums which look like the symbols of rank worn on hats of Qing officials. The poem written on the painting provides the viewer with some hints implied in the picture. The plums on the peacocks were used to ridicule Qing officials; the strangely-shaped and unsteady stone symbolized that the Qing Dynasty was not built on a firm foundation and would eventually be overthrown. When Zheng Banqiao (郑板桥), a later painter, commented on Bada Shanren's works, he said that Bada Shanren's paintings contained more tears than brush strokes done with Chinese ink.

Bada Shanren's method of expression was based on his mastery of the techniques of traditional Chinese painting. However, he did not follow tradition blindly; he tried new trails and sought new ways of expression. He excelled at painting landscapes, flowers, and birds. What characterized his works was simple composition, brief and precise brush strokes, exaggeration, strange images, and the human feelings and attitudes displayed by his subjects. Bada Shanren's style exerted a great influence on later artists. The Eight Eccentrics of Yangzhou (扬州八怪) in the Qing Dynasty and such well-known modern artists as Qi Baishi (齐白石), Xu Beihong (徐悲鸿), Wu Changshuo (吴昌硕), and Li Kuchan (李苦禅) all followed Bada Shanren's example and succeeded in forming their own styles.

New Year Pictures (年画)

In China, when the Spring Festival comes around, people, especially in rural areas, decorate the doors, windows, and walls of their houses with brightly colored pictures. They hope the pictures will bring their families good luck and prosperity. To many, it would not be a "happy" New Year without the New Year pictures. No other Chinese art form has enjoyed such wide-spread popularity.

New Year pictures have a long history and can be traced back to the Eastern Han Dynasty (25—220). Originally, people painted *menshen* (门神, door gods) on their doors with ink and colors to protect their families from devils. During the Tang Dynasty (618—907), pictures of door gods were gradually replaced by those of people from real life. In the Song Dynasty (960—1279) woodblock printed New Year pictures were traded among ordinary people. New Year pictures were gradually popularized and developed into an independent art form. In the 17th century, during the period of great prosperity of the Qing Dynasty (1636—1912), New Year pictures flourished along with other handicrafts.

In China, there are three major kinds of traditional New Year pictures: the Yangliuqing in Tianjin (天津杨柳青年画), the Taohuawu in Jiangsu Province (江苏省桃花坞年画), and the Yangjiabu in Shandong Province (山东省杨家埠年画). Of these three kinds, New Year paintings made by peasants of Yangjiabu seem to be not only the most primitive but also the most original. Yangjiabu New Year pictures feature a combination of classical and folk art techniques. Taohuawu pictures carry on the traditions of previous dynasties and also adopt Western perspectives and shadings.

Yangjiabu New Year Picture

In spite of the difference between the three schools, all the New Year pictures have some common characteristics. The people portrayed in New Year pictures look healthy and happy and usually have complete bodies. Heads are usually a bit larger than natural, so that the face, which is the most expressive part of a person, is emphasized.

New Year pictures portray various topics, from history to daily life. Originally, door gods or kitchen gods (灶神) dominated the pictures. During the Ming and Qing Dynasties, New Year pictures started to draw their themes from people's lives and also from history, folklore, mythology, novels, and operas. The most impressive of the pictures are those from fairy tales and stories. Heroes in Chinese classics such as Zhuge Liang, Guan Yunchang, Zhang Fei, and Cao Cao in *Romance of the Three Kingdoms*, Wu Song, Li Kui, and Song Jiang in *Water Margin* are commonly pictured in New Year paintings. Figures in well-known folk tales like *The White Snake* (《白蛇传》) and *The Butterfly Lovers* (《梁山伯与祝英台》) are also portrayed.

Another characteristic of New Year pictures is the use of symbolism. For example, a chubby and happy baby is often shown embracing a big fish, with a lotus at its side. The word "fish" in Chinese is *yu* (鱼) which sounds like another word meaning "affluence", and the word "lotus" in Chinese is *lian* (莲) which is a homonym of another word meaning "in succession". These symbols express people's hopes for consecutive good harvests. Many other objects employed in New Year pictures also have symbolic meanings. The peony represents wealth and honor, the peach symbolizes longevity, and the pomegranate and red plum reflect auspiciousness, wealth, prosperity, and a large number of children.

People, however, are no longer satisfied merely with healthy babies or more grain and money. They like pictures that are associated with building socialism, modern science, and technology. In one of the most popular pictures, a man is traveling on a spaceship. In another, which is entitled "The Carps Leaps the Dragon Gate (鲤鱼跳龙门)", the term "Four Modernizations" is painted on the gate, expressing people's determination and wishes for the new year and the future.

Four Treasures of the Study (文房四宝)

Four Treasures of the Study, namely brush, ink, paper and ink slab, cannot be ignored when we appreciate and understand Chinese calligraphy and traditional painting because they determine the characteristics and the expressive forms of the artistic work.

It is widely accepted that the best of each of the four items is represented by the *Hu* brush (湖笔), *Hui* ink stick (徽墨), *Xuan* paper (宣纸), and *Duan* ink slab (端砚), all being highly valued in both China and abroad.

Hu brushes are produced in Huzhou, Zhejiang Province. *Hui* ink sticks are produced in Huizhou, Anhui Province. *Xuan* paper was originally produced in the Tang Dynasty in Jing county (泾县), which was under the jurisdiction of Xuanzhou (宣州), hence the name of *Xuan* paper. *Duan* ink slabs were first introduced in Duanzhou, Guangdong Province.

/ Traditional Chinese Operas /

Traditional Chinese opera is one of the shining gems in China's traditional culture treasure-house. In the long history, it has not only shown its exuberant vitality among the Chinese people but also aroused great international interest. Chinese opera is considered one of the three ancient forms of drama in the world, with the other two being Greek tragedy and comedy, and Indian Sanskrit opera. Of these three, only Chinese opera still remains alive.

Different from Western dramas, traditional Chinese operas combine a wide range of different tunes, actions, and musical instruments, depending on where they are being performed.

Traditional Chinese opera is a comprehensive performing art which embraces literature, music, dance, dialogue, martial arts, acrobatics, and pantomime. It represents the culmination and distillation of two thousand years of Chinese civilization.

Traditional Chinese opera has a long history. As far back as the third century, simple plays were performed as part of court entertainment. In the 12th century, during the Southern Song Dynasty (1127—1279), more mature forms of opera such as *zaju* (杂剧) or *zaxi* (杂戏) emerged in Zhejiang Province. Opera flourished during the Yuan Dynasty (1271—1368). The Yuan *zaju* is a landmark in the development of traditional Chinese drama. It took social life as its main subject matter and was very popular at that time. Guan Hanqing is considered the greatest Yuan dramatist. One of his plays, *The Injustice Suffered by Dou E*, is still appreciated by today's audiences.

In the later years of the Yuan Dynasty, Yuan *zaju* was gradually replaced by *nanxi* (南戏), a kind of southern opera. In the middle Ming Dynasty, a combination of Yuan *zaju* and *nanxi*, known as Romance Drama or Poetic Drama, appeared. *The Romance of Peony Pavilion* (《牡丹亭》), which is representative of this type of drama, was written by Tang Xianzu, who is referred to as the "Chinese Shakespeare".

During the late Qing Dynasty, a new type of traditional drama—Beijing Opera (京剧)—came into being. In 1790, for the celebration of the 80th birthday of Emperor Qianlong, the first Huiju Opera troupe, the Sanqing (三庆), was invited to Beijing, then followed by the Siqing (四庆), the Wuqing (五庆), the Sixi (四喜), the Chuntai (春台), the Hechun (和春), the Qixiu (启秀), the Nicui (霓翠) and other troupes. The Sanqing, the Sixi, the Chuntai, and the Hechun were the best of them all and were historically called "the Four Great Anhui Troupes (四大徽班)". Their vigorous performance was very fresh and responsive to the common audience in Beijing as well as that in the Qing court and made a good beginning for them to dominate the Beijing stage in the following years. Based on Anhui Opera, Beijing Opera took shape as an independent opera form between 1840 and 1860. Having incorporated the merits of many other local dramas, Beijing Opera not only appeals to Chinese audiences but is warmly welcomed by people all over the world.

In the course of the development of traditional Chinese opera, mutual borrowing has taken place among various types of local operas and new forms have appeared continually. Recent surveys show there are 368 different forms of opera throughout the country. Each variety takes its name from the place where it originated and enjoyed great popularity. The use of local dialects and unique melodies distinguish the different types of operas. Among the best known forms are Beijing Opera, *Kunqu* Opera (昆曲), Henan Opera or Yu Opera (豫剧), Sichuan Opera or Chuan Opera (川剧), Shaoxing Opera or Yue Opera (越剧), Huangmei Opera (黄梅戏), Shaanxi Opera or Qinqiang (秦腔), Hubei Opera or Han Opera (汉剧), and Ping Opera (评剧).

Beijing Opera

Among the hundreds of forms of opera throughout China, Beijing Opera has the greatest influence, enjoys the greatest reputation, and is therefore regarded as the national opera of China (中国国粹).

As mentioned above, towards the end of the 18th century, folk singers of Anhui and Hubei Provinces, who were performing in Beijing at that time, created Beijing Opera by borrowing some of the plays, tunes, and acting skills from each other and by absorbing some of the folk music and tunes from *Kunqu* Opera and Shaanxi Opera. Over time, it developed into a complete repertoire with its own unique artistic style. It is now known as the crown of Chinese opera (中国戏剧之王).

Beijing Opera is an integrative performing art which combines music, singing, dance, dialogue, pantomime, acrobatics, and martial arts. Singing (唱), recitation (念), acting (做), and acrobatic fighting (打) are the four artistic means and the four basic skills of Beijing Opera. An actor or actress in the Beijing Opera has to meet more requirements than those in other forms of performing art. He has to be a performing artist, a singer, and a dancer at the same time. It usually takes a student more than ten years of training to learn singing and acrobatic skills. Thus, it is difficult to be a qualified performer in the Beijing Opera.

Symbolism prevails in the Beijing Opera. The stage of Beijing Opera knows no limit in space or time. It can be the setting for any action. The performers' acting is mostly pantomime. Footwork, gestures, and various kinds of body movements can portray and symbolize the actions of opening a door, climbing a hill, going upstairs, or rowing a boat. When a girl is doing needle work, she has neither a needle nor thread in her hands. When a lady is riding in a carriage, the actress actually has to walk flanked on each side by a flag with a picture of a wheel on it. A horsewhip with colored tassels represents riding a horse. Four generals and four soldiers stand for an army of thousands. In a word, each action of a performer of the Beijing Opera is highly symbolic.

The music of Beijing Opera combines the *erhuang* (二黄) tune from Anhui Opera, the *xipi* (西皮) tune from Hubei Opera, and tunes and musical accompaniment of *Kunqu* Opera. Typical Chinese musical instruments are used in a Beijing Opera orchestra. The two-stringed fiddles *jinghu* (京胡) and *erhu* (二胡) are two of the main instruments. Other instruments include *sheng* (笙) or reed pipes, *yueqin* (月琴) or moon-shaped mandolin, *pipa* (琵琶) or the Chinese lute, *suona* (唢呐) or the Chinese clarinet, drums, bells, gongs, and hardwood castanets.

Singing in the Beijing Opera consists of a score of melodies based on *xipi* and *erhuang* tunes. The *xipi* tune is usually used for expressing strong emotions while *er huang* is a proper tune for deep and sorrowful feelings. Spoken dialogue is done in two forms: *yunbai* (韵白), which sounds like the Hubei and Anhui dialects, and *jingbai* (京白), which sounds like the Beijing dialect. The former is adopted by main and serious characters and the latter by minor and frivolous roles.

The characters of Beijing Opera are classified according to sex, age, profession, social status, as well as disposition. There are four major roles in the Beijing Opera today: *sheng* (生, male), *dan* (旦, female), *jing* (净, male with a painted face), and *chou* (丑, clown).

Sheng refers to male roles and can be subdivided into *laosheng* (老生), middle-aged or elderly men with artificial beards, also called *xusheng* (须生), *wusheng* (武生, men skilled at martial arts), *xiaosheng* (小生, clean-shaven and handsome young men who sing or speak in real and falsetto voices), and *wawasheng* (娃娃生, children).

Dan refers to various female roles, including *laodan* (老旦), *qingyi* (青衣), *huadan* (花旦), *wudan* (武旦), and *caidan* (彩旦). *Laodan* are elderly women who use their natural voices which are rich, loud, high-pitched and melodious. *Qingyi* are generally young or middle-aged women of a strong character, a refined disposition and a strict moral code. *Huadan* are vivacious young women with a frank and out-going personality. *Wudan* are women skilled at martial arts, including generals, heroic forest outlaws (绿林"好汉") and fairies. *Caidan* are clowns in farces (滑稽戏) and comedies.

The notable "Four Great *Dan* Actors (四大名旦)"—Mei Lanfang (梅兰芳), Shang Xiaoyun (尚小云), Cheng Yanqiu (程砚秋), and Xun Huisheng (荀慧生)—made significant contributions to the performance of *dan* roles and the development of Beijing Opera.

Jing refers to roles with painted faces, also known as *hualian* (花脸). They are usually warriors, heroes, statesmen, or even demons. *Jing* can be further divided into *wenjin* (文净, civilian type), *wujing* (武净, warrior type), *zhengjing* (正净, primary face-painted role), and *fujing* (副净, secondary face-painted role).

Chou refers to a sharp-witted, humorous, honest, and kind-hearted clown who is a comic character and can be recognized at first sight by his special make-up, a patch of white paint on his nose. *Chou* is subdivided into *wenchou* (文丑) and *wuchou* (武丑). The former is a comic civilian role who speaks, acts, and sings. The latter is an acrobatic-fighting comic role whose performance involves both speaking and acrobatic fighting.

In the Beijing Opera, performers wear different types of make-up that are consistent with the characters they perform. Colors are used to paint different patterns and designs on the face.

There are two ways to distinguish a character's personality or role type. The first is to understand the color code of the painted face. For example, red is used for loyal and upright characters; purple for loyal, brave, just, and noble characters; black for faithful, brave, stern, honest, and straightforward characters; green for stubborn, irritable, and not easily controlled characters; yellow for fierce, brutal, and calculating characters; white for cunning, imperious, and treacherous people; gold-silvered make-up for ghosts and gods. White make-up between the eyes and nose is specially used for a clown. The second is to understand the lines and patterns drawn on the face. For example, a distorted face, drawn with asymmetrical lines, generally represents a villain or accomplice or someone whose face has been wounded.

The costumes in the Beijing Opera impress the audience with the bright colors and magnificent embroidery. Some of the costumes used in today's performances have a resemblance to the fashion of the Ming Dynasty. The employment of color in costume designing is also an art. Different robe colors indicate different social status—yellow for the imperial family, red for high nobility, red-and-blue for upright people, white for old officials and black for people of violent nature. There are appropriate costumes for each role. A scholar usually wears a blue gown; a general wears padded armor; an emperor wears a dragon robe. Besides gorgeous clothes and headdresses, jeweled girdles for men and hair ornaments for women are also used in the Beijing Opera.

Mei Lanfang—The Greatest Master of the Beijing Opera

Mei Lanfang, the greatest master of the Beijing Opera, made outstanding contributions to the development of the opera and the spread of the beauty of Chinese theatre all over the world. Mei was born in Beijing into a family of Beijing Opera performers. He started to learn the art of

opera when he was a little boy. He made his debut at the age of

eleven and became well-known before he reached twenty.

Mei not only inherited the fine traditions of the Beijing

Opera, but also improved them with his own creations. In his

actor's career of fifty years, he played more than one hundred

roles, which included emperor's concubines, daughters of noble

families, women generals, and goddesses. In his performances,

Mei Lanfang

he demonstrated the different characters and personalities of these women. He was the first to

change the tradition that female characters paid attention only to singing or acrobatic skills.

Instead he combined singing, dancing, expression, and martial arts to develop comprehensive

roles.

Mei designed various kinds of dances to help to express the roles he played. In the opera

Conqueror Xiang Yu Parts with His Concubine (《霸王别姬》), he used a sort of sword dance (剑

舞). Through the gentle yet forceful movements of the sword, the audience saw the heroine's

bravery, gentleness, and loveliness. For the opera *The Fairy Scattering Flowers* (《天女散花》), he

designed a silk-ribbon dance (长绸舞) based on ancient Buddhist grotto frescoes. With two

colorful ribbons tied to his body he danced with the elegance of a fairy flying in the sky. In

addition, he created a plate dance (盘舞), a horsetail whisk dance (拂尘舞), a feather dance (羽

舞), and a floral sickle dance (花镰舞). The repertory of the Mei Lanfang School (梅派) includes

Conqueror Xiang Yu Parts with His Concubine, *The Fairy Scattering Flowers*, *The Drunken Beauty*

(《贵妃醉酒》), *A Startling Dream of Wandering through the Garden* (《游园惊梦》), *Beauty Defies*

Tyranny (《宇宙锋》), *Mu Guiying Assumes Command* (《穆桂英挂帅》), *The Fisherman's Revenge*

(《打渔杀家》), and *Phoenix Returns to Its Nest* (《凤还巢》).

Mei Lanfang was the first person to introduce the *erhu*, a two-stringed musical instrument,

into the Beijing Opera orchestra. Today more than 100 years since the introduction, *erhu* has

become one of the main orchestral instruments for Beijing Opera. Under Mei's direction, Western

musical instruments were also used in the accompaniment for the Beijing Opera. His other stage

innovations contain changes in hair styles and color of the costumes employed in the opera.

Mei Lanfang was also the first person to introduce Beijing Opera to foreign countries. With

his troupe, Mei Lanfang visited Japan three times. During his first visit to Japan in 1919, he was

praised as an "outstanding performer of Oriental art". In 1930, the master and his troupe toured the United States. In spite of the Great Depression, all the tickets for the two-week premiere were sold out in only three days. Mei's performances were a great success. Justin Brooks Atkinson, the drama critic, said in the *New York Times* (《纽约时报》): "You may feel yourself vaguely in contact, not with the sensation of the moment, but with the strange ripeness of centuries." During his stay in the United States, he met with the famous motion-picture actor Charles Chaplin and the American singer Paul Robeson. Six years later, Mei Lanfang introduced Beijing Opera to the Soviet Union where he had the chance to meet the theatre greats Konstantin Stanislavski (康斯坦丁·斯坦尼斯拉夫斯基), Vladimir Nemirovich-Danchenko (弗拉基米尔·聂米罗维奇-丹钦科), and Vsevolod Meyerhold (弗谢沃洛德·梅耶荷德) as well as other artists. They all felt that they could learn from the superb acting forms in the Beijing Opera.

Kunqu Opera

Kunqu Opera is one of the oldest operas in China and is considered the mother of many other types of traditional operas. At the end of Yuan and the beginning of the Ming Period, the playwright and musician Gu Jian (顾坚) from Kunshan (昆山), with the help of Yang Tiedi (杨铁笛) and others, improved southern songs and music and created this Kunshan Opera, though it was not mature at all at the beginning. Up to the middle of the 16th century, the opera was innovated by the musician Wei Liangfu (魏良辅) who, after 10 years of study, improved and refined the contemporary music, and created a new style of singing called "water mill tunes (水磨调)". It combined the best characteristics of Yiyang Opera (弋阳腔), Haiyan Opera (海盐腔) and other local music and superseded the earlier simple and plain style of singing. Kunshan Opera soon became very popular in the whole country and eventually replaced all other genres of the Romance Drama. It influenced Beijing Opera greatly. *Kunqu* Opera is known for its gentle and clear vocals, beautiful and refined tunes, and dance-like stage performance.

However, towards the end of the Qing Dynasty, *Kunqu* Opera lost its appeal and was on the verge of extinction. Its fate has also attracted worldwide attention. In 2001, it was put on the list of the Oral and Intangible Cultural Heritage (人类口头非物质文化遗产) by the United Nations Educational, Scientific and Cultural Organization (UNESCO, 联合国教科文组织).

With efforts from many aspects, *Kunqu* Opera seems to have escaped from the fate of extinction. Suzhou Kunqu Opera Theatre of Jiangsu Province produced the young lovers' edition of *The Romance of Peony Pavilion* in April 2004, which has been performed over 70 times. There are many other plays that continue to be famous today, including *The Palace of Eternal Life* (《长生殿》).

Du Li'niang and Liu Mengmei in *The Romance of Peony Pavilion*

Henan Opera

Henan Opera, one of the most influential Chinese local operas, is also called Henan *Bangzi* (河南梆子). With Henan Province as its birthplace, Henan Opera is popular mostly in the areas of the Yellow River and Huai River.

Henan Opera is famous for its demanding melodies, strong rhythms and intensive use of spoken language. It is popular among the broad masses for it is full of local features and rich flavors of life.

Chang Xiangyu in *Hua Mulan*

There are over 600 traditional plays in the repertoire of Henan Opera, and among the best-known are Chang Xiangyu (常香玉)'s *Kao Hong* (《拷红》), *White Snake Story* (《白蛇传》), and *Hua Mulan* (《花木兰》), and Ma Jinfeng (马金凤)'s *Mu Guiying Assumes Command* (《穆桂英挂帅》) and *Chaoyang Ditch* (《朝阳沟》).

Sichuan Opera

In the mid-18th century, in Sichuan Province and some parts of Yunnan and Guizhou Provinces, *Kunqu* Opera and High-Pitched Opera (高腔) were commonly performed together with the local operas; sometimes they were shown on the same stage. Influenced by each other, they blended into a new opera category designated as Sichuan Opera.

As a type of local opera, Sichuan Opera has a strong literary quality, and is full of wit, humour and lively dialogue with a pronounced local flavor. It also has its own unique system of stylized movement. Sichuan Opera used stunts (特技) to create characters such as immortals who have a third eye on their forehead that can open suddenly to reveal their supernatural power. Its representative stunts include quick changes of facial masks without changing make-up, spitting fire, jumping through burning hoops, and swallowing swords.

Face Changing in Sichuan Opera

The technique of "face changing (变脸)" is usually performed in Sichuan Opera. The specially trained performers are so agile that just by turning their bodies quickly, they make each change. This is achieved by the performers secretly tearing away a single layer of multiple layers of masks for each change of facial expression. With a swipe of a fan, a turn of the head, a wave of the hand or a blink of the eyes, Sichuan Opera performers change masks instantaneously, seemingly by magic, sometimes in less than a second. Wearing brightly colored costumes and heavy, colorful makeup, performers sing in a high pitch and move to quick, dramatic music, twirling, hopping, rolling, jumping and performing surprising stunts. As they move, they also change masks to reveal characters' changing emotions. It is said that face changing was invented in ancient times to scare away wild animals with frightening masks. Sichuan artists borrowed this practice and integrated it into opera and considered it a secret weapon. The art of face changing has been passed down through families as a closely guarded secret. In 1987, the skills of face changing were listed as a "second-level state secret" by China's Ministry of Culture.

Shaoxing Opera

Shaoxing Opera, as one type of traditional opera, originated in Shengxian county (嵊县), Zhejiang Province, but is popular throughout Zhejiang Province and Shanghai as well as in many large and medium-sized cities throughout China. The soft and gentle music of this opera evokes sentimental emotions, and the acting style is likewise graceful and refined. Most of the themes are from fairy tales, literary classics and historical stories. Representative works of Shaoxing Opera include *The Butterfly Lovers*, *A Dream of the Red Mansions*, *The Romance of the Western Chamber*, and *Chasing the Fish* (《追鱼》).

The Butterfly Lovers

Huangmei Opera

Huangmei Opera, a type of local opera in Anhui Province, has been performed for over 200 years.

The music of *Huangmei* Opera is its core appeal: light and lyrical. *Huangmei* Opera is easy to understand and learn because it adopts simple words and literary traditions. Like other local Chinese operas, *Huangmei* Opera is also sung in the local dialect and its language is a mixture of northern and southern Anhui dialects and therefore easy to imitate while remaining pleasant to native ears. This is beneficial to the spread of *Huangmei* Opera. Its naturalness, simplicity, and passion are what make *Huangmei* Opera an enduring drama appreciated by many people.

Yan Fengying in *Female Son-in-Law of the Emperor*

Versatile *Huangmei* actress Yan Fengying (严凤英) played a variety of roles in different plays including *The Heavenly Maid and the Mortal* (《天仙配》) and *Female Son-in-Law of the Emperor* (《女驸马》).

/ Folk Performing Arts /

China has a wide variety of folk performing arts featuring, among others, acrobatics, *quyi* (曲艺), puppet plays (木偶戏), shadow plays (皮影戏) and so on.

Acrobatics

The acrobatic art, as a pearl in the treasure chest of traditional Chinese performing arts, has existed in China for more than 2,000 years.

In the long course of its development, Chinese acrobatic art has formed its own style. Ancient acrobatics mirrored people's lives. Instruments like tridents (三叉戟), wicker (柳条) rings, tables, chairs, jars, plates, and bowls were used in their performance, like "Flying Trident" "Balance on Chairs" "Jar Tricks" and "Hoop Diving". All of these acts have become commonplace in acrobatic shows throughout China.

Chinese acrobats have been successful in many international competitions over the years and China is playing a dominating part in acrobatics. Moreover, foreign audiences eulogize this art form as mythical and engrossing. These achievements owe greatly to the unique creativity of Chinese acrobatics over the past centuries.

Quyi

Quyi is a general term covering several different types of performances in which speech, singing, or both are adopted. As an independent art, it was formed in the Mid-Tang Dynasty and thrived in the Song Dynasty. Now about 400 forms of *quyi* are popular among all ethnic groups throughout China. They are crosstalk (相声), clapper talk (快板), *pingshu* (评书), short play (小品) and so on.

Quyi possesses a strong Chinese flavor. Excellent *quyi* items reflect people's thoughts, ideals, and moral aspirations, with many works speaking highly of national heroes, honest officials, faithful lovers, and so on.

Crosstalk is one of the most popular and influential types of *quyi*. Its performance is characterized by talking (说), imitation (学), fun-making (逗), and singing (唱). Satire is its main purpose. This humorous and amusing performing art can be classified into three sub-types: comic monologue (单口相声), comic dialogue (对口相声), and group crosstalk (群口相声). Besides, *shuanghuang* (双簧) or two-men act is a special kind of crosstalk, which features a two-man comic show with one acting in pantomime and another hiding behind him doing all the speaking or singing.

A skilled crosstalk performer must have clear enunciation, and be able to imitate various kinds of people and situations with sound effect. He must also have a good singing voice, be able to master opera melodies and have a repertoire of famous songs. Naturally, every artist has his own style, but the basic aim of any crosstalk performance is to amuse the audience.

Clapper talk is a folk art form. Clapper talk performers usually deliver comic rhymes or monologues to the accompaniment of bamboo clappers.

Pingshu is a kind of storytelling, with *pingshu* performers adding their own commentaries on subjects and characters. *Pingshu* performers also explain the origins of the objects within their stories. So, the audience is not only entertained but also educated and enlightened. This simple art form has merely a single performer standing or sitting at a table, using a gavel (醒木) or a folded fan as the prop (道具).

Short play performances, about 15 minutes in length, were first popularized when televised nationally in 1983. It is regarded as one of the most lively and best-received art forms in China. The short, brisk, humorous, and often poignant comic skits (讽刺剧) have become popular items at China's Spring Festival Gala Show (春节联欢晚会) for more than 40 years.

Puppet play is considered to have begun in the Han Dynasty and risen to prominence in the Tang Dynasty. With a history of roughly 2,000 years, the Chinese puppet play combines elements of singing, dancing, painting, and sculpture.

Puppet Play

In puppet plays, actors or specially-trained operations manipulate the puppets with their hands and fingers by means of sticks and strings.

Puppet plays are usually accompanied by tunes from local operas. The spirit of traditional Chinese puppet shows combined with the latest technology has enabled it to develop and play a significant role in religious ceremonies and folk festivities.

Shadow play is one of the most ancient genres of drama in China. It first appeared about 2, 000 years ago and by the Song Dynasty it had become highly developed. The performers manipulate colorful leather or cardboard figures whose silhouettes (侧影) are mirrored on a screen by lantern light. The silhouettes are seen performing on the screen while the real actor who operates the silhouettes sings to the accompaniment of music behind the scene.

Shadow Play

With their strong local characteristics, the shadow puppets are valuable folk handicrafts, which are now being collected by many art museums and shadow play enthusiasts.

/ Traditional Musical Instruments /

The tradition of Chinese music dates back to remote antiquity. Governing the country and nourishing the mind through music are two of the main functions of this tradition.

Governance Through Music

According to ancient Chinese culture, rituals provided the norms of conduct for people. The goal was to maintain social order. Music was for the mind's cultivation and expression. Its purpose was to enhance people's outlook on life and imbue them with energy and creativity, so that they could enjoy a more harmonious and happier spiritual life. Individual contentment would then lead to social harmony, as well as to a more harmonious relationship between people and nature. The highest level of ancient Chinese music was to represent spiritual harmony with nature.

The prominent stature of music in ancient China explains the emergence of sophisticated instruments from early times. Chime bells (编钟) were one example. First used in the Shang Dynasty, they became popular during the Western Zhou Dynasty (1046 B.C.E.—771 B.C.E.). In 1978, a fine set of Chime bells was unearthed in Hubei Province, from the tomb of Marquis Yi (曾侯乙), a local lord in a small state called Zeng during the Warring States Period.

The Marquis Yi chime bells consist of 65 bells arranged in three vows. The first row includes 19 *niu* bells (钮钟), and the second and third rows include 45 *yong* bells (甬钟). The bells in each row differ from one another in shape and size, emanating different tones. In addition, there is a separate and much larger bell used to adjust pitch. Like the bells, the frame is made of bronze, weighing as much as five tons or more. The total weight of the bells is more than 400 kilograms. While the bells bear inscriptions totaling over 2,800 Chinese characters relating to music and the making of the instrument, the frame is carved with exquisite patterns in relief and fretwork (会纹细工). Instruments of such a scale and such fine craftsmanship were quite rare in the world at the time.

Five musicians were needed to play the instrument. Each bell produces two tones when struck at the respective sound points as marked. The entire set of chime bells is able to produce all the tones of a modern piano.

Marquis Yi Chime Bells

The grandeur and precision of the Marquis Yi chime bells epitomize ancient Chinese society's emphasis on music as a means to promote personal cultivation and social harmony. Xun Zi, a great Confucian thinker of the Warring States Period, gave music the same stature as rituals, stating, "Musical education enables people to purify their minds. Rituals are established to temper people's conduct. With music and rituals, people are imbued with clearer, more intelligent and peaceful minds. They also improve their ways and manners. Thus the country enjoys peace, with beauty and compassion complementing each other."

"Music brings harmony" is an important concept that has influenced Chinese culture for several thousand years. It stresses harmony as the culture's core value. The tradition guiding rituals and music is that of a harmonious world order.

Consoling the Mind with Music

One cannot talk about Chinese music without mentioning a seven-stringed musical instrument, the Chinese zither (琴), which represented the zenith of cultivated learning in ancient times, followed by go (围棋), calligraphy and painting. As the most ancient instrument in China, the zither has long been a favorite of the literati (文人学士). While music in general was meant to govern the country by promoting harmony, the Chinese zither was more of an individual instrument for solace and personal appreciation.

Chinese Zither

Ancient Chinese literati considered the zither a prerequisite for their cultivation. Its beautiful melodies helped to maintain peace and balance of the mind.

Ambiance was an important aspect in playing the Chinese zither. Zong Bing (宗炳), a painter and musician of the late Eastern Jin Dynasty (317—420) and early Southern Dynasties (420—589), enjoyed playing the zither by a stream in the mountains. As he plucked the strings gently, he would gradually forget where he was. The sounds of the zither mixed with the echoes from the mountains, until the musician found himself at one with nature.

Playing the Chinese zither in the snow was also a favorite pastime for ancient artists, who regarded the instrument as the purest of its kind in the world. A moonlit night was also considered ideal for playing the zither. Wang Wei (王维), a highly accomplished poet of the Tang Dynasty, liked playing the zither in a bamboo forest on moonlit night.

The Chinese zither tends to create a tranquil air. The composition *Wild Geese Landing on the Shallow Shore* (《平沙落雁》) is such an example.

The zither was also an instrument in communication between ancient scholars and artists. The famous zither composition, *Three Stanzas of Plum Blossoms* (《梅花三弄》), was based on an Eastern Jin Dynasty story of the poet Wang Ziyou (王子猷) and the flute player Huan Yi (桓伊). One day, the poet was taking a boat trip when he overheard someone on the riverbank say Huan Yi was passing by. Although the two had never met before, they admired each other as poet and flute player. Despite his lower rank of office, Ziyou sent a family member to request Huan Yi to play the flute. Without hesitation, Huan Yi dismounted (下车) from his carriage and played *Three Stanzas of Plum Blossoms*, while Ziyou listened from his boat. After finishing, Huan Yi mounted his carriage and drove on. Ziyou, too, continued with his boat journey. The two of them exchanged not a single word, yet both were content with the communication of their hearts through the music. The flute's three stanzas were later converted into a composition for the Chinese zither, which has become one of the best-known musical works—as an expression of otherworldly feelings through its eulogy of the plum flowers' purity, fragrance, and resistance against the cold.

Plucked Instruments (弦乐器)

Pipa is an ancient four/three-stringed plucked musical instrument made of wood, with the fingerboard in the shape of a melon-seed, and a long beautiful neck bending backwards. In performance, the player holds it vertically and plucks its four or three strings with five fingers. The most notable traditional musical pieces for *pipa* are *Ambush on All Sides* (《十面埋伏》) and *Spring Moonlight on the Flowers by the River* (《春江花月夜》).

Guzheng (古筝) is a zither-like 21-stringed or 25-stringed plucked musical instrument. It has been popular since ancient times and is one of the main ensemble and solo instruments of traditional Chinese music. It has a special wooden sound body with strings arched across movable bridges along the length of the instrument for the purpose of tuning.

Guzheng

The *guzheng* player attaches a small plectrum (弦乐器拨子) on each finger. For traditional musical pieces, the player often uses three fingers of the right hand to pluck whereas the left hand is used to press the strings from the other side of the bridge to create a tone. For some contemporary musical pieces, both hands are needed to produce complicated harmonies, which means that even the fingers of the left hand need to wear plectrums. The most popular musical pieces for *guzheng* are *Singing on the Return of Fishing Boats* (《渔舟唱晚》) and *High Mount Flowing Water* (《高山流水》).

Erhu (二胡), sometimes known in the West as the "Chinese violin", is a two-string bowed musical instrument and is used as a solo instrument as well as for small ensembles and large orchestras. The sound body of an *erhu* is a small, drum-like case usually made of ebony (乌木) and snake skin. It has a hexagonal shape with the length of about 13 centimeters. The front opening is covered with snake skin and the back is left open. The neck of an *erhu* is about 81 centimeters long and is manufactured with the same material as the drum. The best-known *erhu* piece is *Two Springs Reflect the Moon* (《二泉映月》).

Erhu

Sanxian (三弦) is another plucked musical instrument which has a long three string stem (柄) attached to a wooden cylinder whose ends are covered with skin of the boa (蟒蛇). There are greater *sanxian* (大三弦), which are used as an accompanying instrument in *dagu* (大鼓), and lesser *sanxian* (小三弦), which are used as an accompanying instrument in *Kunqu* Opera.

Yangqin

Yangqin (扬琴) is a traditional musical instrument with up to 100 strings, but played with light hammers.

Percussion Instruments (打击乐器)

Drum is a type of percussion instrument consisting of a hollow cylinder or hemisphere with a membrane (膜) stretched tightly over the end or ends. It is played by beating the membrane with hands or sticks.

Gong (锣) is also a type of percussion instrument made of copper in the shape of a disk and it is beaten with a wooden hammer.

Wind Instruments (管乐器)

Suona (唢呐) or ceremonial horn, is a woodwind instrument, with its mouthpiece made of brass, and its body made of wood. It has seven holes on the obverse side (正面) and one on the reverse side (反面) of the tube. It can produce resonant sounds and is a principal wind instrument of folk bands. *Suona* can also be used as a solo instrument. The best-known *suona* piece is *One Hundred Birds Serenade the Phoenix* (《百鸟朝凤》), in which the exquisite bird mimicry evokes people's love for nature.

Bamboo flute (竹笛) is also a wind instrument made of bamboo, with a row of holes, bamboo membrane and a sound-adjusting hole. It looks like a thin pipe and is played by holding the instrument horizontally across the player's lips, covering the holes and blowing into one side. A vertical bamboo flute is called *xiao* (箫).

Exercises

Part One Comprehension

Fill in the following blanks with the information you learn in Chapter 7.

1. The development of bronze casting made it possible for bronze _____ to emerge in the late Shang Dynasty.

2. Chines scripts are generally divided into five styles: the seal script, the official script or the clerical script, the cursive script, the _____ script, and the running script.

3. Wang Xizhi from the Eastern Jin Dynasty has been always honored and worshiped as the "Sage of Chinese _____" in history.

4. Among the numerous ancient Chinese painters, Wu Daozi in the Tang Dynasty was regarded as the "Sage of Traditional Chinese Painting" and the _____ master of Tang figure painting.

5. Bada Shanren's paintings look _____ to the public and even to many artists.

6. Singing, _____, acting, and acrobatic fighting are the four artistic means and the four

basic skills of Beijing Opera.

7. *Kunqu* Opera is one of the oldest opera in China and is considered the _____ of many other types of traditional operas.

8. The technique of "_____" is usually performed in Sichuan Opera.

9. A skilled crosstalk performer must have clear enunciation, and be able to _____ various kinds of people and situations with sound effect.

10. *Erhu*, sometimes know in the West as the "Chinese _____", is a two-string bowed musical instrument and is used as a solo instrument as well as for small ensembles and large orchestras.

Part Two   Translation

Passage Translation

　　汉字是从图画和符号演变而来,中国书法艺术则是从其独特的书写方式发展而来。书法通过字的独特结构、字体和运笔的方法,表达了艺术家的道德、性格、感情、审美和文化观,给读者以美的享受。因此,许多人认为"字如其人"。书法也被认为是一种保持健康的有效方法,因为它可以使人放松,也可以自娱自乐。随着书写工具的更新,除传统毛笔书法之外,硬笔书法及其他书法艺术蓬勃兴起。中国书法作为一种高雅的艺术形式已随着中国文化传播到日本、韩国、新加坡和越南等周边国家,成为东方艺术独有的特点。

Part Three   Critical Thinking and Discussion

1. Which calligrapher (s) and what style (s) do you like best? Why?

2. What are the main characteristics of Chinese painting?

3. What is your attitude towards Chinese calligraphy?

4. Suppose you are going to give a performance at a party, in a month's preparation, what kind of traditional Chinese arts would you like to show to other people? How would you practice or learn this kind of art?

Chapter 8
Science & Technology in Ancient China

For more than a millennium, from the Qin Dynasty to the early period of the Ming Dynasty, science and technology in China contributed greatly to the advance of human civilization.

Ancient China had a well-developed agricultural system along with advanced irrigation. It also boasted an independent tradition in medicine and some advanced botanical (植物学的) knowledge.

China's Four Great Inventions (四大发明), namely, the compass, paper-making, gunpowder, and printing, not only changed the world but also accelerated the evolution of world history. China has further contributed to the world with its rich heritage of silk and porcelain.

The world's most detailed and earliest astronomical records (天文记录) were kept by the ancient Chinese. They are the first to take note of such astronomical phenomena as comets, sunspots (太阳黑子) and new stars, producing the most advanced astronomical observatory apparatus of the time.

Ancient China once played a dominant role in metallurgy (冶金学). Cast iron was produced in China as early as the 6th century B.C.E., while it was produced just sporadically in Europe in the 14th century.

Ancient China also made great achievements in mathematics (数学), agronomy (农学), and medicine science (医学).

/ Four Great Inventions /

Westerners may know little about China's feats in the past, but they are familiar with China's Four Great Inventions. These four inventions have become important symbols of China's role in the world's civilization.

Compass

Compass is a device showing geographic directions by using the earth's magnetic field. It enabled trade and exploration to develop on a worldwide scale.

As early as in the Warring States Period, while mining ores and melting copper and iron, Chinese people discovered accidentally a natural magnetite that attracted iron and pointed fixedly north. Referred to as a "south pointer", the spoon- or ladle-shaped compass is made of magnetic lodestone, and the plate is bronze. The circular center represents Heaven, and the square plate represents Earth.

Chinese characters on the plate denote the eight main directions of north, northeast, east, and so on. This type of compass has been scientifically tested and proved to work tolerably well. The earliest record of the use of a compass in navigation was in the Song Dynasty.

Without the invention of compass, many historic ocean voyages such as Zheng He's seven voyages to the Western Seas (郑和七下西洋), Christopher Columbus's discovery of America (克里斯托弗·哥伦布发现美洲), the voyage to India by Vasco da Gama (达·伽马航行到印度), and Ferdinand Magellan's round-the-world voyage (斐迪南·麦哲伦环球航行) would have been inconceivable.

Compass

The compass vehicle was said to have been invented by the Yellow Emperor. It was an ancient Chinese vehicle equipped with many gear wheels and a wooden figure that always pointed south no matter which direction the vehicle went. It is an earlier and more primitive form of compass.

Paper-Making

Paper has been a major medium for recording, transmitting, and storing information throughout human civilization. In Chinese history, the earliest characters were inscribed on bones, tortoise shells, and bronze ware at first and later on silk, bamboo, and wood.

Bamboo slips (竹简) were used as a form of book for the longest time in Chinese history before the invention of paper. Bamboo slips, for the first time, liberated characters from a confined circle of the upper class of society and introduced them into a much broader circle. Hence, bamboo slips played a key role in the spreading of Chinese culture.

But bamboo slips were too clumsy, and thus difficult to handle; a book would need a large number of slips. Emperor Qinshihuang once complained that he had to read intensively and comment on 60 kilograms of official documents every day and a courtier of the Western Han Dynasty was said to have presented a petition to the emperor written on about 3,000 bamboo slips, which had to be carried into the court by two strong men. On the other hand, silk was too expensive for common people to use for writing. Better materials were badly needed.

In the Western Han Dynasty, paper was invented, but in the Eastern Han Dynasty, a court official named Cai Lun (蔡伦) adopted inexpensive materials such as bark, hemp (麻头), rags, fishnet, and other materials to make paper, known as Cai Lun Paper (蔡侯纸). The materials were soaked, cut into pieces, boiled with plant ashes, washed, and grounded with a pestle (杵) in a mortar (臼). The mixture was then poured evenly on a flat surface to dry, or baked to become paper. Cai Lun Paper was relatively cheap, light, thin, durable, and more suitable for brush-writing. In later periods, different materials were used for making paper, and its quality became better and better. The famous Xuan paper (宣

Cai Lun

纸), produced in Xuanzhou, Anhui, first appeared in the Tang Dynasty. Made in an 18-step process from the bark of the wingceltis (青檀) tree and rice straw, Xuan paper is snow-white, soft, durable, absorbent, and moth-proof. Hence, it is a principal type of paper for traditional Chinese calligraphy and painting. During the Song Dynasty, bamboo began to be used for making paper, and the output of bamboo paper increased rapidly.

China's paper-making technique was first introduced to the Korean Peninsula and Vietnam, then to Japan, Arab countries, Europe, and the rest of the world, contributing greatly to the dissemination of knowledge all over the world. One point worthwhile to mention is that Europe knew how to make paper about a thousand years later than China.

Gunpowder

Gunpowder was invented in China, not by people seeking better weapons or even explosives, but by alchemists seeking the elixir of immortality. Ancient Chinese alchemists believed that by putting different elements in a big pot and heating the pot for a long period of time, an element leading to immortality would be distilled.

The Chinese invented gunpowder over 1,100 years ago. Towards the end of the Tang Dynasty, gunpowder was first used in war. In 904, during a battle between local forces, a weapon then called "Flying Fire" was used. It was a packet of gunpowder tied to the head of an arrow. After the fuse was lit, the arrow was shot to the enemy side, and the gunpowder would cause damage or kill men. During the Song, Yuan, and Ming Dynasties, military applications of gunpowder became common and other weapons like the "Bronze Cannon" and "Two-Stage Rockets" were invented. In the Yuan Dynasty, the method of making gunpowder was introduced to the Arab world. In the 14th century, some European countries began to make gunpowder weapons with methods they had learned from the Arabs. The introduction of gunpowder to the world had brought a series of revolutions to weapon manufacturing, as well as to stratagems and tactics on the battlefield.

Printing

Printing, known as the "mother of civilization", was another great invention made by Chinese people. It has a long history and includes block printing (雕版印刷) and movable type printing (活字印刷).

Before printing was invented, people had to rely on handwriting to reproduce a book. It was very slow and errors easily occurred. Block printing first appeared in the early Tang Period. It was developed from the use of seals and stone engraving. Words engraved on stones could last very long, and later, in about the 4th century, the method of rubbing a piece of paper on an engraved stone covered with ink was used to make copies. This gave workers the idea of engraving words on a wood-block and printing them. With the rapid development of the economy and culture in the Tang Dynasty, books and other publications like calendars were needed by the public, and this demand promoted wood-block printing. According to records in certain books, block printing was very common in the late Tang Period.

The world's oldest surviving book made through block printing is *Vajra Sutra* (《金刚经》).

Block printing was inconvenient and time-consuming as blocks had to be engraved each time a new book was printed. It could take several years to finish making the blocks for a thick book, and there had to be large places for storing these blocks. What's more, all the blocks were useless after the printing and a single mistake in engraving could ruin the entire block. To overcome these shortcomings, Bi Sheng (毕昇) invented the movable type printing during the years between 1041 and 1048, which ushered in a major revolution in the history of printing. It was about 400 years earlier than Europe's.

Bi Sheng

Movable type printing involved engraving single words into pieces of clay, heating them by fire until hardened and using them as permanent type. The type was then set into printing plates.

Obviously, movable type printing has its advantages. After being hardened by fire, the type became durable and could be re-used. The pieces of movable type could be glued to an iron plate and later easily detached. Many characters could be assembled to print a page and then broken up and redistributed or stored as needed.

Bi Sheng's invention made printing faster and easier than before. Later, movable type printing developed very quickly with the appearance of wood, tin, copper and lead blocks.

/ Other Impressive Ancient Inventions /

Besides the above-mentioned Four Great Inventions, the ancient Chinese had brought many other valuable inventions to mankind such as fireworks (鞭炮), silk (丝绸), porcelain (瓷器), abacus (算盘), seismograph (地震仪), anaesthetic (麻药), *weiqi* (围棋), and so on.

Fireworks

Fireworks were probably first made by stuffing gunpowder into bamboo sticks. It was generally believed that explosions would scare off evil spirits and ghosts. The tradition of setting off fireworks on holidays is still very popular in China.

Silk

Silk was first produced in ancient China, with some of the earliest found in as early as 3,500 B.C.E. Silk was originally reserved by emperors and nobles for their own use or as gifts to others, and later spread to other countries of the world.

Porcelain

Porcelain is made generally from clay in the form of kaolin (高龄土). It is heated at 1,200—1,400 degrees centigrade while ordinary ceramics (陶器) are baked at about 500 degrees centigrade. The first porcelain pots were usually white- or cream-colored until artists started using glazing paints in the 13th century. The first glazing color was blue from the mineral cobalt (钴).

Abacus

Abacus is an early form of calculator. It is a frame with rows of beads around the rods that are used for calculations. Usually, it is separated into two sections, with two beads above, each representing the number five, and five beads below, each representing the number one. Abacus was used for the four fundamental operations (加减乘除四则运算) of arithmetic. The Chinese invented the abacus sometime in the second century B.C.E.

Seismograph

Zhang Heng (张衡), an outstanding astronomer of the Eastern Han Dynasty, invented a seismograph to indicate the direction of a distant earthquake. The seismograph worked as follows: It dropped a bronze ball from one of eight tuned projections shaped as dragon heads; the ball fell into the mouth of a corresponding metal object shaped as a toad, each representing a direction. It was over 1,700 years later that a similar instrument was invented in Europe.

Zhang Heng and His Seismograph

Anaesthetic

Anaesthetic is necessary for surgical operations. As early as the Warring States Period, Bian Que (扁鹊) had concocted (配制) an anaesthetic called "toxic wine" to be used in surgical operations. In the third century, the most famous surgeon Hua Tuo (华佗) of the Eastern Han Dynasty, the father of Chinese surgery, invented *mafeisan* (麻沸散), a kind of oral anaesthetic which was said to have been used for patients undergoing abdominal surgery.

Weiqi

Weiqi, or go, is a popular board game that originated in China. It is played with black and white pieces on a square wooden board with 361 intersections formed by 19 vertical lines and 19 horizontal lines. The person who has the most pieces walled in will have the most points and be declared as the winner.

/ Mathematics /

China was the first country to establish the decimal counting method (十进位计数法). In the first century, the Chinese had mastered the concepts of fractions (分数) and positive and negative numbers (正负数) and proposed the "Pythagorean Theorem (勾股定理)" for right triangle. In the third century, Liu Hui (刘徽), a mathematician in the Wei and Jin Dynasties, used a special technique called "Circle Segmenting Method (割圆术)" to work out a Pi or circumference ratio of 3.1416. The concept of mathematical limits associated with the "Circle Segmenting Method" was not known to European mathematicians until 1,500 years later. *The Nine Chapters on Mathematical Art* (《九章算术注》) by Liu Hui is the most important work in *Suan Jing Shi Shu* (《算经十书》) and the first mathematics monograph in China. *The Nine Chapters on Mathematical Art* is rich in content, summarizing the mathematical achievements of the Warring States, and Qin and Han Dynasties. It was a comprehensive historical work, the most concise and effective applied mathematics in the world at that time, and its appearance marked the formation of a complete system of ancient Chinese mathematics. During the Northern and Southern Dynasties, remarkable mathematician Zu Chongzhi (祖冲之) refined Pi to 3.1415926—3.1415927, and expressed Pi as a fraction of 355/113. After 1,000 years, the German mathematician Wolter (渥脱) achieved the same result. "Zu Geng's Axiom (祖暅公理)" for calculating the volume of a sphere, invented by Zu Geng (祖暅) who was Zu Chongzhi's son, was also 1,000 years ahead of European mathematicians.

/ Agronomy /

China, as one of the four oldest recorded civilizations in the world, is said to have its advanced agricultural science and technology as its symbol. As early as about 6000 B.C.E.—

5000 B.C.E., China's Yellow River and Yangtze River valleys were farmed. By the Western Zhou Dynasty, the production pattern with agriculture as the main and animal husbandry as the auxiliary had been formed. The rulers have always attached great importance to agricultural production, so China has long formed a unique system of agronomy.

According to *The Book of Changes* (《易经》), Shen Nong (神农氏), a legendary figure, once invented *lei* (耒) and *si* (耜). *Lei* is a wooden handle at the upper end for grasping the wooden shovel; *Si* refers to a sharp-shaped wooden shovel. The classic of *Guan Zi: Sea King* (《管子·海王》) says: "A cultivator must have one wooden-stone plow and a small cooking pan with handles and spout (铫)." When copper and iron were used to make farm tools, the wooden-stone plow became a metal one, reflecting the technical level of agricultural production at that time from the perspective of tools. After the Qin and Han Dynasties, there appeared an "animal-drawn sowing plow (耧车)" which was a high-efficiency tool, combining the two working procedures of ploughing land and sowing seeds together. Animal-drawn sowing plows were driven by cattles, equipped with both the plow for cultivating land and the funnel for holding seeds. As the device moved forward, the ground was ploughed, and the seeds slipped from the funnel into the ground.

Chinese agriculture is characterized by intensive farming. With land being the basis of the planting industry, the Chinese ancestors have long noticed that "soil appropriateness (土宜)" may serve as the key factor for high yield.

China is one of the largest and the earliest countries of origins of fruit trees in the world. Traditionally, the north in China is noted for peach trees (桃树), plum trees (李树), persimmon trees (柿树) and jujube trees (枣树), the south in China for citrus trees (柑橘树) and litchi trees (荔枝树). Peach trees have been cultivated for more than 3,000 years in China. From *The Book of Songs* (《诗经》), the verse "Peach blossoms bloom tens of millions of flowers, bright colors look like red fire." describes the lush peach trees. Roughly in the Han Dynasty, peach trees were introduced into Iran from China's northwestern areas through Central Asia, and then spread to European countries. In the second half of the 19th century, Japan and America introduced honey peach trees and flat peach trees from China.

There are more than 300 kinds of special agricultural books in Chinese cultural classics. *The Book of Si Shengzhi* (《氾胜之书》), *Qi Min Yao Shu* or *Important Arts for Qi People* (《齐民要术》), *The Book of Agriculture* (《农书》) and *The Book of Agricultural Administration* (《农政全书》) are called the Four Agricultural Books (四大农书) in ancient China, which represent the level of agricultural science and technology in ancient China.

The Book of Si Shengzhi is the earliest agricultural book left present. On the basis of summing up the experience of agricultural production, Si Shengzhi (汜胜之) had written an agricultural book containing 18 pieces, which is called *The Book of Si Shengzhi*. The book summarizes the farming experience in northern China, mainly in Guanzhong region (关中地区), and puts forward the "Six-Link Theory (六环节理论)" of agricultural production, namely, farming in time, improving and utilizing land resources, fertilizing, irrigating, weeding in time and harvesting in time, and has made concrete explanations for each link.

Qi Min Yao Shu is the oldest extant agricultural book, written by Jia Sixie (贾思勰) of the Northern Wei Dynasty, who served as the prefecture chief of Gao Yang (today's Linzi County in Shandong Province). In order to write this book, Jia Sixie not only read a lot of literature, but also personally consulted the old farmers, established a more complete agricultural system in it, and made a reasonable division of the agricultural category with the characteristics of practicality. *Qi Min Yao Shu* is a great agricultural work, which brilliantly and thoroughly discusses the key technical problems of

Qi Min Yao Shu

dry land farming in the middle and lower reaches of the Yellow River, regulating basic farming measures such as ploughing land (耕地), harrowing land (耙地), leveling land (耱地), and so on. The detailed discussions on animal breeding and plant growing technology and agricultural products processing, brewing, cooking, and storage are also made in this book. As an encyclopedia of agronomy, *Qi Min Yao Shu* not only laid the foundation for the development of agronomy in China, but also played an important role in the history of the development of agricultural science in the world. Jia Sixie is generally considered the "Sage of Agronomy (农圣)" in Chinese history.

/ Traditional Chinese Medicine (TCM) /

Before Western medicine came into China, traditional Chinese medicine had been the major guarantee for people's health for about 5,000 years. In modern times, it is still a principal means of health care for the Chinese and still provides solutions to some serious diseases which modern medicine has failed to address.

Traditional Chinese medicine (TCM) is an important part of the cultural heritage of the nation. Developed over the course of more than five thousand years, the system is unique because of its complete dialectical theoretical framework, diagnostic methods, pharmacology, and special methods of treatment, including acupuncture and moxibustion, deep breathing, and medical massage.

TCM with a unique and profound theoretical system has a long and independent history of more than 3,000 years. It occupies an important place in the ancient and glorious civilization of the country and has become a shining gem in the eyes of more and more people in the world.

Theoretical Framework of TCM

TCM believes that opposite but unitive phenomena between *yin* (阴, negative) and *yang* (阳, positive) exist between rostral and caudal, inside and outside, exterior and interior, dorsal and ventral aspects of every tissue and structure of the human body (人体上下、内外、表里、前后各组织结构之间，以及每一组织结构本身，无不包含着阴阳对立统一现象). The ancient philosophical concepts of *yin* and *yang* as well as the Five Elements (五行) serve as the theoretical basis of TCM. These concepts are embodied in every aspect of TCM's theoretical system, explaining the tissues and structures, physiology and pathology of the human body, and direct clinical diagnosis and treatment.

So far as the internal organs in the body are concerned, the five viscera (heart, liver, spleen, lung and kidney) are *yin*, because their functions of preserving vital substances tend to be stable, while the six bowel organs (gall-bladder, stomach, large intestine, small intestine, urinary bladder and triple warmer) are *yang*, because their functions of transmitting and digesting water and food tend to be active. When speaking of each organ, its function is *yang* and its substance is *yin* (功能为阳，物质为阴).

The *yin* and *yang* theory holds that everything, or every phenomenon in the universe, consists of two forces, *yin* and *yang* that oppose each other and at the same time complement each other. The human body is also made up of *yin* and *yang* elements. The normal physiological functions of the human body result from the opposite, unitive and coordinate relation between *yang* (function) and *yin* (substance). *Yin* and *yang* are always in a state of dynamic balance. It is known as "*Yin* is even and well while *yang* is firm, hence a relative equilibrium is maintained and health is guaranteed (阴平阳秘，精神乃治)." That is to say, when there is a balance between the two, there is no disease. On the contrary, the imbalance will bring about disease. For example, preponderance of *yang* leads to hyperfunction of the organism and heat manifestations, while the preponderance of *yin* hyperfunction of the organism leads to endogenous cold (阳盛则热, 阴盛则寒). Deficiency of *yang* brings on symptoms of external cold while deficiency of *yin* as the result of exhausted vital essence leads to endogenous heat (阳虚生外寒, 阴虚生内热). *Yang* in excess makes *yin* suffer, while *yin* in excess makes *yang* suffer (阳盛则阴病, 阴盛则阳病).

The theory of the Five Elements assumes that the material world is basically made up of five elements of metal (金), wood (木), water (水), fire (火), and earth (土). Among these elements, there exists an interdependence and inter-restraint which determines their state of constant changes. The human body is regarded as part of the physical world and the internal organs such as the liver, heart, spleen, lungs, and kidney correspond with the five elements of the universe. For instance, the liver is considered to have the quality of wood which can be lit up by fire. Thus, a person with a liver disorder can easily get angry. In this way, the development and change of the physiological and pathological phenomena of humans can be explained in terms of the developments and changes in nature.

Guided by these two theories, doctors of TCM emphasize not only local treatment but treatment of the whole body, which is aimed at readjusting its balance. Attention is also paid to the season of the year, the environment, and living conditions of the patient. It is usually the case that even if two patients have the same symptoms and are diagnosed as having the same disease, doctors of TCM will prescribe different drugs for them because of the differences in the internal and external conditions of the patients. In other words, Chinese practitioners of traditional medicine take a holistic approach to diagnosis. They take the diet, age, habits, emotions, lifestyle and living environment of the patient into consideration. They pay particular attention to the causes of the illness rather than the symptoms. So, to some degree, surgery to relieve symptoms is not encouraged in Chinese medicine.

Another important theory in TCM is the theory of *jing* (经, channel) and *luo* (络, collateral) which is the basis of such therapeutic treatments as acupuncture and moxibustion. According to the theory, the internal organs and the limbs of the human body are related and linked by channels through which blood and *qi* (气, vital energy) circulate. The main channels that run longitudinally are called *jing* while the branches that run latitudinally are called *luo*. If there is a blockage in either *jing* or *luo*, the blood and vital energy cannot pass through. In time, it affects a person's health. To clear the blockage and ensure the free flow of blood and vital energy is the first and fundamental step in curing a disease.

Generally speaking, TCM is based on the premise that the cause of sickness is an imbalance and blockage of the flow of *qi*, a vital force or energy instrumental for the workings of the human body and mind. Treatment focuses on the profile (病历) of the patient and stresses the impact on the patient's *qi*. There are many ways in which imbalance in *qi* can be corrected. These ways include acupuncture, herbal medicine, massage (按摩), diets, and corrective breathing exercises such as *tai chi chuan* (太极拳) or *qigong* (气功).

Fundamental Characteristics of TCM

TCM has a number of characteristics both in the understanding of the human body's physiology and pathology and in the diagnosis and treatment of diseases. These characteristics, however, can be summarized in the following two respects.

The Concept of the Organic Whole

By "organic whole (整体)" we mean the unity within the human body and the unified relations between the human body and the outside world. The human body is made up of viscera, bowels, tissues and other organs. Each of them has its own special physiological function which is a component part of the entire life process of the body. As a unity, all the parts, with the five viscera as centers, are inseparable from each other in structure, related, subsidiary and conditional to each other in physiology, and of certain influence upon each other in pathology. For instance, the heart is interior-exteriorly related to the small intestine, controls blood circulation, and has its "specific opening" in the tongue proper (心合小肠，主血脉，开窍于舌). So the physiological functions and pathological changes of the heart can be known by observing the tongue, for example, pale tongue indicates the blood deficiency of the heart. To cure it, the first important thing of all is to find out where the key pathogenesis (发病机理) is according to the relationship between the heart and the tongue, by taking into consideration the concept of the organism as a whole and by making a comprehensive analysis of the case.

Man lives in nature and takes nature as his vital condition for living. So TCM maintains that man is influenced directly or indirectly by the movements and changes in nature, to which he is bound to make corresponding physiological and pathological responses. For instance, as the climate varies with the four seasons in a year, the normal pulse conditions are also varied: string-like in spring, full in summer, floating in autumn and sunken in winter (春弦、夏洪、秋浮、冬沉). TCM physicians also have observed that along with alteration in early morning, late afternoon, daytime and night in a day, a disease may become severer or milder. More than 2,000 years ago, physicians pointed out in *The Yellow Emperor's Canon of Internal Medicine* (《黄帝内经》): "There are various diseases, most of which become milder in the morning, better during the daytime, worse again in the late afternoon and even severer at night." This is because "in the morning, the vital energy of the human body begins to grow stronger, while the pathogenic factors weaker; at midday, the vital energy of the human body is predominant and lords it over the pathogenic factors; in the late afternoon, the vital energy of the human body begins to become weaker, while the pathogenic factors stronger; at midnight, the vital energy of the human body returns to the internal organs, while the pathogenic factors come into leading place (朝则人气始生,病气衰;日中人气长,长则胜邪;夕则人气始衰,邪气始生;夜半人气入脏,邪气独居于身)." The quotation has its scientific basis because modern researchers have proved that human pulse conditions, temperature, the amount of oxygen consumed, carbon dioxide released and hormones secreted all have biorhythms (生物节律) 24 hours a day.

A Holistic Approach to Diagnosis and Treatment

TCM stresses the practice of analyzing the relevant information, signs and symptoms collected through the four methods of diagnosis in the light of the theory of TCM, having a good idea of the cause, nature and location of a disease, and the relationship between pathogenic factors and vital energy, and summarizing them into the syndrome of a certain nature, and then determining the corresponding therapeutic method according to the conclusion of an overall differentiation of symptoms, signs and others.

That is to say, in clinical treatment, TCM physicians do not focus their main attention on the similarities and dissimilarities between diseases but on the differences between the syndromes they have. Generally speaking, the same syndromes are treated in similar ways, while different syndromes are treated in different ways. Take a cold for example, if it manifests itself in more severe chilliness, slight fever, a tongue with thin and white fur, then it belongs to the exterior syndrome caused by wind and cold (若表现为恶寒重、发热轻、舌苔薄白,属风寒表证), and should be treated with strong sudorific (发汗的) drugs pungent in taste and warm in property, to dispel the wind and cold (辛温解表法); if its manifestations are more severe fever, milder chilliness, a tongue with thin and yellow fur, then it belongs to the exterior syndrome caused by wind and heat, and should be treated with mild diaphoretics pungent in taste and cool in property, to dispel the wind and heat (辛凉解表法). This is called "treating the same diseases with different methods (同病异治)". Sometimes, different diseases have the same syndromes in nature, so their treatments are basically the same. If clinical analysis and differentiation show that persistent dysentery (痢疾), prolapse of the rectum (大肠滑脱), uterus and others belong to the syndrome of "sinking of the *qi* (中气下陷)", then their treating method should be the same one, lifting the *qi* of the middle warmer (提升中气). This is called "treating different diseases with the same method (异病同治)".

Diagnosis

TCM diagnosis includes diagnostic methods and differentiation of syndromes.

Diagnostic methods consist of inspection (望, observing), auscultation and olfaction (闻, listening and smelling), interrogation (问, inquiring), pulse-feeling and palpation (切). All these methods aim mainly at providing an objective basis for differentiation of syndromes by collecting symptoms and signs from the patient.

As one of the four basic diagnostic methods, inspection is to observe, with the doctor's own eyes, the patient's vitality, complexion (面色, 肤色), physical condition and behavior, tongue coating (舌苔), secretion (分泌物), excrement (排泄物) and so on.

Auscultation is to judge pathological changes in the interior of the patient's body by listening to his voices, moans (呻吟), breathing and cough, while olfaction is to differentiate the internal conditions of the disease by smelling the odors emitted by the patient.

Interrogation is to ask the patient or his companion about the history of the diseases, the history of the patient's life and his family, as well as the symptoms he feels.

Pulse-feeling is applied to find out the prosperity or decline of the viscera (脏腑) and bowels, *qi* and blood by feeling the patient's pulse. In other words, palpation means detecting disease conditions by touching or pressing some part of the patient's body by hand.

Of the four diagnostic methods, pulse-feeling is the most important. A doctor uses his three fingers to feel the pulse so as to find out the quality, power, rate, and rhythm of the patient's pulse. A good doctor can distinguish more than twenty types of pulse and through pulse-feeling he can diagnose what the disease is. These four diagnostic methods are believed to have been systematized by Bian Que (扁鹊), a physician who lived in the Warring States Period.

Bian Que

In addition to the four fundamental methods of diagnosis, such laboratory examinations as testing the urine (尿) were used in ancient times. *The Secret Prescriptions Revealed by a Provincial Governor* (《外台秘要》) records the testing of the urine of a jaundice (黄

疸病) patient. In the test, small pieces of silk were used. Then the shades of color of those pieces of silk were compared to find out whether the patient was improving.

The techniques of differentiation of syndromes consist of the methods to differentiate pathological conditions in accordance with the eight principal syndromes (八纲辨证), to differentiate syndromes according to the state of *qi* and blood (气血辨证), to differentiate syndromes according to pathological changes of the viscera and their interrelations (脏腑辨证), to differentiate syndromes of a febrile (发热的) disease in accordance with the theory of the six channels (六经辨证), and to differentiate the development of an epidemic febrile disease by analyzing and studying conditions of the four syndromes, namely, *wei*, *qi*, *ying*, and *xue* systems (卫、气、营、血辨证).

To differentiate pathological conditions in accordance with the eight principal syndromes is to induce and generalize a disease in guidance with such ideas as exterior and interior, excess and deficiency, coldness and heat, *yin* and *yang* to identify the location, the degree of seriousness and nature of a disease, as well as the conditions of the vital *qi* in conflict with pathogenic factors. This method provides the guiding principle for the other methods mentioned above and reflects the common characteristics of all these methods. Therefore, it is applicable to the differentiation of the syndromes of diseases in every clinical branch of medicine.

The second and third differentiations of syndromes are mainly applied to analyze and distinguish miscellaneous diseases due to disorder of the internal organs. These two methods are often used in combination with the first technique.

The last two are designed for diagnosis of exopathic (病因在体外的) febrile diseases.

Pharmacology

Doctors of Chinese medicine adopt a variety of methods to treat diseases. One of them is utilizing medicinal herbs, animals, and minerals. The legend about Shen Nong (神农, God of Husbandry) tasting a hundred kinds of herbs embodies that the ancient Chinese used natural substances to cure diseases. *Shen Nong's Materia Medica* (《神农本草经》), compiled in the first and second centuries, records more than 300 natural drugs, including herbs, fruits, cereals, insects, animals, fish, and metals. Li Shizhen (李时珍), the most outstanding pharmacologist and physician in the 16th century, conducted investigations and researched the effects of different kinds of drugs. In order to learn more about the numerous medicinal herbs, he went into the mountains and wilds and talked with farmers, woodcutters, herb collectors, and hunters. Li Shizhen even planted some herbs himself and tasted them to see their effects. On the basis of his investigation and research, he completed his great work on pharmacology, *Compendium of Materia Medica* (《本草纲目》), in 1578. The 52-volume encyclopedia contains not only descriptions of 1,892 medicines with illustrations but also 11,000 prescriptions in 16 different parts. The monumental masterpiece has been translated into a number of languages and circulated in many countries.

Li Shizhen

Since the establishment of the People's Republic of China (PRC), the Chinese government has made great efforts to promote the development of natural medicines, which are believed to have minor or no side-effects. In 1983, the State Council of PRC organized professional investigative groups with 20,000 members from all over the country to carry out a nation-wide investigation of the varieties of medicines. Their research reveals that of the 30,000 plants existing in China, one third have medicinal value. On the basis of the results of the investigation, experts have written several books, including *Resources of Traditional Chinese Medicine* (《中药资源》), *Divisions of Traditional Medicine in China* (《中国传统医学科》), and *A Collection of Maps of Traditional Chinese Medicine* (《中医药地图集》). All these works enrich mankind's knowledge of using natural medicine against disease.

There are various ways to take herbal medicines in TCM. In ancient times, people just chewed medicinal herbs and swallowed them. With the discovery of the fire, decoction (煎煮) was used. Because boiling can sterilize the herbs and enable the effective ingredients to dissolve, decoction is still the most common way used today. Tincture (酊剂) was also popular in ancient times. Oracle bone inscriptions indicate that wine was once used with herbal medicines as long ago as the Shang Dynasty (1600 B.C.E.—1046 B.C.E.). Doctors of Chinese medicine believe that wine can enhance the therapeutic effect and preserve the property of drugs. Dispersion (涂擦), mentioned in many classical medical books, is another drug-using way. Medical substances are ground into powder and the patient disperses the powder to the affected region of body or takes it. Ointment (膏药) has been used for a long time. Some ointments are employed for relieving pain; some for reducing the inflammation (炎症) of boils; some for the healing of a wound. Drugs are also made into a paste form which can be preserved for a long time. The pellet (丹) form is also popular. What's more, various medicinal herbs are grounded into powder and then made into pills (丸). At present, herbal medicines in TCM are very convenient for patients to take because many of them, used to be taken in the way of decoction, are transformed into pills, powder (散), syrup (糖浆), capsules (胶囊), and even injections (针药).

/ Acupuncture and Moxibustion /

Acupuncture and moxibustion form an indispensable part of TCM with a long history. It is a science dealing with the prevention and treatment of diseases by needling and moxibustion methods. For thousands of years, it has been accepted by the general population for its prompt and appreciable cures, wide range of indications, simple application, low cost and safety.

The Theoretical Basis

Acupuncture and moxibustion, similar to Chinese *qigong*, are based on the theory of points, channels and collaterals (经络). A point means a specific spot on the body surface at which needling or moxibustion is applied to evoke a certain reaction in certain body regions or viscera so as to produce therapeutic effects. The theory of the channels and collaterals maintains that all points are capable of both reflecting functional changes of the viscera on the body surface and passing sensations from the body surface to the viscera.

Of course, the points used nowadays in acupuncture and moxibustion were not discovered all at once but one by one in the course of development. In the embryonic stage, long and repeated practice confirmed that massage, puncture (刺), pressing, or applying heat at a given spot on the body surface often produced proximal or even distal reflexes to relieve or cure certain disease syndromes. Finally, the location of the points became definite by virtue of their therapeutic properties, and names, according to their specifications, were given to facilitate memorization and clinical use.

The discovery of points and their functions marked significant progress in acupuncture. Apart from establishing their positions and therapeutic value, it contributes to the theory of "channels and collateral", which is vital to the further development of acupuncture. Early acupuncturists have repeatedly observed that the sensation produced by a definite needle manipulation at a point is always passed along to other parts of the body along definite routes, and that points in different areas might have similar functions. By linking these points or the closely related ones, lines of points were established and so arose the concept of "channels and collaterals", which implied the relationship among groups of points, and between those points and the respective viscera.

The vertically distributed "trunk lines" were described by physicians in ancient times as "channels" implying "passage", while their large and small branches were referred to as "collaterals", implying a "network". According to traditional Chinese medical books, there are 12 channels, 15 collaterals, and 8 extraordinary channels interwoven into "a system of channels and collaterals" linking the viscera and the body surface, the head and limbs into one integrated whole. The introduction and development of this concept has enriched and elevated acupuncture and moxibustion in both theory and practice.

A Brief History of Acupuncture and Moxibustion

According to historical records and archaeological findings, as early as in the Neolithic Age (新石器时代) in China, the primitive human beings began to use stone piercers (砭石, stone needles), the earliest acupuncture instrument, to treat diseases. With the development of productive forces, bone needles and bamboo needles appeared. Then the development and improvement of metal casting techniques and metal tools brought about metal medical needles, such as bronze, iron, gold and silver ones. At present, stainless steel needles are widely used.

Moxibustion was gradually created after the use of fire. The origin can be traced back to the discovery by ancient men that certain disease symptoms disappeared after warming around a bonfire. Others were alleviated by an accidental burn on the skin. These incidents gradually led to the deliberate application of moxibustion. At first ancient men used dry leaves, and twigs. Then, by repeated practice people selected moxa (艾蒿) as the material, for they found moxa had a better medical effectiveness.

In the Periods of Spring and Autumn and Warring States at least, ancient doctors began to widely use acupuncture and moxibustion to treat diseases. Two silk scrolls recording channels and collaterals, *Moxibustion Classic with Eleven Foot-Hand Channels* (《足臂十一脉灸经》) and *Moxibustion Classic with Eleven Yin-Yang Channels* (《阴阳十一脉灸经》), were discovered in the excavation of the No. 3 Han Tomb at Mawangdui (马王堆3号汉墓), in Changsha City, in 1973, which reflected the earliest outlook of the theory of channels and collaterals. The book *Yellow*

Emperor's Canon of Internal Medicine, the earliest classic of traditional Chinese medicine passed on to now, generally discusses the basic theory of acupuncture and moxibustion and the basic knowledge of point-needling manipulations, especially in "Miraculous Pivot (灵枢)", one part of this book, which describes acupuncture and moxibustion in detail and systematically. Thus, another name of this part of the book is "Canon of Acupuncture".

From the Eastern Han Dynasty to the Three Kingdoms Period, the science of acupuncture and moxibustion developed further. Hua Tuo, a famous physician at that time, selected only one to two points in acupuncture treatment and paid much attention to propagation of needling sensation. He was ascribed to the authorship of *Canon of Moxibustion and Acupuncture Preserved in Pillow* (《枕中灸刺经》) which has been early lost. Zhang Zhongjing (张仲景), another physician in this period, also elaborated the methods of acupuncture, moxibustion, fire needling, warm needling, and management of erroneous treatment in acupuncture. In his book *Treaties on Febrile and Miscellaneous Diseases* (《伤寒杂病论》), he stressed on combining acupuncture with medicinal herbs in the treatment according to the differentiation of symptom complex.

Zhang Zhongjing

The famous medical doctor Huangfu Mi (皇甫谧) in the Jin Dynasty compiled the book *A-B Classic of Acupuncture and Moxibustion* (《针灸甲乙经》) by collecting the materials of acupuncture and moxibustion from ancient books *Plain Questions* (《素问》), *Canon of Acupuncture* (《针经》) and *Essentials of Points, Acupuncture and Moxibustion* (《明堂孔穴治要》). The work consists of 12 volumes with 128 chapters, including 349 acupoints (穴位). It tells the locations, indications and manipulations of these points, manipulating techniques and precautions of acupuncture and

Huangfu Mi

moxibustion, and the treatment of common diseases by acupuncture and moxibustion. It is the earliest exclusive book on acupuncture and moxibustion which has been one of the most influential works in the history of acupuncture and moxibustion.

During the Tang Dynasty, China was undergoing the process of economic and cultural prosperity of the feudal society. The science of acupuncture and moxibustion also witnessed great development. In late Sui and early Tang Dynasties, the famous Sun Simiao (孙思邈)

compiled *Prescriptions Worth a Thousand Gold for Emergencies* (《备急千金要方》) and *A Supplement to the Prescriptions Worth a Thousand Gold* (《千金翼方》), in which a great deal of clinical experience in acupuncture treatment of various schools were included, and the location and application of *Ashi points* (阿是穴) were introduced for the first time. He also designed and made three multicolored hanging charts of acupuncture and moxibustion—Charts of Three Views (《明堂三人图》), which are the earliest multicolored charts of channels and points, but have been lost. Soon after, Wang Tao (王焘) drew

Sun Simiao

twelve multicolored hanging charts. He also wrote the book *The Secret Prescriptions Revealed by a Provincial Governor* (《外台秘要》), in which a host of moxibustion methods were recorded. In the Imperial Medical Bureau (太医局) of the Tang Dynasty, the department of acupuncture was an independent one, which housed personnel in this field, such as professors of acupuncture, assistant professors, instructors and students.

In the Song Dynasty, the extensive application of movable type printing technique greatly promoted the wide application and development of acupuncture and moxibustion. The famous medical doctor Wang Weiyi (王惟一) revised the locations of acupoints and their related channels, and made a supplement to the indications of acupuncture points. In 1026, he wrote the book *Illustrated Manual on the Points for Acupuncture and Moxibustion on a New Bronze Figure* (《新铸铜人腧穴针灸图经》). The next year, two life-size bronze figures designed by Wang Weiyi were manufactured. These were excellent medical teaching models of the ancient times, and an important invention of visual teaching in the educational history.

Hua Shou (滑寿), a famous doctor of the Yuan Dynasty, did textual research on the pathways of channels and collaterals as well as their relationship with acupuncture points. He wrote the book *Exposition of the Fourteen Channels* (《十四经发挥》) in which the *du* and *ren* channels (督任二脉), and the twelve regular channels are mentioned in the same breath, making up fourteen channels.

The famous acupuncturists He Ruoyu (何若愚), Dou Hanqing (窦汉卿), and others of the Yuan Dynasty suggested that the acupuncture points should be selected according to midnight-noon ebb-flow (子午流注针法). They explained the close relationship between selection and compatible application of acupuncture points and the time.

In the Ming Dynasty, acupuncture and moxibustion were worked up to a climax. Many outstanding doctors specializing in this field have emerged with many exclusive books on acupuncture and moxibustion, such as *A Complete Collection of Acupuncture and Moxibustion* (《针灸大全》) by Xu Feng (徐凤), and *An Exemplary Collection of Acupuncture and Moxibustion* (《针灸聚英》) and *Essentials of Acupuncture and Moxibustion* (《针灸节要》) by Gao Wu (高武). But the most important one was the book *Compendium of Acupuncture and Moxibustion* (《针灸大成》) by Yang Jizhou (杨继洲), which was a new milestone in the history of the development of acupuncture and moxibustion science. Yang Jizhou wrote the book on the basis of his ancestor's work *Mysterious Secrets of Acupuncture and Moxibustion* (《针灸玄机秘要》) combined with the summing up of his own clinical experience. His book describes the channels and collaterals, acupuncture points, manipulation methods of acupuncture and their indications. It also introduces the experience of the treatment of diseases by acupuncture combined with herbal medicines, and records the cases of success and failure of acupuncture and moxibustion, a comparatively comprehensive summary of the achievements of acupuncture and moxibustion before the Ming Dynasty. Interestingly, Li Shizhen, in his *Compendium of Materia Medica*, once indicated that "Moxa has the effect of warming the spleen and stomach and dispelling cold and damp." Modern science has also proved that moxa leaves contain volatile oil and burning them can eliminate pathogenic strain.

In the Qing Dynasty, certain progress was made in the development of the science of acupuncture and moxibustion. There came the book *Golden Mirror of Medicine: Essentials of Acupuncture and Moxibustion in Verse* (《医宗金鉴·刺灸心法要诀》) compiled by Wu Qian (吴谦) and his collaborators, and *The Source of Acupuncture and Moxibustion* (《针灸逢源》) compiled by Li Xuechuan (李学川) and some others.

During the middle and late period of the Qing Dynasty, however, the authorities of the Qing Dynasty issued a decree to abolish the acupuncture-moxibustion department from the Imperial Medical College (太医院) under the pretext that "acupuncture and moxibustion are not suitable to be applied to the Emperor (针刺火灸, 究非奉君之所宜)". So acupuncture and moxibustion were restrained to a certain extent. But the treatment of acupuncture and moxibustion was widely accepted and used among common people.

Since the founding of the People's Republic of China, the science of acupuncture and moxibustion has developed vigorously because of the implementation of the polices for TCM. The therapy of acupuncture and moxibustion has been popularized extensively in China. What's more, new techniques of acupuncture have been invented. One of them is electrical stimulation, in which a weak electric current is connected with the needle. Another is the point laser stimulation, in which a laser is concentrated on certain points. This kind of therapy can increase the patient's immunity. The point magnetic therapy combining acupuncture and magnetic treatment is used to cure sprains (扭伤) and bruises (瘀伤), rheumatic arthritis (风湿性关节炎) and high blood pressure (高血压). Ear acupuncture (耳针疗法) has been popular in recent years. More than 200 acupoints have been found on the ears and 40 of them have turned out to be effective.

International Dissemination of Acupuncture and Moxibustion

Playing a significant role in the advance of Chinese medical science, acupuncture and moxibustion have also served to promote medicine and treatment world-wide.

Along with China's friendly trade relations and cultural exchanges with Korea, Japan and the southeastern and central Asian countries which dated from the 3rd century B.C.E., Chinese medical science, essentially acupuncture and moxibustion, was introduced into those countries at that time and won recognition by both the rulers and the common people. The Chinese doctor Yang Er (杨尔) went to Japan as a professor of medicine in 513, while Zhi Cong (知聪) took medical writings and acupuncture and moxibustion diagrams to Japan when he went as a doctor in 550. In 552, Emperor Wu of the Liang Dynasty presented the *Canon of Acupuncture* to the Japanese court. This was followed by visits to China by Japanese students of medical science, including acupuncture and moxibustion. The Taiho Code promulgated by the Imperial Government of Japan in 701 stipulated that medical institutes include compulsory courses based on *The Yellow Emperor's Classic on Acupuncture and Moxibustion* (《黄帝明堂经》) and *A-B Classic of Acupuncture and Moxibustion*. Measures were appended to ensure enforcement of this stipulation. There thus grew up in Japan a circle of Japanese physicians and writers specializing in these methods, and institutes of acupuncture and moxibustion were founded.

In what is now the Republic of Korea, the ancient kingdoms of Silla (新罗), Paekche (百济) and Koguryo (高句丽) adopted a civil examination system comparable to China's between the 7th and 10th centuries, making *Canon of Acupuncture*, *The Yellow Emperor's Classic on Acupuncture and Moxibustion* and *Classic of Acupuncture and Moxibustion* compulsory reading books for medical students.

The development of navigation after the 10th century favored China's trade and other exchanges with Africa and Europe. Acupuncture and moxibustion were among the Chinese techniques taken to those parts of the world. English, French, German, Dutch and Austrian physicians took up these techniques in their clinical practice and research. Textbooks on these branches of medical science have been translated from Chinese into a host of other languages.

Exercises

Part One   Comprehension

Fill in the following blanks with the information you learn in Chapter 8.

1. China's Four Great Inventions, namely, the compass, paper-making, _____, and printing, not only changed the world but also accelerated the evolution of world history.

2. Printing, known as "mother of _____", was another great invention made by Chinese people.

3. Silk was _____ produced in ancient China, with some of the earliest found in as early as 3500 B.C.E.

4. Anaesthetic is necessary for surgical operations. As early as the Warring States Period, Bian Que had concocted an anaesthetic called "_____ wine" to be used in surgical operations.

5. China was the first country to establish the _____ counting method.

6. Jia Sixie is generally considered the "Sage of _____" in Chinese history.

7. The *yin* and *yang* theory holds that everything, or every phenomenon in the universe, consists of two forces, *yin* and *yang* that oppose each other and at the same time _____ each other.

8. Diagnostic methods consist of inspection (observing), auscultation and olfaction (listening and smelling), interrogation (inquiring), pulse-feeling and _____.

9. Li Shizhen, the most outstanding _____ and physician in the 16th century, conducted investigations and researched the effects of different kinds of drugs.

10. In his book *Treaties on Febrile and Miscellaneous Diseases*, he stressed on combining _____ with medicinal herbs in the treatment according to the differentiation of symptom complex.

Part Two   Translation

Passage Translation

    中国以创造各种方式、方法来方便人类的生活而闻名。在中国古代的发明中，四大发明不仅为中国的发展，还为世界经济和文化的发展，作出了巨大贡献。中国古代的四大发明，即指南针、造纸术、火药、印刷术,不仅改变了世界,也加速了世界历史的演进。西方人可能对中国过去的壮举知之甚少,但他们对中国的四大发明却很熟悉。中国古代的四大发明也是中国作为世界文明大国的重要象征。

Part Three Critical Thinking and Discussion

1. What are the characteristics of TCM?

2. What do you know about Zhang Zhongjing and Li Shizhen?

3. What do you think of the future of TCM?

Chapter 9
Traditional Chinese Festivals

China's major traditional festivals consist of the Spring Festival, the Lantern Festival, the Qingming Festival (or Clear and Bright Day), the Dragon Boat Festival, the Double Seventh Festival, the Mid-Autumn Festival and the Double Ninth Festival.

/ Spring Festival /

The Spring Festival, also called the Chinese New Year or *guonian* (过年, keeping the monster *nian* away), is China's most important festival which falls on the first day of the first lunar month each year. Family members gather just as westerners do on Christmas. The celebration of the Spring Festival has a history of over 2,000 years. It became known as "the Spring Festival" to distinguish it from the Western New Year, when China adopted the Western calendar after the Revolution of 1911.

Legend about the Spring Festival

There are many legends about the origin of *nian*. According to one of the most famous legends, in ancient China, *nian* was believed to be a fierce monster resembling a bull with a lion's head. *Nian* lived deep at the bottom of the sea all the year round and climbed up to the shore only on New Year's Eve to devour domestic animals and even people. The red color, bright flames, and exploding were what *nian* feared the most. Thus to drive the monster away, that night people gathered together, lit bonfires and threw dry bamboo sticks into the fire. The crackling of the burning bamboo sticks indeed frightened the monster away. After the night passed and the new day arrived, people felt safe, and then brought out a great array of food to celebrate their victory over the monster. From then on, on each New Year's Eve, every family sticks on their doors Spring Festival couplets (春联) written on red paper, sets off firecrackers, keeps their houses brilliantly illuminated and stays up late or all night (守岁). Early in the morning of the first day of the first lunar month, people go to visit their relatives and friends to send their regards and congratulations. These customs are spreading far and wide and handed down from generation to generation.

Nian

Preparations for the Spring Festival

Preparations for the Spring Festival begin on *laba* (腊八), the eighth day of the 12th lunar month. On this day, Chinese people usually eat *laba* porridge (腊八粥) made with glutinous rice (糯米), millet (小米), seed of Job's tears (薏米), dates (枣), lotus seeds (莲子), raisins (葡萄干), beans (豆子), peanut kernels (花生仁), and so on. Besides eating *laba* porridge, Chinese people also put cloves of garlic (蒜瓣) into vinegar to make *laba* vinegar (腊八醋) and use it as a condiment.

After *laba*, Chinese people busy themselves with the preparations for the Spring Festival: cleaning and decorating the house, and shopping and cooking. They wash their clothes and bedclothes, clean the entire house as well as all their cooking utensils. It is believed that if people clean their houses on the 24th day of the 12th lunar month with new brooms and dustpans, they will have good luck in the coming year. In addition, before the Spring Festival, people traditionally take a bath and have their hair cut, once thought to be a protection against misfortune and disease in the new year.

House decorations vary in different regions of China. In rural areas, people put up Spring Festival couplets and New Year pictures. The tradition of Spring Festival couplets dates back to ancient times when people carved or painted the gods Shen Tu (神荼) and Yu Lei (郁垒), who were believed to safeguard people from devils and evil spirits, on *taofu* (桃符) or peach wood, and place them on either side of their doorways. Later, *taofu* were replaced by couplets flanking the doors. The couplets usually contain two lines of poetic musings transcribed by a calligrapher on red paper, expressing the feeling of life's renewal and the return of spring. New Year pictures are a special kind of folk art. They are brightly colored and convey propitious messages. The Spring Festival would not be the Spring Festival without these colorful images. What's more, traditional Chinese paper-cuts are also pasted on windows or doors for decoration. The paper used for paper-cuts is usually red; and the figures may include fish, birds, flowers, animals, scenery, and auspicious characters. Interestingly, some Chinese people even paste inverted drawings of the characters for "spring", "wealth", and "blessing" since the Chinese for "inverted" is a homonym in Chinese for "arrive", thus signifying that spring, wealth or blessing has arrived.

Paper-cut (福 , Happiness)

Weeks before the Spring Festival, supermarkets, department stores, shopping malls, and commercial streets are thronged with people who are busy buying meat, chicken, eggs, duck, fish, vegetables, fruits, candies, new clothes, flowers, Spring Festival couplets, and paper-cuts for decorating their houses. Some people will buy new chopsticks, new rice bowls and plates in the hope of welcoming new family members.

Celebrations of the Spring Festival

The celebration of the Spring Festival begins on the 23rd of the 12th lunar month when the Kitchen God (灶神) was once believed to visit heaven to give his yearly report about the family. On this day, people used to make sacrifices to their Kitchen God, but later the custom switched to smearing the Kitchen God's mouth with sticky malt, either to sweeten his report or to seal his lips. Nowadays, many families eat malt sugar sticks or pumpkin-shaped candies in memory of this old custom. By the way, the 23rd day of the 12th lunar month is called Preliminary Eve (小年).

The highlight of the Spring Festival is lunar New Year's Eve. Traditionally, houses are brightly lit, all the family members sit down together to enjoy the important reunion dinner, a sumptuous feast with a variety of dishes and beverages. Dishes such as chicken, fish, and tofu (豆腐, bean curd) must be included, for in Chinese, their pronunciations, respectively *ji*, *yu*, and *doufu* are similar to those of the Chinese characters which mean "auspicious" "abundant" and "blessed". In southern China, people eat *niangao* (年糕), New Year cake made of glutinous rice flour. *Niangao* means "higher and higher, one year after another". In northern China, *jiaozi* (饺子), or dumplings, are "bidding farewell to the old and ushering in the new (辞旧迎新)". The shape of the dumplings is reminiscent of gold nuggets (金元宝) from ancient times. People eating *jiaozi* wish for money and treasure.

Nowadays, on the lunar New Year's Eve there are exciting programs on television which last from 7:30 PM until midnight. Thus, after the ample dinner that night, all the family members usually sit around watching TV, chatting, playing cards or "mahjong (麻将)". In recent years, the Spring Festival Gala (春节联欢晚会) on CCTV is an essential entertainment for the Chinese both at home and abroad. According to customs, every family sets off firecrackers and fireworks at midnight to drive away evil spirits and to see the New Year in. After midnight, some people may go to bed, others prefer to sit up for the rest of the night playing cards or other games.

After waking up on New Year's Day in the lunar calendar, everybody dresses up. The younger members of the family first extend greetings such as "Happy New Year" to the elder members. Then each child will get money as a New Year gift, wrapped up in red paper. The money is called "lucky money for the Spring Festival (压岁钱)", which is believed to guarantee children's healthy growth in the new year. A married daughter should return to her parents' home on the 2nd day of the lunar New Year. During the Spring Festival holiday, people hurry around visiting relatives and friends, especially those whom they have not seen all year.

It is worth mentioning that burning firecrackers was once the most typical custom on the Spring Festival because people believed that the sound could help frighten away evil spirits. However, nowadays, this activity is completely or partially forbidden in big cities since the government took security and pollution factors into consideration. As a replacement, some buy tapes with firecracker sounds to listen to, some break little balloons to get the sound, and others buy firecracker handicrafts to hang in the living room.

The lively happy atmosphere not only fills every household, but permeates streets and lanes. Activities such as lion dancing (舞狮), dragon dancing (舞龙), and temple affairs (庙会) are held for days. The Spring Festival then comes to an end when the Lantern Festival is finished.

/ Lantern Festival /

The Lantern Festival, celebrated on the 15th day of the first lunar month, is closely related to the Spring Festival. It marks the end of the New Year's festivities, following which people return to their normal routines. The most prominent activity of the Lantern Festival is the grand display of beautiful lanterns. In cold areas, especially in the northeastern part of China, people usually enjoy making ice lanterns (冰灯).

Lanterns of various shapes and sizes are hung in the streets, attracting countless visitors. Excited children hold lanterns as they walk along the streets. Guessing riddles pasted onto lanterns is a Lantern Festival tradition from the Tang and Song Dynasties. Visitors who solve a riddle may get a prize.

The custom of hanging lanterns dates back to the early Han Dynasty. Emperor Wen suppressed a rebellion on the 15th day of the first lunar month. On that night, Emperor Wen went out to celebrate his victory with his subjects. He later named the day *Yuan Xiao Jie* (元宵节). *Yuan* refers to the first lunar month, *xiao* means "night" and *jie* signifies "festival".

The Lantern Festival has always been observed with great enthusiasm. History records a celebration of the festival during the reign of Emperor Xuanzong of Tang (唐玄宗). On the top of a hill, 100 giant trees were decorated with lanterns. Each tree was about 27 meters tall. When all the lanterns were lit, they could be seen from hundreds of miles away. Lantern-making reached its height under the Ming and Qing Dynasties. Folk artists competed to improve their techniques, and lantern-making became a handicraft in its own right. In the Qing Dynasty, lanterns were hung everywhere: at court, in private residences, in stores, and in workshops. At night, people tour the displays of lanterns. Even young women were allowed to go out to look at lanterns.

The Lantern Festival

Custom demands the eating of *yuanxiao* (also called *tangyuan*), or rice dumplings on this day. That's why the Lantern Festival can also be called the "*Yuan Xiao* Festival". *Tangyuan* are small dumpling balls made of glutinous rice flour with sesame (芝麻), bean paste, date paste (枣泥), walnut meat (核桃肉), dried fruit, or sugar and edible oil as filling. *Tangyuan* can be boiled, fried, or steamed. They taste sweet and delicious. What's more, *tangyuan* in the Chinese language has a similar pronunciation to "*tuanyuan*", meaning reunion. So people eat them in the hope of bringing union, harmony, and happiness to the family.

Today, people maintain the tradition of celebrating the Lantern Festival. They go to big parks to watch dragon dances, lion dances, boat dances, and masked dramas, often performed on stilts. In addition, many big cities hold exhibitions of lanterns of various shapes and colors. They are made of paper and gauze on plastic in the shape of fish, frogs, roses, lotus flowers, and others. The most popular lanterns are inspired by the animal designated by the Chinese lunar calendar for the year. For example, in the Year of the Dragon, dragon-theme lanterns are hung in the parks and on both sides of the streets. In addition to lantern exhibitions, people also go to guess lantern riddles and appreciate fireworks. The Lantern Festival is an enjoyable and exciting day for children who go out after dark carrying lanterns. In the evening, people have a grand dinner to mark the end of the Spring Festival celebrations.

/ Qingming Festival /

The Qingming Festival (or Clear and Bright Day) is a day for mourning the dead. It is one of the 24 seasonal division points (24 节气) in the Chinese lunar calendar, falling on 4—6 April each year. After the festival, the temperature rises and rainfall increases in readiness for spring plowing (春耕) and sowing.

Legend about the Qingming Festival

The *Han Shi* Day (寒食节, Cold Food Day) is the day before the Qingming Festival, when no fire or smoke is permitted and people only eat cold food. Its origin is a touching story.

The *Han Shi* Day is in memory of Jie Zitui (介子推) who lived in the Spring and Autumn Period. Jie Zitui was a loyal official in the State of Jin (晋国), working for Crown Prince Chong Er (太子重耳). During a period of turmoil, Chong Er was forced to leave Jin with his court, including Jie Zitui. In exile, they suffered a lot of hardships and difficulties. To save the starving Chong Er, Jie Zitui cut the flesh off his own leg and boiled it for Chong Er. After Chong Er became a king, Jie Zitui noticed that Chong Er liked to hear sweet things instead of criticisms, so he left the court and went to live in mountains with his mother.

Chong Er went in person to the mountains to look for Jie Zitui. It was impossible to find Jie Zitui in the endless trees and hills. Chong Er ordered to set the mountains on fire to force Jie Zitui out. Unfortunately, Jie Zitui did not emerge; he and his mother were found dead in each other's arms with a note written in Jie's blood: "I cut off my own flesh and dedicated it to you, only to hope my king will always be clear and bright (割肉奉君尽丹心，但愿主公常清明)." In honor of Jie Zitui, Chong Er issued an order that every family put out their kitchen fire and eat just cold food that day.

Jie Zitui

The custom of crushing out the kitchen fire before the Qingming Festival has vanished, but the habits of planting willow twigs (柳条) and paying respect to ancestors at their tombs have continued to the present day.

Activities of the Qingming Festival

The major custom of the Qingming Festival is tomb sweeping (扫墓). According to the folklore, the spirits of dead ancestors still live under the ground and look after the family, and the tombs are said to be their houses, so it is vital to keep the tombs clean. On this day, people visit their family graves to remove any underbrush that has grown. They would uproot weeds (除草) near the grave sites, wipe the tombstones and decorate the tombstones with fresh flowers. And then they will burn incenses and candles (烧香烛), set out offerings of food and paper gifts, which include paper money, houses, furniture, household electric appliances, and so on.

The Qingming Festival is also known as an occasion for kite flying (放风筝) and playing on the swing (荡秋千) in China.

/ Dragon Boat Festival /

The Dragon Boat Festival, also known as the *Duan Wu* Festival, falls on the 5th day of the 5th lunar month and is celebrated everywhere in China. During this festival there are dragon boat races, and people eat *zongzi* (粽子), pyramid-shaped dumplings wrapped in bamboo or reed leaves. *Zongzi* are made of glutinous rice and stuffed with pork, ham, chicken, dates, or sweet bean paste, and so on. There are many legends describing the evolution of the festival, the most popular one being in memory of Qu Yuan (屈原).

Origin of the Dragon Boat Festival

Qu Yuan, a renowned poet, politician, and thinker who lived over two thousands years ago in the State of Chu (楚) during the Warring States Period. In the face of great pressure from the powerful State of Qin (秦), Qu Yuan, as an important minister, advocated the union of the six states against Qin as well as political and economic reforms. His suggestions, however, were opposed by aristocrats. Qu Yuan was later deposed (被免职) and exiled by King Huai (怀王) to what is now the eastern part of Hunan Province. During his banishment, Qu Yuan still cared much for his country and people, which was expressed in his poems such as *Sorrow After Departure* (《离骚》) and *Questions to Heaven* (《天问》). When Qu yuan heard that the Qin troops had finally conquered the Chu capital, he was plunged into such a deep despair that he drowned himself in the Miluo River (汨罗江) in Hunan Province on the 5th day of the 5th lunar month, 278 B.C.E.

Legend says that when the news of Qu Yuan's drowning spread, people from the State of

Chu gathered along the banks of the Miluo River to pay their respect. The fishermen sailed their boats up and down the river searching for his body. Since everyone was anxious to be the first to find Qu Yuan, the search soon became a race. What's more, in ancient China, superstitious people believed that a man's soul would not be permitted to enter heaven if his body was not intact; thus, to divert fish and shrimps from attacking Qu Yuan's body, people of the State of Chu threw *zongzi* and eggs into the water; an old doctor poured a jug of Realgar wine (雄黄酒) into the water, hoping to make all aquatic beasts drunk.

Although the story about Qu Yuan is popular, some say that the Dragon Boat Festival originated before his time. Then people considered themselves descendants of the dragon and worshiped the God Totem. After they threw into the river food which had been put in hollowed-out bamboo or wrapped in leaves, they boarded boats and raced in the river to the accompaniment of drums.

Customs of the Dragon Boat Festival

It has become a popular tradition to eat *zongzi* and drink Realgar wine on the 5th day of the 5th lunar month. It is also a custom to hang wormwood (艾草) and carry "fragrant pouches (香袋)" made of pieces of cloth with colored silk threads. All these have a common aim—to keep evil spirits away.

Dragon boat racing is an indispensable part of the festival, held all over the country, especially along waterways in many southern cities and towns. On the day of the festival, boats are decorated in the shape of a dragon with a drum and a gong on each boat to set the pace. With a shout of "dragon away (飞龙出发)", the race starts and the dragon boats skim over the water, powered by teams of skilled oarsmen who have been practicing for months. Strength, teamwork, and split-second timing are all important in the race. The oarsmen often sing songs with an emphatic, drum-beat rhythm as they race for the finish line to the excited cheers from spectators on both banks of the river.

Dragon Boat Racing

Categories of *Zongzi*

There are two main categories of *zongzi*—Guangdong (广东) style and Jiagxing (嘉兴) style. Although they are both in the shape of a pyramid, Guangdong *zongzi* are longer and have various kinds of stuffings. Jiaxing *zongzi* are smaller and are usually stuffed with pork or bean paste.

There are a number of famous *zongzi* stores in China. Wufang *Zongzi* Store (五芳斋粽子店) in Jiaxing city, Zhejiang Province, is one of them. Wufang *Zongzi* Store has existed for more than 50 years and is well-known for the high quality ingredients, the distinctive flavor and the careful preparation of its *zongzi*.

To make zongzi, first, you wash the glutinous rice quickly without allowing it to macerate (浸软), drain it for about 15 minutes, and then mix it with soy sauce, sugar, and a little salt. Many master chefs use cane sugar (蔗糖) to sweeten the rice and make the dumpling look brighter. Next, you dice the pork for the stuffing and marinate (腌泡) it in a mixture of soy sauce, sugar, fine salt, kitchen wine, and MSG (味精). Then, the wrapping begins. You fold the bamboo or the reed leaves into a cone (圆锥体), fill it about one third full with rice, and bind it tightly with thread. Finally, you put *zongzi* into a pot and boil *zongzi* for 4 hours before eating.

At the Dragon Boat Festival, *zongzi* make good presents for relatives and friends. They are also an inexpensive and delicious snack. Because some of the best ones, such as Wufang *zongzi*, can be preserved for over 3 months, they can be exported to foreign countries.

/ Double Seventh Festival /

The Double Seventh Festival falling on the 7th day of the 7th lunar month is a traditional Chinese festival replete with romance.

This festival is in mid-summer (仲夏) when the weather is hot and the grass and trees display their luxurious green. At night, when the sky is dotted with stars, people can see the Milky Way (银河) spanning from the north to the south. On each bank of the Milky Way there is a bright star looking at each other from afar. One of the stars is conceived to be the Weaver Maid (织女) and the other the Cowherd (牛郎). There exists a beautiful love story about them passed down from generation to generation.

Long, long ago, there was an honest and kind-hearted fellow named Niulang (牛郎, Cowherd) who led a miserable life. He had only one companion—an old ox. One day, a fairy named Zhinü (织女, Weaver Maid) fell in love with Niulang and came down to Earth to marry him. They lived a happy life and gave birth to a boy and a girl. Unfortunately, the Empress of Heaven discovered their union and ordered the troops from Heaven to take the Weaver Maid back.

With the help of his ox, the Cowherd flew to Heaven with his son and daughter. At the moment when he was about to catch up with his wife, the Empress of Heaven took off one of her hairpins (发簪) and drew a line with it in the air. Immediately a celestial river (天河) appeared in the sky. The Cowherd and the Weaver Maid were separated by the river forever and could only burst into tears. Their true and deep love moved magpies (喜鹊), so tens of thousands of magpies came to build a bridge for them to meet each other. The Empress of Heaven was eventually touched and she allowed them to meet each other on the 7th day of the 7th lunar month every year. Hence, their meeting date has been called *qixi* (七夕, the evening of the 7th day of the 7th lunar month).

The Cowherd and The Weaver Maid

Today, although some traditional customs are still followed in rural areas of China, many have been weakened or diluted (冲淡) in cities. However, the legend of the Cowherd and the Weaver Maid has taken root in the hearts of Chinese people. And the 7th day of the 7th lunar month has also been known as China's Valentine's Day.

/ Mid-Autumn Festival /

The Mid-Autumn Festival falls on the 15th day of the 8th lunar month. It has been believed that the moon is at its fullest and roundest on this day, so the festival is also regarded as an occasion for family reunions. Watching the moon is an important part of the Mid-Autumn Festival celebration. At night, people watch and worship the full moon while eating moon cakes (月饼). Delighted by the beautiful sight, people who are steeped in Chinese classical poetry recite well-known verses or poems of their own.

In ancient times, the emperors held ceremonies to offer sacrifices to the sun in spring and to the moon in autumn. Later, the rites became prevalent among ordinary people. Today, the Mid-Autumn Festival has become a time for peasants to celebrate their harvests and enjoy themselves.

Legends about Mid-Autumn Festival

Of many legends about the Mid-Autumn Festival, the story concerning Hou Yi (后羿) and Chang E (嫦娥) is perhaps the most popular.

In the distant past, there were 10 suns in the sky, whose boiling heat burnt all the crops, dried up all the lakes and put people at death's door. A hero named Hou Yi was deeply worried about this predicament (困境). He climbed Mount Kunlun (昆仑山), drew his extraordinary bow, and shot down 9 suns one after another with his superman strength. He also ordered the last sun to rise and set regularly. For this reason, he was respected and loved by people.

On a visit to Mount Kunlun with his beautiful and kind-hearted wife, Chang E, Hou Yi happened to meet the Empress of Heaven, who gave him an elixir (仙丹, pill of immortality). Whoever eats the elixir would immediately ascend (升) to Heaven and become a celestial being (神仙). Hou Yi, not wishing to be separated from his wife, gave the elixir to Chang E for safekeeping. She hid the elixir in a case of her dressing table where Peng Meng (彭蒙), Hou Yi's disciple, later noticed it.

One day when Hou Yi went out hunting, Peng Meng, with sword in hand, rushed into the inner chamber (卧室) to demand the elixir from Chang E. Knowing the impossibility of protecting the elixir, Chang E fetched it from the case and swiftly swallowed it. Suddenly, her body floated out of the window and flew towards Heaven.

Chang E's Flight to the Moon

Overcome with grief, Hou Yi looked up into the sky and called out the name of his beloved wife when, to his surprise, he found that the moon was particularly clear and bright and on it appeared a shimmering shadow looking exactly like his wife. But he could not reach the moon to be with his wife.

In memory of his wife, Hou Yi erected an incense table in Chang E's beloved garden, and laid on it her favorite moon cakes and fresh fruits. So, the custom of worshiping the moon spread among people.

Another legend about an emperor's journey to the moon adds charm to the festival. On a mid-autumn evening, Emperor Xuanzong of Tang (唐玄宗) was invited to see the moon palace by a Taoist named Luo Gongyuan (罗公远). Just as the emperor wondered how he could get to the moon, Luo Gongyuan threw his magic stick into the air and immediately there appeared a silver bridge leading to the moon. The emperor crossed the bridge and saw a big palace named "Guanghan Gong (广寒宫, Vast Cold Palace)". By the gate there was a fragrant osmanthus tree (桂花树) under which a white rabbit was pounding out the elixir of life. When he entered the gate, the emperor was fascinated by the magnificent jade buildings. To melodious music, hundreds of beautifully dressed fairies danced around him and served him some delicious cakes which were as round as the full moon. When he came back to earth, the emperor ordered the chefs in the palace to make cakes similar to the ones he had eaten on the moon. Gradually, eating moon cakes evolved into a desirable cultural tradition.

The 15th day of the 8th lunar month is in the season when crops and fruits ripen and the weather is pleasant. On this evening, family members or friends meet outdoors, with food on tables, and appreciate the full and bright moon. People away from home often recite Li Bai's famous poem lines: "I raise my head, the splendid moon I see; Then droop my head and sink to the dreams of my hometown (举头望明月，低头思故乡)." Others who are hopeful for their future prefer Su Shi's lines: "My one wish for you, then, is long life; And a share in this loveliness (the moon) far, far away (但愿人长久，千里共婵娟)."

/ Double Ninth Festival /

The Double Ninth Festival, or *Chong Yang* Festival, is celebrated on the 9th day of the 9th lunar month.

This festival began as early as the Warring States Period. The Chinese view of life was recorded in an ancient and mysterious work, *The Book of Change* (《易经》). It depicts *yin* (阴) as the element of darkness and *yang* (阳) as life and brightness. The number "6" stands for the feminine (阴性的) or negative *yin*, while the number "9" the masculine (阳性的) or positive *yang*. So the number "9" in both month and day creates the Double Ninth Festival, or *Chong Yang* Festival. The Chinese ancestors regarded it as a propitious day worthy of celebration. That's why the Chinese people began to celebrate this festival from ancient times, exactly from the Western Han Dynasty.

The celebration of this festival is diverse and colorful, usually including activities of going out and enjoying the scenery, climbing mountains, appreciating chrysanthemum (菊花), wearing dogwood (茱萸), eating *Chong Yang* pastry (重阳糕点), drinking chrysanthemum wine (菊花酒), and so on.

Climbing Mountains and Appreciating Chrysanthemum

In 1989, the Chinese government designated the Double Ninth Festival as "Senior Citizen's Day (老人节)". Since then, the Double Ninth Festival has become a day for revering and caring about the aged nationwide. All the government units, organizations, and communities would arrange autumn trips for the elderly. Younger generations may take their elders for trips or send them gifts.

Exercises

Part One　Comprehension

Fill in the following blanks with the information you learn in Chapter 9.

1. The Spring Festival, also called the Chinese New Year or *guonian* (keeping the monster *nian* away), is China's _____ festival which falls on the first day of the first lunar month each year.

2. The Lantern Festival, celebrated on the 15th day of the first _____ month, is closely related to the Spring Festival.

3. The Qingming Festival is also known as an occasion for _____ and playing on the swing in China.

4. It has become a popular tradition to eat *zongzi* and drink _____ wine on the 5th day of the 5th lunar month.

5. And the 7th day of the 7th lunar month has also been known as China's _____'s Day.

6. The Mid-Autumn Festival falls on the 15th day of the 8th lunar month. It has been believed that the moon is at its fullest and roundest on this day, so the festival is also regarded as an occasion for family _____.

7. In _____, the Chinese government designated the Double Ninth Festival as "Senior Citizen's Day".

Part Two　Translation

Passage Translation

　　中国人自古以来就在中秋时节庆祝丰收。过中秋节的习俗于唐代早期在中国各地开始流行。农历八月十五是人们拜月的节日。这天夜晚皓月当空，人们阖家团聚，共赏明月。远离家人的游子经常背诵李白的著名诗句:"举头望明月,低头思故乡。"那些对未来满怀憧憬的人则更喜欢苏轼的诗句:"但愿人长久,千里共婵娟。"

2006年,中秋节被列为中国的文化遗产,2008年又被定为公共假日。月饼被视为中秋节不可或缺的美食,人们将月饼作为礼物馈赠亲友或在家庭聚会上享用。传统的月饼上带有"寿"(longevity)、"福"或"和"等字样。

Part Three　Critical Thinking and Discussion

What's your favorite traditional Chinese Festival? Why?

Chapter 10
Traditional Chinese Cuisine

Chinese cuisine has a tremendously long history. Archaeological findings show that the ancestors of modern Chinese were already using pottery wares for cooking food during the Period of the Longshan Culture (龙山文化) of the Neolithic Age (新石器时代). People realized the importance of diversity and balance in diet as early as over 2,000 years ago. *The Yellow Emperor's Canon of Internal Medicine* (《黄帝内经》), a well-known medical book composed at that time, says: "Cereals supply men with necessary nutrition, fruits are subsidiary, meat is an added benefit and vegetables are nutritional enrichment (五谷为养,五果为助,五畜为益,五菜为充)." The book also indicates that a diversified diet helps maintain the function of the organs. One cookbook circulated in China about 1,500 years ago shows that cooking had become an art and something worth studying. Over the following centuries, Chinese cooking continued to develop. Now it is one of the world's greatest cuisines.

/ Features of Chinese Food /

Three Standards for Judging Chinese Cooking

Generally speaking, there are three essential standards by which Chinese cooking is judged, namely, color (色), aroma (香), and taste (味), with taste being the most important. Color refers not only to the beautiful color of the food, but also to the layout and design. Aroma means the fragrant and appetizing (开胃的) smell of the dishes served on the table before eating. Taste is not only associated with tasting the food itself, but also with the appreciation of seasonings (调味品) and texture (质地).

Preparation of Raw Materials

Chinese dishes are rich in raw materials, which may include chicken, duck, fish, red meat, seafood, eggs, vegetables, soybean products, fruits, dried food, and nuts. Different dishes have different requirements as regard to the selection and preparation of the main ingredients. For Beijing Roast Duck, only force-fed ducks raised on the duck farms near the city are suitable.

Besides selection and preparation, Chinese chefs also pay attention to the combination of main ingredients and auxiliary materials. They see to it that the combination looks beautiful, tastes good, and is nutritious. Stir-fried shrimp is an example. If shrimp and broccoli are fried together, the colors are very appealing to the eye, and the dish is named Sautéed Shrimp with Broccoli (翡翠虾仁). Similarly, bean curd and green vegetables, fish fillet (鱼片) and tomato sauce, chicken and mushroom all make good combinations. In Chinese dishes, meat and vegetables are often cooked together so that they not only look good and taste delicious but are nutritious as well.

Cutting and Seasonings

Cutting has always been a distinctive feature of Chinese culinary art. The ingredients of a given dish can be cut into slices (丝), strips (条), shreds (碎片), cubes (方块), segments (节段), dices (丁), grains (细粒), or minced (剁碎) into a uniform small size. Some materials like turnip (大头菜), radish (小萝卜), and potato (土豆), can be carved into the artistic shapes of chrysanthemums (菊花), peonies (牡丹), phoenixes (凤凰), and peacocks (孔雀). Chinese characters can also be carved in food for special banquets to celebrate birthdays or weddings.

Taste, to some extent, relies on the seasonings. There are many tastes—salty (salt, soy sauce), sweet (sugar, honey), sour (vinegar), fragrant (sesame oil, coriander wine), spicy (chili, garlic, ginger), tangy (MSG), bitter (dried tangerine, bitter apricot kernel), and so on. The suitable application of seasonings will produce a variety of dishes to suit a variety of tastes.

Seasonings are quite important to Chinese cooking. The number of spices and herbs used is estimated at more than 100. Those adopted in various geographical regions have helped to shape the different styles of Chinese cooking, and all kinds of salty, sweet, sour, fragrant, spicy, tangy, bitter flavors can be found in those cuisines. Changes resulting from cooking are carefully watched. Chinese chefs see to it that seasonings are added at the right time so that the natural flavors of the main materials are preserved.

Cooking Techniques

Locality and climate play a vital role in cooking. Both of them affect people's choice of cooking materials and preference of cooking process. Over the centuries, Chinese people have acquired many cooking techniques, which include boiling (煮), stewing or braising (炖, 煨, 焖), frying (煎), stir-frying (炒), quick-frying (爆), deep-frying (炸), frying and simmering (扒),

sautéing (嫩煎), smoking (熏), roasting or barbecuing (烤), baking (烘), steaming (蒸), scalding (白灼), stewing in soy sauce (卤), stewing in syrup (上蜜汁), and so on.

Different culinary materials require different cooking techniques, and different ways of cooking produce different flavors. Let's take chicken for example. If the meat is tender, it is suitable for quick-frying or stir-frying. If the meat is tough, braising or stewing will be the best way to cook it. Steaming is often used in Chinese cooking because it helps to preserve the flavor and nutrients in the food regardless of the fact that it is a slower process than boiling.

Cooking Temperature

The texture of the raw materials for Chinese cuisine is varied. They can be hard, soft, crisp, or tender. The cut shapes are also different. Different ingredients require different cooking times and temperatures. They can be cooked at high, moderate, or low temperatures. Dongpo Pork (东坡肉), a famous dish of Zhejiang Cuisine (浙菜), is a good example. This dish is named after a distinguished Song poet and painter, Su Dongpo (Su Shi). Su, an excellent amateur cook, was especially good at making Braised Pork in

Dongpo Pork

Brown Sauce (红烧猪肉). He even wrote a poem to describe the cooking process. According to his recipe, the pork is simmered slowly over low heat in a covered pot. When done, the meat is tender and delicious but not greasy at all.

On the other hand, the dish Fried Sliced Chicken and Chicken Liver (凤肝鸡片) is stir-fried at a high temperature for only a few seconds. The cooked meats turn out to be tender and tasty. But a low temperature would make the meats tough and hard.

Yin-Yang Principle

Chinese people believe that everything in the universe is either positive or negative, hot or cold, wet or dry, and so on. So they think that the food they eat should keep a harmonious balance of these cosmic forces if they want to stay physically, emotionally and spiritually healthy. Each type of food has its own characteristics of *yin* or *yang*. *Yin* foods are thin, cold, and low in calories. *Yang* foods are rich, spicy, hot, and high in calories. Boiling makes food *yin*; frying makes food *yang*. So Chinese cuisine always seeks a balance between the two. It is believed that all main food colors should be included in a meal to ensure a range of nutrients.

Medicinal Function

Great importance is attached to nutrition in Chinese cuisine. Based on the practice of traditional Chinese herbal medicine, medicinal cuisine combines strictly processed traditional Chinese medicine with traditional culinary materials to produce delicious food with health-restoring functions. Over the centuries, Chinese people have explored the world of plants, roots, herbs, fungi (菌菇) and seeds to find life-giving elements. They have discovered that many items have medicinal value and that improper cooking can destroy the nutritional value of some items. For example, ginger, one of people's favorite condiments (佐料), is also used to soothe (舒缓) an upset stomach and as a remedy to relieve cold.

In China, people hold the belief that a food tonic (滋补品) is much better than a medicine for fortifying one's health. To cook medicinal food, one has a variety of fine materials to select from and each ingredient (原料) has its own unique flavor. Slow cooking methods such as stewing are adopted to extract more of the herb's healing properties.

/ Eight Regional Cuisines /

China is a vast country with diverse geographic conditions, climates, customs, products, and habits. Favored dishes vary from region to region. Dwellers in coastal areas prefer seafood and aquatic products, whereas those in central and northwestern China eat more domestic animals and poultry. Tastes also differ regionally because of the climate differences. One popular summary of Chinese food is "sweet in the south, salty in the north, sour in the west and spicy in the east (南甜北咸, 西酸东辣)".

Despite the differences in choice of dishes, people throughout the whole country adopt the traditional cooking style prevalent in their respective regions. Generally speaking, there are eight schools of cuisine: Shandong, Sichuan, Guangdong, Fujian, Jiangsu, Zhejiang, Anhui, and Hunan cuisines. These regional cuisines have evolved over centuries, so their designations have no specific geographical boundaries.

Shandong Cuisine

Shandong Cuisine, also known as *Lucai* (鲁菜), is representative of northern China's cooking and its techniques are widely practiced in northeast China.

Shandong Cuisine features its emphasis on aroma, freshness, crispness (脆), tenderness (软), and the use of minimal fat. Seasonings such as sauce paste, onion, and garlic are frequently used, so Shandong dishes usually taste a little pungent. In addition, Shandong Province lies on China's eastern seaboard, so it is natural that Shandong Cuisine includes many well-known seafood dishes which are fresh, tasty, but not greasy.

Shandong's most famous dishes are Deep-fried Red-scale Fish (干炸赤鳞鱼), Yellow River Carp in Sweet and Sour Sauce (糖醋黄河鲤鱼), Stewed Sea Cucumber (红烧海参), and Sautéed Pickled Fish Slices (糟溜鱼片). When meat or seafood is cooked, only small amounts of cooking oil and mild spices are used so that the natural flavor of the food is preserved. Dezhou Braised Chicken (德州扒鸡) is known throughout the whole country for it is so well-cooked that the meat is easily separated from the bone while the shape of the chicken is preserved.

Stewed Sea Cucumber

Shandong Cuisine has also been influenced by the "Confucius Family Dishes (孔府菜)". Confucius was born in Qufu (曲阜), Shandong Province. As a great educator, thinker, and statesman in the late Spring and Autumn Period, Confucius holds a special place in Chinese history. His descendants enjoyed a number of privileges and preferred delicate taste. Their cooks constantly improved their skills and gradually the repertoire of "Confucius Family Dishes" took shape. The dishes are renowned for their taste, aroma, color, shape, and the dinnerware used. A restaurant in Beijing's Xicheng District (西城区) offers more than 40 dishes based on recipes from the kitchen of the Confucius Family in Qufu. Among them are Shark Fin with Broccoli (翡翠鱼翅), Sea Cucumber with Ham (玛瑙海参), Shrimp with Yam and Celery (玉带虾仁), Chicken with White Fish, Sea-ear or Abalone, Shrimp, Shark fin, Sea Cucumber, Asparagus, and Ham (八仙过海).

Sichuan Cuisine

Sichuan Cuisine, also known as *Chuancai* (川菜), is generally regarded as the most famous of Chinese cuisines, especially for its being spicy (辣的) and flavorful (香的). With a myriad of tastes, Sichuan Cuisine emphasizes the use of chili (红辣椒). Hot pepper (辣椒) and Chinese prickly ash (花椒) are always in accompaniment, producing typical exciting tastes. Ginger, garlic, scallion (葱), and fermented soybean (豆瓣) are often used in the cooking process. Yet the highly distinctive pungency is not its only characteristic. In fact, Sichuan Cuisine boasts a great variety of flavors and different methods of cooking. A Sichuan dish can be hot (辣的), sweet, sour, salty, or tongue-numbing.

The raw materials for Sichuan Cuisine are delicacies from the land and river, edible wild herbs, and the meat of domestic animals and poultry. Beef is more common in Sichuan Cuisine than it is in other Chinese cuisines, perhaps due to the widespread use of oxen in the region. The principal cooking methods of Sichuan Cuisine include frying, frying without oil, braising, and so on.

Fish-flavored Pork Shreds

Among the most well-known dishes of Sichuan Cuisine are Hot Pot (火锅), Twice Cooked Pork Slices (回锅肉), Spicy Diced Chicken with Peanuts (宫保鸡丁), Fish-flavored Pork Shreds (鱼香肉丝), Sauteed Vermicelli with Spicy Minced Pork (蚂蚁上树), and Dry-fried Shark Fin (干烧鱼翅). One of the popular dishes is Mapo Tofu (麻婆豆腐) which was invented by a Chengdu chef's pockmarked wife decades ago. The dish, though not expensive, has been made into a gourmet delight. The cubed bean curd is cooked over a low flame in a sauce which contains ground beef, chili, and pepper. When served, the bean curd is tender, spicy, and appetizing.

Guangdong Cuisine

Guangdong Cuisine is also known as *Yuecai* (粤菜) in China and Cantonese Cuisine in the West. It was developed in Guangzhou (广州), Huizhou (惠州), Chaozhou (潮州) and on Hainan Island. The majority of overseas Chinese, especially in Southeast Asia, are from Guangdong, so Guangdong Cuisine is perhaps the most widely available Chinese regional cuisine outside China.

As the climate of Guangdong Province is hot, the dishes are fresh, tender, and lightly seasoned. The basic cooking methods of Guangdong Cuisine consist of roasting, stir-frying, deep-frying, sautéing, stewing, and steaming. The raw material for Guangdong Cuisine is very rich and includes snakes. A cooked snake is considered a delicacy. Stewed Snake and Wild Cat

(龙虎斗) is one of the most famous Guangdong dishes, for which poisonous snake, cat, and over 20 spices (香料, 调味品) are used. Roast Snake with Chrysanthemum Blooms (金菊银蛇) is provided in autumn. The dish is white in color and is garnished with beautiful petals of chrysanthemum, mushrooms, and various flavorings (调味品). Other delicacies in Guangdong Cuisine include Roast Piglet (烤乳猪), Duck Web in Oyster Sauce (蚝油鸭掌), Braised Chicken Feet with Wild Herbs (鸡脚炖山瑞), Steamed Sea Bass (蒸海鲈鱼), Steamed Turtle with Chive Sauce (美味蒸甲鱼), and Double-stewed Soup (老火靓汤).

Steamed Sea Bass

Fujian Cuisine

Fujian Cuisine, also known as *Mincai* (闽菜), is noted for its light taste, sweet and sour flavor. It has the characteristics of strictly selected ingredients, and is thus particularly apt in preparing seafood dishes.

Typical dishes of Fujian Cuisine are Crisp Pomfret with Litchi (荔枝鲳鱼), Pork Roll with Rice Flour Steamed in Lotus Leaf (荷叶米粉肉), Fried Prawn Shaped as a Pair of Fish (太极明虾).

Fried Prawn Shaped as a Pair of Fish

Jiangsu Cuisine

Jiangsu Cuisine, also known as *Sucai* (苏菜), is popular in the middle and lower reaches of the Yangtze River and is characteristically sweet. In this school of cooking, cutting technique and temperature control are emphasized. It also pays attention to the preservation of the original flavor of cooking materials and the strict selection of ingredients, exquisite workmanship, and elegant shapes.

Yincai Cooked with Chicken Slices

Some of the best dishes of Jiangsu Cuisine are Jinling Salted Dried Duck (金陵盐水鸭), Clear Crab and Pork Meatballs (清炖蟹肉狮子头), *Yincai* Cooked with Chicken Slices (银菜鸡丝), Triple Combo Duck (三套鸭), Crystal Pork (水晶肴肉), Braise Shark Fin in Brown Sauce (红烧鱼翅), and Simmered Pig's Head (扒烧猪头).

Zhejiang Cuisine

Zhejiang Cuisine or *Zhecai* (浙菜) has won a reputation for its freshness, tenderness, softness, and smoothness with mellow fragrance. It contains the specialties (特色菜) of Hangzhou, Ningbo and Shaoxing in Zhejiang Province, with Hangzhou Cuisine being the most noted one.

Each of these sub-cuisine traditions is famous for its distinctive flavor and taste, but they are all characterized by the careful selection and preparation of ingredients, and their unique, fresh and tender tastes. Chefs of Zhejiang Cuisine are adept at retaining the natural flavor and taste of the food by quick frying, stir-frying, deep-frying, simmering and steaming. The special attention paid to the cooking process ensures that the food is fresh, crispy and tender. With their graceful presentation, the dishes are merely a pleasure for the eyes and a comfort for the stomach.

The most well-known dishes of Zhejiang Cuisine are Beggar's Chicken (叫花鸡), Dongpo Pork, West Lake Fish in Vinegar Sauce (西湖醋鱼), and Shelled Shrimps Cooked with Longjing Tea Leaves (龙井虾仁).

Beggar's Chicken

Anhui Cuisine

Anhui Cuisine, also known as *Huicai* (徽菜), is highly distinctive not only for its elaborate selection of cooking ingredients but also for its strict control of the cooking process.

Anhui chefs pay much attention to the taste, color, and cooking temperature of their dishes. They are particularly skilled at braising and stewing, and are experts in cooking delicacies from the mountain and the sea. Anhui dishes preserve most of the original taste and nutrition of the ingredients. The food is slightly spicy and salty. Some typical dishes are stewed in a heavy brown oily sauce. Ham and sugar are often added to improve the taste and enhance freshness.

High up on the menu of Anhui Cuisine are Stewed Soft-shell Turtle with Ham (火腿炖甲鱼), Huangshan Braised Pigeon (黄山炖鸽), Crisp Pork with Pine Nuts (松子米酥肉), and Li Hongzhang Hotchpotch (李鸿章大杂烩).

Li Hongzhang Hotchpotch

Hunan Cuisine

Hunan Cuisine or *Xiangcai* (湘菜) is similar to the chili-rich Sichuan Cuisine. It is also characterized by a dense pungent flavor. Chili, pepper and shallot (葱) are necessities in Hunan Cuisine.

Hunan Cuisine is famous for hot and sour flavor, fresh aroma, greasiness, and deep color.

Local people eat hot peppers to help fight dampness and cold. The main cooking methods for Hunan dishes are braising, double-boiling, steaming and stewing. It is also renowned for its frequent use of preserved meat in cooking.

Special menu items of Hunan Cuisine are Dong'an Chicken (东安子鸡), Peppery and Hot Chicken (麻辣子鸡), Steamed Fried Pork in Black Bean Sauce (走油豆豉扣肉), and Braised Dried Pork with Eel Slices (腊肉焖鳝片).

Braised Dried Pork with Eel Slices

Obviously, the above-mentioned eight schools of cuisine are not enough to cover all types of Chinese food. Beijing Cuisine, Henan Cuisine, Hubei Cuisine, Muslim Cuisine and vegetarian cuisine are also popular. China abounds with a variety of local food; even a county or a small village can have its own distinctive local dishes.

/ Top 10 Chinese Dishes Most Missed by Overseas Chinese /

With 56 ethnic groups, eight recognized major cuisines and countless cooking styles, this menu of Chinese favorites could run longer than a finely pulled noodle. But these 10 dishes are almost guaranteed to waken the homesick bug in most Chinese living or traveling abroad.

In no particular order, these are the real deals, hard to find at the local Chinese restaurants in the United States.

Street Kebabs (烤串)

The most unforgettable meals in China don't come from Michelin-starred restaurants (米其林星级餐厅). They're eaten in the streets in noisy, crowded, pungent food quarters in the heart of cities. Lamb kebabs with cumin (孜然羊肉串), teppanyaki-style squid with five-spice sauce (抹上五香酱的鱿鱼铁板烧), gigantic "swords" of mind-blowing spicy chicken wings (硕大的辣鸡翅烤串), grilled fresh oysters (烤生蚝), fried pork tenderloin slices (炸里脊肉片) and razzle-dazzle exhibitions of vegetables-on-sticks (令人眼花缭乱的蔬菜烤串).

Lamb kebabs

Every bite of China's street kebabs is a combination of good food and a street-side buzz (街头小吃文化) unique to the country.

Spicy Crayfish (麻辣小龙虾)

Cities all over the country go gaga over the crustaceans (小龙虾), which are simmered in a broth with chili and abundant spices, and then served dry. From spring to early autumn, Crayfish-Night-Outs (小龙虾夜宵) have become a ritual for many. Groups of friends find a jam-packed stall (大排档), sit on tiny plastic stools and order a bucket or two of bright red crayfish.

Spicy Crayfish

No chopsticks needed, digging in with the hands is preferred. The preferred beverage to go with these tasty freshwater lobsters (龙虾) is ice cold Chinese beer (中国冰啤) such as Reeb (力波), Tsingtao (青岛), and Yanjing (燕京), depending on the city.

Lamb Hot Pot (涮羊肉)

Outside of China, spicy Sichuan hot pot (辛辣的四川火锅) and nourishing Cantonese hot pot (滋养的广东火锅) are well known.

Lamb Hot Pot

But in China, Lamb Hot Pot is hugely popular, especially in the north during the bitterly cold winter.

Guilin Rice Noodles (桂林米粉)

Located in southern China among clear rivers and the Karst Mountains (卡斯特山脉), Guilin isn't only famous for its heavenly landscape, but for bowls of rice noodles.

Guilin Rice Noodles

There are noodles stalls (米粉摊位) everywhere in Guilin and surrounding areas.

Yan Du Xian Soup (腌笃鲜)

Yan Du Xian is a nutritious soup known as the great comfort food of the Yangtze River Delta in early spring.

Yan Du Xian Soup

Lanzhou Hand-Pulled Noodles (兰州拉面)

Lanzhou Hand-Pulled Noodles

The flagship halal dish (招牌清真菜肴) from China, hand-pulled noodles hail from the wild, sandy lands of northwest China.

Sugar-Coated Haws (Candied Haws, Tang Hu Lu 糖葫芦)

Sugar-Coated Haws

This is an iconic snack (典型的小吃) in northern China, especially in Beijing.

Stinky Tofu (臭豆腐)

Fried, braised, steamed or grilled—Stinky Tofu is delicious no matter how it's prepared.

Stinky Tofu

Stinky Tofu is most popular in Hunan Province in central China, the Yangtze River Delta region (especially Shaoxing) and Taiwan.

Shanghai Hairy Crab (上海大闸蟹)

For Shanghai people, autumn isn't complete without a steamed, roe-laden hairy crab (清蒸、带卵的大闸蟹).

Shanghai Hairy Crab

The traditional beverage to drink with a steamed hairy crab is warm yellow rice wine (温热的黄米酒).

Harbin Red Sausage (哈尔滨红肠)

Harbin Red Sausage is a hugely popular cold cut (冷切菜) in China. People get it from delicatessens (熟食店) and eat it on its own as a snack, with bread as a picnic food (郊游食物) or cook it with vegetables (especially cabbage).

Harbin Red Sausage

The texture is more tender than salami (意大利蒜味腊肠), firmer than an American hotdog (美国热狗) and drier than cooked British sausages (熟英国香肠).

/ Table Manners /

Chinese people are famous for their hospitality. They like to invite friends to their homes for dinner. Usually, they cook as many special dishes as they can, which is a normal practice of Chinese people. At a formal banquet, table manners are virtually important and should be observed.

Arrangement of Seats

At a formal banquet, the host usually prepares adequate seats for guests. For a large number of guests, the elderly or people of high status are allocated specific seats, which are at the northern side of the table or directly face the entrance to the room. The concept of "honored north, humble south (尊北卑南)" is closely related with traditional Chinese etiquette since buildings in China are traditionally located in north while facing south.

Toasts

Once the guests are seated, the host proposes a toast to the guests while saying "Drink first to show respect (先干为敬)". The host and guests empty their glasses, which are refilled in readiness for the next of many toasts.

The Chinese toast with the word *ganbei* (干杯, bottoms up), and traditionally the guests are expected to drain their glass in one swig (一口喝干) and to drink one glass with each person present. For those with low alcohol tolerance, it is witty to declare this beforehand in order to avoid awkward situations. It is completely acceptable to have three toasts with the entire company rather than one separate toast for every individual present. Some other toasts can also be offered, such as "Toast to your health" "Toast to our friendship", and so on.

Serving Courses

The serving order of courses is from cold to hot. Hot entrees (主菜) should be served starting on the left of the seat across the main guests. The meal then begins with a set of at least four cold dishes followed by the main courses of hot meat and vegetable dishes. Soup is served next (except in Guangdong-style restaurants); and the local staples (主食) such as rice, noodles, and dumplings are served last. Hosts tend to cook abundant food to avoid the embarrassment that all the food should be consumed.

/ Chinese Chopsticks /

Chopsticks are a symbol of Chinese culture, and the Chinese people are proud of them. Chopsticks are mentioned in many ancient Chinese books. It is commonly accepted that chopsticks originated in China, but when they were invented remains a mystery. Historical documents show that the use of chopsticks dates back to 3,000 years ago. Dr. Li Zhengdao (李政道), Nobel Prize winning physicist, states that chopsticks were invented as early as the Spring and Autumn Period (770 B.C.E.—475 B.C.E.). This seemingly simple tool illustrates the wonder of the lever principle.

Chopsticks were called *zhu* (箸) in ancient China. This word refers to taboo on ships because it is a homonym for another Chinese word meaning "to stop"; ships stopping on route would mean an accident or disaster. In order to avoid the ominous sound, fishermans called chopsticks *kuai* (快) denoting "fast" in Chinese. And, following the way small things and other kitchen utensils were referred to, people added the suffix *zi* (子) to *kuai*. Thus, chopsticks began to be called *kuaizi* (筷子).

Kuaizi

Apart from bamboo and wood, jade, ivory, plastic, aluminum, silver, and gold can all be used to make chopsticks. They are roughly the same length throughout China (about 25 centimeters). Special long bamboo chopsticks are used in the kitchen.

Chinese people use chopsticks every day, and they are very skillful at handling them, which seems a wonder and a mystery to many foreigners. Foreign visitors have to learn to use chopsticks if they want to eat Chinese food in China. It is not very difficult to learn, but practice is needed.

To use chopsticks, first take up a pair of sticks horizontally with your right hand, and hold them with your thumb and forefinger. The thick ends of the sticks will naturally rest upon the junction (接合点) of the thumb and your forefinger. Then, insert your middle finger between the two sticks about one third of the way down. Rest the lower one upon the first joint of your ring finger and keep it stationary (不动的). Move the upper stick up and down with the forefinger and the middle finger so that the tips of the sticks meet and separate like a crab's claw. After some practice, you will be able to pick up something from a dish and put it into your mouth with these mysterious sticks.

As the Chinese use chopsticks every day, they are greatly careful about the way chopsticks are handled. The correct way of holding chopsticks is to hold chopsticks in the middle, making sure that the ends are even. There are some taboos (禁忌) about using chopsticks in Chinese culture. Don't stick your chopsticks upright in the rice bowl because, in most parts of China, it indicates the food for the dead. Lay them beside your bowl or plate. Don't wave chopsticks above the dishes. Don't rummage through the food in a dish with chopsticks searching for your favorite pieces. Don't tap on your bowl with your chopsticks. Beggars tap on their bowls, so this is impolite. Avoid sucking the ends of your chopsticks or keeping them in your mouth for a long time. Never point at someone with your chopsticks and do not use them to prick food in order to pick it up. These behaviors are generally viewed as bad table manners.

Traditionally, to demonstrate his hospitality, the host may pick up some dishes for the guests with his own chopsticks. This is a sign of politeness. The appropriate thing to do is to eat whatever it is and say how delicious it is.

Chinese people are taught from childhood to "stand properly, sit properly and eat properly", and receive training about table manners. The training includes seat selection, being courteous to the elderly, how to handle chopsticks, and when to speak cheerfully and humorously.

Chopsticks are not only used as eating tools. They have many other functions. In the past, silver chopsticks or wooden chopsticks inlaid (镶嵌) with silver thread were used to test whether a dish had been poisoned or not. The silver would turn black if it touches poisonous food. Wang Xifeng (王熙凤), one of the main characters in the classical novel *A Dream of the Red Mansions* (《红楼梦》), once said, "If there is poison in the dish, the chopsticks will tell." There are many legends about how emperors used chopsticks to make decisions. A Tang Dynasty emperor found it difficult to decide who should be his prime minister. He wrote the names of the candidates on small pieces of paper, folded them into small balls, and put them into a tube. Then he shook the tube and, with a pair of chopsticks, he picked out the lucky name. Chopsticks made of ivory, bamboo, or silver, with decorations or carvings, often serve as ornaments or gifts.

Chopsticks are also used in Mongolian dancing. In certain dances, Mongolian girls have a bundle of red chopsticks in each hand. As they dance, they beat the sticks against their shoulders, arms, waists, legs, feet, or each other. Last but not least, using chopsticks proves to be good physical exercise. According to an investigation, chopsticks exercise many joints and muscles and stimulate the nervous system, thus helping to make a person more nimble (敏捷) and intelligent.

Chopsticks Dance

/ Chinese Tea /

China has a rich and sophisticated tea culture. Chinese people have a popular saying, "Seven things in the house: firewood, rice, oil, salt, soy sauce, vinegar, and tea". It can be drawn from the saying that tea plays an important role in Chinese people's daily life.

It is commonly recognized that China is the first country to grow, produce, and drink tea.

Drinking tea has become a daily habit of Chinese people. The art of tea making and drinking, after evolving through different dynasties, now focuses on the method of brewing (泡) tea, the drinking utensils, and the serving etiquette.

Tea Classification

Although there are hundreds of varieties of Chinese tea, they can be classified into five basic categories according to their different processing techniques. The five types are green tea (绿茶), black tea (红茶), oolong tea (乌龙茶), compressed tea (砖茶), and scented tea (花茶). Some minor types are white tea and yellow tea.

Green tea, which is unfermented (未发酵的), is the most natural of all types of Chinese tea. It is called green tea because the tea liquid and tea leaves are greenish. Compared with other types of Chinese tea, it has the most medicinal value and the least caffeine content. It can help people reduce their inner heat.

The most famous among various types of green tea are *longjing* of West Lake (西湖龙井) in Zhejiang Province, *maofeng* of Mount Huangshan (黄山毛峰) in Anhui Province, *biluochun* (碧螺春) produced in Jiangsu and *yunwu* from Mount Lushan (庐山云雾) in Jiangxi Province.

The main difference between green tea and black tea is that green tea keeps the original color of tea leaves without fermentation when being processed, whereas black tea is fermented before being baked. Black tea is so named because the tea liquid and tea leaves are reddish black. It tastes sweet and can facilitate the fostering of *yang* energy and erase the greasiness in the human body.

The best types of black tea include *qihong* tea of Anhui (祁红茶), *dianhong* tea of Yunnan (滇红茶), *suhong* tea of Jiangsu (苏红茶), *chuanhong* tea of Sichuan (川红茶), and *huhong* tea of Hunan (湖红茶).

Oolong tea sits half way between green tea and black tea because it is semi-fermented. Typical oolong tea leaves are green in the middle and red on the edges as a result of being softened. Oolong tea is the chosen tea for the famous *gong fu* tea (功夫茶) brewing process. Its aroma ranges from mild to medium. Beginners of oolong tea should take care, as even though its flavor seems only mild to medium, the tea may be quite strong.

Oolong tea is also favored for its medicinal functions. Fujian, Guangdong, and Taiwan are the major producers of this kind of tea.

Oolong tea can be grouped into three grades based on its light, medium or heavy fermentation. Lightly fermented oolong tea has the characteristics of strong aroma and high refinement, making a golden-colored drink. Medium fermented oolong tea includes *tieguanyin* (铁观音) which is brown in color and steady in taste. Heavily fermented oolong tea is orange-colored with the sweetness and fragrance of ripe fruits.

Compressed tea is made by compressing steamed tea leaves into molds such as bricks, cakes, columns, and so on. Compressed tea can be stored for years. Aged compressed tea possesses a gentle flavor.

Chinese scented tea is a unique category. It is a mixture of flowers such as roses, jasmine and orchids, and tea leaves, mostly green but also with elements of black or oolong tea. The two are finely blended and sealed for a time to let the sweet scent of flowers pervade the tea leaves. Chinese scented tea has a light-to-medium aroma and a medium-to-strong aroma.

White tea is non-roasted and non-rubbed tea with natural fragrance. Well-known varieties include *baihao yinzhen* (白毫银针) and *baimudan* (白牡丹).

Yellow tea has yellow leaves and yellow tea color. It is an uncommon class of Chinese tea. The flavor is mild and refreshing.

Tea Etiquette

In China, it is customary for people to serve guests tea. Serving a cup of tea is more than mere politeness. It is a symbol of togetherness, a sharing of something enjoyable, and a way of showing respect to guests.

A Chinese host usually asks the preference of the guest before making tea. The water should not be too hot, otherwise it will scald the guest. When pouring tea, Chinese hosts often follow the rule of "full cup of wine and half cup of tea (满杯酒半杯茶)". Custom dictates that a host will only fill a teacup to seven-tenths of its capacity. It is said that the other three-tenths will be filled with friendship and affection. When offered tea, the guest should take a sip at least, which is considered polite by Chinese people. Moreover, it is a bad manner that the spout (壶嘴) of the teapot is facing someone. The proper way is to direct it outwards from the table.

/ Chinese Wine /

Wine has a long history in China and plays an important role in the lives of Chinese people. It is comparable with such daily necessities as rice, salt, oil, and water.

In ancient China, since wine was regarded as a kind of sacred liquid, it was only used as sacrificial offerings to Heaven, Earth, or ancestors. Later, along with the development of distilling (蒸馏) and brewing (酿造) techniques, wine became an ordinary, daily drink. Chinese wine culture, with its unique national characteristics, has been constantly enriched and developed. More and more kinds of wine have been brewed, and more and more customs concerning wine have emerged accordingly.

Wine Feasts

Chinese drinking customs were born almost at the same time as wine was invented. Some customs have survived till today.

The marriage wine feast (喜宴) has long been synonymous with weddings. To drink marriage wine (喝喜酒) means "going to attend a wedding". At a wedding banquet, the new couple must propose toasts to their parents and the guests present. They must also drink arm-crossed wine (交杯酒), which will bless them with a hundred years of happy marriage.

The one-month-old wine feast (满月酒宴) and hundredth-day wine feast (百日酒宴), which are for newly born babies, are popular banquets. When a baby is a month or one hundred days old, his family will hold a wine feast to celebrate and those guests who take part in the feast usually give the baby some gifts or a red packet, which is a red paper envelop with some money wrapped inside.

The longevity wine feast (寿宴) is a birthday feast prepared for elders in the family. The 50th, 60th and 70th birthdays are entitled to great celebrations. Participants include family members, relatives, and close friends.

The wine feast for setting a roof beam in place (安放挑梁酒宴) and for moving into a new house (乔迁新居酒宴) originate in the countryside of China. Setting a roof beam in place is a remarkable process in building a house. Moving into a new house is also a vital event in one's life. So such feasts are unavoidable.

There are a variety of reasons for Chinese people to organize wine feasts, such as a feast for opening a business (开张宴), a feast for division of dividends (分红宴), and a feast for farewell (告别宴), and so on.

In addition, Chinese people offer different wine feasts on different occasions. On Chinese New Year's Eve, people drink New Year's wine (团年酒), wishing good health and closeness in the family in the coming year. On the Dragon Boat Festival, Chinese people drink *changpu* wine (菖蒲酒) to ward off evil spirits and hope for peace and security. On the Mid-Autumn Festival, drinking while appreciating the full moon is a part of the celebration. This is also the time when sweet-scented osmanthus flowers (桂花) are in full bloom. So, drinking osmanthus wine (桂花酒) is also a tradition of the festival.

Chinese people tend to urge their guests to drink in order to express their sincerity and friendship. The more the guests drink, the more cheerful they feel, because they believe the guests have good opinions of them. If the guests refuse to drink, they will feel disgraced.

Drinkers' Wager Game (酒令)

A drinkers' wager game is a special method in China to help create a more joyous atmosphere while drinking. In general, a drinkers' wager game is adopted as a penalty to urge drinkers to drink more, but its main purpose is to produce a more cheerful ambiance. Drinkers' wager wine has many forms, depending on the drinkers' social status, literacy status, and interest. Generally, there are three types—general games, literary games, and competing games.

General Games

Ladies attending banquets may play general games such as telling jokes and passing down a flower to the beats of a drum (击鼓传花). The latter game requires diners to pass a flower round to the accompaniment of drumbeats. When the drumbeats suddenly stop, the diner found with the flower still in his hand will have to pay a forfeit by drinking a cup of wine (受罚喝一杯). While the flower is being passed round, the great tension adds fun and excitement to the game.

Literary Game

Literary games are more popular with scholars and intellectuals, since their education equips them with the knowledge to compete. They play it by composing poems, solving word puzzles, guessing riddles, and so on.

Competing Games

Competing games include archery, arrow pitching, dice throwing (掷骰子), finger guessing (猜拳), and so on. The most common and simplest way of playing the wager game is the finger-guessing game performed by two drinkers. Both of them should stretch out their fingers at the same time to indicate a certain number from one to ten, while they both shout out the sum of the two numbers at the same time. The one who guesses right is the winner, and the other has to pay a forfeit by drinking a cup of wine.

Exercises

Part One   Comprehension

Fill in the following blanks with the information you learn in Chapter 10.

1. Generally speaking, there are three essential standards by which Chinese cooking is judged, namely, color, aroma, and taste, with _____ being the most important.

2. Shandong Cuisine, also known as *Lucai*, is representative of northern China's cooking and its techniques are widely practised in _____ China.

3. Sichuan Cuisine, also known as *Chuancai*, is generally regarded as the most famous of Chinese cuisines, especially for its being spicy and _____.

4. Chinese people are taught from childhood to "stand properly, sit properly, and eat properly", and receive training about _____ manners.

5. It is commonly recognized that China is the _____ country to grow, produce, and drink tea.

6. Drinkers' _____ game is a special method in China to help create more joyous atmosphere while drinking.

Part Two   Translation

Passage Translation

中国是世界公认的最早种茶、产茶和饮茶的国家。饮茶已经成为中国人的一种日常生活习惯。经过历朝历代的发展，制茶与饮茶的艺术现在集中在泡茶（brewing tea）的方法、茶具（drinking utensils）和上茶礼节（serving etiquette）上。在中国，饮茶是一种仪式（ritual）和一种精致品位（refined taste）的展示。中国人在饮茶的同时，也领略着（take delight in）品茶的惬意。喝茶聊天是中国人中非常流行的打发时间的方式。过去，他们从走进一家有名的茶馆（tea house）来开始一天的生活。中国的茶馆相当于法国的咖啡馆（cafe）和英国的酒馆（pub）。中国人到这里不仅是为了喝茶，也是为了社交。

Part Three Critical Thinking and Discussion

1. Of the eight regional cuisines, which one do you like most? Why?

2. Compared to cafes, tea houses have less appeal to young Chinese people. Discuss with your partner whether coffee, which is popular with young Chinese people, poses a great threat to Chinese tea culture.

Chapter 11
Traditional Chinese Handicrafts

/ Ceramics /

Ceramics (制陶工艺) is the general art of heating common clay to produce a utilitarian or ornamental object. All pottery (陶器) and porcelain (瓷器) are considered ceramic (陶瓷制品).

Pottery

Pottery or earth-ware is, technically, any object made from a porous clay and baked at a temperature ranging from hot, direct sunlight to baking, or firing, in a kiln at a temperature of about 1,000 degrees centigrade. Often, pottery is neither hard nor stable. Pigments or colors, and a glossy glaze can be applied to pottery before firing, producing beautiful results. Or, pottery after firing can be painted with almost any pigment, although the unprotected painted decoration is susceptible to damage.

When, then, did pottery first touch the life of mankind actually? Archaeological findings set the date in the Neolithic Age (新石器时代) in Chinese primitive society (approximately 8000 B.C.E.—2000 B.C.E.). Agriculture and stock breeding began to develop from that time and farm production led to a fairly settled life for the ancient Chinese. Pottery was needed for convenience and improvement in their life, and they experimented with making vessels, gradually developing the art of firing pottery out of clay. In the Neolithic Age, people created three different types of earthenware. They were a coarse pottery with a yellowish brown sandy body, a red pottery and a painted pottery decorated with motifs (基本图案) painted with an iron-oxide pigment. The excellence of the last has given the name Painted Pottery (彩陶) to this Neolithic Culture, which is also called the Yangshao Culture (仰韶文化) after the Yangshao Village in Mianchi County (渑池县), Henan Province,

Painted Pottery

where the first discovery of painted pottery was made. Besides the Yangshao Culture on the Central Plains in the Yellow River valley, others which were well-known were the Qingliangang (青莲岗) in the Huaihe River valley and Daxi (大溪) cultures in the Yangtze River valley, the Qujialing Culture (屈家岭文化) in the region around the confluence of the Yangtze River and Hanshui River, all of which took place about the same period.

It is not possible to date the exact duration of painted pottery production, but those pieces discovered at the Yangshao sites: Banpo Village (半坡村)in Xi'an, Miaodigou (庙底沟) in Shanxian County (陕县), Henan Province, are considered to have been produced sometime between 5000 B.C.E. and 3000 B.C.E.

Painted pottery was followed by black pottery, which was due to a relatively high charcoal content, the tiny holes in the paste being filled with charcoal grains. Its first discovery was made in Longshan Town (龙山镇) of Shandong Province in 1928; hence this ware is referred to as the pottery of the Longshan Culture (龙山文化). Excavations show that Longshan black pottery evolved from the Yangshao painted pottery.

Some of the distinguished characteristics of painted pottery, thin construction and a well-polished surface, for example, are inherited from the black pottery, but there are also major improvements to be seen in the newer ware. One is that its shapes are much more varied. Another is its concise and fresh contour (外形) and simple decoration. The third is the development of the potter's wheel, which both marked a great advance in ceramic production and also allowed for mass production. The pottery worked out with wheels was more precisely formed and had thinner walls; some were as thin and smooth as an egg shell, so this type was called the eggshell black pottery (薄胎黑陶) and it is very well-known in the history of Chinese pottery.

The Longshan black pottery culture developed in the region centering around Shandong and Henan Provinces but spread to the surrounding areas, such as today's Jiangsu, Anhui, Hebei and Liaoning.

From the beginning of the Xia Dynasty, the black pottery turned by and by into gray pottery, which prevailed through the slavery society and on to the early feudal society in the Warring States Period. This drab, gray pottery is not as aesthetically pleasing as the bright and colorful red and painted potteries, but its durability insured it a place of importance in Chinese ceramics history.

Many pieces of gray pottery have been unearthed from the site of Erligang (二里岗) in

Zhengzhou and other sites in Luoyang, Anyang and Xi'an. Major shapes include *li* (鬲, hollow-legged tripod vessels), *zeng* (甑), *jia* (斝, wine goblets), *gui* (簋, high-footed bowls) and *zhi* (觯, goblets). Many of them were fashioned after the bronze vessels of the Shang and Zhou Dynasties and were elaborately and delicately decorated with a variety of new decorative techniques. For instance, incise design of trellises (格架) and zigzag lines into the surface of the vessels, and impressions in the clay with stamps carved in a simple geometric pattern.

There is a certain type of white pottery that was produced at the same time as the gray and black pottery of the Shang Period, though it was started as early as the Dawenkou Culture (大汶口文化) of 5,000 years ago. This white pottery was made from almost pure kaolin clay (高岭土) which gave white color and hard texture. Common shapes are the *lei* (罍, urn-like vessels), *dou* (豆, stemmed vessels) and *zun* (尊, wine vessels), decorated with stamped imprints (盖印) of key-frets (键槽), coiling dragons, and other motifs that are identical with but more simplified than the ritual bronzes of that time. This white ware is extremely rare compared to the gray and black wares. Most of those that we have are from the tombs of kings. Obviously, this fine white pottery was owned exclusively by the nobility and slave-owners, as funeral objects.

During the Shang and Zhou Dynasties, pottery also took its place in architecture when plate and tube tiles (瓦片) and bricks for balustrade (栏杆) construction were made. This marked a great innovation in pottery production, as, from then on, bricks and tiles have been important building materials.

Greater concentration in pottery production and a more specialized division of labor marked the Warring States Period, which passed from slavery into feudal society. The pottery of this period was of four varieties: gray, red, dull-brown (暗褐色), and black. They surpassed wares of any previous period in variety, quantity and quality.

The Qin and Han Dynasties did not see a great development in producing pottery wares of daily necessity, but witnessed the production of large pottery sculptures. In the summer of 1974, a vast underground vault (墓穴) filled with life-sized terra-cotta figures of warriors and horses (兵马俑) was discovered east of the mausoleum of the First Emperor of the Qin Dynasty in Lintong County (临潼县), Shaanxi Province. The several

Terra-Cotta Figures of Warriors and Horses

thousand stalwart (强壮的), life-like figures of warriors 1.8 meters tall and of life-size horses

1.63 meters high were unearthed from an area of 1,260 square meters. The warriors are in battle-dress, armor and helmets, and carry bows and arrows or swords and lances (长矛). Every one, looking powerful and mighty, is distinctly different, both in mien (外表) and posture (姿势). The plump pottery horses have ears pointed in intent attention. The successful firing of this huge contingent of life-size and life-like pottery warriors was unprecedented in the history of China's ancient pottery-making art and marked an important stage in the production of large sculptures in ancient China.

Pottery sculpture advanced also in the Han Dynasty. Various kinds of figurines and images show that craftsmen had attained a high level of skill and the objects gradually tended more and more to reflect reality. The most outstanding is the figure of a ballad singer unearthed near Chengdu, Sichuan Province. The figure holds a drum in his left hand and points downward with the forefinger of his right hand; his head is drawn back between shrugged shoulders while a broad smile narrows his eyes. Raised eyebrows and the creases (皱纹) on his forehead tell of long experience of misery. Its vividness surpassed all the equivalents before the era.

What must be mentioned here is the glazed pottery (釉陶). It is called pottery because it is only glazed on the outside. Some scholars take it that Chinese glazed pottery made its first appearance sometime in the Shang Period, flourished from the Spring and Autumn Period all the way through the Han Dynasty. This pottery usually requires a firing temperature of more than 1,100℃, so it is also called high-fired glazed pottery. This was over 3,000 years earlier than that produced in West Asia and Europe for they did not produce it until the 18th century. This great gap may be attributed to differences in kiln construction and firing methods. The ancient Chinese invented a more efficient kiln and reduction firing, both of which helped to bring about superior glazing techniques as well. The benefits of these inventions extended into countries in Southeast Asia.

The glazed pottery, which was green, yellow, black or brown, developed in two directions; one is its evolvement into porcelain during the Eastern Han Dynasty, so we say it is in fact the fore-runner of porcelain; the other is its more delicate refinement.

The appearance of the Tri-Colored Glazed Pottery of the Tang Dynasty (唐三彩) was, in a sense, the zenith of the development of glazed pottery. Of all the wares in China's long history of pottery production, it is the most admired for its ornate beauty.

The wares of the Tri-Colored Glazed Pottery of the Tang Dynasty are made of kaolin. Though some have a slightly red tinge (色调), many are fine, smooth and spotlessly white. The primary decorative elements are, of course, the glazes containing lead silicate (硅酸盐). Various metal oxides (氧化物) are used to prepare pigments: brownish red and brownish yellow from iron, bright yellow from iron or antimony (锑), various greens from copper or chromium (铬), purple from manganese (锰), and so on, among which white, yellow and green are the chief colors. Aluminum is used as flux to enhance the luster (光泽) of colors. These glazes and pigments are not applied in distinctly separate color fields. Rather, the different

The Tri-colored Glazed Pottery of the Tang Dynasty

colors run into and mingle with (混合) each other, creating a dreamy, fantastic color scheme (色彩设计).

　　The tri-colored glazed ware showsa diversity in shape, such as *zun* (尊) wine cups, ewers (大口水壶), jars, bowls, plates, vases, cosmetics or ointment (油膏) boxes, spittoons (痰盂), incense burners (香炉), pillows, houses, storerooms and mortars (研钵). Human figures included warriors, officials, aristocrat ladies, young women, boys, attendants, musicians and dancers, and riders and hunters on horseback. Among animal figures were horses, camels, donkeys, oxen, lions, tigers, sheep, dogs, chickens, ducks and rabbits. The rich variety, on the one hand, shows the complexity of the Tang society, and on the other hand, reflects its wide use in life. Some of them were for daily use, some as funerary objects and some for decoration.

　　The Tri-Colored Glazed Pottery of the Tang Dynasty, or Tang Tri-Color, with the rich variety of shapes, the complicated structure, the vividness of images, the brilliancy of colors and the magnificence of appearance, attained a craftsmanship that was remarkable in ancient ceramic art. It is a shining pearl rarely seen in the arts and crafts history of the world.

/ Porcelain /

　　Unlike pottery, porcelain is made from a mixture of special clays, often kaolin and feldspar (长石); it is fired at a very high temperature of over 1,200 degrees. It is hard and is more durable than pottery. After firing, porcelain can be painted in a rainbow of colors and glazed, and then fired at a low temperature to seal the color and harden the glaze.

　　Porcelain is one of China's great inventions. When was Chinese porcelain invented? Scholars are still exhaustively discussing this question. Some scholars place its origin in the Wei and Jin Dynasties, though a number of others think that the Eastern Han Dynasty or the Three Kingdoms Period are more appropriate dates. The most recent idea, however, based on new data and findings, is that porcelain goes back as far in Chinese history as the 16th century B.C.E. It is, in fact, no other than the glazed pottery as we have just mentioned, more exactly speaking, a kind of proto-porcelain (原型瓷器).

This glazed pottery that developed in the Shang and Zhou Period went into a decline, for reasons unknown, in the Spring and Autumn Period, but recent excavations in our country point to a revival of its production in the early Han Period. In some sense, the proto-porcelain glaze did not in fact completely fulfill the function of a glaze in that it did not coat both the interior and exterior of the vessel. Only when during the Eastern Han Dynasty did it develop into a kind of mature porcelain which had very little difference from the celadon (青瓷) of the Three Kingdoms Period and the Jin Dynasty.

From very early on, the production of ceramics was generally centralized. A production center at that time required, besides advanced techniques, an abundance of fine clay, wood for fuel, proper glazes, and good conditions to transport the final products for widespread distribution. The region of Yuezhou (越州), present Shangyu (上虞), Yuyao (余姚) counties, centered in Shaoxing (绍兴), Zhejiang Province, apparently met these qualifications. So large groups of kilns were established in the counties around. It was these kilns that marked the establishment of the celadon kilns, commonly known as Yuezhou kilns and their products as Yuezhou ware. Examinations have verified that the Yue ware of the Shangyu kilns in the Eastern Han Period has only a 0.16 to 0.18 percent water-absorption rate, proving that these examples are of the same quality as perfect celadon wares.

The Yue ware is held in high esteem because of its great superiority that lies in the quality of the glaze. It displays two types of glazes, one highly transparent and glossy (有光泽的), the other translucent (半透明的) with a dull luster (阴暗的色泽).

Yue Porcelain

Areas along the Yellow River, such as Hebei, Henan and Shandong Provinces, became porcelain producers on a fairly large scale too, though it was perhaps not until the late Northern Wei Period that the celadon ware was first produced.

Northern celadon differs most notably from its southern equivalent in the glaze tone. Its glaze was highly vitreous (玻璃质的) and bluish green in color, some showing a slight yellow tinge. Chemical analysis reveals the northern glazes were of different materials from those of southern celadon. The vessels were also more forceful and magnificent in shape. Representatives of this ware were four large celadon jars decorated with molded lotus petals in high relief unearthed from the Feng Family Tombs (封氏墓) in Jingxian County (景县), Hebei Province.

The development of northern celadon brought about two new types of ware: the white and the black porcelains.

Northern celadon clay is fairly white, containing little iron. The quality is the prime reason that northern ceramics later surpassed the southern celadon. This same white clay had given birth to white ware near the end of the Northern Dynasties. Some pieces of the ware were found in the tomb of Fan Cui (范粹), dated 575 and located in Anyang, Henan Province. These pieces have a refined white clay-body, which is firmly contracted by high firing and coated with a finely crackled transparent glaze.

White porcelain held an important place in daily life and laid the basis for subsequent ware with painted designs and for modern porcelain.

During the Sui and Tang Dynasties, ceramics developed greatly. The Tang rulers allowed craftsmen to pay money into the imperial coffers (金库) as a substitute for conscript labor (兵役) and to work as hired laborers. An independent stratum (社会阶层) of handicraftsmen thus appeared in society and handicraft workshops in their real sense sprang up and Tang ceramics became even more flourishing.

So far as celadon was concerned, the achievements lay mainly in the widening of producing areas and the appearance of kilns in different styles. The Tang hermit (隐士) Lu Yu (陆羽) wrote in his *Classic of Tea* (《茶经》) in the 8th century after his study of many porcelain vessels he saw from all over the country, "The best tea-bowls are those of the celadon of Yuezhou. Next comes Dingzhou (鼎州) and Wuzhou (婺州), and then Yuezhou (岳州), Shouzhou (寿州) and Hongzhou (洪州)."

Another prevailing school of ware was white porcelain which, as mentioned above, evolved from the northern celadon. The glaze was lustrous (光亮的) and mostly white, though some pieces had a light yellow tinge. The most common shapes are jars, bowls, vases, plates and lamps and other vessels. Its producing centers were

Neiqiu White Porcelain

chiefly Xingzhou (邢州), today's Neiqiu County (内丘县) and Dingzhou, today's Quyang County (曲阳县) in Hebei Province.

In Henan Province there were the Gongxian (巩县) kilns, the Xiguan (西关) kilns in Mixian (密县) County, the Quhe (曲河) kilns in Dengfeng (登封), and the Jiaxian (郏县) kilns.

In addition to the white porcelain and celadon, Tang black ware was also significant and its craftsmanship far surpassed that of the Eastern Jin and Northern Dynasties.

The black ware was mostly produced in kilns in the Henan area, some vessels and shards (碎片) being found in the Jiaxian kilns, the Duandian (段店) kilns in Lushan (鲁山). Its achievements lay chiefly in glazes and decoration. The glaze was even and the black color had the sheen (光泽) of lacquer (漆). Some were decorated with yellow, greyish blue and brownish green splashes (色块). The splashes were natural and unrestrained, resembling colored clouds or tree leaves. Some were decorated with various flower designs painted with a liquid black glaze. These decorative methods of distinctive artistic style contributed much to making Tang black glaze porcelain the best of its time.

Black Porcelain from Duandian Kiln

The Song Dynasty saw a still greater advance in porcelain manufacture. Various schools, each with a distinctive style, appeared in different places of China, depending on the characteristics of the raw materials and fuels, traditions of workmanship and people's customs and habits in the areas. There were celadon, white porcelain, black porcelain, misty blue, white porcelain with black designs, copper-red glaze, ever-changing crystalline glaze and furnace transmutation (窑变) of the various porcelain schools, namely, Ding Porcelain (定瓷), Yaozhou Porcelain (耀州瓷), Ru Porcelain (汝瓷), Guan Porcelain (官瓷), Jun Porcelain (钧瓷), Longquan Porcelain (龙泉瓷), and Misty Blue Porcelain (影青瓷).

Ding Porcelain

Ding kilns produced mainly white porcelain except a few vessels of green, black and dark brown glazes. Its central kiln site was located in Jianci Village (涧磁村), Quyang County, Hebei Province. Other kilns in Hebei and Shaanxi Provinces also produced wares of the same type.

Ding ware was made of extremely fine kaolin-type clay.

Ding Porcelain

When fired at a high temperature, the silicate and alumina in the clay crystallized, increasing the hardness of the clay. This quality and plasticity of the clay allowed it to be fashioned into extremely thin-walled wares. Its transparent glaze was so well suited to the clay that here was very little crazing.

The rims (轮缘) of many Ding vessels were bound with gold, silver or copper, for the rims were unglazed and sandy. The decoration was usually applied by impressing (铭记), incising and carving patterns, sometimes by moulding (线条装饰).

Yaozhou Porcelain

The Yaozhou kiln sites are located in Tongchuan (铜川), Shaanxi Province, with the present-day Huangbaozhen (黄堡镇) as the center. The basic glaze color is olive green (橄榄绿) ranging in tone from dark to light, but without any bluish tinge. Carved decoration is its most attractive feature. The most common style is an obliquely (倾斜地) carved, or beveled, motif embellished with combed decoration (精梳装饰), no matter what they are: peonies (牡丹), lotus flowers, or leaves. The style of carving is somewhat different from that of the Ding kilns. Ding motifs are usually

Yaozhou Porcelain

carved with shallow, oblique cuts and floral scrolls (花卷) of vines or flower petals are simply incised with narrow lines. Yaozhou motifs, on the other hand, are deeply carved, even thin vines and sprays of flowers. This technique gives a relief effect caused by the celadon glaze collecting in the grooves (沟纹).

Ru Porcelain

Ru ware was another major celadon school of the Song Dynasty. Its kilns were believed to have been in Linru County (临汝县), but recent discoveries prove that Qingliangsi Village (清凉寺村) in Baofeng County (宝丰县) should be the center.

With the Ru ware, the formerly olive-green celadon glaze developed a blue tint (色彩) which appeared softened, delicate and clear. In other words, a true, perfect celadon color has at last been achieved. Some of the Tang and the Five Dynasties

Ru Porcelain

Yue celadon wares were fired in an almost perfect reduction atmosphere, and yet they lacked the requisite bluish tintand deepness of color that mark true celadon. Then Ru celadon was the last step in the long process of evolving a perfect celadon ware and demonstrated maturity in celadon manufacture.

Guan Porcelain

The so-called Guan ware here is none other than that produced in the kilns officially established in Bianliang (汴梁), the present-day Kaifeng, and Lin'an (临安), the present-day Hangzhou during the Northern and Southern Song Dynasties.

Guan Porcelain

Most of Guan ware was made of a blackish, rather sandy clay with a high iron content. The quite thick glaze coating gave it the lustrous and bright finish. Their color was paler than the celadon of Ru ware. As the glaze was fired at a high temperature, it melted and streamed down the vessels, leaving the glaze on the mouth-rims thinner so the paste color showed through. And, as the mouth-rims were separated by the vitreous glaze (玻璃釉), the color had a purplish tinge. The foot-rim was unglazed with the iron-colored paste fully exposed, showing its special feature of "purple mouth-rim and iron foot"—an important factor in identifying Guan Porcelain.

Because of different contraction rates the glaze on the blackish clay ware is patterned with large and small crackles. The crazing of the glaze always creates subtle variations of gloss and color. This kaleidoscope effect of the Guan celadon strongly resembles the surface of a natural jade stone.

Jun Porcelain

There are still different ideas about why the ware is called Jun Porcelain. One is that Yuxian County (禹县) of Henan Province was renamed Junzhou (钧州) in 1184 (the 24th year of the Dading reign) in the Jin Dynasty. Another theory says that Yuxian County was the capital of Yu of the Xia Dynasty. When his son Qi (启) came the throne he held a great

Jun Porcelain

celebration banquet on a platform called "Juntai (钧台)" where the kilns were located in the Song Dynasty.

The most attractive feature of Jun celadon is the peculiar type of celadon glaze. Because of the silicate in the glaze something unique appears as small white mottles (斑点, 杂色) when the ware is fired. The effect of the white mottles suffused (布满) throughout the blue glaze is reminiscent of the bluish white light of the moon, and thus this glaze is called "moon white" or opaque blue mottled glaze (不透明蓝花釉). Some Jun wares have reddish purple splotches (斑点) on the moon white glaze. These were created by spotting the vessels with copper-oxide before glazing and firing in a reduction kiln. The splotches vary from subdued purple to a vivid rose purple, depending on the thickness of the opaque blue mottled overglaze. Jun ware is a gem in the Song porcelain history.

Longquan Porcelain

The name Longquan is a general one encompassing kilns in many different locations, including Lishui (丽水), Suichang (遂昌), Yunhe (云和), Qingtian (青田), Yongjia (永嘉), and Longquan, with Dayao (大窑) and Jincun (金村) of Longquan County as its center.

Longquan Porcelain

The Longquan kilns probably began production sometimes in the Five Dynasties Period, and flourished during the Southern Song, for by the end of the Northern Song it was still on a very small scale.

Longquan ware was also known as *ge* (哥, elder brother) and *di* (弟, younger brother) ware (哥弟瓷). It was said that two brothers, the elder named Zhang Sheng the First (章生一), and the younger Zhang Sheng the Second (章生二), were both skilled at porcelain making, each representing a different style.

Vessels from Zhang Sheng the Second's Kiln were remarkably blue and transparent like fine jade. Its bluish green glaze was of many varieties, the best being kingfisher green (翠鸟绿的), powder blue (粉蓝的) and plum green (梅子绿的). The paste was white with a blue tinge, fine, compact and durable.

Ge wares from Zhang Sheng the First's Kiln were light in color, powder blue, pale white or the yellow of parched rice (炒米黄). Its glaze was often crackled (有裂纹的), large and small crackles interspersed, the large ones jet black (墨黑色的) and the small ones brownish yellow (棕黄色的). So "golden wires and iron threads" was the popular description.

Misty Blue Porcelain

The Jingdezhen (景德镇) kilns in Jiangxi Province have been outstanding in ceramics productions. Wares produced at these kilns from the Late Tang Period include celadon and white porcelain. But they were rather coarse. It was not until the Northern Song Dynasty that Jingdezhen began to receive public acclaim. The ware of this period is known as "misty blue (影

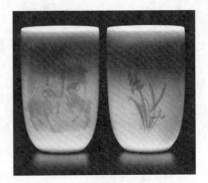

青)" or "clear blue (青白)" porcelain. Its unique glaze falls somewhat between blue and white, more bluish green and has a better lustre compared with Song white porcelain. The ware is so delicate, and its swiftly etched (蚀刻的) design and paper-like surface so fine that "white as jade, thin as paper, bright as a mirror, ringing like a stone chime (白如玉, 薄如纸, 明如镜, 响如石钟)" are epithets (词语) applied to this famous ware.

Misty Blue Porcelain

Unfortunately the Southern Song Period saw the decline of the Jingdezhen ware though the decline continued only a short period.

Besides the wares mentioned above, some other porcelains of the Song Dynasty were also well-known, such as Cizhou (磁州, the present-day Handan area, Hebei Province) ware. The most outstanding achievement of Cizhou Porcelain which came in many glaze colors—white, black, yellow, brown, green, and also a blended glaze—was its applying of the traditional Chinese art of painting on porcelain, which paved the way for a still better decoration of porcelain vessels in the future.

The Song porcelain surpassed its predecessors in variety, quantity and quality as well. So it is not at all exaggerated to say it reached the zenith in the ceramics history of feudal China if we take it as a whole, though the wares in the Ming and Qing Dynasties developed to a higher level in some ways.

At the end of the Song Dynasty, even some years after the founding of the Yuan Dynasty, wars continued for many years. Song porcelain schools in the north went downhill one after another. But areas south of the Yangtze River suffered comparatively less from the wars. In some respects, some porcelain wares surpassed those of the Song Dynasty. Take for instance, Jingdezhen porcelain.

What is most worth mentioning is that from the early Yuan Period, potters in Jingdezhen kilns were experimenting with new techniques and variations of their wares. Besides incised, engraved and impressed decorative designs, the more complicated technique of molded decoration had developed to a higher level and a new under-glaze painting technique had been invented, that is, blue decorative designs painted under the glaze of white porcelain. Thus a decorative blue-and-white porcelain was produced.

The emergence of this kind of under-glaze blue decoration is significant in the history of

Chinese ceramics. The under-glaze iron painted white ware of the Cizhou kilns had appeared much earlier, but it was a monochrome (单色的) ware. The new blue-and-white ware represented a move toward polychrome decoration with green, purple, yellow, and red enamels (珐琅). Its appearance marked the first step toward a transition from a classical absorption with glaze tone to the modern concept of expressive painting.

In the Ming Period, the Jingdezhen wares were the only ones to show a steady development, though there were, of course, other types of wares being produced at the same time. Jingdezhen became the national porcelain center and nearly 300 kilns were set up in the town. "White smoke covered the sky by day and flames rose into the air at night." This description provided us with an unprecedentedly flourishing scene of that time.

There was also a great advance in producing technique. One of the prime factors was the establishment of official kilns.

First of all, white porcelain surpassed that of any previous time. White porcelain of different periods in Ming had its own predominant characteristics. In the Yongle reign (永乐统治时期) it had a thin paste and lustrous glaze known as "sweet white (甜白)" for its soft and pleasant whiteness. It was, in the Xuande reign (宣德在位时期), praised as "moist and smooth as lard and lustrous as fine jade (润滑如猪油, 光泽如美玉)," that of the Jiajing reign (嘉靖时期, 1522—1566) as "pure without blemish (纯洁无瑕的)" while the Wanli white porcelain (万历白瓷) was lauded as "translucent and bright (透明光亮的)."

Secondly, blue-and-white porcelain ranked first and predominated during the Ming Dynasty, with that of the Yongle and Xuande Periods at its best. The high-quality smalt (颜料) imported from Persia (波斯, 现称伊朗) was used as pigment and the clay was improved. Corresponding to these was the refinement in painting techniques and decorations. Motifs in the sophisticated literati style increased: large plates decorated with a painting of trees and rocks surrounded by grasses, vases on which depicted birds perched on trees and so on. Some were so wonderfully painted that one could feel musical tempo in them: water plants

Blue-and-White Porcelain

quivering in a running stream, and floral scrolls undulating in a rhythmic pattern across the surface of a vessel, which was none other than a valuable work of art.

Thirdly, a true polychrome enameled ware called "contending colors (斗彩)" was invented in the Chenghua reign (成化时期, 1465—1487). In producing this ware, an outline of designs in an under-glaze blue was sketched onto the unglazed surface of a vessel, and the whole was coated with a transparent over-glaze and then fired until the vessel was firmly contracted. The next step was to paint designs of yellow, green, purple and red enamels (红釉) with a blue-and-white outline and fire them again. These multiple layers of colors "contending for beauty (斗彩)" and created an exquisitely

Contending Colors Porcelain

elegant effect. Just on this basis, a type of five-color ware made its appearance during the reign of Hongzhi (弘治时期).

In the Qing Dynasty, the reigns of Kangxi (康熙), Yongzheng (雍正) and Qianlong (乾隆), from 1662 to 1795, were the golden age of Chinese ceramics. The Qing laws demanded that the employers and the employees be equal. This change in productive relations provided good conditions for developing the productive force. Ceramics, like other trade, took a step ahead of what the Ming Dynasty had achieved.

Beginning from the Kangxi reign (1662—1722) Qing resumed porcelain-making at Jingdezhen and striking progress was made in porcelain craftsmanship, which reached its ultimate peak in the Yongzheng and Qianlong Periods. Besides the development of the blue-and-white, "contending colors", and other traditional wares of fine varieties were created, such as *famille rose* (粉彩).

It is usually assumed that *famille rose* began to be produced in the last years of the Kangxi reign and attained its peak in the Yongzheng reign. It developed from the "contending colors". common *famille rose* painting subjects include birds and flowers, grasses and insects, trees and rocks, and landscapes and scenes with human figures. Bird and flower, and grass and insect motifs were apparently considered most suitable for the *famille rose* enameling technique. They were in fact the most finely executed. Their startling reality is such that one tries to brush away the insects on a vessel before realizing that they are only painted on.

***Famille Rose* Porcelain**

During the Qing Dynasty, monochrome-glaze porcelain was also greatly improved. In Jingdezhen alone, there were porcelains of powder blue, red glaze, furnace transmutation (窑变),

crab-shell green (蟹壳青), eel yellow (鳝鱼黄), aubergine (茄皮紫), turquoise (青绿) and many other glaze colors.

Since the 1840's Opium War, because of political darkness and imperialist aggression, Chinese porcelain began to decline. The founding of the People's Republic of China in 1949 brought about a new life to ceramic art, and producing centers have been set up all over the country.

Chinese pottery and porcelain play a vital role in the economic, cultural and friendly exchanges which have long existed between China and other countries. Entering the international market very early, they were well known to the world for their exquisiteness and usefulness so that the word china had become synonymous with ceramics itself. As early as more than 2,000 years ago, the Silk Road was opened and China's pottery, porcelain and silk fabrics were transported west. At about the same time, Chinese north-south coastal shipping lanes linked China with many countries via the sea. After Emperor Wu of the Han Dynasty, sea voyages between China and Japan became more frequent, while in the south, sea navigation developed between Chinese ports and Indian Ocean ports and also pointed west. Many vessels of pottery and porcelain of the Han Period or earlier have been discovered and unearthed in Japan, Korea, the Middle East, Southeast Asia, and even Europe.

Since the early Tang Dynasty, Chinese ceramics began to be exported in large quantities to almost the whole world. Foreigners were so fascinated by Chinese ceramics that they took great pride in owning beautiful Chinese porcelain ware and they were also spurred to learn and emulate the art of Chinese porcelain-making. The wares carried the wisdom and friendship of Chinese people to people of other countries and added splendour to the civilization of mankind.

/ Embroidery /

Embroidery is a traditional Chinese handicraft featuring flowers, birdsand scenery on silk or other cloth with colored silk threads. Chinese embroidery dates back over 2,000 years. It has distinct regional and ethnic characteristics, and appeals to people both at home and abroad.

Once there was a rule that on ceremonial occasions, people should wear dresses with embroidered designs; thus, embroidery became very important in ancient China. The embroidery of the Warring States Period shows that the lockstitch (双线连锁缝法) was the principal stitch used during that period. Decorative embroidery developed during the Southern and Northern Dynasties. In the Song and Yuan Dynasties, embroidery shops were established in Bianliang (汴

梁, the present-day Kaifeng), Dadu (大都, the present-day Beijing), and Suzhou by the courts. In the Ming and Qing Dynasties, the art of embroidery had its heyday, and the embroidered works began to be exported. Household embroidery has also developed greatly.

Embroidery is done with colored silk threads in different stitiches. There are many kinds of hand-embroidery (手工刺绣). Some of them use seven or eight different stitiches and more than 100 varieties of colored threads. Sometimes the thread has to be split into many thin filaments (长丝). The finer the thread is, the better the effect is. To become a good embroiderer, one has to learn first of all how to divide a thread into a fine floss (绣花丝线).

Today, silk embroidery is practised nearly all over China. There are four important embroidery centers in China, namely, Hunan, Jiangsu, Guangdong, and Sichuan. Each of the four embroidery centers is famous for its own particular style.

Hunan embroidery or Xiang embroidery (湘绣), famous for its rich colors, has a history spanning more than 2,500 years. It was first developed by local women to decorate skirts, pouches (小袋), and other articles. The designs show birds, animals, flowers, and landscapes. Embroidered tigers and lions look fierce, imposing, and lifelike. These animals are embroidered with a unique method known as the "loose hair stitch." Originally, Xiang embroidery was

Xiang Embroidery

done on a single side of a piece of fabric. Later craftsmen adopted the technique of double-sided embroidery in which both sides display the same design in the same colors. In 1979, a new breakthrough was made: embroidery experts succeeded in embroidery pictures that were different in designs, colors, and stitches on either side of a piece of silk.

Suzhou embroidery or Su embroidery (苏绣) is famous for its delicate workmanship, beautiful designs, and tasteful colors. In the past, many families in the south of the Yangtze River raised silkworms and did embroidery. Girls began to learn this skill when they were very young. Suzhou's double-sided embroidery has a distinct pattern on either side. The two sides bear different patterns

Su Embroidery

with different stitches and colors. There are some famous samples of this kind of embroidery. "Kitten and Lapdog (小猫和哈巴狗)" is a two-sided piece showing a kitten and a lapdog embroidered in different stitches. "Rose" is another piece of double-sided embroidery. The colors of one side differ from those of the other side.

Guangdong embroidery or Yue embroidery (粤绣), which is famous for its complicated patterns and is usually done in bright colors, includes woollen needlepoint, cotton embroidery, and embroidery with gold and silver thread. The superb workmanship of the Yue embroidery enabled it to win prizes at international fairs in Panama and London in 1915 and 1923 respectively. In recent years, other places have also begun to produce Yue embroidery and the number of workers in this industry has increased greatly. "I Love the Chickens of Our Commune (我喜欢公社的鸡)" is a typical piece done in the Yue style. The picture is well composed and lifelike, showing a good sense of perspective.

Yue Embroidery

Sichuan embroidery or Shu embroidery (蜀绣) is famous for its simplicity. A typical sample is "Hibiscus and Carps (木槿和鲤鱼)". Smooth, beautiful and exquisitely stitched, it shows a hibiscus tree growing on the river bank and carps swimming in the clear water.

Shidao embroidery (石岛刺绣) in Shandong Province should not be neglected. As early as the Sui and Tang Dynasties (581—907), embroidery had become popular among the people in the

Shu Embroidery

part where Shidao is located. Shidao embroidery has inherited the cream (精华) of oriental art in its designs and patterns while taking in the good points of Western painting, thus forming its own artistic style. Shidao embroidery has been named a national product of the best quality by the Ministry of Light Industry and is highly praised in many foreign countries.

Although machines have replaced human hands in many arenas, fortunately, the art and craft of embroidery have been preserved as part of China's great cultural heritage. Today, Chinese embroidery handicraft has not only come into ordinary people's homes, but also stepped onto the world stage.

/ Carpets /

Rugs and carpets originated in prehistorical times in various areas of Central Asia. There are now dozens of carpet-making countries all over the world. Carpets may be subdivided into two categories: hand-made (手工的) and machine-made (机织的). Hand-made carpets are mainly produced in some Asian countries along the old Silk Road from the Far East to the Near East. That is why hand-made carpets are also known as Oriental carpets (东方地毯). Machine-made carpets are mostly made in developed countries such as the United States, Japan, and some European countries.

Tianjin Carpet

China is one of the biggest hand-made carpet producers in the world, with a history of more than 3,000 years. Chinese carpets are celebrated for their gorgeous designs, exquisite craftsmanship, and full range of specifications. Chinese carpets were highly acclaimed and awarded a gold medal in the world exposition held in St. Louis in the United States in 1904. In the international competition held in Leipzig (莱比锡) in 1965, Tianjin carpets were universally praised and awarded a gold medal. The same brand of carpets won another gold medal at a world fair held in Hungary in 1980.

Main Designs

The main designs of Chinese carpets are Peking design (北京式), aesthetic design (美术式), floral design (彩花式), and plain design (素凸式).

Peking design is derived from the rich traditional Chinese arts such as Chinese painting, architecture, religious emblems (标记; 徽章), and embroidery. It features symmetrical patterns, elegant color tones, and a classical style. Aesthetic design is a recent modification of Western decorative art which consists mainly of roses, buds, scroll leaves and tulips (卷叶和郁金香). The pattern is well-disposed and in good perspective. The colors are bright and rich. The overall design looks elegant and magnificent. Carpets with a floral design look like a traditional Chinese realistic painting of flowers and birds in beautiful colors. The composition is full of varieties, including diagonal corner (斜角) flower pattern, three flower

Carpet with the Allusion of "Dragon and Phoenix Bringing Luck and Fortune"

pattern, four flower pattern and an all-round pattern. It gives one a feeling of freshness and loveliness. Carpets in plain embossed (浮雕的) design have a single color with patterns fashioned in relief. They look elegant and sedate (静肃的).

Chinese carpets are rich in allusions and legends such as "Dragon and Phoenix Bringing Luck and Fortune (龙凤呈祥)" "The Eight Celestial Objects (八仙法器)", and "The Eight Lucky Omens (八宝)", which prompts a large number of users to study their details and symbolism.

Craftsmanship

Chinese carpets are made from indigenous wool of high quality, carefully selected and scientifically blended and spun exclusively for carpet-making. Carpet yarn (纱线) is colored by experienced technicians so that the colors are even and fast on the fibers and will not fade after a long time or after chemical cleaning. Pattern design and the enlargement of the layout lay the foundation for carpet making. Experts first draft the form of the pattern and then enlarge the layout according to the form and the required size. Weavers then sketch the outline of the enlarged layout design on the warps (描经, which is also known as "tracing on warps") as a blueprint for the actual weaving process.

Weaving is the most important process in carpet-making. It includes four steps: knot-tying (打结, known as hand-knotting), locking of the edge (撩边), passing the wefts (过纬) and cutting the excessive length of wool (剪荒毛). When a carpet is woven, carpet smoothing workers use special tools to peel off the excessive thickness of the knotted layers, making the surface smooth and lustrous. After shearing (修剪), clipping workers use scissors to make the patterns on a carpet stand out distinctively. Finally, in washing the carpet, various chemical washing agents are used to alter the form and arrangement of the carpet fibers, making the surface as smooth and glossy as velvet (丝绒).

China also produces aesthetic hanging carpets or tapestries (美术挂毯), latex-back full-cut woolen rugs (胶背全片地毯), Tibetan rugs (西藏地毯), and Xinjiang carpets (新疆地毯), in addition to other varieties. Among them, Tianjin aesthetic hanging carpets are celebrated for the unique effect of combination of art and carpet-making. "The Great Wall", a tapestry that decorates the headquarters of the United Nations, was woven by Tianjin carpet-making artists.

/ Ivory Carving /

The art of carving a whole piece of elephant tusk can be traced back to the Shang Dynasty. The ivory carvers make imaginative use of the shape of the raw material. The items carved are usually animals, birds, figurines, landscapes, floral baskets, boats, and even articles for daily use, such as brooches (饰针), seals, chopsticks, powder-boxes, and cigarette-holders.

In Beijing, an anonymous amateur ivory carver once made an exact copy of a piece of writing by the famous calligrapher Wang Xizhi (王羲之) on a piece of ivory which was five millimeters in diameter. Another anonymous technical adviser to the Suzhou Sandalwood (檀香木) Fan Factory once successfully created an ivory and sandalwood miniature carving of the scene depicted in the famous poem "Anchored by Night". The ivory and sandalwood miniature brings the scene alive. In front of the temple, there is the river, the arched Maple (枫树) Bridge, the little boat and the poet sitting in the boat. The temple houses are so exquisitely made that they resemble the real ones in every minute detail: the carved railings in front of each house, the winding passage, the upturned eaves (上翘的屋顶), and even the bells on them. It is a masterpiece.

Ivory Pendant

Guangzhou is well-known for intricate hollowed-cut ivory balls. There, a master artisan (工匠), Weng Rongbiao (翁荣标), has surpassed his father who could carve an ivory pendant (象牙吊坠) with an ivory ball in twenty eight layers. Weng Rongbiao can now work out a revolvable ivory ball with forty-five layers.

It is worth mentioning that in order to protect elephants, traditional ivory carvings have mostly been replaced by dog tooth carvings or bone carvings.

/ Jade Carving /

Jade has been cherished by the Chinese as a symbol of many virtues. Its hardness suggests firmness and loyalty, and its luster projects purity and beauty. In China, jade carving dates back to the late Old Stone Age, the period of the "Upper Cave Man." By the late New Stone Age, jade ornaments such as *bi* (壁, pierced discs), zhui (坠, pendants), earrings (耳环) and beads (珠子) had appeared. In the Shang and Zhou Dynasties, jade articles were used as ritual objects and symbols of personal morality or political authority. Jade carvings are made by chiseling (凿, 雕, 琢), grinding (磨), and boring (钻). Typical subjects of jade carving are flowers, birds, animals, vases,

Jade Carving

incense burners, and human figures, especially beautiful women from popular fairy tales and legends. The skill of the craftsman is shown in his ability to make the best use of the natural color and the shape of the raw material.

Some artisans are renowned for their special skills. Zhou Shouhai (周寿海), a master in Shanghai, succeeded in carving from a block of jade 16 centimeters high an incense burner decorated with chains of interconnecting links. Wang shusen (王树森), a master in Beijing, is known for his carvings of arhats (阿罗汉), the Goddess of Mercy, celestial beings, and beautiful women in ancient costumes. Zhang Yunhe (张云和) is the founder of the art of bird carving. An emerald green (翠绿色的) bird resting on a plum branch with a yellow leaf in its mouth is his masterpiece. The birds he carved are so exquisite and lifelike that he acquired the nickname "Bird Zhang (鸟儿张)". Up to now, Bird Zhang has handed down his skill to more than a hundred apprentices.

People used to think the best jade sculptures were those made in the Qing Dynasty. But four newly carved giant jadeite ornaments show that jade carving reached a new level after the founding of the People's Republic of China. The four pieces are on permanent display at the Chinese Arts and Crafts Museum (中国工艺美术展览馆). One of them is a miniature (微型的) Taishan Mountain. The craftsmen created the peak, trees, temples, bridges, waterfalls, people and animals by following the natural shape, veining (叶脉形状), and colors of the stone. The most interesting part is a shining sun on the side of the cliff. The most magnificent of the four pieces is the screen carved with nine dragons. The designers made the best use of the jade's nuances of color to depict the writhing dragons (扭动巨龙), flying clouds, and the turbulent sea. The four brownish streaks (条纹) in the stone were turned into water jets (水射流) from the dragons' mouths. The four sculptures represent the development of jade carving in the People's Republic of China.

/ Wood Carving /

Wood carving can be divided into many different categories due to its wide range in application and decoration, diversity in methods of representation and difference in wood texture. In terms of application and decoration, architecture, furniture and display art, wood carving occupies a very important position in the daily lives

Wood Carving: Seven Fairy Maidens

of Chinese people. In term of technical methods, there is piercing (镂空) carving, basso-relievo (浮雕), solid tondo (立体圆雕), piercing decal (镂空贴花), etc. In terms of wood texture, hard, often called rosewood (红木) and soft wood are usually two types of wood harnessed by wood craftsmen.

Dong Yang Wood Carving

Wood carving varies from one place to another in pattern of woodwork, design of carving decoration, and carving technique. For example, both rosewood carving furniture in Suzhou, Jiangsu Province and Dongyang wood carving furniture in Zhejiang Province are world-famous, while they differ from each other in the former being elegant and luxurious and the latter being exquisite and unique.

/ Clay Modeling /

Clay modeling is a folk art popular in both rural and urban areas. Colored clay figurines (彩色泥人) are put on sale in cities, towns, and at rural fairs during the Spring Festival and other traditional festivals. Today, workshops and enterprises have been established specializing in this kind of folk art. There are even research groups in some institutes of arts and crafts. The clay modeling of Beijing, Tianjin and Wuxi (无锡) each has its own style and characteristics.

Tianjin Colored Clay Figurine

In Tianjin, everybody knows the name "Ni Ren Zhang (泥人张)" or "Clay-Figurine Zhang". Traditionally, clay modeling was only a source of children's toys, but thanks to the efforts of "Clay-Figurine Zhang", clay modeling has become a respectable art, and some of his products are among the treasures in Beijing's museums and the China Art Gallery (中国美术馆). The name "Clay-Figurine Zhang" is used to refer to Zhang Mingshan (张明山) who was the first person to make colored clay figurines in Tianjin. He transformed clay modeling into an art. People later began to use the name to refer to the Zhang family. Now people sometimes use it to mean the workshop which was set up in 1959 and which has more than 40 craftsmen whose surnames are not Zhang.

Tianjin colored clay figurines are characterized by a sense of motion. All the figures look vivid and lifelike. Some of the themes are taken from legends and myths while others are taken from everyday life.

Now, Zhan Naiying (张乃英), the fifth generation of the Zhang family, has made a breakthrough. He has combined clay modeling and modern sculpture to create eighty colored clay figurines based on the characters in the novel *Water Margin* (《水浒传》). All the figurines are only a few centimeters in height, but each has its unique posture, clothing, and facial expression.

Clay figurines have been popular in Wuxi, Jiangsu Province, for more than 600 years. Today multi-colored clay figurines made Wuxi stand on desks or in shops around the world. They are called "Ah Fu (阿福)". "Fu (福)" in Chinese means fortune or happiness, and "Ah (阿)" is merely a meaningless auxiliary sound. The name was first used by local people to describe cherubic children. Now it refers to all clay figurines made in Wuxi, especially those made at the Wuxi Clay Figurine Mill (无锡泥人厂). Today "Ah Fu" comes in more than 100 designs: children in various postures, Lao

Ah Fu Colored Figurine

Shouxing (老寿星, an old man of longevity), historical and legendary figures, and animals of all kinds. All these clay figurines are made of dark clay from the foot of the Hui Hills (惠山) near the city of Wuxi.

The products of the Wuxi Clay Figurine Mill enjoy a wide market. Ah Fu colored figurines are sold not only in Wuxi but also in shops in more than 50 countries. Businessmen from the United States, Canada, Japan, Eastern Europe and Southeast Asia buy wholesale from the mill.

The mill pays great attention to training young apprentices. The young people are each assigned to a master craftsman. New recruits have to spend all their time learning the basic skills, and, at the same time, taking related cultural courses. Nowadays, former apprentices have become the main force in the mill. Many of them have gone abroad on several occasions to demonstrate their clay modeling skills.

/ Cloisonné /

Cloisonné (Jingtai Blue, 景泰蓝) is a variation of an enamel work (搪瓷制品). During the reign of Jingtai of the Ming Dynasty, the making of Chinese cloisonné developed to meet the needs of the imperial households. Thus, this enamel ware obtained the name "Jingtai", meaning blue ware of the Jingtai reign.

Cloisonné

The process of producing cloisonné is complicated. First, delicate copper strips are bent into designs and soldered onto the surface of a metal art object. Then, enamel pastes of different colors are poured into the compartments (隔层) formed by the copper strips. Then the object is baked in several firings, polished, and gilded. The finished article is a splendid sight with islands of brilliant color separated by gilded copper wire.

Patterns for cloisonné articles include dragons, phoenixes, and flowers. Craftsmen have also introduced patterns based on ordinary objects such as grasshoppers (蚂蚱), frogs, horses, cranes, and grapes. They are attractive and full of vitality. Cloisonné is used to make not only ornamental objects but also articles for daily use, such as desk sets, smoking sets, vases, table lamp bases, food containers, fruit bowls, incense burners, jewelry boxes, mirror frames, folding screens and buttons.

Recently a newly-developed cloisonné called Yinjing (Silver and Crystal) Blue (银晶蓝) has appeared. It has a three dimensional effect, with patterns designed around silver wires. Its high-gloss luster (高光泽) makes it very beautiful. The process of making Yinjing Blue is similar to that of making traditional high-gloss cloisonné, but much more complicated. First, bronze is cast into the desired shapes—bowls, vases, cups, ornamental plates, melon-shaped pots, bells, ashtrays (烟灰缸), or other shapes. To make the pattern, flat silver wires are soldered to the bodies. The hollows are then filled with enamels of different colors. Usually, a cloisonné piece has to be baked five times and a new coat of enamel is added each time. After baking, the pieces are ground and polished. Now craftsmen are doing their utmost to solve some technical problems and trying to make patterns more interesting and shapes more elegant and diverse.

/ Lacquer-Ware /

Chinese lacquer-ware (漆器) has a very long history. A vermilion lacquer bowl (朱砂漆碗) unearthed at a site in Yuyao (余姚), Zhejiang Province, was among the findings identified as relics of the Hemudu Culture (河姆渡文化, 5000 B.C.E.—3300 B.C.E.). This bowl proves that lacquer-ware had been in use before that period. According to archaeologists, the earliest example of lacquer-ware with a colored pattern is a stringed musical instrument unearthed in Xinyang (信阳),

Chinese Lacquer ware

Henan Province. It dates back to the Warring States Period (475 B.C.E.—221 B.C.E.). On this instrument there are pictures of dragons, snakes, and a scene of dancing in different colors, including bright red, dark red, yellow, green, blue, white and gold. The coffins unearthed in 1972 at Mawangdui (马王堆) in Hunan Province near Changsha (长沙) prove that lacquer-ware as an art reached a new height in the Han Dynasty (202 B.C.E.—220 A.D.). One of the coffins is decorated with a lacquer picture showing people, deities, animals, and clouds.

Chinese lacquer is a natural varnish (清漆) made from the sap (树液) of the lacquer tree. It dries on exposure to air to form a plastic coat which is resistant to water and acid or alkaline (碱) corrosion (腐蚀). It may be applied with or without a coloring agent to a body made of wood, bamboo, leather, or metal. The lacquer is applied in numerous coats, each of which must be allowed to dry before the next is added. Early lacquer-ware was mostly restricted to only two colors, black and vermilion. Today lacquer-making techniques are so advanced that lacquer is not only multi-colored but also combined with gilding, silver, jade, and mother-of-pearl inlay (珍珠母镶嵌).

Lacquer-ware today is produced in Beijing, Shanghai, Fuzhou, Yangzhou, Yichun (宜春), Chongqing, Pingyao (平遥), and other places. Beijing lacquer-ware, for instance, is developed from the techniques used in the imperial workshops of the Ming and Qing Dynasties. Up to one hundred layers of lacquer are applied to an object which is then ready to be finely carved. The end effect is a combination of carving with painting. Emperor Qianlong of the Qing Dynasty had a special fondness for carved lacquer. During his reign, lacquer thrones, screens, and tables were produced; he was even buried in a carved lacquer coffin. Fujian lacquer-ware is known for its multi-colors, gold tracery (黄金窗饰), silver-inlay, and filigree (金银丝).

Chinese lacquer-ware is elaborate in workmanship (工艺精湛), elegant in appearance (外观典雅), and harmonious in color (色彩和谐). Objects made of lacquer are works of art as well as articles for daily use, including screens, cabinets, and coffee tables. They have enjoyed popularity with people at home and abroad for many centuries.

/ Batik /

Batik (蜡染) is a traditional Chinese folk art which combines painting and dyeing. It is made by dipping a specially designed knife into melted wax and painting various patterns on pieces of white cloth. The wax stays on the cloth and often cracks after it hardens. The cloth is then dyed and the dyes seep into the cracks and make fine lines. When the wax is boiled away, beautiful patterns appear on the cloth. Batik cloth can be made into garments (服装), scarfs (围巾), bags, table-cloths, bedspreads (床罩), curtains, and other decorative items.

The history of batik can be traced back to the Western Han Dynasty (202 B.C.E. —24 A.D.). Batik used to be popular both in central and southwest China, but it has been handed down from generation to generation among the ethnic people in Guizhou (贵州), a Province in Southwest China. Nobody knows how batik was invented, but a folk tale about "batik girl" tells us something about it. The story relates that long, long ago, there was a girl living in a stone village called Anshun (安顺), now a city in Guizhou Province. She was fond of dyeing white cloth blue and purple. One day, while she was working, a bee happened to alight (降落) on her cloth. After she took away the bee, she found there was a white dot left on the cloth, which looked very pretty. Her finding led to the use of wax in dyeing.

Among the Miao nationality (苗族), an ethnic group in Southwest China, young girls have to learn to make batik, to weave, and to embroider (刺绣). Custom demands that they make their own garments, from wedding dresses to funeral shrouds (寿衣). Like all other Miao girls, Yang Jinxiu (杨金秀), a native of Anshun in Guizhou, learned batik skill when she was a little girl. At twenty, she had already formed her own style which was characterized by a combination of realism and romanticism. In 1981, she was chosen by the China Association

Miao Nationality Batik

for Science and Technology (中国科技协会) to exhibit her art of batik making at an exhibition abroad. Later she took the exhibition to Canada in 1982 and the United States in 1984. Her works were praised as "gems of ancient folk art (古代民间艺术之瑰宝)" and "flowers of legendary oriental art (东方传奇艺术之花)". In 1986, she went to Guiyang (贵阳), capital of Guizhou Province, and established a batik handicraft mill which expanded a year later into the Yang Jinxiu Batik Joint Corporation. Yang is the manager and chief designer. The corporation exports batik goods to a number of foreign countries, including the United States, Canada, France, Austria (奥地利), Australia, Argentina, Brazil, Japan, and Singapore.

Wang Yao (王曜), a contemporary Chinese Batik Craftsman, is also well-known for his batik experience shop named "Batik Soul" in the ancient city of Phoenix, Hunan Province.

/ Kite-Making /

Kite-making (风筝制作) in China has a history of over 2,000 years. The earliest kites were made of wood in the shape of a hawk; they were called wooden hawks. In the Han Dynasty, paper was used to replace wood, and paper hawks appeared. During the Five Dynasties (907—960), bamboo whistles (竹哨) were fastened to the kite and when the wind blew through the whistles, the kite sounded like a "zheng (筝)", a Chinese musical instrument similar to the zither. From then on, the kite was called "fengzheng (风筝)" in Chinese.

Kite-making and flying are old traditions in China. At first, kites were used by the military to drop propaganda messages on enemies. It is believed that Gongshun Ban (公孙般), a notable carpenter in the Warring States Period, made the first kite, a wooden hawk, which flew for three consecutive days without falling down. During the Five Dynasties, kite-flying became a recreational activity for imperial families, but it was in the Northern Song Dynasty (960—1127) that kite-flying became popular among ordinary people. In many places, people flew kites to celebrate the Qingming Festival, a traditional holiday for honoring ancestors and celebrating the coming of the spring. Kites were flown by people of all ages, rich and poor. After flying high for a while, the kites were released in the hope that they would fly away with all of their adversities (苦难). Nowadays, however, flying kites is not only a form of recreation, but also an enjoyable physical exercise. It helps the old to prolong life, adults to keep fit, and children to grow healthily.

Being the motherland of the kite, China enjoys a worldwide reputation for kite-making.

Beijing, Tianjin, Weifang (潍坊) in Shandong Province and Nantong (南通) in Jiangsu Province are the major centers of kite-making. "Kite Ha (风筝哈)" of Beijing and "Kite Wei (风筝魏)" in Tianjin were awarded a gold medal at the 1915 Panama Pacific International Exposition and those made by "Kite Ha" won a silver medal and a certificate of merit at that fair.

Kite Ha

Chinese kites have unique national styles in craftsmanship, modeling, designs, and colors. Making a kite usually has three steps. First, the frame is made with bamboo strips; then the frame is covered with paper or silk, and after that, designs are hand-painted on the paper or silk. The painting skills of Chinese painting and New Year pictures are used so that the designs on kites have clear outlines and bright colors. The shapes of fish, birds, dragons, eagles, swallows (燕子), butterflies, phoenixes, and fairies are generally used for patterns because they all symbolize good luck or prosperity. For example, the double swallow pattern symbolizes devotion between husband and wife and the wish that their love will last all their lives. Kites vary in size, ranging from those of tens of square meters to tiny ones less than ten centimeters in width. The framework is exquisite and flexible, simple to fix and easy to fold and carry. All these characteristics have enabled Chinese kites to enjoy great popularity around the world.

In Weifang, which is known as the "City of Kites", the International Kite Festival (国际风筝节) has been held annually since 1984. The festival is jointly sponsored by the Shandong Tourism Corporation and the Weifang Kite Association. This event has attracted kite enthusiasts from many countries, including Australia, Britain, Canada, Germany, Japan, Singapore, and the United States.

/ Paper-Cutting /

Paper-cutting is one of the most popular forms of Chinese traditional folk art. Its materials are easy to get and low in cost. The history of paper-cutting can be dated back to the Han Dynasty, which became quite popular in the Northern and Southern Dynasties and prospered during the Qing Dynasty. Paper-cutting can be seen all over the country.

Paper-cuts are patterns cut on paper by scissors or engraving knife. These patterns were used as the ornaments of offerings to sacrifice ancestors. Nowadays, paper-cuts are mainly used for interior decoration. People paste paper-cuts on walls, doors, windows, poles, mirrors, lamps and lanterns at wedding ceremonies or festivals to beautify the surroundings and enhance the festive atmosphere. These patterns are rich in content and usually have symbolic meanings, as one can see in the Chinese character "福" in paper-cutting, which means happiness and luck. The designs of children, lotuses and bottle gourds suggest a happy family with a large number of children and grandchildren. Zodiac animals, fruits, fish, and flowers are all familiar objects depicted by paper-cutting artists. Qi Xiumei (祁秀梅) was regarded as a "divine

Paper-Cutting: Tree of Life

by Qi Xiumei

scissors" because she is so skillful as to paper-cut anything at her own will. The People's Daily, the most influential newspaper, introduced her in a special column in 1986, when one of her master pieces, "Tree of Life", was cast into popularity in society.

Exercises

Part One　Comprehension

Fill in the following blanks with the information you learn in Chapter 11.

1. Pottery or earth-ware is, technically, any object made from a porous clay and baked at a temperature ranging from hot, direct sunlight to baking, or firing, in a _____ at a temperature of about 1,000 degrees centigrade.

2. In the summer of 1974 a vast underground vault filled with life-sized _____ figures of warriors and horses was discovered east of the mausoleum of the First Emperor of the Qin Dynasty in Lintong County, Shaanxi Province.

3. The appearance of the Tri-Colored Glazed Pottery of the Tang Dynasty was, in a sense, the _____ of the development of the glazed pottery.

4. Unlike pottery, porcelain is made from a mixture of special clays, often kaolin and feldspar; it is fired at a very high temperature of over _____ degrees.

5. Secondly, _____ porcelain ranked first and predominated during the Ming Dynasty, with that of the Yongle and Xuande Periods at its best.

6. Sichuan embroidery or Shu embroidery is famous for its _____.

7. China is one of the biggest _____ carpet producers in the world, with a history of more

than 3,000 years.

8. The art of carving a whole piece of elephant tusk can be traced back to the _____ Dynasty.

9. _____ colored clay figurines are characterized by a sense of motion. All the figures look vivid and lifelike.

10. Cloisonné (Jingtai Blue) is a variation of _____ work.

Part Two   Translation

Passage Translation

周二,距离冬奥会开幕还有100天,北京2022年冬奥会和冬残奥会的官方奖牌首次亮相,令人印象深刻。奖牌名为"同心",寓意"团结一致",其灵感来源于精美的"玉璧",一件距今约5 000年的中国古代玉器。每枚奖牌的正面中心都刻有奥林匹克五环,周围刻有英文"XXIV Olympic Winter Games Beijing 2022(北京2022年第24届冬季奥林匹克运动会)"。外圈布满了祥云纹、冰雪纹和冰痕。围绕中心的同心环代表了中国文化对团结与和谐的追求,同时也呼应了促进人类团结、包容与和平的奥林匹克价值观。奖牌背面中央印有北京2022年冬奥会会徽,外圈点缀着由圆圈串在一起的24颗星星,代表第24届冬奥会,并印有奖牌项目的名称。

Part Three   Critical Thinking and Discussion

1. How many sorts of porcelain are there in China? Which one do you like best? Why?

2. What do you know about present-day Chinese ceramics?

3. Have you ever practiced some Chinese handicrafts such as paper-cutting or knotting? How do you like these practices?

Chapter 12
Chinese Folk Sports

/ Sports in Ancient China /

As an important part of popular culture, sports in China began to take shape during the Qin, Han and Three-Kingdoms Periods. Sporting scenes have been recorded over the dynasties in sepulchral (阴森森的) mural paintings (壁画), stone paintings, brick paintings, poems, and so on.

During the Tang Dynasty, equestrian polo (击鞠, 马球) was prevalent in the palace, the army, and among the men of letters (文人墨客). Even women took delight in playing it. The princess in the famous ancient drama *Beating the Princess While Drunk* (《醉打金枝》) is described as being addicted to the game.

In the Song Dynasty, *cuju* (蹴鞠), a primitive soccer game using a leather ball filled with hair or something else, was so prevailing that everyone from the emperor to ordinary people participated in it. In the novel *Water Margin* (《水浒传》), Gao Qiu (高俅), a vulgar villain (市井流氓), was promoted to a high official position by the emperor just because he was a skillful *cuju* player.

Cuju

In the Yuan Dynasty, people liked playing a game called *Chuiwan* (捶丸), which was similar to golf as shown in the mural painting *Hitting Balls*. At that time, people used a stick that was crooked at one end to hit balls into a hole. The one who hit most balls into the hole won the game.

Besides all the games mentioned above, wresting (摔跤), dancing, chess playing (下棋), horse racing (赛马), and other forms of sports were part of the ancient people's daily pastimes.

/ Ethnic Sports /

Owing to their unique lifestyles, ethnic groups play sports with their own characteristics.

Since the founding of the People's Republic of China, Chinese government has promoted the development of traditional ethnic sports. Among the 1,000 or so such sports, some of the well-known ones are Mongolian wrestling, horsemanship (马术) and archery; Hui shuttlecock kicking (踢毽子) and tug-of-war (拔河); Tibetan yak (牦牛) racing; Miao swinging (荡秋千) and dragon boat racing; Zhuang colored silk ball throwing (抛绣球); Korean see-saw jumping (跳跷跷板); Man skating; Dong walking on stilts (踩高跷); and Yao top whipping (打陀螺).

Dragon boat racing, kite flying, *yangge* (秧歌), *weiqi* (围棋), *qigong* (气功) and *Taiji quan* (太极拳, shadow boxing) are also traditional sports popular among both Han people and people from ethnic minorities.

/ Traditional Physical Activities /

Among traditional Chinese physical activities, *wushu* (武术) or martial arts may be the most representative and typical. Martial arts, also known in the West as kongfu (功夫), is a traditional folk sport characterized by various bare-handed and armed combat techniques.

According to the formation of Chinese characters, "武 (wǔ)" is made up of "止" and "戈". The former means "stop" while the latter refers to "dagger-axe" or "any kind of weapons". The combination of the two means "stop martial actions". The character "术 (shù)" denotes strategies. Therefore, the term "武术" means "using methods and skills to stop martial actions and activities". Another meaning of the term is martial activities between two people or two groups with weapons.

Chinese martial arts may be traced back to prehistoric times when Chinese ancestors used stones and wooden clubs (棍棒) in hunting for subsistence (生存) and self-defense. They are the forms of fighting sports that combine kicking, hitting, wrestling (摔, 拧, 扭), seizing (抓), tumbling (翻), striking (撞), chopping (砍, 劈), and so on, bare-handed or with weapons. Martial arts have been created and developed by Chinese people and are a precious national cultural legacy.

With various graceful movements, martial arts provide practitioners with elegance and strength. People are attracted to martial arts for many reasons: to improve their mental discipline, to have fun and to participate in martial arts competitions.

/ Categories of Modern Chinese Martial Arts /

Modern Chinese martial arts consist of the following five categories:

- boxing, including long boxing (长拳), shadow boxing, southern boxing (南拳), form boxing (形拳), Eight-Trigram boxing (八卦掌), Shaolin boxing (少林拳), and drunkard boxing (醉拳);

- weapon exercises, including exercises with long weapons (长兵器), such as spears (长矛) and staffs (拐杖), short weapons (短兵器), such as swords and sabers (军刀), double weapons (双兵器), such as double-swords, double-hooks, and soft weapons (软兵器), such as nine-section whips (九节鞭) and three-section sticks (三节棍).

- sparring exercises (拳击练习), including sparring exercises bare-handed (徒手对练), with weapons (器械对练), and bare-handed against weapons (徒手对器械);

- actual combat (技击术), including free sparring (散打), hand-pushing (推手), and fighting with long or short weapons;

- teamwork, including exercises or performances by six or more people working together with or without weapons.

Modern Chinese martial arts can also be classified into the following styles:

- northern vs southern styles

　　The Yellow River is used as the rough demarcation (分界) line. The practitioners of the southern style often utter shouts and cries to make their movements more forceful. The northern style is characterized by its short, swift and vigorous routines.

- internal vs external styles

　　The difference between internal and external styles lies in which parts are trained, the inner organs of the body or organs like wrists, arms, shoulders, legs, and so on. The words "external" and "internal" are commonly misconceived, inaccurately and poorly applied. Some people hold that martial arts styles are either exclusively hard (external) or exclusively soft (internal).

This tendency is incorrect, because any good martial arts style requires a balanced combination of the inseparable internal and external principles: hard and soft, relaxed and tense, up and down, opening and closing, thought and action. Yin and yang principles are demonstrated in the training theories, techniques, and philosophies of all styles of martial arts.

With hundreds of styles, Chinese martial arts are diverse and complex, each possessing unique characteristics and all coming from a rich cultural legacy. However, there is a good saying, "Martial arts originate in China, but it belongs to the world."

/ A Brief History of Chinese Martial Arts /

Chinese martial arts have a long history. Far back in primitive society about four thousand years ago, hard living conditions compelled the ancient people to use their stone and wooden tools as weapons to hunt and to defend themselves. Their fighting skills with bare hands and in using weapons formed the basis of primitive wushu. During the Shang and Zhou Dynasties, with the development of productive forces, especially that of the techniques in bronze casting, the variety of weapons increased and their quality improved.

In the Han Dynasty, *wushu* became quite popular. A *wushu* competition which was held in the spring of 108 B.C.E. attracted thousands of spectators. Through competitions, *wushu* further developed. There appeared various forms of martial arts, such as sword-play, broadsword-play, and halberd (戟) play. During the Tang Dynasty, both military men and scholars were required to practice wushu. Sword-play was often performed at parties and other social gatherings. The boxing style of Shaolin Temple (少林寺) became very popular because, in the early period of the Tang , the Shaolin monks had helped Li Shimin (Emperor Tai Zong) conquer Wang Shichong (King of the Zheng Kingdom); thus Emperor Tai Zong gave the Shaolin Temple special permission to train monks in *wushu*.

The Ming Dynasty saw the all-round development of Chinese martial arts. Various boxing schools appeared, each named after its master. In addition, scores of routines of weapon-play movements have evolved. Many high-ranking officers and *wushu* masters, such as Tang Shunzhi (唐顺之), Yu Dayou (俞大猷), Zheng Ruozeng (郑若增) and Qi Jiguang (戚继光) wrote books on wushu. Among those works, two books by Qi Jiguang are better-known; they are *New Martial Arts* (《纪效新书》) and *Military Training Record* (《练兵实纪》).

In order to keep its ruling position, the government of the Qing Dynasty once restricted wushu practice, but that could not prevent wushu from spreading among the people. Many popular schools of boxing styles, including *Taiji quan* or shadow boxing, *nanquan* or southern boxing, and *xingyi quan* (形意拳) were formed and each had its own guiding theories.

In spite of its rich variety, *wushu* has four main types: bare-handed boxing (徒手拳术), the wielding of weapons (器械), combat (对练) and collective performance (集体练习). There are over one hundred schools of boxing in the Yellow River valley area and about eighty in the Yangtze River basin. Each school has its own characteristics. *Changquan* or long boxing demands quickness and valor (勇猛), and it is liked by young people. *Taiji quan*, characterized by its slow rhythm and gentle movements, is suitable for people of all ages, especially elderly people. *Xingyi quan*, vigorous in its balanced motions and poised steps (稳健的步伐), is popular with young and middle-aged people. *Nanquan* is wide-spread in China's southern areas. Its practitioners utter shouts and cries now and then to make their movements more forceful. *Shaolin quan* or Shaolin boxing, popular in the north, is known for its short routines of movements and swiftness and vigour. In certain styles, such as *tanglang quan* (螳螂拳) or Mantis boxing, and *zuiquan* (醉拳) or Drunkard boxing, the practitioner imitates animals and birds as well as drunken humans.

/ Distinguished Forms of Chinese Martial Arts /

Shaolin Boxing

Shaolin boxing is named after the Shaolin Temple on Mount Songshan (嵩山) where the monks practiced in the early years of the Tang Dynasty. During that time, when Li Shimin was besieged (围困) by his enemy near Luoyang (洛阳), 13 monks from the Shaolin Temple rescued him. After Li became emperor of the Tang Dynasty, he rewarded the 13 monks and granted land and silver to the Shaolin Temple.

Shaolin Boxing

From then on, the Shaolin Temple and Shaolin boxing became well known.

Shaolin boxing is the representative boxing style of long boxing. It is characterized by sturdiness, fast attacks, and coordinated forward and backward movements. Its serial movements are mostly short and straight.

Taiji quan

Taiji quan is a popular school of Chinese martial arts marked by slow and gentle movements that are designed for defense, strengthening of the physique and prevention of diseases.

Taiji Quan

In this art, it is essential that the mind guide the body through graceful, gentle and firm movements. It originates in Chenjiagou (陈家沟) in Wenxian county (温 县), Henan Province. There are different schools, including Chen (陈), Yang (杨), Wu (吴), Sun (孙), and He (和) styles.

At the spectacular opening ceremony of the 11th Asian Games, the sheer magnificence of the *Taiji quan* performance given by 1,400 players from China and Japan created an amazing sensation (轰动).

Chenjiaogou—Birthplace of *Taiji Quan*

Chenjiagou is well-known not only for its *wushu* masters but also for being the birthplace of Taiji quan. Chen Wangting (陈王庭), a Ming Dynasty general and a 9th-generation descendant of the Chen family of boxers, returned to his home in Chenjiagou after he retired. Drawing on the principles of traditional medicine and dialectics of ancient Chinese philosophy as well as other disciplines in boxing, he created a system of movements which became the earliest form of *Taiji quan* of the Chen school. It branched into other types of *Taiji quan* after Chen Changxing (陈长兴), the 14th generation descendant of the Chen family, taught *Taiji quan* to Yang Luchan (杨露禅), and the Yang Luchan, Wu Jianquan

Chen Wangting

(吴鉴泉), Sun Lutang (孙禄堂), and He Zhaoyuan (和兆元) schools started to appear one after another.

According to some wushu masters of Chenjiagou, the Chen school is characterized by firmness in gentleness, the combination of fastness and slowness, and continuity of movements. Besides these principles, which have also been adopted by other schools, the Chen school has its own special features like jumping, leaping, stamping (跺脚), and the use of weapons such as the sword, double-sword, broadsword, double broadsword and mace (权杖).

Taiji quan is very popular in Chenjiagou, where half of the 2,000 villagers practice boxing. Those who are unable to box are fans of *Taiji quan* and fond of commenting on the performances. The village has a Taiji quan sports school which accepts students from the local area and other places. Even the students of the village's primary and junior middle schools practice Taiji quan both at school, especially in their physical culture classes, and at home.

The village has produced many famous boxers. At present, Chen Xiaowang (陈小旺), Zhu Tiancai (朱天才), Wang Xi'an (王西安), and Chen Zhenglei (陈正雷) are known as the four eminent Taiji masters of Chenjiagou. Chen Xiaowang learned his skills from his father, Chen Zhaoxu (陈照旭), one of the best boxers in the village. But it was at the Chenjiagou Sports School that he received systematic training. He has won three awards at national *wushu* performance contests. Later, he became a coach in the provincial *wushu* center in Zhengzhou (郑州). The other three *Taiji* masters are also boxing coaches, working in the village or other places. The villagers expect the four masters to surpass their ancestors in *Taiji* quan and make new contributions to its further development.

Looking back at the history of the development of *Taiji quan* in the village of Chenjiagou, one could draw the conclusion that whenever the country was prosperous and the society was stable, *Taiji quan* developed vigorously and *Taiji* masters were produced. Nowadays, with great support from the government and society, *Taiji quan* of the Chen school is certain to reach a new peak.

Qigong

Qigong (气功), also called deep breathing exercise, is practiced by the Chinese on a regular basis to keep fit. "*Qi*" literally means "air" and implies "life force". The purpose of qigong is to coordinate the health of the mind and body. The practitioner does *qigong* for self-reliance, self-adjustment, body building, resistance of premature aging, and prolongation of life.

Theoretical Basis of *Qigong*

Being a traditional art of the self-training of body and mind and a prophylactic (预防的) method, qigong, created by Chinese people in the long process of life, labor and fight against diseases and senium (衰老), can prevent and cure diseases, strengthen health and prolong life. It is one of the gems in the treasure-house of China's cultural heritage as well as an important part of traditional Chinese medicine.

Qigong is an art and skill to train qi. To be exact, it is a method by which the practitioner gets physical and mental self-exercise through bringing his initiative into play. To achieve this aim, the practitioner must integrate his mind with postures and respiration (揉合意念、姿势和呼吸) and act on the whole organism. On the one hand, it actively and intrinsically self-regulates the functional activities of the organism and maintains a dynamic equilibrium. On the other hand, it enables the body to produce an "energy-storing" reaction ("储能性"反应), reduce energy consumption and increase energy accumulation, which results in the regulating of *yin* and *yang*, dredging (疏浚) the channels and collaterals (经络) and emitting external *qi* (外气).

The basic theory of *qigong* is closely related with the *yin-yang* theory (阴阳学说), viscera theory (脏腑学说) and the theory of channels and collaterals of traditional Chinese medicine (中医经络学说). According to traditional Chinese medicine, the viscera govern all of the activities of a person's body. *Qigong* may achieve different effects through the viscera.

The heart governs mental activities (心主神明). To exercise *qigong* can concentrate the mind and bring the brain into a tranquil state (使大脑入静) so as to achieve the purpose of regulating and recuperating the "mental activities" (达到调节和调理"精神活动"的目的). The heart also governs blood circulation and has its outward manifestation in the face. *Qigong* exercise may affect the exuberance of the heart-*qi* manifested by even, gentle and forceful pulse, and ruddy and lustrous complexion (气功锻炼可使心气旺盛,脉搏平缓有力,面色红润).

The lung governs *qi* and is in charge of respiration. The breathing exercise (呼吸练习) can inhale the essence *qi* in heaven and earth (吸入天地之精气) and exhale the turbid *qi* in the viscera (吐出脏腑浊气). The inhaled essence *qi* not only enriches the genuine *qi* (真气), but also directly promotes the circulation of *qi* and blood so that the qi and blood throughout the body can flow freely and all the viscera, the limbs (肢) and bones can function normally.

The kidney governs the reception of respired air through the lung. When the practitioner sinks the respired air into *dantian* (丹田, elixir field) through deep, long abdominal respiration, he can further strengthen the lowering function of the lung and the receptive function of the kidney, thus achieving a state of deep, long, gentle respiration. At this time, the inhaled essence *qi* of heaven and earth sinks to meet and combine with the congenital essence *qi* of the kidney (先天肾气) to transform into the genuine qi of the human body, thus enabling the internal *qi* and strength of the body to condense and strengthen rapidly.

Inside the kidneys locates the gate of life (命门), which is the root of primordial *qi* (元气之根) and the residence of water and fire (水火之宅). The exercise of qigong can make the gate of life fire sufficient, the spleen earth warmed, the viscera nourished, food and air transported, *yang-qi* lifted and the constitution strengthened (气功练习可使命门火旺,暖脾土,滋脏腑,运食气,升阳气,强身健体).

The liver stores blood and is in charge of thinking (肝藏血,主谋虑). It prefers cheerfulness and magnanimity (宽宏大量) and is averse to gloominess and depression. Gloomy mood and stagnation of the liver-*qi* (肝气) may cause the abnormal dispersing and dredging function of the liver (情绪低落, 肝气郁结, 可能导致肝脏疏泄功能异常), while through relaxation and tranquilization (放松与安定) *qigong* dirigation (疏通) can stabilize the moods and recover the normal dispersing and dredging function.

The spleen has the function to transport and transform nutrients (脾之运化). Saliva is its excretion (唾液是它的分泌物). *Qigong* dirigation can, on the one hand, directly strengthen the spleen's function and bring about an increase in saliva and appetite; on the other hand, qigong lays stress on abdominal respiration which strengthens the superior-inferior movement of the diaphragm (气功强调腹式呼吸, 加强横膈膜的上下运动), thus producing a massaging effect on the stomach and promoting the peristaltic and digestive functions of the stomach (促进胃的蠕动和消化功能).

Contents of *Qigong*

The contents of *qigong* are varied, but they mainly involve the following aspects: regulation of the body (身体调节), regulation of breathing (呼吸调节), and regulation of mind (精神调节).

Regulation of body refers to the adjustment of body postures and relaxation exercise for it is essential to assume suitable postures in *qigong* dirigation. Correct postures are the preconditions to guarantee smooth respiration and induce mental relaxation and tranquilization. The theory that if the postures are not correct, the flow of qi cannot be smooth (形不正则气不顺); that if the flow of *qi* is not smooth, the mind cannot be concentrated (气不顺则意不守); and that if the mind is not concentrated, *qi* will be in disorder (意不守则气散乱) shows the importance of regulation of the body.

The postures commonly assumed are plain sitting posture (平坐式), free knee-crossing posture (自由盘膝式), single knee-crossing posture (单盘膝式), supine lying posture (仰卧式), latericumbent lying posture (侧卧式), standing posture, and walking posture.

Regulation of breathing is the regulation and exercise of respiration. It is a very important link in training *qi*, an essential method to cause genuine *qi* in the human body to accumulate, initiate and circulate. Regulation of breathing not only achieves the effects of regulating *qi* and blood and massaging the internal organs of the organism, but it is also helpful to mental tranquilization and physical relaxation.

Breathing regulation methods usually adopted are natural respiration method (自然呼吸法), orthodromic abdominal respiration method (顺腹式呼吸法), counter-abdominal respiration method (逆腹式呼吸法), pausing-closing respiration method (停闭式呼吸法) which requires to pause and close *qi* for a little while after each inhalation/exhalation and then exhale/inhale, nose-inhaling and mouth-exhaling method (鼻吸口呼法), reading word respiration method (读字呼吸法), sole breathing method (踵息法) that is to conduct qi through deep breathing to the acupoint Pouring Spring (涌泉穴) in the center of the sole while respiring, small heavenly circuit respiration method (小周天呼吸法) or method of *qi* circulation through ren and du channels (气通任督脉法), genuine breathing method (真息法), latent respiration method (潜呼吸法), and opening-closing respiration method (开合呼吸法) or sweat pore respiration method (毛孔呼吸法).

Regulation of mind refers to the regulation of mental activities: the exercise of mental tranquilization and mind concentration. Its key link is to, through exertion of mind-will (通过意志的运用), concentrate the mind (专心), get rid of all stray thoughts (除杂念), replace myriads of thoughts with one thought (以一念代替万念), thus gradually induce into tranquilization (渐入静) and enter a state of void (渐入空). This is the so-called "training the mind to return to void (练神还虚)", which is the most essential exercise in *qigong* dirigation. The effect of the training practice is mainly determined by the degree of tranquilization.

There are six major tranquilizing methods, namely, mind concentration method (意守法), breath-following method (随息法), breath-counting method (数息法), silent reading method (默念法), breath-listening method (听息法), and mental looking method (观想法).

Mind Concentration Method

The mind (意念) is highly concentrated on certain parts of the body, certain acupoint (穴位) or certain object outside the body, usually concentrated on the elixir field.

Breath-Following Method

The mind is highly concentrated on respiration, concentrated only on the rise and fall of the abdominal respiration without the conduct of mind-will so as to form a unification of mind-will and qi and reach a tranquil state of mind.

Bread-Counting Method

During the training, count silently the times of breath till the ear fails to hear, the eyes fail to see and the mind fails to think, thus naturally reaching a tranquil state of mind.

Silent Reading Method

Read silently certain single word or phrase, one for exhalation and one for inhalation, to replace the myriads of thoughts with one thought, gradually achieving a state free from stray thoughts and full of relaxation and joyousness, and comfortably reaching a tranquil state of mind.

Breath-Listening Method

Listen to your own breathing sound made by the passing current of respired air (聆听呼吸气流通过时自己发出的呼吸声). It will be better to hear nothing, but fancy in the mind to listen so as to help tranquilize.

Mental Looking Method

During the training practice, fancy in the mind to conduct your eyes to look inwardly at certain parts inside your own body or certain objects outside your body so as to induce youself into a tranquil state of mind.

Schools of *Qigong*

The schools of Chinese *qigong* are various. Some people classify them into five major schools, namely, medical, Confucian, Buddhist, Taoist, and martial art (气功五派：医、儒、释、道、武术). Each of them might be subdivided into minor schools and has its own characteristics. The medical school aims at strengthening one's health and is good for treating and preventing diseases. The intention of the Confucian School is self-cultivation and the training of one's temperament and morality, while the Taoist school is to cultivate one's moral characters and seek longevity. As for the Buddhist school, which essentially involves the mind, there are two branches, one of which is called "Samadhi (三昧)" claiming that all matters in the world (dhata) are illusory (sunyata), and the other is called "meditation (冥想)" which stresses the cultivation of the mind and the need to save all living organisms on earth. The martial art school is mainly for the purpose of physical training and the improvement of health. Though differing in purpose and method, these diverse schools have one thing in common, that is, the training of the mind and the strengthening of vital energy.

By appearance and posture, Chinese *qigong* can be divided into two kinds, the static (静功) and the dynamic (动功). Externally the static *qigong* adopts three types of positions, namely, the supine, the sitting and the standing (从外表看，静气功采用卧、坐、立三种体位). It stresses the training from inside the body itself and is thus termed "internal *qigong* (内功)". The dynamic *qigong* combines the training of mental consciousness and qi with the movements of four extremities (四肢), such as walking exercise, *Taiji quan*, and self massage, to activate the circulation of *qi* and blood, and to mould one's temperament. It is also named "external *qigong* (外功)" due to its visible active movements of the body.

A Brief History of *Qigong*

Chinese *qigong* has a history which can be traced back to remote antiquity several thousand years ago. As tradition has it, in the times of Yao (尧), people has already realized that dancing could strengthen health. For instance, *The Spring and Autumn Annals of Master Lü* (《吕氏春秋》) recorded, "From as early as the origin of the previous Tao and Tang tribes (陶、唐氏), *yin* tends to stagnate and incubate latently and accumulate in the depth of the body; the water passages are thus blocked up and water no longer flows in its original right passages; *qi* smoulders (郁积) and stagnates (停滞) within the body; the muscles and bones cower (畏缩) and shorten and cannot extend properly, and then dancing is created accordingly to remove the stagnancy and obstruction (消除停滞和阻塞)." Later on some dance gradually evolved into physical and breathing therapies. In the process of fight against nature, ancient people realized that certain actions, breathing and utterance of certain sound can regulate some functions of the human body, such as extending the limbs being able to dissipate heat (伸展四肢能够散热), huddling up the body to keep out cold (蜷缩身躯御寒), and the sound ha to subdue and discharge physical strength (声"哈"音可克制和释放体力). The ancient theory that "the bear will contract itself when climbing a tree and the bird will stretch its legs when flying in the air" was formed in this way in practice.

In the Zhou Dynasty, there had already been records on qigong in the inscriptions on bronze. Lao Zi suggested the methods of "blowing (吹)" and "puffing (呴)". His follower, Zhuang Zi, carried it further and said, "Blowing and puffing, exhaling and inhaling helps to rid one of the stale and take in the fresh. Moving as a bear and stretching as a bird can result in longevity (吹呴呼吸,吐故纳新,熊经鸟伸,为寿而已矣)."

"Jade Pendant Inscription on *Qigong* (行气玉佩铭)", a 12-side cylinder (12面圆柱) and a historical relic of the early Spring and Autumn Period, recorded the training method and theory of *qigong* in 45 Chinese characters: In promoting and conducting qi, depth promises storage, storage promises extension, extension promises descent, descent promises stability, stability promises solidity, solidity promises germination, germination promises growth, growth promises retreat, and retreat leads to heaven. Heavenly *qi* functions from above, earthly *qi* from below. Conformity to this leads to life while adverseness to this leads to death (行气,深则蓄,蓄则伸,伸则下,下则定,定则固,固则萌,萌则长,长则退,退则天。天几春在上,地几春在下。顺则生,逆则死). Here not only is the training process of the small heavenly circuit clearly explained, but the health-preserving principles of qigong are also expounded.

Among the historical relics unearthed from the Han tombs at Mawangdui Village, Changsha, Hunan Province, there was a silk book *On Abandoning Food and Living on Qi* (《却谷食气篇》) and a silk painting *Daoyin Illustrations* (《导引图》) of the early Western Han Dynasty. The former is about a method of "inducing, promoting, and conducting *qi*"; the latter displays 44 colored "*daoyin* illustrations" of training exercises. This shows that China already used the form of illustrations to teach *qigong* no later than the early Western Han Dynasty.

The Yellow Emperor's Canon of Internal Medicine (《黄帝内经》) systematically expounded *qigong*'s principles, exercising methods and its effects. For instance, "Exhale and inhale essence qi, concentrate the spirit to keep a sound mind, the muscle and flesh unite as one (呼吸精气,独立守神,肌肉若一)." Those who suffer from a lingering kidney disease can face the south in the early morning, clear the mind of all worries and stray thoughts, hold breath without respiration for seven times, and then swallow the breath by slightly craning the neck to send it down smoothly, just as swallowing very hard objects. Having done this for seven times, gulp down the plenty of sublingual saliva (肾有久病者,可以寅时面向南,净神不乱思,闭气不息七遍,以引颈咽气顺之,如咽甚硬物,如此七遍后,饵舌下津无数).

Viewed from the development of the history of traditional Chinese medicine, doctors through the ages all paid great attention to and had great attainments in *qigong*. In *Treatise on Febrile and Miscellaneous Disease* (《伤寒杂病论》) by Zhang Zhongjing (张仲景), there are accounts of employing qigong to treat diseases. One of them is "As soon as the limbs feel heavy and sluggish, resort to such treatments as *daoyin* (导引, inducing and conducting *qi*), *tuna* (吐纳, expiration and inspiration), acupuncture and massage by rubbing with ointment so as not allow the nine orifices to close up (针灸膏抹,勿令九窍闭塞)." The renowned physician Hua Tuo (华佗), inheriting the ancient *qigong* and *daoyin*, created a set of fitness exercises called "The Five-Animal Play (五禽戏)" mimicking the movements and gestures of the tiger, the deer, the bear, the ape and the bird. It is exercised to attain the goal of free circulation of blood and prevention of disease.

Ge Hong (葛洪), a renowned physician in the Eastern Jin Dynasty, held that the methods of daoyin should be diversified. He pointed out in his book *The Man Who Holds to Simplicity·Inner Treatise* (《抱朴子·内篇》), "Flexing or stretching, bending or up-facing, walking or lying, leaning or standing, pacing or strolling, chanting or breathing are all methods of daoyin (屈伸、弯腰或仰卧、行

Ge Hong

卧、卧立、蹀步或走动、念诵或呼吸，都是导引的方法)." He believed that the function of qigong is "to cure disease not yet contracted and dredge discordant *qi* (疗未患之病，通不和之气)". "Once it gets working, *qi* will flow in an unimpeded way everywhere (一旦它起作用了，气就会到处畅通无阻)." He also commented on applying exhalation and inhalation, expiration and inspiration to "conducting *qi*", which can "maintain good health internally and eliminate pathogenic factors externally (他还评论将呼气和吸气与"行气"结合起来，可以"内养身体，外祛病因")."

Since the Eastern Han Dynasty, with the introduction of Buddhism, the Indian Buddhists' yoga was combined with the ancient *daoyin* of China, thereby contributing to the development of *qigong* both in theory and practice.

Chao Yuanfang (巢元方), a famous doctor in the Sui Dynasty, pointed out in his *General Treatise on the Causes and Symptoms of Diseases* (《诸病源候论》) that when a man had mastered *qigong*, he could release through his palm a kind of qi to cure diseases for others. Records on *qigong* are also found in *Prescriptions Worth a Thousand Gold for Emergencies* (《千金方》) by the renowned physician Sun Simiao (孙思邈), *The Secret Prescriptions Revealed by a Provincial Governor* (《外台秘要》) by Wang Tao (王焘) during the Tang Dynasty, the well-known medical formulary *General Collection for Holy Relief* (《圣济总录》) of the Northern Song Dynasty and medical books written by the four eminent physician in the Jin and Yuan Dynasties, namely, Liu Wansu's *On Keeping Fit* (刘完素，《摄生论》), Zhang Zihe's *Clinical Experience of A Scholar* (张从正，《儒门事亲》), Li Dongyuan's *Medical Secrets of the Orchid Chamber* (李东垣，《兰室秘藏》) and Zhu Danxi's *On Inquiring the Properties of Things* (朱丹溪，《格致余论》).

In the Ming Dynasty, the renowned physician and pharmacologist Li Shizhen (李时珍) said in his *A Study on the Eight Extra Channels* (《奇经八脉考》), "The inner scene and channels can be perceived clean and clear only by those who can see inwards (内景隧道，唯返观者能照查之)." He also pointed out in his *Guidebook to Acupuncture and Moxibustion* (《针灸指南》) that those who learn acupuncture and moxibustion should practice still-sitting exercise first, thus "in the human body the circulation of *qi* and blood in the channels and the opening and closing of the functional activities of *qi* can have a reliable foundation."

Collection of Prescriptions with Notes (《医方集解》) compiled by the well-known physician Wang Ang (汪昂) of the early Qing Dynasty and *Shen's Work on the Health Preservation* (《沈氏尊生书》) written by Shen Jin'ao (沈金鳌) both have special records of the training methods of *qigong*. Shen proposed 12 principles of movement and described therapeutic *qigong*. After the

Revolution of 1911, some intellectuals advocated still-sitting exercises. Their representative works include Jiang Weiqiao's *Yinshi Zi Still-Sitting Exercises* (蒋维乔,《因是子静坐法》), Ding Fubao's *Essence of Still-Sitting Exercises* (丁福保,《静坐法精义》) and Chen Qianming's *The Health Preserving Method of Tranquility* (陈乾明,《静的修养法》).

After the founding of the People's Republic of China, many experts, inheriting the traditional qigong, further tapped (进一步挖掘), systematized and formulated a multitude of new training maneuvers (系统制定了许多新的练功手法). Some *qigong* sanatoriums (气功疗养院) were founded. Quite a few training courses and academic conferences were held. In recent years, *qigong* has been widely used to treat many chronic diseases, such as chronic hepatitis (慢性肝炎), hypertension (高血压), pyknocardia (心搏过速), bronchial asthma (支气管哮喘) and neurasthenia (神经衰弱). At present, the application and research of *qigong* have gone far beyond the scope of medical hygienics (医疗卫生). It has been found to have relatively high application value in agriculture, military affairs, physical culture, education and many other aspects. It is certain that the application and research of *qigong* may bring even larger profits to human beings and play a more important role in probing the secrets of the human body and life.

Exercises

Part One　Comprehension

Fill in the following blanks with the information you learn in Chapter 12.

1. In the Song Dynasty, *cuju*, a primitive _____ game using a leather ball filled with hair or something else, was so prevailing that everyone from the emperor to ordinary people participated in it.

2. In the Yuan Dynasty, people liked playing a game called Chuiwan, which was similar to _____ as shown in the mural painting Hitting Balls.

3. Among traditional Chinese physical activities, wushu or martial arts may be the most _____ and typical.

4. Chenjiagou is well-known not only for its wushu masters but also for being the birthplace of _____.

5. The renowned physician Hua Tuo, inheriting the ancient qigong and daoyin, created a set of fitness exercises called "The Five-Animal Play" mimicking the movements and gestures of the tiger, the _____, the bear, the ape and the bird.

Part Two   Translation

Passage Translation

中国传统体育文化有着极其丰富的内容,历史悠久,自成体系。它以自己的体育文化方式发展、传承,是人类体育文化的杰出代表之一。从以武术为主体的武艺到以调节呼吸方法为主体的导引养生,从以身体活动形式满足人们娱乐需求为主体的民间乡土游戏,到少数民族传统体育,中国传统体育文化记载着人类社会的发展进程。

Part Three   Critical Thinking and Discussion

1. How many major schools of qigong are there in history? What are they?

2. Do you like practicing qigong? Why or why not?

3. Some people think that the vigor of China traditional sports is languishing in real life. How to solve this problem?

Chapter 13
Chinese Classical Gardens

Chinese classical gardens are considered a chief component of traditional Chinese culture. Some people say that if you have never walked through a Chinese classical garden, you cannot say that you have really visited China.

Traditional Chinese gardens are held in high esteem in the history of Chinese culture. As a form of art, they arose from the fertility of ancient Chinese civilization, assembled and blended with the ideas and approaches of traditional Chinese painting and were also intimately related to poetry and music. They originated and developed over 3,000 years ago and were valued as a living environment with naturalistic beauty, meeting the sophisticated daily and socio-political needs of ancient garden owners.

/ A General History of Chinese Classical Gardens /

Before the Qin Dynasty, there were three main kinds of Chinese classical gardens: those of the imperial palaces, private gardens and temple ones.

Lingyou

Of the three kinds, the imperial gardens appeared earliest, and can be traced back, according to written records, to King Wen Wang of the Zhou Dynasty (周文王), who built a vast garden of about 1,000 square kilometers called *Lingyou* (灵囿). Then many gardens followed throughout the dynasty and the Warring States Period. At first, most of them were called *you* (囿) which meant animal farms; later, more and more of them became known as *yuan* (苑) which meant gardens. Imperial gardens before the Qin and Han Dynasties harbored wild animals, birds and fish, which were the chief source of entertainment, mainly as objects to be admired, but also as game for hunting parties. As agriculture developed to a higher level from the Qin Dynasty, wild-life was gradually replaced by exotic plants and flowers, although some animals were still retained for hunting. Take for instance, Long Pond (长池). It was built by the First Emperor of the Qin Dynasty around the present-day Xiangyang (襄阳), with a large extension measuring about 100 kilometers east to west and 10 kilometers north to south. This enormous, labor-consuming construction included the introduction of water from the Weihe River (渭河) to fill the gigantic pond. The legendary island, Penglai Mountain (蓬莱山), supposed to be the magical dwelling of the immortals, was constructed with soil excavated from the pond. In the Han Period, the change was more obvious. Emperor Wu constructed the Grand Fluid Pond (大液池), embracing three legendary immortal mountains: Penglai, Fangzhang (方丈) and Yingzhou (瀛洲). This became a pattern since then and was repeated in later imperial gardens with varied designs and modified versions. In their function there was also a little change. They were not only for the owner's enjoyment, but also places for the emperors to offer sacrifices to heaven and earth, to pray for prosperity, and to hold other religious activities.

During this period, landscape gardens were basically full-sized reproductions of natural mountain and water scenes. The style was believed to have started in the late Zhou Dynasty, and came into vogue during the Qin and Han Dynasties, and continued for a certain period of time.

After the Han Dynasty, imperial gardens developed rapidly. Influenced by religions, most imperial gardens began to contain temples and Buddhist pagodas, which stressed the religious flavor.

Private gardens, though arising probably in the Spring and Autumn Period, began to develop in the Han Dynasty. They were mainly built by bureaucrats (官僚) and rich nobles, such as the prime minister Cao Can (曹参), the general Huo Guang (霍光) and the wealthy man Yuan Guanghan (袁广汉) in Maoling (茂陵). At first, private gardens were also quite large-sized. Then they were limited not only by building costs but also by the hierarchical regulations of the feudal society molded by Confucianism. Nothing should surpass the imperial possessions in any way, including the size of a garden, or the owners would be accused of violating the hierarchical order. So, private gardens were restricted to a medium or small size.

These early private gardens were basically diminished imitations of palatial gardens. Only till the period of Wei and Jin and of the Northern and Southern Dynasties, did the style change a little. The tumult (骚动, 心烦意乱) of successively changing dynasties distressed some court officials on the one hand. On the other hand, some talented scholars could not realize their ambition and were even persecuted, so they had a strong desire to escape from reality. Influenced by the Taoist and Buddhist idea of going back to nature, they built their own gardens as retreats or ideal environments for scholastic activities, such as studying, painting, composing verses, and cultivating plants, fish, and birds.

At that time, landscape painting and lyrical poetry appeared. It was recorded that some celebrated paintings depicted "a height of 8,000 feet with 3 inches in vertical compositions and hundreds of miles within several feet in horizontal composition (竖画三寸, 当千仞之高; 横墨数尺, 体百里之回)." The lyrical poets, especially Tao Yuanming (陶渊明), in the Jin Dynasty, described the beauty of mountains, rivers and rural scenery. Later the paintings and poems became the chief source of inspiration for landscape designers of private gardens which were graceful and refined and close to the subtle harmony of the wilderness, with modesty and simplicity fostering a tone of restrained elegance. The most outstanding examples were the garden of Tao Yuanming, the Garden of the Fool's Stream (愚溪园) of the Tang scholar Liu Zongyuan (柳宗元), the Thatched Manor Hall on the Lushan Mountains (庐山草堂) that belonged to the Tang poet Bai Juyi (白居易), the Garden of the Painted Boat (画舫斋) of the Song scholar Ouyang Xiu (欧阳修), the Garden of the Humble Administrator or the Humble Administrator's Garden (拙政园) of the Ming celebrity Wang Xianchen (王献臣) and other exquisite ones.

The Garden of the Humble Administrator

Here one point must be made clear: most of the extant private gardens (现存私家园林) are located in Suzhou (苏州), Hangzhou (杭州), Wuxi (无锡), and Yangzhou (扬州)—cities south of the lower reaches of the Yangtze River, especially Suzhou. Suzhou, famed as the "city of gardens", is endowed with over a hundred high-quality surviving gardens, which are famous not only for being the most beautiful and distinctive but also for representing the most clear ideas of Chinese garden design. The earliest Suzhou garden still in existence, dating back to the 10th century, is the Blue-Wave Pavilion (沧浪亭). Most of the others were built in the Ming or Qing Dynasties.

The Blue-Wave Pavilion

In the Tang and Song Dynasties, the number of imperial gardens increased greatly, most being built in Chang'an (长安) and Luoyang (洛阳), but almost all of them were completely destroyed.

From the 13th century, Beijing, the ancient capital of Yuan, Ming, and Qing Dynasties, became the center of garden building. In fact, the predominance of its imperial gardens was chiefly accomplished in the last feudal dynasty. They tend toward staidness and resplendence consistent with a sense of palatial grandeur (它们倾向于沉稳和辉煌，与富丽堂皇的感觉相一致). Special approaches are employed in dealing with form, coloring, and the sense of beauty. Roofs of yellow-glazed tiles are set off by green foliage, blue sky, and an extensive span of water surfaces (黄琉璃瓦屋顶被绿叶、蓝天和广阔的水面衬托). Multicolored beams and brackets under the embellished eaves are supported by rows of brilliant vermilion pillars (缀饰檐下的五彩梁柱，由一排排艳丽的朱红色台柱支撑).

Many scenes in the imperial gardens are reproductions of distinguished gardens throughout the country, especially gardens south of the Yangtze River. Emperor Qianlong of the Qing Dynasty, after his legendary visit to Southern China, demanded that the greatest landscape views and garden scenes be reproduced and included in his gardens. For instance, the Kunming Lake

(昆明湖) in the Summer Palace (颐和园) was constructed to reproduce scenic West Lake (西湖) in Hangzhou; the Garden of Harmonious Interests (谐趣园) in the northeastern corner is an imitation of the Garden of the Free Spirit (寄畅园) in Wuxi (无锡). This "garden within a garden" is small and elegant, with pavilions and walking galleries winding around a placid pond. It successfully reproduced the beauty of its model. Nevertheless, these reproductions were not simply copies of the originals but had been revised according to the peculiarities of their site and style. Therefore, the Qing imperial gardens remained innovative by retaining the garden designing canon (保留园林设计准则): Follow the environmental context and manifest the best.

The Summer Palace

Another thing worth mentioning is that in ancient China there were few professional garden designers, which resulted in very few books on garden building. The best one was *Garden Building* (《园冶》) compiled by Ji Cheng (计成) of the Ming Dynasty. Ji Cheng was a painter and rockery artisan (假山工匠). His book was honored as the earliest masterpiece of garden books, which provided a comprehensive survey, including the basic idea, general layout, design methods, and components of the garden with distinctive national characteristics. In spite of all the detailed instructions covered in the book, it is emphasized that a garden is not constituted by any regulating rules but is an expression of nature's pulsating life (自然脉动生命的表达). So any principles are elastic. His book was translated into Japanese over 50 years ago.

Immediately after Taoism became a religion and Buddhism entered China, temples of the religions were built one after another. They are the best models of nature reformed into the constructed environment that integrated the beauty of the natural landscape with artifacts (人工制品), for the most fascinating scenic spots in China's mountainous regions were chosen for monasteries (寺院) and temples (寺庙). That's why we have the saying "No mountain is ever devoid of monks (没有一座山没有僧侣)." In the temples, buildings were erected to accommodate the religious requirements and the daily needs of the monks. The buildings highlight the mountain scape (山景) and, in the meantime, provide a command of the serene (宁静) and peaceful (祥和的) landscape in the vicinity (附近).

During the long history of Chinese gardens, only a few of the distinguished gardens have been preserved and they have been repeatedly praised and depicted by Chinese classic literature and antique paintings. Many exquisite gardens were devastated or totally destroyed by natural calamities and all the successive warfare in the changing of dynasties in ancient China.

The Garden of Perfectness and Brightness

Because of the European invasions of the last hundred years, none of the resplendent imperial gardens (金碧辉煌的皇家园林) that took generations to elaborate escaped from being burned and looted (掠夺, 洗劫). Among these, the Summer Palace and Beihai Park (北海公园) have been restored to their original magnificence. The Garden of Perfectness and Brightness (圆明园) was the most imposing and beautiful imperial garden of the Qing Dynasty. Celebrated as the "garden of gardens", the extensive and fabulous garden was built for almost 100 years, beginning in 1709. It was first completely destroyed in 1869 by invading Anglo-French forces. Shortly after partial restoration, the garden was again looted and burned by an army of eight allied Western powers in 1900. Only a few ruins of the once exuberant architecture bear witness to its existence (曾经繁华的建筑只剩几处废墟, 见证着它的存在).

After the fall of the Qing Dynasty, garden building had come to a halt, due to continuous national warfare, economic depression, and other reasons. The gardens, both imperial and private, began to disintegrate under ill use and negligence. Since 1949, most of the surviving traditional gardens have been excavated and restored to their original magnificence in an effort at cultural preservation.

/ Components of Chinese Classical Gardens /

Hills

The artificial hill is Chinese classical garden's most unconventional, fascinating scenic feature, indispensable to its unique style. "Hill molding and rockery manipulation (筑山叠石)" was a term in ancient China for garden construction.

There are usually three methods of hill molding in regard to the use of soil and rocks. The first type, the earth hill (土山), is suitable for gardens with large tracts of land, such as those of the palatial gardens (宫殿式园林). It is often large enough to be cultivated extensively with plants that make it seem like a natural mountain. The second type is the composite use of soil and rocks (土石复合利用). The third is the rock hill which is best applied in smaller constructions and in confined areas.

Artificial hills, both molded hills (筑山) and rockery, are essentially structural garden components. They are built to simulate the distilled and enhanced beauty of natural mountain views—peak (峰顶), cliff (悬崖), precipice (峭壁), gorge (峡谷), and cave (洞穴), but are often asymmetric in shape, with a steeper slope on one end that contrasts with a moderate slope on the other. They also function to divide space, to screen, and to serve as foils for garden views. For instance, elegant sets of hills are often used as ornamental screens at garden gates or as very effective transitions between artifacts and the natural garden landscape. When organized appropriately in relation to other garden features, the hill is always the most appreciated art presentation of the Chinese garden.

Rocks

According to historical records, rock collection was a sophisticated hobby for gentlemen and scholars as early as the Spring and Autumn Period. The use of rocks in the Chinese garden can be traced back to the Sui Dynasty. The love of rock came into vogue during the Tang Period. Gardens in the city of Chang'an used lots of rocks hauled from Zhongnan Mountain (终南山).

The "grotesque" rocks (奇石) used in Chinese gardens can be mainly divided into two kinds: the graceful and elegant light-gray lake rock (雍容华贵的浅灰色湖石) and the sturdy and staid yellow mountain rock (粗犷沉稳的黄色山石), each with its own individual style. The lake rock is the highly prized variety (珍贵品种) quarried from the shores and bottom of the Taihu

Lake in Jiangsu Province. It is limestone (石灰岩) eroded by waves, with irregular shapes and sculptured cavities (空洞) and holes (孔洞). The aesthetic criteria established for excellence are that the rock be perforated (穿孔), slender (细长的), and corrugated (波纹状). The yellow rock appears more geometrical and angular in form. As it is available within almost all the territories of China, yellow rock compositions are extensively used. These arrangements are characterized by an air of majestic magnificence. A good example is the hill of the Yuyuan Garden (豫园) in Shanghai.

Yuyuan Garden

Rockery presentations are expected to evoke personal feelings through abstract beauty that inspires the unlimited enjoyment of reminiscence and thus allow for different interpretations, varying with moods or perspectives, as do the changing clouds in the sky.

Water

Water is as important in creating moods and emotional appeal in the garden as eyes are in the human face. In building a garden in ancient China, sources of water were the essential site-selecting factor. Natural springs and wells were often the main sources. Some ponds were connected with rivers, and when water supply was totally absent in a garden site, rainfall water was collected from the gutters (排水沟) of nearby buildings to fill small ponds. The water surface is often found boldly dominating an area exceeding more than half of the entire garden. To be precise, in Beijing's Summer Palace, water surface dominates up to 3/4 of its plot, and the central pond occupies 3/5 of the total garden area and over 80% of the buildings are along the watercourses in the Garden of the Humble Administrator.

The Chinese have many clever and different ways of playing with reflection on water, which greatly contributes to the individual garden's intended character. A water pavilion commanding water scenes in different directions, boat-like buildings berthing (停泊) by a corner of a large pond, walking galleries meandering (蜿蜒) along the embankment (堤岸), tiny bridges with streamlets running under them, and grotesque rocks and exotic flowers (奇石和异草) dotting on all sides are typical water scenes of Chinese gardens.

A body of water most effectively unifies the garden by focusing the observer's attention on itself as well as on the features around it and provides beholders a pleasing, serene and fascinating world for their enjoyment.

Architecture

Greatly different from that of Western gardens in which architecture is sometimes not taken as a component, architecture predominates over plant life in the Chinese garden scene and there is no Chinese garden devoid of architecture.

In China, a series of genuine garden architectures have evolved and crystallized through thousands of years of practice. A large variety of building types were developed to fit particular situations in the garden as well as to facilitate the daily and occasional needs of habitation. Each building type has an individually characteristic form of its own—with special size, proportion, and details that yield to modification without losing their individuality.

The disposition and design of garden architecture are guided by dual criteria: architecture functions both as a viewing-point and as a part of the garden scene.

Garden architecture, in general, takes the form of open shelters and defines space from overhead without blocking up the continuity of space. The columns and beams of the open shelters serve as picture frames that focus and greatly enhance the magnificence of garden scenes. The Lingering Garden (留园) in Suzhou is one of the many excellent examples.

The Lingering Garden

The Chinese garden architecture is composed of many types of buildings, among which the following are the main ones.

Main Hall

The main hall (厅堂), which is sometimes called the flower hall (花厅) to distinguish it from the main hall of the traditional courtyard house, is a sizable structure with a comparatively lofty space occupying a key position as the accent of the garden composition and the center for activities held in the garden. It is south-oriented and has a relatively formal appearance according to tradition. It could be fenestrate (开窗的) on all sides or walled on two or three sides to cope with the scenic dispositions around it.

Pavilion

The pavilion, small in size and varied in form, is the basic and ubiquitous feature of the Chinese garden (亭子小巧玲珑，形式多样，是中国园林的基本特征). "亭", which originated from the character "停", clearly indicates its function as a rest stop. Being light and open, the pavilion acquires the ideal form of garden architecture. It is interspersed with scenic views, blends well into the naturalistic landscape, and at the same time, serves as a sheltered vantage point commanding views in all directions (一个俯瞰四面八方的隐蔽制高点). Pavilions are usually built free-standing on a hill-side, half hidden in groves or a rockery, or on the watercourse (亭子通常建在山坡上，半隐藏在小树林或假山中，或在水道上). They can be cut in half, connected with galleries, and attached to a wall. The plan of a pavilion can be square (正方形的), rectangular (长方形的), hexagonal (六角形的), octagonal (八角形的), circular (圆形的), fan-shaped (扇形的), or any shape selected by the designer.

The roof further contributes to the structure's fascinating appearance with its vast variety of shapes and styles. Pyramidal (金字塔形的), conical (圆锥形的), hipped (四坡的), half-hipped (半坡的) and half-gabled (半山墙的) roofs are the most popular ones.

Mansion

As a sizable building, a mansion is usually avoided in private garden. It is mostly limited to two stories, with diminished ceiling height, in order to maintain a proportional relation with the surrounding space and garden features. It is most often located in remote corners of the garden to avoid overpowering the garden with building mass. The positive use is to provide an elevated viewing point with a wide sight range of enjoying scenes.

Tower

A garden tower can be either one or two stories but is always raised in position, sustaining a floating appearance, and most often fenestrate on four sides to provide viewing opportunities in different directions.

Walking Gallery

Connected with paths, bridges, and garden buildings, the walking gallery (步行画廊) is a prime garden touring route and a most spectacular building type in the Chinese garden. It also serves as a space-confining device. While dividing, it unites the different scenic sections by being open and smooth, greatly adding to the depth and sequence of the garden views. It tends to be long and crooked (修长而弯曲的), undulates horizontally and vertically with land contour (陆地轮廓), and ascends freely upon a hill or flies dramatically over a water-course.

Bridges

The bridge, doing double duty, is carefully located and designed both to command a view of the water scene around it and as a decorative feature for the scenery. It is often erected along a touring route, giving diversity to the visitor who crosses a stream or gains access to an island. It is also a vantage point for viewing a waterfall or a stream of extraordinary serenity leading to an imaginary fountain hidden in the woods, which increases curiosity and urges viewers to continue further in their trip beyond the bridge.

The forms of garden bridges are diversified and most of them are made of stones with simple but elegant design or with intricately carved patterns congruent with their surroundings. The simple plank bridge (简约木板桥) is preferred for a small span of water in a confined area. Over the larger ponds, bridges are broken up into segments in a zigzag form (锯齿形) for a better sense of scale. In lakes of vast area, ornamentation is often better than simplicity, for articulate forms and eye-catching bright colors (清晰的形式和引人注目的鲜艳色彩) produce dramatic effects. Bridges with gorgeous pavilions (华丽亭台) and even clusters of pavilions (一群亭台), such as the Five-Pavilion Bridge (五亭桥) in the Slender West Lake (瘦西湖) of Yangzhou (扬州), are appreciated as scenery as well as for the enchanting picture frames that offset (补偿) views in the vicinity. When a pond or lake is large enough for boating, an arched bridge with a graceful curvature (优美曲度) is often erected to permit a boat to pass under it.

The Five-Pavilion Bridge

In short, the form and detail of bridges, like all other garden architecture, are designed to conform to the individual garden's general concept and the immediate surrounding context. Thus, innumerable types of bridges flourish in Chinese gardens.

Plant Material

With the extraordinary number of buildings and rockeries within Chinese gardens, there are relatively fewer plants than in gardens of other traditions. Plants do, however, retain their importance as a unifying garden element that blends the artifacts with their surroundings, creating a naturalistic landscape.

Plants in Chinese gardens are carefully selected and appropriately applied in accordance with their surroundings. Plants with open foliage (树叶) are ranked over bulky shrubs or hedges with dense foliage (茂密的灌木或树篱); bosquet (矮树) and copse (杂树林) are cultivated for space division in large gardens only; shrubs are often planted on hills of larger scale to serve as foils; trees are favored in smaller areas and said to be "occupying the sky but not the land", as the trunk (树干) takes little space and the crown (树冠) spreads above human height.

Plants in scenic compositions (风景作品中的植物), when intended for close-up viewing (近距离观看), are not chosen merely for their posture. The detailed elegance of branches, the texture of leaves, the color, and the fragrance are all taken into careful consideration (枝条的细腻雅致,树叶的质感,色泽,香气,无一不考究). Antiquity, distinctiveness, and gracefulness are the criteria for plant selection (古老、独特和优雅是植物选择的标准). A variety of examples are presented here. The crept myrtle (桃金娘) and the redbud (紫荆花) are chosen for their artistically twisted and turned stems and branches; bamboo groves (竹林) are widely favored for their singular translucent effect (奇特的透光效果) and their unusual texture and jade-green color; different species of orchids (兰花), lilies (百合花), and ferns (蕨类植物) with graceful drooping leaves are extensively planted in rock-and-plant composition (岩石和植物组合) as an unfailing transitional feature that integrates rocks to each other and to the ground.

Some species of plants are preferred for, beside the above merits, the symbolic significance. Pomegranates (石榴) and finger lemon (手指柠檬), called "Buddha's hand (佛手)" in Chinese, are planted as auspicious symbols of prosperous offspring (繁荣后代) and longevity (长寿); soaring pines and junipers (高耸的松柏), valued for their age and indomitable spirit (历久弥新，坚韧不拔), and as a symbol of longevity, are the ever sought-after models for cultivation (一直备受追捧的栽培典范); a variety of dwarfed plum trees with crooked, knuckled branches, blooming gorgeously during a severe winter snow, symbolize an unconquerable spirit such as the struggle of human kind with hardships and difficulties (各种矮小的梅树，弯弯曲曲的枝条，在严冬的大雪中绽放出绚丽的花朵，象征着人类在艰难困苦中奋斗的不屈不挠的精神); the chrysanthemum (菊花), endearingly described as the "late fragrance (晚香)", is extensively cultivated as a symbol for "those who defy frost (不畏严寒)" and "those who survive all others"; the lotus flower (莲花), the captivating center of a summer scene, is adored as a symbol of purity and truth as it rises spotless from mud (出淤泥而不染); orchids (兰花) are loved for their subtle fragrance (微妙的香气), blossoms of refined beauty (精致美丽的花朵), and especially their sheath-like leaves (鞘状的叶子) that suggest both strength and gracefulness; and plum, orchids, bamboo and chrysanthemum (梅、兰、竹、菊), famed together as the "four virtuous gentlemen (四君子)", symbolize the praise of sincere friendship. In the mind of the Chinese people, the personalized qualities of these plants are just as important as their functional and decorative advantages. Therefore, the presence of plants in Chinese gardens not only affords aesthetic satisfaction (审美上的满足) but exhilarates the spirit (振奋精神) and imbues viewers with the traditionally sophisticated taste (令观者感受到传统的精致品位).

On the whole, although the Chinese garden is chiefly made up of hills, rocks, water, and plants, it never means a copy and miniature of nature (自然的复制和缩影) or casual placement of these favorite components. As mentioned above, the Chinese garden, since the Wei and Jin Dynasties, has been closely associated with the art and literary realms (领域), and governed by theories of artistic creation. Many successful scenes were constructed with famous paintings as models while the theme or tone of a garden depicted the enchantment of a poem. So the Chinese garden is also celebrated as impressionistic painting and embodied poetry to express particular emotions and concepts (中国园林也被誉为印象派绘画和具象诗歌，以表达特定的情感和概

念). In fact, Chinese gardens were designed to be "read" as romantic novels are (中国园林被设计成可以像言情小说一样被"阅读"). The garden touring routes organize Chinese gardens into sequential compositions (游园路线将中国园林组织成连续的构图). For instance, in the Garden of the Humble Administrator and the Lingering Garden, invitational prelude, exciting climax and thought-provoking postlude are beautifully practiced (邀约的前奏、激动人心的高潮、发人深省的后奏都被演绎得淋漓尽致). The integration of poetry, painting, and garden is the culmination of Chinese garden art (诗、画、园的融合，是中国园林艺术的巅峰). The unique and fascinating characteristics could only be originated and nurtured in a country with an exceedingly long history and profound cultural achievements (这种独特而迷人的特色，只有在一个历史极其悠久、文化底蕴深厚的国家才能发扬光大).

/ The Summer Palace /

The Summer Palace, or Yiheyuan (颐和园, Garden of Harmonious Unity), is one of the largest and finest imperial resorts in China. The history of the Summer Palace dates back to the time of the first emperor of the Jin Dynasty (金朝, 1115—1234) when he built the "Gold Mountain Traveling Palace (金山行宫)" at the present site of Longevity Hill (万寿山). During the reign of Emperor Qianlong (1735—1796), the name of the mountain was changed to the Longevity Hill and the lake to the Kunming Lake (昆明湖). The entire area was called Qingyiyuan (清漪园, the Park of Pure Ripples).

The Longevity Hill

Located on the northwestern outskirts of Beijing, the Summer Palace covers an area of about 3 square kilometers, three-fourths of which is covered with shallow lakes. Most of its buildings were burned and looted by the Anglo-French joint forces in 1860 during the Second Opium War. In 1888, Empress Dowager Cixi (慈禧太后) ordered the Summer Palace to be rebuilt and enlarged with funds originally designated for the Chinese navy. She renamed it Yiheyuan. The work took eight years to finish, and consequently, a new garden appeared. The best examples of classical landscape gardening—palaces, halls, pavilions, pagodas, covered corridors, and bridges were included. It became a public park in 1924 after Puyi (溥仪), the last Qing emperor, abdicated and was ousted (驱逐) from the Forbidden City.

The Summer Palace is grand in scale and contains the differing styles of famous Chinese gardens. Its center is the Longevity Hill, which faces the Kunming Lake; other places of interest are located around the hill and the lake. The whole garden may be divided into three areas: the royal palaces, the residential quarters, and the garden.

Facing the main entrance, Renshoudian (仁寿殿, the Hall of Benevolence and Longevity) is the main palace hall where Cixi held court and received foreign envoys. North of the Hall of Benevolence and Longevity stands Deheyuan (德和园, the Palace of Virtue and Harmony) where Cixi watched opera performances. The stage is built in the form of a three-storied tower with a traditional double-eaved roof (舞台采用传统重檐屋顶的三层塔楼形式建造).

Lying behind the Hall of Benevolence and Longevity, the residential area consists mainly of three quadrangles of one story houses (住宅区位于仁寿殿后面，主要由三个平层四合院组成). They were the places where Emperor Guangxu (光绪) used to live. The houses are furnished as they were in the days of Cixi. In the Hall of Joy and Longevity (乐寿堂), the living-room of Cixi, visitors obtain a glimpse of the life of the empress. The interior furnishings include imperial seats, long shaft fans, large blue-and-white porcelain fruit plates, and four gold plated bronze burners (室内陈设有御座、长柄扇、青花瓷大果盘、四个镀金铜炉).

The park is the most beautiful part of the Summer Palace; it is dominated by the Longevity Hill and the Kunming Lake. On the southern slope of Longevity Hill is a large group of buildings. The main structure is Paiyundian (排云殿, Cloud-Dispelling Hall) which was built in celebration of Cixi's seventieth birthday. In the hall hangs a portrait of Empress Dowager Cixi done by Katherine Augusta Carl (凯瑟琳·奥古斯塔·卡尔) in 1903. The covered staircases on either side of Paiyundian lead up to Foxiangge (佛香阁, the Pavilion of Buddha's Fragrance) which is 41 meters high. On top of the hill, behind Foxiangge stands Zhihuihai (智慧海) which is a well-known beamless Buddhist shrine. It is built of glazed bricks and tiles. Because no wood was used, the building was not destroyed by fire during invasions by foreigners. On the right of this group of buildings is the magnificent bronze pavilion which is a rare treasure of the country's legacy. It is 7.55 meters in height and 200 tons in weight.

Seventeen-Arch Bridge

To the south of the Longevity Hill lies the Kunming Lake which occupies most of the area of the park. Among the islands in the lake, the largest is the Southern Lake Island (南湖岛) on which stands the Temple of the Dragon King (龙王庙). The island is connected to the eastern shore by the magnificent Seventeen-Arch Bridge (十七孔桥).

Along the north side of Kunming Lake stretches a 728-meter Long Corridor (长廊). Its beams and girders are decorated with more than 8,000 paintings of natural views, historical stories, and legends. It is the longest corridor in China.

Long Corridor

At the back of the hill, near the eastern end of the palace, there is an interesting spot called Xiequyuan (谐趣园, the Garden of Harmonious Interests) where Cixi used to amuse herself occasionally by fishing in the pond. The layout of the garden is an imitation of the famous Jichang Garden (寄畅园) of Wuxi (无锡), Jiangsu Province, and for that reason it is known as "the garden within the garden (园中之园)".

There is a newly-restored scene in the middle of the Back Lake (后湖) area north of the Longevity Hill. It is called Suzhou Street (苏州街) or "the Emperor's Shopping Street". The street used to be one of the attractions of the Summer Palace. During his tours of the south, Emperor Qianlong was so impressed by the commercial prosperity that he ordered shops to be built in the styles of those along the waterways in Suzhou, a city in Jiangsu Province known as the "Venice of the East". The original shopping street, like other structures in the garden, was destroyed by foreign invaders in 1860.

Suzhou Street

Restoration of the Emperor's shops began in 1986. The design is faithful to the original style and based on historical relics and documents preserved in the state archives. The interior and exterior decorations (内部和外部装饰), shop signs (商店招牌), facades (正面), and horizontally inscribed boards (铭牌) have been fashioned to reflect the 18th century Chinese social and economic life. The street extends for 300 meters along the Back Lake. As of old it is characterized by a small temple, 6 bridges, and nearly 30 wooden arch-ways. Many of the over 60 shops along the street are unique because they portray trades and skills which cannot be found today: an incense shop (香店), a dye house (染坊), and a wooden comb shop (木梳店). The restored shopping street serves as a major tourist attraction of the Summer Palace, and undoubtedly adds charm to this world-famous imperial palace.

/ The Imperial Summer Resort in Chengde /

Bishu Shanzhuang (the Imperial Summer Resort) is in the north of Chengde (承德) which is 250 kilometers northeast of Beijing. Historically, it was called the Rehe Imperial Palace (热河行宫) and known as the largest imperial landscape garden in China. Originally, the resort served as a grand and elegant pied-a-terre (驿站) for the Qing Dynasty emperors on their way to the hunting reserves. Emperor Kangxi (康熙) was fascinated by the beautiful scenery of Chengde. In 1703, he ordered the large scale construction of a summer resort; the project was not completed until 1792, during the reign of Emperor Qianlong (乾隆).

The Imperial Summer Resort in Chengde

The resort built on mountain slopes occupies an area of 5.6 square kilometers, about twice the size of the Summer Palace in Beijing. The resort is surrounded by a solid wall 10 kilometers long, often referred to as the "Lesser Great Wall (小长城)".

The style of the resort is simple and elegant. Unlike other imperial buildings or traditional temples which commonly adopt bright colors, most structures here are built of greyish bricks (灰砖) to make the grand resort (宏伟的度假胜地) a place of royal glamour (皇家魅力) with an atmosphere of serenity (宁静氛围).

For about 130 years, the Qing emperors, from Qianlong to Xianfeng (咸丰), spent as long as 6 months each year in Chengde, living and conducting state affairs from the resort. Consequently, it became known as the second capital of the country. It was also a beautiful summer retreat (美丽的避暑胜地). Its 72 scenic spots, whose names were bestowed by emperors Kangxi and Qianlong, were and still are the gems of the resort.

The whole resort is divided into two parts—the palace area and the scenic park. The palace area is in the south part of the resort and contains 4 groups of buildings: the Principal Palace (正宫), the Pine and Crane Hall (松鹤斋), the Pine Soughing Valley Hall (万壑松风), and the East Palace (东宫). The main hall of the Principal Palace is called the Hall of Rectitude and Sincerity (澹泊敬诚殿). Because the building is made of *nanmu* (楠木), a hard wood, it is popularly known as the Nanmu Hall (楠木殿). It was the place where the emperors received leaders of ethnic groups and foreign diplomats. It was also used for solemn ceremonies.

The scenic park covers all kinds of terrains—plains, lakes, and mountains. The western part of the plain features lush grass while trees predominate in the east. The scenery has the charm of the Inner Mongolian grassland. The emperors staged horse racers, hunting parties, and picnics on the plain.

The lakes to the north of the palace area are dotted with eight islets (小岛), big and small. The Rehe (Hot River) Spring (热河泉) is in the northeast corner. The emperors used to enjoy the beautiful scenery around the area from the Water Center Pavilion (水心榭), the Moonlight and Gurgling Water Hall (月色江声), the Good Luck Plain (如意洲) and the Misty Rain Tower (烟雨楼). Along the lake shore there are four pavilions in different shapes. In the north lies Garden of Multiple Trees (万树园), where Emperor Qianlong once received the first British envoy to China. The mountain area lies in the north west covering four fifths of the resort. It is distinguished by valleys and peaks.

The Rehe Spring

The Imperial Summer Resort in Chengde is a combination of the landscape gardening styles of both South and North China, which reflects how the Qing emperors dreamed of uniting the beautiful scenery of all China into a man-made garden resort.

The imperial life extended beyond the walls of the park. Outside the resort on the lower slopes of the hills to the north and east of Chengde scattered a number of temples known as the Eight Outer Temples (外八庙) or the Outer Eight. They are called "outer" temples because they are situated outside the resort. Originally there are eleven temples, but only seven (instead of eight) have survived the natural wear and tear (磨损) of the past two hundred years. They were built in the styles of the Mongolian, Tibetan, Uygur and Han nationalities to make ethnic group leaders feel at home when they visited the Qing court in Chengde. Not surprisingly, these gestures made the ethnic group leaders less inclined to raise a rebellion and did much to promote the cause of national unity.

The names of the Outer Eight symbolize beauty and good wishes for human society, such as the Pervading Benevolence Monastery (溥仁寺), the Monastery of Universal Tranquility (普宁寺), the Monastery of Quiet Remoteness (安远庙), and the Monastery of Universal Joy (普乐寺). The largest among the Eight Outer Temples is Putuozongcheng Monastery (普陀宗乘之庙) which means "palace" or "potala" as pronunciated in Sanskrit. It is also known as the small

Potala Palace (小布达拉宫) for it replicates the Potala Palace of Tibet. Covering an area of twenty-two hectares, it is architecturally typical of Tibetan religious buildings. Its period of construction lasted from 1767 to 1771; it was built to commemorate the 60th birthday of Emperor Qianlong and the 80th birthday of the Emperor's mother. The central structure is the Great Red Platform (大红台) which serves as a base for the golden roofed Wan Fa Gui Yi Hall (万法归一殿), or Multiplicity-Return-to-Universality Hall. To the south is the White Platform (白台), the living quarters of the monks, Five-Pagoda White Platform (五塔白台), and Single-Pagoda White Platform (单塔白台).

The Monastery of Universal Tranquility

The Monastery of Universal Tranquility or Pu Ning Temple (普宁寺), known as the Giant Buddha Temple, was constructed between 1755 and 1759. Its design was inspired by the Samaya Monastery (桑耶寺) in Tibet. It is unique because the temple is divided into two parts; the front is in the style of the Han nationality while the rear incorporates Tibetan designs. In a pavilion behind the main hall stands a huge wooden statue known as the "thousand-armed- Buddha (千臂佛)". It is 22.28 meters in height and 110 tons in weight and is known as the largest wooden image in the world. This rare Buddha has 42 hands, holding 40 magical instruments. As many as 40 eyes look out from the face and palms. On top of the head sits a small Buddha which is 1.52 meters high. The statue is impressive with its vivid life-like pose.

/ The Humble Administrator's Garden in Suzhou /

In 1522, an imperial censor (御史), Wang Xianchen (王献臣), grew unhappy with his colleagues in the court of the Ming Emperor Jiajing (明朝嘉靖). Wang lost royal favor, resigned, and retired to Suzhou where he built a garden and named it Zhuozhen Yuan (拙政园, Humble Administrator's Garden). Situated in the north of Suzhou, Jiangsu Province, Zhuozheng Yuan is the largest of the private gardens in the city and is considered a masterpiece among China's classical gardens.

Wang named his creation the "Humble Administrator's Garden" because he felt the only thing left for him was to cultivate plants and grow vegetables. In the mid-nineteenth century, the garden became part of the official residence of Li Xiucheng (李秀成) of the Taiping Heavenly Kingdom. It was renovated (翻新) after the founding of the the People's Republic of China in 1949, and has been open to the public since 1952.

The garden occupies five hectares; three fifths of it is devoted to a lake. It reflects the simplicity of the Ming Dynasty artistic style. Halls, pavilions, and corridors are all built around the lake. The buildings are decorated with low wooden railings (低矮木栏杆). Bridges zigzag at right angles across the many ponds. Water flows under little bridges in the shade of lush trees. Many delicately trimmed trees (许多精心修剪的树木) grace the garden in green. It is typical of the scenery south of the Yangtze River.

The garden is roughly divided into three parts: the east, central and west sections. Visitors usually enter by the eastern section; a few structures meet their eyes: the Pavilion of Heaven Fountain (天泉亭) and the Hut of Sorghum Fragrance (秫香馆), both presenting the typical pastoral scene of the country in South China. A corridor with windows separates this part from the rest of the garden. But one may get glimpses of the beautiful views of the central section. This is a good example of one of the principles employed by classical garden designers: "to separate but not to cut off". The central part, about one hectare in area, is the principal compound of the garden. The layout is neat and open, with interconnected ponds as its main feature.

The Pavilion of Heaven Fountain

Yuanxiang Tang (远香堂, the Distant Fragrance Hall), the chief scenic attraction of the garden, is set across a pond from an artificial hill. This arrangement agrees with the principle of "concealing a scene before presenting it" in garden designing. Inside the hall no pillars are visible as can be seen in similar structures. On four sides, symmetrical latticed glass windows (格子玻璃窗) overlook the scenery. The interior of the hall is decorated year-round with potted plants (盆栽植物). A lotus pond lies in front of the hall, the fragrance of flowers in which permeates the hall in summer, thus giving it its name.

The Distant Fragrance Hall

West of the Distant Fragrance Hall stands a small stone bridge called Xiaofeihong (小飞虹, Little Flying Rainbow). Slightly curved with pillars supporting its roof, it is the only roofed bridge in a Suzhou Garden. The name was inspired by its shining reflection in the moving water, which provides a charming scene.

Little Flying Rainbow

Places of interest in the western section include Shiba Mantuoluohua Guan (十八曼陀罗花馆, the Hall of Eighteen Datura Blossoms) and Sanshiliu Yuanyang Guan (三十六鸳鸯馆, Thirty-six Pairs of Mandarin Ducks Hall). The former is so named because eighteen datural plants once grew in the yard; the latter is a reminder that this number of ducks once lived in the water north of the hall.

The buildings of the Humble Administrator's Garden are both functional and ornamental. Halls were built for entertaining guests, towers and pavilions for viewing far-off scenery, studios for reading, and chambers and lounges for rest (为招待宾客而建堂,为观望远景而建塔亭,为读书而建书房,为休憩而建阁楼). They are simple in style and harmonized with the surroundings.

The Hall of Eighteen Datura Blossoms

　　Zhuozheng Yuan is not only a traditional garden typical of South China; it is also a museum of the traditional arts of architecture, calligraphy, epigraphy (碑文), sculpture, and painting. It is one of the important cultural relics under the official protection of the state.

Exercises

Part One　Comprehension

Fill in the following blanks with the information you learn in Chapter 13.

1. Of the three kinds, the _____ gardens appeared earliest, and can be traced back, according to written records, to King Wen Wang of the Zhou Dynasty, who built a vast garden of about 1,000 square kilometers called *Lingyou*.

2. Private gardens, though arising probably in the Spring and Autumn Period, began to develop in the _____ Dynasty.

3. The _____ hill is Chinese classical garden's most unconventional, fascinating scenic feature, indispensable to its unique style.

4. Garden _____ , in general, takes the form of open shelters and defines space from overhead without blocking up the continuity of space.

5. The forms of garden bridges are _____ and most of them are made of stone with simple but elegant design or with intricately carved patterns congruent with their surroundings.

6. Along the north side of the _____ Lake stretches a 728-meter covered Long Corridor.

7. Bishu Shanzhuang (the Imperial Summer Resort) is in the north of Chengde which is 250 kilometers northeast of Beijing. Historically, it was called the Rehe Imperial Palace and known as the largest imperial _____ garden in China.

8. The buildings of the Humble Administrator's Garden are both functional and _____ .

Part Two   Translation

Passage Translation

"筑山叠石"是中国古代园林建设的一个术语。就土壤和岩石的使用而言,有三种筑山的方法。第一种类型是土山,适用于占用大片土地的园林,比如宫殿式园林。它通常足够大,可以广泛种植植物,使它看起来像一座天然的山。第二种是土壤和岩石的综合利用。第三种是石山,它最适用于小型园林建筑和空间受限的区域。

Part Three   Critical Thinking and Discussion

1. Why do people say that Chinese classical garden art is the integration of traditional painting, poetry, and the nature?

2. Describe one Chinese classical garden that you have ever visited.

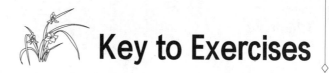

Key to Exercises

Chapter 1

Part One

1. founder   2. supreme   3. ethical   4. virtue   5. elicitation

Part Two

Term Translation

1. When Facing an Opportunity to Exercise Benevolence, Do Not Yield.

2. Think of Righteousness in the Face of Gain

3. When Seeing a Person of High Caliber, Strive to Be His Equal.

4. Restrain Yourself and Follow Social Norms

5. Harmony Is the Most Precious.

Passage Translation

Confucius was a thinker, statesman, educator, and the founder of Confucianism. Fung You-lan, one of the great 20th century authorities on the history of Chinese thought, compares Confucius's influence in Chinese history with that of Socrates in the West. As man has a moral nature, adhereing to moral principles should be everyone's first consideration. Moral principles are more important than all other things, including position, wealth, and even life. Confucius said, "Wealth and high position are desired by all men, but I would not have them if they were not won in the right way. Poverty and low positions are hated by all men, but I would not leave them if they could not be rid of in the right way."

Part Three

(open)

Chapter 2

Part One

1. 5,000   2. origin   3. contradictions   4. naturalness   5. non-action

Part Two

Term Translation

1. *Dao* Operates Naturally.

2. Influence Others without Preaching

3. Fortune and Misfortune Are Intertwined.

4. Maintain Originality and Embrace Simplicity

5. Great Virtue Is Like Water.

Passage Translation

  Lao Zi, also commonly known as *Dao De Jing*, was written by Lao Dan in the Spring and Autumn Period. It mainly studied political philosophy and life philosophy. Due to the influence of its thoughts, Taoism came into being in ancient China, which is the most influential indigenous religion in China. The ideas of *Lao Zi* have a direct impact on the national characteristics, ideological tendencies and aesthetic tastes of the Chinese people. Even now, *Lao Zi* is still an element of our national ideology. In addition, *Lao Zi* is also one of the ancient Chinese philosophical classics with most translated versions.

Part Three

1. (open)

2. (open)

Chapter 3

Part One

1. morale   2. original   3. equally   4. methodology

5. laws   6. Orthodox   7. reality   8. Buddhism

Part Two

Term Translation

1. Have Love for the People, and Cherish All Things

2. Protect the People and Then Rule as a King

3. Give One's Life to Uphold Righteousness

4. A Just Cause Enjoys Abundant Support While an Unjust Cause Finds Little Support.

5. Proper Ranking Leads to Collaboration.

6. Carry or Overturn the Boat / Make or Break

7. Promises Must Be Kept; Actions Must Be Resolute.

8. Effortless Ease

9. Promote the Beneficial; Eliminate the Harmful

10. The Law Does Not Favor the Rich and Powerful.

Passage Translation

The Hundred Schools of Thought lasted from 770 B.C.E. to 222 B.C.E. Known as the Golden Age of Chinese thought and the Contention of a Hundred Schools of Thought, this period saw the rise of many different schools of thought. Confucianism is the body of thought that has arguably had the most enduring effect on Chinese life; Legalism greatly influenced the philosophical basis for the imperial form of government; The focus of Taoism is on the individual within the natural realm and claims that the goal of life for each individual is to seek to adjust oneself and adapt to the rhythm of the natural world, to follow the Way of the universe, and to live in harmony; The school of Mohism was founded upon the doctrine of Mozi, which was seen as a major rival of Confucianism in this period. The emergence of various schools of thought and their exponents, such as Lao Zi and Confucius, occupies a very important position in the world history of philosophy.

Part Three

1. (open)

2. (open)

Chapter 4

Part One

1. elixir   2. Celestial   3. Confucian   4. sacred   5. zoology

Part Two

Passage Translation

Dao, originally, meant "road" and then implied to "rule" and "principle". Lao Zi used *Dao* to propound his ideological system; therefore, his school of thinking is called Taoism. During the Eastern Han Dynasty, it became a religion. This religion pursues immortality and the preservation of health; its uttermost goal is to become an immortal being.

Dao is *wuwei*, namely non-action. Non-action is to follow the rule of nature instead of overriding it. By conforming to the natural rules, *Dao* does nothing but it can do everything. *Dao* makes everything run smoothly, but it does not boast about its own achievements.

This religion has its drawbacks. For example, Chinese intellectuals resort to a hermitic way of life whenever they meet setbacks; when they are successful, they would say, "The less hermitry is to live in the remote areas while the great hermitry is to live in the court". The inner worldly and outer worldly attitudes made the Chinese intellects hover between active Confucianism and passive Taoism.

Part Three

1. (open)

2. (open)

Chapter 5

Part One

1. enlightened   2. reincarnation   3. Han   4. Chan   5. pagodas

Part Two

Passage Translation

Around the first century AD, Buddhism started to spread from ancient India to central

China via the Silk Road. After that, many sutras were introduced into China, and dignitaries from India were invited to preach Buddhist teachings. In the same century, the first Buddhist shrine in China—the White Horse Temple (Baima)—was built in Luoyang, Henan Province.

In the early days of Buddhism, it was highly praised by Chinese royalty, but rejected and disputed by common people, who preferred Confucianism and Taoism.

Huineng (638—713), the Sixth Patriarch of Chan Buddhism, prompted the development of Chinese Buddhism by introducing Confucianist concepts into the religion. Huineng believed that everybody had a Buddha nature and could become a Buddha. He insisted that Buddhist followers could attain Buddhahood without reciting sutras and observing other ceremonial rituals, as long as they could keep Buddha in their heart. His propositions were well received by scholars, bureaucrats and common people. With his efforts, Buddhism finally became popular and spread quickly in China.

Part Three

1. (open)

2. (open)

3. (open)

Chapter 6

Part One

1. classical	2. mythology	3. Hou Yi	4. dragon	5. folk songs
6. realism	7. romanticism	8. pastoral	9. biggest-ever	10. romantic
11. realistic	12. prolific	13. irregular	14. first	15. poetess
16. vigorous	17. official	18. general	19. criticism	20. plot
21. peasant	22. fantastic	23. greatest	24. unjust	25. playwrights

Part Two

Term Translation

1. Use Stones from Another Mountain to Polish One's Jade

2. Coexistence of All in Harmony

3. Complacency Leads to Failure; Modesty to Success.

4. Universal Harmony

5. Reciprocity as a Social Norm

6. Without Sincerity, Nothing Is Possible.

7. Self-Cultivation, Family Regulation, State Governance, Bringing Peace to All under Heaven

8. Teaching and Learning Promote Each Other

9. Work Diligently and Keep Good Company with Others

10. Seek to Benefit the Country Rather than Personal Wealth and Position

11. Once the Lips Are Gone, the Teeth Will Feel Cold.

12. Leather Thongs Binding Wooden Strips Break Three Times.

13. When the Granaries Are Full, People Follow Appropriate Rules of Conduct.

14. Part Ways and Part Company

15. Spend-and-Tax / Expenditure Should Be Carefully Calculated before Making a Plan to Gather Revenue.

16. No Fish Can Survive If Water Is Too Clear.

17. Living in Peace and Working in Contentment

18. Hanging a Gourd (Practicing Medicine) to Help the World

19. Past Experience, If Not Forgotten, Is a Guide for the Future.

20. Writing That Runs Counter to Its Author's Aspirations Is Worthless.

Passage Translation

A Dream of the Red Mansions by Cao Xueqin reached the pinnacle of Chinese classical novels. It has long been acknowledged as the greatest novel in Chinese literature and a gem of world literature. The author was born into a noble and powerful family which declined from extreme prosperity to extreme poverty. The reason why he was able to create the novel lies in that he achieved understanding of life, had progressive ideas, took a serious attitude to writing, and possessed excelling writing skills.

A Dream of the Red Mansions described the life and the declining fortune of a big feudal family. The central thread of the novel is the tragic love story between Jia Baoyu and Lin Daiyu. Instead of just telling the love story itself, the novel taps the social origin of the tragedy through probing deeply into the characters' minds and complicated relationship. The plot of the novel is ingeniously arranged. Its narratives use mature colloquial language, plain but elegant, explicit but expressive. The novel is really a panorama of Chinese feudal society and has been considered an encyclopedia of Chinese literature.

Part Three

1. (open)

2. (open)

3. (open)

4. (open)

5. (open)

Chapter 7

Part One

1. inscriptions   2. regular   3. calligraphy   4. greatest   5. strange

6. recitation   7. mother   8. face changing   9. imitate   10. violin

Part Two

Passage Translation

    Chinese characters evolved from pictures and signs, and the Chinese art of calligraphy developed naturally from its unique writing system. Calligraphy, through its unique word structures, writing styles and way of handling brush, conveys the moral integrity, character, emotions, esthetic feelings and culture of the artist to readers and charms them with appealing beauty. So it is believed among a lot of people that we can tell a person's character through his handwriting. Calligraphy is also considered an active way of keeping oneself fit and healthy, for the practice is relaxing and self-entertaining. The modernization of writing tools has given rise to many types of calligraphy other than traditional brush-writing, for example, pen-writing. Today, Chinese calligraphy is still considered an elegant art form even in such neighboring countries as Japan, the Republic of Korea, Singapore and Vietnam. It has become a unique feature of Oriental art.

Part Three

1. (open)

2. (open)

3. (open)

4. (open)

Chapter 8

Part One

1. gunpowder   2. civilization   3. first   4. toxic   5. decimal
6. Agronomy   7. complement   8. palpation   9. pharmacologist   10. acupuncture

Part Two

Passage Translation

China is well known for its introduction of ways and means to help ease the life of mankind. Among the inventions of ancient China, four emerged as great contributions to the developments not only of the country, but also of the world's economy and culture. The Four Great Inventions of ancient China, namely, the compass, paper-making, gunpowder, and printing, not only changed the world but also accelerated the evolution of world history. Westerners may know little about China's past feats, but they are familiar with China's Four Great Inventions. Ancient China's Four Great Inventions are also important symbols of China's role as a great world civilization.

Part Three

1. (open)

2. (open)

3. (open)

Chapter 9

Part One

1. most important   2. lunar   3. kite flying   4. Realgar
5. Valentine   6. reunions   7. 1989

Part Two

Passage Translation

Since ancient times, the Chinese people usually celebrated harvest in mid-autumn. The tradition of celebrating the Mid-Autumn Festival became popular throughout China in the early

Tang Dynasty. August 15 in the lunar calendar is a day for people to worship the moon. On this day, under the dazzling bright moon, families reunite and enjoy the moon's beauty. People away from home often recite Li Bai's famous poem lines: "I raise my head, the splendid moon I see; Then droop my head and sink to the dreams of my hometown." Others who are hopeful for their future prefer Su Shi's lines: "My one wish for you, then, is long life; And a share in this loveliness (the moon) far, far away."

In 2006, Mid-Autumn Festival was listed as one of China's cultural heritage, and in 2008, it was designated as a public holiday. Moon cakes, as indispensable delicious food of the festival, are gifts for people to send to their families and friends during the festival, and are usually eaten on family gatherings. There are characters of "longevity" "good fortune" and "harmony" on the traditional moon cakes.

Part Three

(open)

Chapter 10

Part One

1. taste   2. northeast   3. flavorful   4. table   5. first   6. wager

Part Two

Passage Translation

It is universally acknowledged that China is the first country to grow, produce and drink tea. Drinking tea has become a daily habit of Chinese people. The art of tea making and drinking, after evolving through different dynasties, now focuses on the method of brewing tea, the drinking utensils and the serving etiquette. Tea drinking in China is a ritual and a demonstration of the refined taste. While drinking tea, Chinese people also take delight in the leisure of this kind of activity. Chatting over a pot of tea is a very popular way of pastime among Chinese people. In the past, they would start a day with a visit to a well-known tea house. Chinese tea houses would be the equivalent of French cafes and English pubs. Chines People come here not just for tea drinking, but also for social communication.

Part Three

1. (open)

2. (open)

Chapter 11

Part One

1. kiln   2. terra-cotta   3. zenith   4. 1,500   5. blue-and-white

6. simplicity   7. hand-made   8. Shang   9. Tianjin   10. enamel

Part Two

Passage Translation

The official medals of the Beijing 2022 Olympic and Paralympic Winter Games made an impressive debut on Tuesday, 100 days from the start of the gala event. Named "Tongxin", meaning "together as one", the medals are inspired by the exquisite "yubi", an ancient Chinese jade artifact dating back some 5,000 years ago. Each medal features carvings of the Olympic rings at its heart on the front with the words "XXIV Olympic Winter Games Beijing 2022" etched around them. Engravings of cloud patterns and snowflakes and ice scratches fill the outer rings. The concentric rings around the center represent the pursuit of unity and harmony common in Chinese culture, while echoing the Olympic values of promoting solidarity, inclusiveness and peace among mankind. The reverse side bears the Beijing 2022 emblem at the center, with the outer rings dotted with 24 stars strung together by circles, representing the 24th edition of the Winter Olympics, and featuring the name of the medal event.

Part Three

1. (open)

2. (open)

3. (open)

Chapter 12

Part One

1. soccer   2. golf   3. representative   4. *Taiji quan*   5. deer

Part Two

Passage Translation

Traditional Chinese sports culture has extremely rich content and a long history, forming its own system. It has developed and been passed down in its own way, making it an outstanding representative of human sports culture. From martial arts representing the main form of combat to guidance of health maintenance through breathing techniques, from folk games satisfying people's entertainment needs through physical activities to traditional sports of ethnic groups, traditional Chinese sports culture records the development process of human society.

Part Three

1. (open)

2. (open)

3. (open)

Chapter 13

Part One

1. imperial   2. Han   3. artificial   4. architecture

5. diversified   6. Kunming   7. landscape   8. ornamental

Part Two

Passage Translation

"Hill molding and rockery manipulation" was a term in ancient China for garden construction. There are three methods of hill molding in regard to the use of soil and rocks. The first type, the earth hill, is suitable for gardens with large tracts of land, such as those of the palatial gardens. It is often large enough to be cultivated extensively with plants that make it seem like a natural mountain. The second type is the composite use of soil and rocks. The third is the rock hill, which is best applied in smaller constructions and in confined areas.

Part Three

1. (open)
2. (open)

References

BAI Shouyi. An outline history of China [M]. Beijing: Foreign Languages Press, 1982.

CHEN Jingpan. Confucius as a teacher [M]. Beijing: Foreign Languages Press, 1990.

MACKERRAS C. Chinese theatre [M]. Hawaii: University of Hawaii Press, 1983.

NEEDHAM J. Science and civilization in China: Vol. 2 [M]. London: Cambridge University Press, 1956.

LI Zhiyan, CHENG Wen. Chinese pottery and porcelain [M]. Beijing: Foreign Languages Press, 1984.

LU Xun. A brief history of Chinese fiction [M]. Translated by YANG Xianyi and YANG Gladys. Beijing: Foreign Languages Press, 1976.

EDWARDS P. Encyclopedia of philosophy [M]. New York: Macmillan Press, 1967.

LAURENCE T. Chinese religion: an introduction [M]. California: Belmont Wadsworth Publishing Company, 1989.

REESE W L. Dictionary of philosophy and religion [M]. New Jersey: Humanities Press, 1980.

ZHANG Enqin. Basic theory of traditional Chinese medicine [M]. Shanghai: Publishing House of Shanghai College of Traditional Chinese Medicine, 1990.

ZHANG Enqin. Chinese qigong [M]. Shanghai: Publishing House of Shanghai College of Traditional Chinese Medicine, 1990.

丁往道. 中国文化掠影 [M]. 北京：外语教学与研究出版社, 2006.

雷镇闾. 宗教概论 [M]. 郑州：河南人民出版社, 1984.

廖华英. 中国文化概况：修订版 [M]. 北京：外语教育与研究出版社, 2015.

刘法公. 商贸汉英翻译专论 [M]. 重庆：重庆出版社, 1999.

潘伯鹰. 中国书法简论 [M]. 上海：上海人民美术出版社, 1983.

沈知白. 中国音乐史纲要 [M]. 上海：上海文艺出版社, 1982.

谭家健. 中国文化史概要 [M]. 北京：高等教育出版社, 1988.

严北溟.哲学大辞典:中国哲学史卷 [M].上海:上海辞书出版社,1985.

叶朗,朱良志.中国文化英语教程 [M].北京:外语教育与研究出版社,2010.

张秀平,王乃庄.中国文化概览 [M].北京:东方出版社,1988.

"中华思想文化术语传播工程"秘书处.一百词解读中国智慧 [M].北京:外语教学与研究出版社,2020.